MASSIMO DI PIERRO

WEB2PY

COMPLETE REFERENCE MANUAL, 5TH EDITION

EXPERTS4SOLUTIONS

For more information about appropriate use of this material contact:

Massimo Di Pierro
School of Computing
DePaul University
243 S Wabash Ave
Chicago, IL 60604 (USA)
Email: massimo.dipierro@gmail.com

Library of Congress Cataloging-in-Publication Data:

ISBN: 978-0-578-12021-8
Build Date: March 3, 2013

to my family

Contents

3 Overview   **73**

8

14

Preface

I believe that the ability to easily build high quality web applications is of critical importance for the growth of a free and open society. This prevents the biggest players from monopolizing the flow of information.

Hence I started the web2py project in 2007, primarily as a teaching tool with the goal of making web development easier, faster, and more secure. Over time, it has managed to win the affection of thousands of knowledgeable users and hundreds of developers. Our collective effort has created one of the most full-featured Open Source Web Frameworks for enterprise web development.

As a result, in 2011, web2py won the Bossie Award for best Open Source Development Software, and in 2012 it won the Technology of the Year award from InfoWorld.

As you will learn in the following pages, web2py tries to lower the barrier of entry to web development by focusing on three main goals:

Ease of use. This means reducing the learning and deployment time as well as development and maintenance costs. This is why web2py is a full-stack framework without dependencies. It requires no installation and has no configuration files. Everything works *out of the box*, including a web server, database and a web-based IDE that gives access to all the main features. The API includes just 12 core objects, which are easy to work with and memorize. It can interoperate with most web servers, databases and all Python libraries.

Rapid development. Every function of web2py has a default behavior (which can be overridden). For example, as soon as you have specified your data models, you will have access to a web-based database administration panel. Also, web2py automatically generates forms for your data and it allows you to easily expose the data in HTML, XML, JSON, RSS, etc. web2py provides some high level widgets such as the wiki and the grid to rapidly build complex applications.

Security.   The web2py Database Abstraction Layer (DAL) eliminates SQL Injections.   The template language prevents Cross Site Scripting vulnerabilities. The forms generated by web2py provide field validation and block Cross Site Request Forgeries. Passwords are always stored hashed. Sessions are stored server-side by default to prevent Cookie Tampering. Session cookies are UUID to prevent Session Hijacking.

web2py is built from the user perspective and is constantly being optimized internally to become faster and leaner, whilst always maintaining *backwards compatibility.*

web2py is free for you to use. If you benefit from it, I hope you will feel encouraged to *pay it forward* by contributing back to society in whatever form you choose.

1

Introduction

web2py [1] is a free, open-source web framework for agile development of secure database-driven web applications; it is written in Python [2] and programmable in Python. web2py is a full-stack framework, meaning that it contains all the components you need to build fully functional web applications. web2py is designed to guide a web developer to follow good software engineering practices, such as using the Model View Controller (MVC) pattern. web2py separates the data representation (the model) from the data presentation (the view) and also from the application logic and workflow (the controller). web2py provides libraries to help the developer design, implement, and test each of these three parts separately, and makes them work together. web2py is built for security. This means that it automatically addresses many of the issues that can lead to security vulnerabilities, by following well established practices. For example, it validates all input (to prevent injections), escapes all output (to prevent cross-site scripting), renames uploaded files (to prevent directory traversal attacks). web2py takes care of main security issues, so developers have less chances of introducing vulnerabilities. web2py includes a Database Abstraction Layer (DAL) that writes SQL [3] dynamically so that you, the developer, don't have to. The DAL knows how to generate SQL transparently for SQLite [4], MySQL [5], PostgreSQL [6], MSSQL [7], FireBird [8], Oracle [9], IBM DB2 [10], Informix [11], Ingres [12], and MongoDB [13]. The DAL can also generate function calls for the Google Datastore when running on the

Google App Engine (GAE) [14]. Experimentally we support more databases and new ones are constantly added. Please check on the web2py web site and mailing list for more recent adapters. Once one or more database tables are defined, web2py automatically generates a fully functional web-based database administration interface to access the database and the tables. web2py differs from other web frameworks in that it is the only framework to fully embrace the Web 2.0 paradigm, where the web is the computer. In fact, web2py does not require installation or configuration; it runs on any architecture that can run Python (Windows, Windows CE, Mac OS X, iOS, and Unix/Linux), and the development, deployment, and maintenance phases for the applications can be done via a local or remote web interface. web2py runs with CPython (the C implementation) and PyPy (Python written in Python), on Python versions 2.5, 2.6, and 2.7. web2py provides a ticketing system for error events. If an error occurs, a ticket is issued to the user, and the error is logged for the administrator. web2py is open source and released under the LGPL version 3 license.

Another important feature of web2py is that we, its developers, commit to maintain backward compatibility in future versions. We have done so since the first release of web2py in October, 2007. New features have been added and bugs have been fixed, but if a program worked with web2py 1.0, that program will work even better today.

Here are some examples of web2py statements that illustrate its power and simplicity. The following code:

```
db.define_table('person', Field('name'), Field('image', 'upload'))
```

creates a database table called "person" with two fields: "name", a string; and "image", something that needs to be uploaded (the actual image). If the table already exists but does not match this definition, it is altered appropriately.

Given the table defined above, the following code:

```
form = SQLFORM(db.person).process()
```

creates an insert form for this table that allows users to upload images. It also validates the submitted form, renames the uploaded image in a secure way, stores the image in a file, inserts the corresponding record in the database, prevents double submission, and eventually modifies the form itself by adding error messages if the data submitted by the user does not pass validation.

This code embeds a fully working wiki with tags, search, tag cloud, permissions, media attachments, and oembed support:

```
1  def index(): return auth.wiki()
```

The following code instead:

```
1  @auth.requires_permission('read','person')
2  def f(): ....
```

prevents visitors from accessing the function f unless the visitor is a member of a group whose members have permissions to "read" records of table "person". If the visitor is not logged in, the visitor gets directed to a login page (provided by default by web2py). web2py also supports components, i.e. actions which can be loaded in a view and interact with the visitor via Ajax without re-loading the entire page. This is done via a LOAD helper which allows very modular design of applications; it is discussed in chapter 3 in the context of the wiki and, in some detail, in the last chapter of this book.

This 5th edition of the book describes web2py 2.4.1 and later versions.

1.1   Principles

Python programming typically follows these basic principles:

- Don't repeat yourself (DRY).

- There should be only one way of doing things.

- Explicit is better than implicit.

web2py fully embraces the first two principles by forcing the developer to use sound software engineering practices that discourage repetition of code. web2py guides the developer through almost all the tasks common in web application development (creating and processing forms, managing sessions, cookies, errors, etc.).

web2py differs from other frameworks with regard to the third principle, which sometimes conflicts with the other two. In particular, web2py does not import user applications, but executes them in a predefined context. This context exposes the Python keywords, as well as the web2py keywords.

To some this may appear as magic, but it should not. Simply, in practice, some modules are already imported without you doing so. web2py is trying to avoid the annoying characteristic of other frameworks that force the developer to import the same modules at the top of every model and controller. web2py, by importing its own modules, saves time and prevents mistakes, thus following the spirit of "don't repeat yourself" and "there should be only one way of doing things".

If the developer wishes to use other Python modules or third-party modules, those modules must be imported explicitly, as in any other Python program.

1.2 Web frameworks

At its most fundamental level, a web application consists of a set of programs (or functions) that are executed when the corresponding URL is visited. The output of the program is returned to the visitor and rendered by the browser.

The purpose of web frameworks is to allow developers to build new apps quickly, easily and without mistakes. This is done by providing APIs and tools that reduce and simplify the amount of coding that is required.

The two classic approaches for developing web applications are:

- Generating HTML [15] [16] programmatically.

- Embedding code into HTML pages.

The first model is the one that was followed, for example, by early CGI scripts. The second model is followed, for example, by PHP [17] (where the code is in PHP, a C-like language), ASP (where the code is in Visual Basic), and JSP (where the code is in Java).

Here is an example of a PHP program that, when executed, retrieves data from a database and returns an HTML page showing the selected records:

```
1  <html><body><h1>Records</h1><?
2    mysql_connect(localhost,username,password);
```

```
3   @mysql_select_db(database) or die( "Unable to select database");
4   $query="SELECT * FROM contacts";
5   $result=mysql_query($query);
6   mysql_close();
7   $i=0;
8   while ($i < mysql_numrows($result)) {
9     $name=mysql_result($result,$i,"name");
10    $phone=mysql_result($result,$i,"phone");
11    echo "<b>$name</b><br>Phone:$phone<br /><br /><hr /><br />";
12    $i++;
13  }
14  ?></body></html>
```

The problem with this approach is that code is embedded into HTML, but the very same code also needs to generate additional HTML and to generate SQL statements to query the database, entangling multiple layers of the application and making it difficult to read and maintain. The situation is even worse for Ajax applications, and the complexity grows with the number of pages (files) that make up the application.

The functionality of the above example can be expressed in web2py with two lines of Python code:

```
1   def index():
2       return HTML(BODY(H1('Records'), db().select(db.contacts.ALL)))
```

In this simple example, the HTML page structure is represented programmatically by the HTML, BODY, and H1 objects; the database db is queried by the select command; finally, everything is serialized into HTML. Notice that db is not a keyword but a user defined variable. We will use this name consistently to refer to a database connection to avoid confusion.

Web frameworks are typically categorized as one of two types: A "glued" framework is built by assembling (gluing together) several third-party components. A "full-stack" framework is built by creating components designed specifically to be tightly integrated and work together. web2py is a full-stack framework. Almost all of its components are built from scratch and are designed to work together, but they function just as well outside of the complete web2py framework. For example, the Database Abstraction Layer (DAL) or the template language can be used independently of the web2py framework by importing gluon.dal or gluon.template into your own Python applications. gluon is the name of the web2py module that contains system libraries. Some web2py libraries, such as building and processing forms from database tables, have dependencies on other portions of web2py. web2py can also work with third-party Python libraries, including other template languages and DALs, but they will not be as tightly integrated as the original components.

1.3   Model-View-Controller

web2py encourages the developer to separate data representation (the model), data presentation (the view) and the application workflow (the controller). Let's consider again the previous example and see how to build a web2py application around it. Here is an example of the web2py MVC edit interface:

The typical workflow of a request in web2py is described in the following diagram:

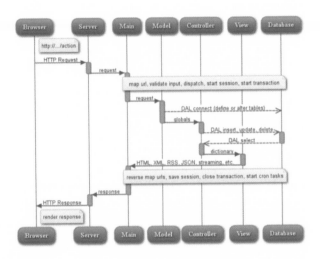

In the diagram:

- The Server can be the web2py built-in web server or a third-party server, such as Apache. The Server handles multi-threading.

- "main" is the main WSGI application. It performs all common tasks and wraps user applications. It deals with cookies, sessions, transactions, URL routing and reverse routing, and dispatching.

It can serve and stream static files if the web server is not doing it already.

- The Models, Views and Controller components make up the user application.

- Multiple applications can be hosted in the same web2py instance.

- The dashed arrows represent communication with the database engine(s). The database queries can be written in raw SQL (discouraged) or by using the web2py Database Abstraction Layer (recommended), so that web2py application code is not dependent on the specific database engine.

- The dispatcher maps the requested URL to a function call in the controller. The output of the function can be a string or a dictionary of symbols (a hash table). The data in the dictionary is rendered by a view. If the visitor requests an HTML page (the default), the dictionary is rendered into an HTML page. If the visitor requests the same page in XML, web2py tries to find a view that can render the dictionary in XML. The developer can create views to render pages in any of the already supported protocols (HTML, XML, JSON, RSS, CSV, and RTF) or in additional custom protocols.

- All calls are wrapped into a transaction, and any uncaught exception causes the transaction to be rolled back. If the request succeeds, the transaction is committed.

- web2py also handles sessions and session cookies automatically, and when a transaction is committed, the session is also stored, unless specified otherwise.

- It is possible to register recurrent tasks (via cron) to run at scheduled times and/or after the completion of certain actions. In this way it is possible to run long and compute-intensive tasks in the background without slowing down navigation.

Here is a minimal and complete MVC application, consisting of three files:

"db.py" is the model:

```
1  db = DAL('sqlite://storage.sqlite')
2  db.define_table('contact',
3      Field('name'),
4      Field('phone'))
```

It connects to the database (in this example a SQLite database stored in the storage.sqlite file) and defines a table called contact. If the table does not exist, web2py creates it and, transparently and in the background, generates SQL code in the appropriate SQL dialect for the specific database engine used. The developer can see the generated SQL but does not need to change the code if the database back-end, which defaults to SQLite, is replaced with MySQL, PostgreSQL, MSSQL, FireBird, Oracle, DB2, Informix, Interbase, Ingres, and the Google App Engine (both SQL and NoSQL).

Once a table is defined and created, web2py also generates a fully functional web-based database administration interface, called **appadmin**, to access the database and the tables.

"default.py" is the controller:

```
1  def contacts():
```

```
2    grid=SQLFORM.grid(db.contact, user_signature=False)
3    return locals()
```

In web2py, URLs are mapped to Python modules and function calls. In this case, the controller contains a single function (or "action") called contacts. An action may return a string (the returned web page) or a Python dictionary (a set of key:value pairs) or the set of local variables (as in this example). If the function returns a dictionary, it is passed to a view with the same name as the controller/function, which in turn renders the page. In this example, the function contacts generates a select/search/create/update/delete grid for table db.contact and returns the grid to the view.

"default/contacts.html" is the view:

```
1   {{extend 'layout.html'}}
2   <h1>Manage My Contacts</h1>
3   {{=grid}}
```

This view is called automatically by web2py after the associated controller function (action) is executed. The purpose of this view is to render the variables in the returned dictionary (in our case grid) into HTML. The view file is written in HTML, but it embeds Python code delimited by the special {{ and }} delimiters. This is quite different from the PHP code example, because the only code embedded into the HTML is "presentation layer" code. The "layout.html" file referenced at the top of the view is provided by web2py and constitutes the basic layout for all web2py applications. The layout file can easily be modified or replaced.

1.4   Why web2py

web2py is one of many web application frameworks, but it has compelling and unique features. web2py was originally developed as a teaching tool, with the following primary motivations:

- Easy for users to learn server-side web development without compromising functionality. For this reason, web2py requires no installation and no configuration, has no dependencies (except for the source code distribution, which requires Python 2.5 and its standard library modules), and exposes most of its functionality via a Web interface, including an Integrated Development Environment with Debugger and database interface.

- web2py has been stable from day one because it follows a top-down design; i.e., its API was designed before it was implemented. Even as new functionality has been added, web2py has never broken backwards compatibility, and it will not break compatibility when additional functionality is added in the future.

- web2py proactively addresses the most important security issues which plague many modern web applications, as determined by OWASP [18] below.

- web2py is lightweight. Its core libraries, including the Database Abstraction Layer, the template language, and all the helpers amount to 1.4MB. The entire source code including sample applications and images amounts to 10.4MB.

- web2py has a small footprint and is very fast. It uses the Rocket [19] WSGI web server developed by Timothy Farrell. It is as fast as Apache with mod_wsgi, and supports SSL and IPv6.

- web2py uses Python syntax for models, controllers, and views, but does not import models and controllers (as all the other Python frameworks do) - instead it executes them. This means that apps can be installed, uninstalled, and modified without having to restart the web server (even in production), and different apps can coexist without their modules interfering with one another.

- web2py uses a Database Abstraction Layer (DAL) instead of an Object Relational Mapper (ORM). From a conceptual point of view, this means that different database tables are mapped into different instances of one Table class and not into different classes, while records are mapped into instances of one Row class, not into instances of the corresponding table class. From a practical point of view, it means that SQL syntax maps almost one-to-one into DAL syntax, and there is no complex metaclass programming going on under the hood as in popular ORMs, which would add latency.

WSGI [20] [21] (Web Server Gateway Interface) is an emerging Python standard for communication between a web server and Python applications).

Here is a screenshot of the main web2py **admin** interface:

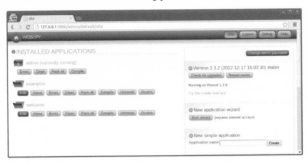

1.5 Security

The Open Web Application Security Project [18] (OWASP) is a free and open worldwide community focused on improving the security of application software.

OWASP has listed the top ten security issues that put web applications at risk. That list is reproduced here, along with a description of how each issue is addressed by web2py:

- "Cross Site Scripting (XSS): XSS flaws occur whenever an application takes user supplied data and sends it to a web browser without first validating or encoding that content. XSS allows attackers to execute scripts in the victim's browser which can hijack user sessions, deface web sites, possibly introduce worms, etc." *web2py, by default, escapes all variables rendered in the view, preventing XSS.*

- "Injection Flaws: Injection flaws, particularly SQL injection, are common in web applications. Injection occurs when user-supplied data is sent to an interpreter as part of a command or query. The attacker's hostile data tricks the interpreter into executing unintended commands or changing data." *web2py includes a Database Abstraction Layer that makes SQL injection impossible. Normally, SQL statements are not written by the developer. Instead,*

SQL is generated dynamically by the DAL, ensuring that all inserted data is properly escaped.

- "Malicious File Execution: Code vulnerable to remote file inclusion (RFI) allows attackers to include hostile code and data, resulting in devastating attacks, such as total server compromise." *web2py allows only exposed functions to be executed, preventing malicious file execution. Imported functions are never exposed; only actions are exposed. web2py uses a Web-based administration interface which makes it very easy to keep track of what is exposed and what is not.*

- "Insecure Direct Object Reference: A direct object reference occurs when a developer exposes a reference to an internal implementation object, such as a file, directory, database record, or key, as a URL or form parameter. Attackers can manipulate those references to access other objects without authorization." *web2py does not expose any internal objects; moreover, web2py validates all URLs, thus preventing directory traversal attacks. web2py also provides a simple mechanism to create forms that automatically validate all input values.*

- "Cross Site Request Forgery (CSRF): A CSRF attack forces a logged-on victim's browser to send a pre-authenticated request to a vulnerable web application, which then forces the victim's browser to perform a hostile action to the benefit of the attacker. CSRF can be as powerful as the web application that it attacks." *web2py prevents CSRF as well as accidental double submission of forms by assigning a one-time random token to each form. Moreover web2py uses UUID for session cookie.*

- "Information Leakage and Improper Error Handling: Applications can unintentionally leak information about their configuration, internal workings, or violate privacy through a variety of application problems. Attackers use this weakness to steal sensitive data, or conduct more serious attacks." *web2py includes a ticketing system. No error can result in code being exposed to the users. All errors are logged and a ticket is issued to the user that allows error tracking. But errors and source code are accessible only to the administrator.*

- "Broken Authentication and Session Management: Account credentials and session tokens are often not properly protected. Attackers compromise passwords, keys, or authentication tokens to assume other users' identities." *web2py provides a built-in mechanism for administrator authentication, and it manages sessions independently for each application. The administrative interface also forces the use of secure session cookies when the client is not "localhost". For applications, it includes a powerful Role Based Access Control API.*

- "Insecure Cryptographic Storage: Web applications rarely use cryptographic functions properly to protect data and credentials. Attackers use weakly protected data to conduct identity theft and other crimes, such as credit card fraud." *web2py uses the MD5 or the HMAC+SHA-512 hash algorithms to protect stored passwords. Other algorithms are also available.*

- "Insecure Communications: Applications frequently fail to encrypt network traffic when it is necessary to protect sensitive communications." *web2py includes the SSL-enabled [22] Rocket WSGI server, but it can also use Apache or Lighttpd and mod_ssl to provide SSL encryption of communications.*

- "Failure to Restrict URL Access: Frequently an application only protects sensitive functionality by preventing the display of links or URLs to unauthorized users. Attackers can use this weakness to access and perform unauthorized operations by accessing those URLs directly." *web2py maps URL requests to Python modules and functions. web2py provides a mechanism for declaring which functions are public and which require authentication and authorization. The included Role Based Access Control API allow developers to restrict access to any function based on login, group membership or group based permissions. The permissions are very granular and can be combined with database filters to allow, for example, to give access to specific tables and/or records. web2py also allows digitally signed URL and provides API to digitally sign Ajax callbacks.*

web2py was reviewed for security and you can find the result of the review in ref. [23].

1.6   In the box

You can download web2py from the official web site:

```
http://www.web2py.com
```

web2py is composed of the following components:

- **libraries**:   provide core functionality of web2py and are accessible programmatically.

- **web server**: the Rocket WSGI web server.

- the **admin** application: used to create, design, and manage other web2py applications. **admin** provides a complete web-based Integrated Development Environment (IDE) for building web2py applications. It also includes other functionality, such as web-based testing and a web-based shell.

- the **examples** application: contains documentation and interactive examples. **examples** is a clone of the official web2py.com web site, and includes epydoc documentation.

- the **welcome** application: the basic scaffolding template for any other application. By default it includes a pure CSS cascading menu and user authentication (discussed in Chapter 9).

web2py is distributed in source code, and in binary form for Microsoft Windows and for Mac OS X.

The source code distribution can be used in any platform where Python runs and includes the above-mentioned components. To run the source code, you need Python 2.5 or 2.7 pre-installed on the system. You also need one of the supported database engines installed. For testing and light-demand applications, you can use the SQLite database, included with Python 2.7.

The binary versions of web2py (for Windows and Mac OS X) include a Python 2.7 interpreter and the SQLite database. Technically, these two are not components of web2py. Including them in the binary distributions enables you to run web2py out of the box.

The following image depicts the overall web2py structure:

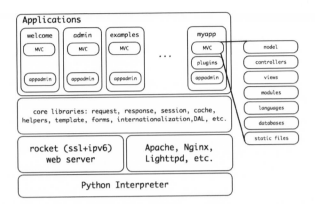

At the bottom we find the interpreter. Moving up we find the web
server (rocket), the libraries, and the applications. Each application consists
for its own MVC design (models, controllers, views, modules, languages,
databases, and static files). Each application includes it own database
administration code (appadmin). Every web2py instance ships with three
applications: welcome (the scaffolding app), admin (the web based IDE),
and examples (copy of website and examples).

1.7   About this book

This book includes the following chapters, besides this introduction:

- Chapter 2 is a minimalist introduction to Python. It assumes knowledge of
  both procedural and object-oriented programming concepts such as loops,
  conditions, function calls and classes, and covers basic Python syntax. It
  also covers examples of Python modules that are used throughout the
  book. If you already know Python, you may skip Chapter 2.

- Chapter 3 shows how to start web2py, discusses the administrative
  interface, and guides the reader through various examples of increasing
  complexity: an application that returns a string, a counter application, an
  image blog, and a full blown wiki application that allows image uploads
  and comments, provides authentication, authorization, web services and
  an RSS feed. While reading this chapter, you may need to refer to Chapter

2 for general Python syntax and to the following chapters for a more detailed reference about the functions that are used.

- Chapter 4 covers more systematically the core structure and libraries: URL mapping, request, response, sessions, caching, schedulre, cron, internationalization and general workflow.

- Chapter 5 is a reference for the template language used to build views. It shows how to embed Python code into HTML, and demonstrates the use of helpers (objects that can generate HTML).

- Chapter 6 covers the Database Abstraction Layer, or DAL. The syntax of the DAL is presented through a series of examples.

- Chapter 7 covers forms, form validation and form processing. FORM is the low level helper for form building. SQLFORM is the high level form builder. In Chapter 7 we also discuss Create/Read/Update/Delete (CRUD) API.

- Chapter 8 covers communication with as sending emails and SMSes.

- Chapter 9 covers authentication, authorization and the extensible Role-Based Access Control mechanism available in web2py. Mail configuration and CAPTCHA are also discussed here, since they are used for authentication. In the third edition of the book we have added extensive coverage of integration with third-party authentication mechanisms such as OpenID, OAuth, Google, Facebook, LinkedIn, etc.

- Chapter 10 is about creating web services in web2py. We provide examples of integration with the Google Web Toolkit via Pyjamas, and with Adobe Flash via PyAMF.

- Chapter 11 is about web2py and jQuery recipes. web2py is designed mainly for server-side programming, but it includes jQuery, since we have found it to be the best open-source JavaScript library available for effects and Ajax. In this chapter, we discuss how to effectively use jQuery with web2py.

- Chapter 12 discusses web2py components and plugins as a way to build modular applications. We provide an example of a plugin that implements many commonly used functionality, such as charting, comments, and tagging.

- Chapter 13 is about production deployment of web2py applications. We specifically discuss the deployment on a LAMP web server (which we consider the main deployment alternative). We discuss alterantive web servers, and configuration of the PostgreSQL database. We discuss running as a service on a Microsoft Windows environment, and deployment on some specific platforms including Google Applications Engine, Heorku, and PythonAnywhere. In this chapter, we also discuss security and scalability issues.

- Chapter 14 contains a variety of other recipes to solve specific tasks, including upgrades, geocoding, pagination, the Twitter API, and more.

This book only covers basic web2py functionalities and the API that ships with web2py. This book does not cover web2py appliances (i.e. ready made applications).

You can download web2py appliances from the corresponding web site [24].

You can find additional topics discussed on the usergroup [25]. There is also AlterEgo [26], the old web2py blog and FAQ. This book has been written using the markmin syntax and automatically converted to HTML, LaTeX and PDF.

1.8 Support

The main support channel is the usergroup [25], with dozens of posts every day. Even if you're a newbie, don't hesitate to ask - we'll be pleased to help you. There is also a formal issue tracker system on http://code.google.com/p/web2py/issue. Last but not least, you can have professional support (see the web site for details).

1.9   Contribute

Any help is really appreciated. You can help other users on the user group, or by directly submitting patches on the program (at the GitHub site https://github.com/web2py/web2py). Even if you find a typo on this book, or have an improvement on it, the best way to help is by patching the book itself (which is under the source folder of the repository at https://github.com/mdipierro/web2py-book).

1.10   Elements of style

PEP8 [27] contains good style practices when programming with Python. You will find that web2py does not always follow these rules. This is not because of omissions or negligence; it is our belief that the users of web2py should follow these rules and we encourage it. We chose not to follow some of those rules when defining web2py helper objects in order to minimize the probability of name conflict with objects defined by the user.

For example, the class that represents a <div> is called DIV, while according to the Python style reference it should have been called Div. We believe that, for this specific example that using an all-upper-case "DIV" is a more natural choice. Moreover, this approach leaves programmers free to create a class called "Div" if they choose to do so. Our syntax also maps naturally into the DOM notation of most browsers (including, for example, Firefox).

According to the Python style guide, all-upper-case strings should be used for constants and not variables. Continuing with our example, even considering that DIV is a class, it is a special class that should never be modified by the user because doing so would break other web2py applications. Hence, we believe this qualifies the DIV class as something that should be treated as a constant, further justifying our choice of notation.

In summary, the following conventions are followed:

- HTML helpers and validators are all upper case for the reasons discussed above (for example DIV, A, FORM, URL).

- The translator object T is upper case despite the fact that it is an instance of a class and not a class itself. Logically the translator object performs an action similar to the HTML helpers, it affects rendering part of the presentation. Also, T needs to be easy to locate in the code and must have a short name.

- DAL classes follow the Python style guide (first letter capitalized), for example Table, Field, Query, Row, Rows, etc.

In all other cases we believe we have followed, as much as possible, the Python Style Guide (PEP8). For example all instance objects are lower-case (request, response, session, cache), and all internal classes are capitalized.

In all the examples of this book, web2py keywords are shown in bold, while strings and comments are shown in italic.

1.11 License

web2py is licensed under the LGPL version 3 License. The full text of the license if available in ref. [28].

In accordance with LGPL you may:

- redistribute web2py with your apps (including official web2py binary versions)

- release your applications which use official web2py libraries under any license you wish

Yet you must:

- make clear in the documentation that your application uses web2py

- release any modification of the web2py libraries under the LGPLv3 license

The license includes the usual disclaimer:

THERE IS NO WARRANTY FOR THE PROGRAM, TO THE EXTENT PERMITTED BY APPLICABLE LAW. EXCEPT WHEN OTHERWISE STATED IN WRITING THE COPYRIGHT HOLDERS AND/OR OTHER

PARTIES PROVIDE THE PROGRAM "AS IS" WITHOUT WARRANTY OF ANY KIND, EITHER EXPRESSED OR IMPLIED, INCLUDING, BUT NOT LIMITED TO, THE IMPLIED WARRANTIES OF MERCHANTABILITY AND FITNESS FOR A PARTICULAR PURPOSE. THE ENTIRE RISK AS TO THE QUALITY AND PERFORMANCE OF THE PROGRAM IS WITH YOU. SHOULD THE PROGRAM PROVE DEFECTIVE, YOU ASSUME THE COST OF ALL NECESSARY SERVICING, REPAIR OR CORRECTION.

IN NO EVENT UNLESS REQUIRED BY APPLICABLE LAW OR AGREED TO IN WRITING WILL ANY COPYRIGHT HOLDER, OR ANY OTHER PARTY WHO MODIFIES AND/OR CONVEYS THE PROGRAM AS PERMITTED ABOVE, BE LIABLE TO YOU FOR DAMAGES, INCLUDING ANY GENERAL, SPECIAL, INCIDENTAL OR CONSEQUENTIAL DAMAGES ARISING OUT OF THE USE OR INABILITY TO USE THE PROGRAM (INCLUDING BUT NOT LIMITED TO LOSS OF DATA OR DATA BEING RENDERED INACCURATE OR LOSSES SUSTAINED BY YOU OR THIRD PARTIES OR A FAILURE OF THE PROGRAM TO OPERATE WITH ANY OTHER PROGRAMS), EVEN IF SUCH HOLDER OR OTHER PARTY HAS BEEN ADVISED OF THE POSSIBILITY OF SUCH DAMAGES.

Earlier versions

Earlier versions of web2py, 1.0.*-1.90.*, were released under the GPL2 license plus a commercial exception which, for practical purposes, was very similar to the current LPGLv3.

Third party software distributed with web2py web2py contains third party software under the gluon/contrib/ folder and various JavaScript and CSS files. These files are distributed with web2py under their original licenses, as stated in the files.

1.12 Acknowledgments

web2py was originally developed by and copyrighted by Massimo Di Pierro. The first version (1.0) was released in October, 2007. Since then it has been adopted by many users, some of whom have also contributed bug reports, testing, debugging, patches, and proofreading of this book.

Some of the major developers and contributors are, in alphabetical order by first name:

Adam Bryzak, Adam Gojdas, Adrian Klaver, Alain Boulch, Alan Etkin, Alec Taylor, Alexandre Andrade, Alexey Nezhdanov, Alvaro Justen, Anand Vaidya, Anatoly Belyakov, Ander Arbelaiz, Anders Roos, Andrew Replogle, Andrew Willimott, Angelo Compagnucci, Angelo and Villas, Annet Vermeer, Anthony Bastardi, Anton Muecki, Antonio Ramos, Arun Rajeevan, Attila Csipa, Ben Goosman, Ben Reinhart, Benjamin, Bernd Rothert, Bill Ferret, Blomqvist, Boris Manojlovic, Branko Vukelic, Brent Zeiben, Brian Cottingham, Brian Harrison, Brian Meredyk, Bruno Rocha, CJ Lazell, Caleb Hattingh, Carlos Galindo, Carlos Hanson, Carsten Haese, Cedric Meyer, Charles Law, Charles Winebrinner, Chris Clark, Chris May, Chris Sanders, Christian Foster Howes, Christopher Smiga, Christopher Steel, Clavin Sim, Cliff Kachinske, Corne Dickens, Craig Younkins, Dan McGee, Dan Ragubba, Dane Wright, Danny Morgan, Daniel Gonz, Daniel Haag, Daniel Lin, Dave Stoll, David Adley, David Harrison, David Lin, David Marko, David Wagner, Denes Lengyel, Diaz Luis, Dirk Krause, Dominic Koenig, Doug Warren, Douglas Philips, Douglas Soares de Andrade, Douglas and Alan, Dustin Bensing, Elcio Ferreira, Eric Vicenti, Erwin Olario, Falko Krause, Farsheed Ashouri, Felipe Meirelles, Flavien Scheurer, Fran Boon, Francisco Gama, Fred Yanowski, Friedrich Weber, Gabriele Alberti, Gergely Kontra, Gergely Peli, Gerley Kontra, Gilson Filho, Glenn Caltech, Graham Dumpleton, Gregory Benjamin, Gustavo Di Pietro, Gyuris Szabolcs, Hamdy Abdel-Badeea, Hans C. v. Stockhausen, Hans Donner, Hans Murx, Huaiyu Wang, Ian Reinhart Geiser, Iceberg, Igor Gassko, Ismael Serratos, Jan Beilicke, Jay Kelkar, Jeff Bauer, Jesus Matrinez, Jim Karsten, Joachim Breitsprecher, Joakim Eriksson, Joe Barnhart, Joel Carrier, Joel Samuelsson, John Heenan, Jon Romero, Jonas Rundberg, Jonathan Benn, Jonathan Lundell, Jose Jachuf, Joseph Piron, Josh Goldfoot, Josh Jaques, José Vicente de Sousa, Jurgis Pralgauskis, Keith Yang, Kenji Hosoda, Kenneth Lundstr, Kirill Spitsin, Kyle Smith, Larry Weinberg, Limodou, Loren McGinnis, Louis DaPrato, Luca De Alfaro, Luca Zachetti, Lucas D'Ávila, Madhukar R Pai, Manuele Presenti, Marc Abramowitz,

Marcel Hellkamp, Marcel Leuthi, Marcello Della Longa, Margaret Greaney, Maria Mitica, Mariano Reingart, Marin Prajic, Marin Pranji, Marius van Niekerk, Mark Kirkwood, Mark Larsen, Mark Moore, Markus Gritsch, Mart Senecal, Martin Hufsky, Martin Mulone, Martin Weissenboeck, Mateusz Banach, Mathew Grabau, Mathieu Clabaut, Matt Doiron, Matthew Norris, Michael Fig, Michael Herman, Michael Howden, Michael Jursa, Michael Toomim, Michael Willis, Michele Comitini, Miguel Goncalves, Miguel Lopez, Mike Amy, Mike Dickun, Mike Ellis, Mike Pechkin, Milan Melena, Muhammet Aydin, Napoleon Moreno, Nathan Freeze, Niall Sweeny, Niccolo Polo, Nick Groenke, Nick Vargish, Nico de Groot, Nico Zanferrari, Nicolas Bruxer, Nik Klever, Olaf Ferger, Oliver Dain, Olivier Roch Vilato, Omi Chiba, Ondrej Such, Ont Rif, Oscar Benjamin, Osman Masood, Ovidio Marinho Falcao Neto, Pai, Panos Jee, Paolo Betti, Paolo Caruccio, Paolo Gasparello, Paolo Valleri, Patrick Breitenbach, Pearu Peterson, Peli Gergely, Pete Hunt, Peter Kirchner, Phyo Arkar Lwin, Pierre Thibault, Pieter Muller, Piotr Banasziewicz, Ramjee Ganti, Richard Gordon, Richard Ree, Robert Kooij, Robert Valentak, Roberto Perdomo, Robin Bhattacharyya, Roman Bataev, Ron McOuat, Ross Peoples, Ruijun Luo, Running Calm, Ryan Seto, Salomon Derossi, Sam Sheftel, Scott Roberts, Sergey Podlesnyi, Sharriff Aina, Simone Bizzotto, Sriram Durbha, Sterling Hankins, Stuart Rackham, Telman Yusupov, Thadeus Burgess, Thomas Dallagnese, Tim Farrell, Tim Michelsen, Tim Richardson, Timothy Farrell, Tito Garrido, Tyrone Hattingh, Vasile Ermicioi, Vidul Nikolaev Petrov, Vidul Petrov, Vinicius Assef, Vladimir Donnikov, Vladyslav Kozlovsky, Vladyslav Kozlovskyy, Wang Huaiyu, Wen Gong, Wes James, Will Stevens, Yair Eshel, Yarko Tymciurak, Yoshiyuki Nakamura, Younghyun Jo, Zahariash.

I am sure I forgot somebody, so I apologize.

I particularly thank Anthony, Jonathan, Mariano, Bruno, Vladyslav, Martin, Nathan, Simone, Thadeus, Tim, Iceberg, Denes, Hans, Christian, Fran and Patrick for their major contributions to web2py and Anthony, Alvaro, Brian, Bruno, Denes, Dane Denny, Erwin, Felipe, Graham, Jonathan, Hans, Kyle, Mark, Margaret, Michele, Nico, Richard, Roberto, Robin, Roman, Scott, Shane, Sharriff, Sriram, Sterling, Stuart, Thadeus, Wen (and others) for proofreading various versions of this book. Their contribution was invaluable. If you find any errors in this book, they are exclusively my fault, probably introduced by a last-minute edit. I also thank Ryan Steffen of Wiley Custom Learning Solutions for help with publishing the first edition of this book. web2py contains code from the following authors, whom I would like to thank:

Guido van Rossum for Python [2], Peter Hunt, Richard Gordon, Timothy Farrell for the Rocket [19] web server, Christopher Dolivet for EditArea [29], Bob Ippolito for simplejson [30], Simon Cusack and Grant Edwards for pyRTF [31], Dalke Scientific Software for pyRSS2Gen [32], Mark Pilgrim for feedparser [33], Trent Mick for markdown2 [34], Allan Saddi for fcgi.py, Evan Martin for the Python memcache module [35], John Resig for jQuery [36].

I thank Helmut Epp (provost of DePaul University), David Miller (Dean of the College of Computing and Digital Media of DePaul University), and Estia Eichten (Member of MetaCryption LLC), for their continuous trust and support.

Finally, I wish to thank my wife, Claudia, and my son, Marco, for putting up with me during the many hours I have spent developing web2py, exchanging emails with users and collaborators, and writing this book. This book is dedicated to them.

2

The Python language

2.1 About Python

Python is a general-purpose high-level programming language. Its design philosophy emphasizes programmer productivity and code readability. It has a minimalist core syntax with very few basic commands and simple semantics, but it also has a large and comprehensive standard library, including an Application Programming Interface (API) to many of the underlying operating system (OS) functions. Python code, while minimalist, defines built-in objects such as linked lists (`list`), tuples (`tuple`), hash tables (`dict`), and arbitrarily long integers (`long`).

Python supports multiple programming paradigms, including object-oriented (`class`), imperative (`def`), and functional (`lambda`) programming. Python has a dynamic type system and automatic memory management using reference counting (similar to Perl, Ruby, and Scheme).

Python was first released by Guido van Rossum in 1991. The language has an open, community-based development model managed by the non-profit Python Software Foundation. There are many interpreters and compilers that implement the Python language, including one in Java (Jython) but, in this brief review, we refer to the reference C implementation created by Guido.

You can find many tutorials, the official documentation and library references of the language on the official Python website. [2]

For additional Python references, we can recommend the books in ref. [37] and ref. [38].

You may skip this chapter if you are already familiar with the Python language.

2.2   Starting up

The binary distributions of web2py for Microsoft Windows or Apple OS X come packaged with the Python interpreter built into the distribution file itself.

You can start it on Windows with the following command (type at the DOS prompt):

```
web2py.exe -S welcome
```

On Apple OS X, enter the following command type in a Terminal window (assuming you're in the same folder as web2py.app):

```
./web2py.app/Contents/MacOS/web2py -S welcome
```

On a Linux or other Unix box, chances are that you have Python already installed. If so, at a shell prompt type:

```
python web2py.py -S welcome
```

If you do not have Python 2.5 (or later 2.x) already installed, you will have to download and install it before running web2py.

The -S welcome command line option instructs web2py to run the interactive shell as if the commands were executed in a controller for the **welcome** application, the web2py scaffolding application. This exposes almost all web2py classes, objects and functions to you. This is the only difference between the web2py interactive command line and the normal Python command line.

The admin interface also provides a web-based shell for each application. You can access the one for the "welcome" application at.

```
http://127.0.0.1:8000/admin/shell/index/welcome
```

You can try all the examples in this chapter using the normal shell or the web-based shell.

2.3   help, dir

The Python language provides two commands to obtain documentation about objects defined in the current scope, both built-in and user-defined.

We can ask for help about an object, for example "1":

```
 1  >>> help(1)
 2  Help on int object:
 3
 4  class int(object)
 5   |  int(x[, base]) -> integer
 6   |
 7   |  Convert a string or number to an integer, if possible.  A floating point
 8   |  argument will be truncated towards zero (this does not include a string
 9   |  representation of a floating point number!)  When converting a string, use
10   |  the optional base.  It is an error to supply a base when converting a
11   |  non-string. If the argument is outside the integer range a long object
12   |  will be returned instead.
13   |
14   |  Methods defined here:
15   |
16   |  __abs__(...)
17   |      x.__abs__() <==> abs(x)
18  ...
```

and, since "1" is an integer, we get a description about the int class and all its methods. Here the output has been truncated because it is very long and detailed.

Similarly, we can obtain a list of methods of the object "1" with the command dir:

```
 1  >>> dir(1)
 2  ['__abs__', ..., '__xor__']
```

2.4   Types

Python is a dynamically typed language, meaning that variables do not have a type and therefore do not have to be declared. Values, on the other hand, do have a type. You can query a variable for the type of value it contains:

```
1  >>> a = 3
2  >>> print type(a)
3  <type 'int'>
4  >>> a = 3.14
5  >>> print type(a)
6  <type 'float'>
7  >>> a = 'hello python'
8  >>> print type(a)
9  <type 'str'>
```

Python also includes, natively, data structures such as lists and dictionaries.

2.4.1   str

Python supports the use of two different types of strings: ASCII strings and Unicode strings. ASCII strings are delimited by '...', "..." or by '..' or """...""". Triple quotes delimit multiline strings. Unicode strings start with a u followed by the string containing Unicode characters. A Unicode string can be converted into an ASCII string by choosing an encoding for example:

```
1  >>> a = 'this is an ASCII string'
2  >>> b = u'This is a Unicode string'
3  >>> a = b.encode('utf8')
```

After executing these three commands, the resulting a is an ASCII string storing UTF8 encoded characters. By design, web2py uses UTF8 encoded strings internally.

It is also possible to write variables into strings in various ways:

```
1  >>> print 'number is ' + str(3)
2  number is 3
3  >>> print 'number is %s' % (3)
4  number is 3
5  >>> print 'number is %(number)s' % dict(number=3)
6  number is 3
```

The last notation is more explicit and less error prone, and is to be preferred.

Many Python objects, for example numbers, can be serialized into strings using str or repr. These two commands are very similar but produce slightly different output. For example:

```
1 >>> for i in [3, 'hello']:
2       print str(i), repr(i)
3 3 3
4 hello 'hello'
```

For user-defined classes, str and repr can be defined/redefined using the special operators __str__ and __repr__. These are briefly described later on; for more, refer to the official Python documentation [39]. repr always has a default value.

Another important characteristic of a Python string is that, like a list, it is an iterable object.

```
1 >>> for i in 'hello':
2       print i
3 h
4 e
5 l
6 l
7 o
```

2.4.2 list

The main methods of a Python list are append, insert, and delete:

```
1 >>> a = [1, 2, 3]
2 >>> print type(a)
3 <type 'list'>
4 >>> a.append(8)
5 >>> a.insert(2, 7)
6 >>> del a[0]
7 >>> print a
8 [2, 7, 3, 8]
9 >>> print len(a)
10 4
```

Lists can be sliced:

```
1 >>> print a[:3]
2 [2, 7, 3]
3 >>> print a[1:]
4 [7, 3, 8]
5 >>> print a[-2:]
```

```
6  [3, 8]
```

and concatenated:

```
1  >>> a = [2, 3]
2  >>> b = [5, 6]
3  >>> print a + b
4  [2, 3, 5, 6]
```

A list is iterable; you can loop over it:

```
1  >>> a = [1, 2, 3]
2  >>> for i in a:
3          print i
4  1
5  2
6  3
```

The elements of a list do not have to be of the same type; they can be any type of Python object.

There is a very common situation for which a *list comprehension* can be used. Consider the following code:

```
1  >>> a = [1,2,3,4,5]
2  >>> b = []
3  >>> for x in a:
4          if x % 2 == 0:
5              b.append(x * 3)
6  >>> b
7  [6, 12]
```

This code clearly processes a list of items, selects and modifies a subset of the input list, and creates a new result list, and this code can be entirely replaced with the following list comprehension:

```
1  >>> a = [1,2,3,4,5]
2  >>> b = [x * 3 for x in a if x % 2 == 0]
3  >>> b
4  [6, 12]
```

2.4.3   tuple

A tuple is like a list, but its size and elements are immutable, while in a list they are mutable. If a tuple element is an object, the object attributes are mutable. A tuple is delimited by round brackets.

```
1  >>> a = (1, 2, 3)
```

So while this works for a list:

```
>>> a = [1, 2, 3]
>>> a[1] = 5
>>> print a
[1, 5, 3]
```

the element assignment does not work for a tuple:

```
>>> a = (1, 2, 3)
>>> print a[1]
2
>>> a[1] = 5
Traceback (most recent call last):
  File "<stdin>", line 1, in <module>
TypeError: 'tuple' object does not support item assignment
```

A tuple, like a list, is an iterable object. Notice that a tuple consisting of a single element must include a trailing comma, as shown below:

```
>>> a = (1)
>>> print type(a)
<type 'int'>
>>> a = (1,)
>>> print type(a)
<type 'tuple'>
```

Tuples are very useful for efficient packing of objects because of their immutability, and the brackets are often optional:

```
>>> a = 2, 3, 'hello'
>>> x, y, z = a
>>> print x
2
>>> print z
hello
```

2.4.4 dict

A Python dict-ionary is a hash table that maps a key object to a value object. For example:

```
>>> a = {'k':'v', 'k2':3}
>>> a['k']
v
>>> a['k2']
3
>>> a.has_key('k')
True
```

```
8  >>> a.has_key('v')
9  False
```

Keys can be of any hashable type (int, string, or any object whose class implements the __hash__ method). Values can be of any type. Different keys and values in the same dictionary do not have to be of the same type. If the keys are alphanumeric characters, a dictionary can also be declared with the alternative syntax:

```
1  >>> a = dict(k='v', h2=3)
2  >>> a['k']
3  v
4  >>> print a
5  {'k':'v', 'h2':3}
```

Useful methods are has_key, keys, values and items:

```
1  >>> a = dict(k='v', k2=3)
2  >>> print a.keys()
3  ['k', 'k2']
4  >>> print a.values()
5  ['v', 3]
6  >>> print a.items()
7  [('k', 'v'), ('k2', 3)]
```

The items method produces a list of tuples, each containing a key and its associated value.

Dictionary elements and list elements can be deleted with the command del:

```
1  >>> a = [1, 2, 3]
2  >>> del a[1]
3  >>> print a
4  [1, 3]
5  >>> a = dict(k='v', h2=3)
6  >>> del a['h2']
7  >>> print a
8  {'k':'v'}
```

Internally, Python uses the hash operator to convert objects into integers, and uses that integer to determine where to store the value.

```
1  >>> hash("hello world")
2  -1500746465
```

2.5 About indentation

Python uses indentation to delimit blocks of code. A block starts with a line ending in colon, and continues for all lines that have a similar or higher indentation as the next line. For example:

```
1  >>> i = 0
2  >>> while i < 3:
3  >>>     print i
4  >>>     i = i + 1
5  >>>
6  0
7  1
8  2
```

It is common to use four spaces for each level of indentation. It is a good policy not to mix tabs with spaces, which can result in (invisible) confusion.

2.6 for...in

In Python, you can loop over iterable objects:

```
1  >>> a = [0, 1, 'hello', 'python']
2  >>> for i in a:
3          print i
4  0
5  1
6  hello
7  python
```

One common shortcut is xrange, which generates an iterable range without storing the entire list of elements.

```
1  >>> for i in xrange(0, 4):
2          print i
3  0
4  1
5  2
6  3
```

This is equivalent to the C/C++/C#/Java syntax:

```
1  for(int i=0; i<4; i=i+1) { print(i); }
```

Another useful command is enumerate, which counts while looping:

```
1  >>> a = [0, 1, 'hello', 'python']
```

```
2  >>> for i, j in enumerate(a):
3         print i, j
4  0 0
5  1 1
6  2 hello
7  3 python
```

There is also a keyword range(a, b, c) that returns a list of integers starting with the value a, incrementing by c, and ending with the last value smaller than b, a defaults to 0 and c defaults to 1. xrange is similar but does not actually generate the list, only an iterator over the list; thus it is better for looping.

You can jump out of a loop using break

```
1  >>> for i in [1, 2, 3]:
2         print i
3         break
4  1
```

You can jump to the next loop iteration without executing the entire code block with continue

```
1  >>> for i in [1, 2, 3]:
2         print i
3         continue
4         print 'test'
5  1
6  2
7  3
```

2.7   while

The while loop in Python works much as it does in many other programming languages, by looping an indefinite number of times and testing a condition before each iteration. If the condition is False, the loop ends.

```
1  >>> i = 0
2  >>> while i < 10:
3         i = i + 1
4  >>> print i
5  10
```

There is no loop...until construct in Python.

2.8 if...elif...else

The use of conditionals in Python is intuitive:

```
1 >>> for i in range(3):
2 >>>     if i == 0:
3 >>>         print 'zero'
4 >>>     elif i == 1:
5 >>>         print 'one'
6 >>>     else:
7 >>>         print 'other'
8 zero
9 one
10 other
```

"elif" means "else if". Both elif and else clauses are optional. There can be more than one elif but only one else statement. Complex conditions can be created using the not, and and or operators.

```
1 >>> for i in range(3):
2 >>>     if i == 0 or (i == 1 and i + 1 == 2):
3 >>>         print '0 or 1'
```

2.9 try...except...else...finally

Python can throw - pardon, raise - Exceptions:

```
1 >>> try:
2 >>>     a = 1 / 0
3 >>> except Exception, e:
4 >>>     print 'oops: %s' % e
5 >>> else:
6 >>>     print 'no problem here'
7 >>> finally:
8 >>>     print 'done'
9 oops: integer division or modulo by zero
10 done
```

If the exception is raised, it is caught by the except clause, which is executed, while the else clause is not. If no exception is raised, the except clause is not executed, but the else one is. The finally clause is always executed.

There can be multiple except clauses for different possible exceptions:

```
1 >>> try:
2 >>>     raise SyntaxError
```

```
3  >>> except ValueError:
4  >>>     print 'value error'
5  >>> except SyntaxError:
6  >>>     print 'syntax error'
7  syntax error
```

The else and finally clauses are optional.

Here is a list of built-in Python exceptions + HTTP (defined by web2py)

```
1   BaseException
2   +-- HTTP (defined by web2py)
3   +-- SystemExit
4   +-- KeyboardInterrupt
5   +-- Exception
6       +-- GeneratorExit
7       +-- StopIteration
8       +-- StandardError
9       |   +-- ArithmeticError
10      |   |   +-- FloatingPointError
11      |   |   +-- OverflowError
12      |   |   +-- ZeroDivisionError
13      |   +-- AssertionError
14      |   +-- AttributeError
15      |   +-- EnvironmentError
16      |   |   +-- IOError
17      |   |   +-- OSError
18      |   |       +-- WindowsError (Windows)
19      |   |       +-- VMSError (VMS)
20      |   +-- EOFError
21      |   +-- ImportError
22      |   +-- LookupError
23      |   |   +-- IndexError
24      |   |   +-- KeyError
25      |   +-- MemoryError
26      |   +-- NameError
27      |   |   +-- UnboundLocalError
28      |   +-- ReferenceError
29      |   +-- RuntimeError
30      |   |   +-- NotImplementedError
31      |   +-- SyntaxError
32      |   |   +-- IndentationError
33      |   |       +-- TabError
34      |   +-- SystemError
35      |   +-- TypeError
36      |   +-- ValueError
37      |   |   +-- UnicodeError
38      |   |       +-- UnicodeDecodeError
39      |   |       +-- UnicodeEncodeError
```

```
40                |    |              +-- UnicodeTranslateError
41          +-- Warning
42              +-- DeprecationWarning
43              +-- PendingDeprecationWarning
44              +-- RuntimeWarning
45              +-- SyntaxWarning
46              +-- UserWarning
47              +-- FutureWarning
48              +-- ImportWarning
49              +-- UnicodeWarning
```

For a detailed description of each of them, refer to the official Python documentation. web2py exposes only one new exception, called HTTP. When raised, it causes the program to return an HTTP error page (for more on this refer to Chapter 4).

Any object can be raised as an exception, but it is good practice to raise objects that extend one of the built-in exception classes.

2.10   def...return

Functions are declared using def. Here is a typical Python function:

```
1  >>> def f(a, b):
2          return a + b
3  >>> print f(4, 2)
4  6
```

There is no need (or way) to specify types of the arguments or the return type(s). In this example, a function f is defined that can take two arguments.

Functions are the first code syntax feature described in this chapter to introduce the concept of *scope*, or *namespace*. In the above example, the identifiers a and b are undefined outside of the scope of function f:

```
1  >>> def f(a):
2          return a + 1
3  >>> print f(1)
4  2
5  >>> print a
6  Traceback (most recent call last):
7    File "<pyshell#22>", line 1, in <module>
8      print a
9  NameError: name 'a' is not defined
```

Identifiers defined outside of function scope are accessible within the function; observe how the identifier a is handled in the following code:

```
1  >>> a = 1
2  >>> def f(b):
3          return a + b
4  >>> print f(1)
5  2
6  >>> a = 2
7  >>> print f(1) # new value of a is used
8  3
9  >>> a = 1 # reset a
10 >>> def g(b):
11         a = 2 # creates a new local a
12         return a + b
13 >>> print g(2)
14 4
15 >>> print a # global a is unchanged
16 1
```

If a is modified, subsequent function calls will use the new value of the global a because the function definition binds the storage location of the identifier a, not the value of a itself at the time of function declaration; however, if a is assigned-to inside function g, the global a is unaffected because the new local a hides the global value. The external-scope reference can be used in the creation of *closures*:

```
1  >>> def f(x):
2          def g(y):
3              return x * y
4          return g
5  >>> doubler = f(2) # doubler is a new function
6  >>> tripler = f(3) # tripler is a new function
7  >>> quadrupler = f(4) # quadrupler is a new function
8  >>> print doubler(5)
9  10
10 >>> print tripler(5)
11 15
12 >>> print quadrupler(5)
13 20
```

Function f creates new functions; and note that the scope of the name g is entirely internal to f. Closures are extremely powerful.

Function arguments can have default values, and can return multiple results:

```
1  >>> def f(a, b=2):
2          return a + b, a - b
```

```
3 >>> x, y = f(5)
4 >>> print x
5 7
6 >>> print y
7 3
```

Function arguments can be passed explicitly by name, and this means that the order of arguments specified in the caller can be different than the order of arguments with which the function was defined:

```
1 >>> def f(a, b=2):
2         return a + b, a - b
3 >>> x, y = f(b=5, a=2)
4 >>> print x
5 7
6 >>> print y
7 -3
```

Functions can also take a runtime-variable number of arguments:

```
1 >>> def f(*a, **b):
2         return a, b
3 >>> x, y = f(3, 'hello', c=4, test='world')
4 >>> print x
5 (3, 'hello')
6 >>> print y
7 {'c':4, 'test':'world'}
```

Here arguments not passed by name (3, 'hello') are stored in the tuple a, and arguments passed by name (c and test) are stored in the dictionary b.

In the opposite case, a list or tuple can be passed to a function that requires individual positional arguments by unpacking them:

```
1 >>> def f(a, b):
2         return a + b
3 >>> c = (1, 2)
4 >>> print f(*c)
5 3
```

and a dictionary can be unpacked to deliver keyword arguments:

```
1 >>> def f(a, b):
2         return a + b
3 >>> c = {'a':1, 'b':2}
4 >>> print f(**c)
5 3
```

2.10.1   lambda

lambda provides a way to create a very short unnamed function very easily:

```
1  >>> a = lambda b: b + 2
2  >>> print a(3)
3  5
```

The expression "lambda [a]:[b]" literally reads as "a function with arguments [a] that returns [b]". The lambda expression is itself unnamed, but the function acquires a name by being assigned to identifier a. The scoping rules for def apply to lambda equally, and in fact the code above, with respect to a, is identical to the function declaration using def:

```
1  >>> def a(b):
2          return b + 2
3  >>> print a(3)
4  5
```

The only benefit of lambda is brevity; however, brevity can be very convenient in certain situations. Consider a function called map that applies a function to all items in a list, creating a new list:

```
1  >>> a = [1, 7, 2, 5, 4, 8]
2  >>> map(lambda x: x + 2, a)
3  [3, 9, 4, 7, 6, 10]
```

This code would have doubled in size had def been used instead of lambda. The main drawback of lambda is that (in the Python implementation) the syntax allows only for a single expression; however, for longer functions, def can be used and the extra cost of providing a function name decreases as the length of the function grows. Just like def, lambda can be used to *curry* functions: new functions can be created by wrapping existing functions such that the new function carries a different set of arguments:

```
1  >>> def f(a, b): return a + b
2  >>> g = lambda a: f(a, 3)
3  >>> g(2)
4  5
```

There are many situations where currying is useful, but one of those is directly useful in web2py: caching. Suppose you have an expensive function that checks whether its argument is prime:

```
1  def isprime(number):
2      for p in range(2, number):
```

```
3        if (number % p) == 0:
4            return False
5    return True
```

This function is obviously time consuming.

Suppose you have a caching function `cache.ram` that takes three arguments: a key, a function and a number of seconds.

```
1  value = cache.ram('key', f, 60)
```

The first time it is called, it calls the function `f()`, stores the output in a dictionary in memory (let's say "d"), and returns it so that value is:

```
1  value = d['key']=f()
```

The second time it is called, if the key is in the dictionary and not older than the number of seconds specified (60), it returns the corresponding value without performing the function call.

```
1  value = d['key']
```

How would you cache the output of the function **isprime** for any input? Here is how:

```
1  >>> number = 7
2  >>> seconds = 60
3  >>> print cache.ram(str(number), lambda: isprime(number), seconds)
4  True
5  >>> print cache.ram(str(number), lambda: isprime(number), seconds)
6  True
```

The output is always the same, but the first time `cache.ram` is called, `isprime` is called; the second time it is not.

> Python functions, created with either `def` or `lambda` allow re-factoring existing functions in terms of a different set of arguments. `cache.ram` and `cache.disk` are web2py caching functions.

2.11 class

Because Python is dynamically typed, Python classes and objects may seem odd. In fact, you do not need to define the member variables (attributes) when declaring a class, and different instances of the same class can have different attributes. Attributes are generally associated with the instance, not the class (except when declared as "class attributes", which is the same as "static member variables" in C++/Java).

Here is an example:

```
1 >>> class MyClass(object): pass
2 >>> myinstance = MyClass()
3 >>> myinstance.myvariable = 3
4 >>> print myinstance.myvariable
5 3
```

Notice that pass is a do-nothing command. In this case it is used to define a class MyClass that contains nothing. MyClass() calls the constructor of the class (in this case the default constructor) and returns an object, an instance of the class. The (object) in the class definition indicates that our class extends the built-in object class. This is not required, but it is good practice.

Here is a more complex class:

```
1 >>> class MyClass(object):
2 >>>     z = 2
3 >>>     def __init__(self, a, b):
4 >>>         self.x = a
5 >>>         self.y = b
6 >>>     def add(self):
7 >>>         return self.x + self.y + self.z
8 >>> myinstance = MyClass(3, 4)
9 >>> print myinstance.add()
10 9
```

Functions declared inside the class are methods. Some methods have special reserved names. For example, __init__ is the constructor. All variables are local variables of the method except variables declared outside methods. For example, z is a *class variable*, equivalent to a C++ *static member variable* that holds the same value for all instances of the class.

Notice that __init__ takes 3 arguments and add takes one, and yet we call them with 2 and 0 arguments respectively. The first argument represents, by convention, the local name used inside the method to refer to the current object. Here we use self to refer to the current object, but we could have used any other name. self plays the same role as *this in C++ or this in Java, but self is not a reserved keyword.

This syntax is necessary to avoid ambiguity when declaring nested classes, such as a class that is local to a method inside another class.

2.12   Special attributes, methods and operators

Class attributes, methods, and operators starting with a double underscore are usually intended to be private (i.e. to be used internally but not exposed outside the class) although this is a convention that is not enforced by the interpreter.

Some of them are reserved keywords and have a special meaning.

Here, as an example, are three of them:

- `__len__`

- `__getitem__`

- `__setitem__`

They can be used, for example, to create a container object that acts like a list:

```
 1 >>> class MyList(object):
 2 >>>     def __init__(self, *a): self.a = list(a)
 3 >>>     def __len__(self): return len(self.a)
 4 >>>     def __getitem__(self, i): return self.a[i]
 5 >>>     def __setitem__(self, i, j): self.a[i] = j
 6 >>> b = MyList(3, 4, 5)
 7 >>> print b[1]
 8 4
 9 >>> b.a[1] = 7
10 >>> print b.a
11 [3, 7, 5]
```

Other special operators include `__getattr__` and `__setattr__`, which define the get and set attributes for the class, and `__sum__` and `__sub__`, which overload arithmetic operators. For the use of these operators we refer the reader to more advanced books on this topic. We have already mentioned the special operators `__str__` and `__repr__`.

2.13   File input/output

In Python you can open and write in a file with:

```
>>> file = open('myfile.txt', 'w')
>>> file.write('hello world')
>>> file.close()
```

Similarly, you can read back from the file with:

```
>>> file = open('myfile.txt', 'r')
>>> print file.read()
hello world
```

Alternatively, you can read in binary mode with "rb", write in binary mode with "wb", and open the file in append mode "a", using standard C notation.

The read command takes an optional argument, which is the number of bytes. You can also jump to any location in a file using seek.

You can read back from the file with read

```
>>> print file.seek(6)
>>> print file.read()
world
```

and you can close the file with:

```
>>> file.close()
```

In the standard distribution of Python, which is known as CPython, variables are reference-counted, including those holding file handles, so CPython knows that when the reference count of an open file handle decreases to zero, the file may be closed and the variable disposed. However, in other implementations of Python such as PyPy, garbage collection is used instead of reference counting, and this means that it is possible that there may accumulate too many open file handles at one time, resulting in an error before the gc has a chance to close and dispose of them all. Therefore it is best to explicitly close file handles when they are no longer needed. *web2py* provides two helper functions, read_file() and write_file() inside the gluon.fileutils namespace that encapsulate the file access and ensure that the file handles being used are properly closed.

When using web2py, you do not know where the current directory is, because it depends on how web2py is configured. The variable request.folder contains the path to the current application. Paths can be concatenated with the command os.path.join, discussed below.

2.14   exec, eval

Unlike Java, Python is a truly interpreted language. This means it has the ability to execute Python statements stored in strings. For example:

```
1  >>> a = "print 'hello world'"
2  >>> exec(a)
3  'hello world'
```

What just happened? The function exec tells the interpreter to call itself and execute the content of the string passed as argument. It is also possible to execute the content of a string within a context defined by the symbols in a dictionary:

```
1  >>> a = "print b"
2  >>> c = dict(b=3)
3  >>> exec(a, {}, c)
4  3
```

Here the interpreter, when executing the string a, sees the symbols defined in c (b in the example), but does not see c or a themselves. This is different than a restricted environment, since exec does not limit what the inner code can do; it just defines the set of variables visible to the code.

A related function is eval, which works very much like exec except that it expects the argument to evaluate to a value, and it returns that value.

```
1  >>> a = "3*4"
2  >>> b = eval(a)
3  >>> print b
4  12
```

2.15   import

The real power of Python is in its library modules. They provide a large and consistent set of Application Programming Interfaces (APIs) to many system libraries (often in a way independent of the operating system).

For example, if you need to use a random number generator, you can do:

```
1 >>> import random
2 >>> print random.randint(0, 9)
3 5
```

This prints a random integer between 0 and 9 (including 9), 5 in the example. The function randint is defined in the module random. It is also possible to import an object from a module into the current namespace:

```
1 >>> from random import randint
2 >>> print randint(0, 9)
```

or import all objects from a module into the current namespace:

```
1 >>> from random import *
2 >>> print randint(0, 9)
```

or import everything in a newly defined namespace:

```
1 >>> import random as myrand
2 >>> print myrand.randint(0, 9)
```

In the rest of this book, we will mainly use objects defined in modules os, sys, datetime, time and cPickle.

> All of the web2py objects are accessible via a module called gluon, and that is the subject of later chapters. Internally, web2py uses many Python modules (for example thread), but you rarely need to access them directly.

In the following subsections we consider those modules that are most useful.

2.15.1   os

This module provides an interface to the operating system API. For example:

```
1 >>> import os
2 >>> os.chdir('..')
3 >>> os.unlink('filename_to_be_deleted')
```

> Some of the os functions, such as chdir, MUST NOT be used in web2py because they are not thread-safe.

os.path.join is very useful; it allows the concatenation of paths in an OS-independent way:

```
1 >>> import os
```

```
2 >>> a = os.path.join('path', 'sub_path')
3 >>> print a
4 path/sub_path
```

System environment variables can be accessed via:

```
1 >>> print os.environ
```

which is a read-only dictionary.

2.15.2 sys

The sys module contains many variables and functions, but the one we use the most is sys.path. It contains a list of paths where Python searches for modules. When we try to import a module, Python looks for it in all the folders listed in sys.path. If you install additional modules in some location and want Python to find them, you need to append the path to that location to sys.path.

```
1 >>> import sys
2 >>> sys.path.append('path/to/my/modules')
```

When running web2py, Python stays resident in memory, and there is only one sys.path, while there are many threads servicing the HTTP requests. To avoid a memory leak, it is best to check if a path is already present before appending:

```
1 >>> path = 'path/to/my/modules'
2 >>> if not path in sys.path:
3         sys.path.append(path)
```

2.15.3 datetime

The use of the datetime module is best illustrated by some examples:

```
1 >>> import datetime
2 >>> print datetime.datetime.today()
3 2008-07-04 14:03:90
4 >>> print datetime.date.today()
5 2008-07-04
```

Occasionally you may need to time-stamp data based on the UTC time as opposed to local time. In this case you can use the following function:

```
1 >>> import datetime
2 >>> print datetime.datetime.utcnow()
3 2008-07-04 14:03:90
```

The datetime module contains various classes: date, datetime, time and timedelta. The difference between two date or two datetime or two time objects is a timedelta:

```
1 >>> a = datetime.datetime(2008, 1, 1, 20, 30)
2 >>> b = datetime.datetime(2008, 1, 2, 20, 30)
3 >>> c = b - a
4 >>> print c.days
5 1
```

In web2py, date and datetime are used to store the corresponding SQL types when passed to or returned from the database.

2.15.4   time

The time module differs from date and datetime because it represents time as seconds from the epoch (beginning of 1970).

```
1 >>> import time
2 >>> t = time.time()
3 1215138737.571
```

Refer to the Python documentation for conversion functions between time in seconds and time as a datetime.

2.15.5   cPickle

This is a very powerful module. It provides functions that can serialize almost any Python object, including self-referential objects. For example, let's build a weird object:

```
1 >>> class MyClass(object): pass
2 >>> myinstance = MyClass()
3 >>> myinstance.x = 'something'
4 >>> a = [1 ,2, {'hello':'world'}, [3, 4, [myinstance]]]
```

and now:

```
1 >>> import cPickle
2 >>> b = cPickle.dumps(a)
3 >>> c = cPickle.loads(b)
```

In this example, b is a string representation of a, and c is a copy of a generated by de-serializing b. cPickle can also serialize to and de-serialize from a file:

```
1 >>> cPickle.dump(a, open('myfile.pickle', 'wb'))
2 >>> c = cPickle.load(open('myfile.pickle', 'rb'))
```

3

Overview

3.1 Startup

web2py comes in binary packages for Windows and Mac OS X. They include the Python interpreter so you do not need to have it pre-installed. There is also a source code version that runs on Windows, Mac, Linux, and other Unix systems. The source code package assumes that Python is already installed on the computer. web2py requires no installation. To get started, unzip the downloaded zip file for your specific operating system and execute the corresponding web2py file.

On Unix and Linux (source distribution), run:

```
1 python web2py.py
```

On OS X (binary distribution), run:

```
1 open web2py.app
```

On Windows (binary web2py distribution), run:

```
1 web2py.exe
```

On Windows (source web2py distribution), run:

```
1 c:/Python27/python.exe web2py.exe
```

> Attention, to run web2py on Windows from source you must install first Mark Hammond's win32 extensions from http://sourceforge.net/projects/pywin32/.

The web2py program accepts various command line options which are discussed later.

By default, at startup, web2py displays a startup window and then displays a GUI widget that asks you to choose a one-time administrator password, the IP address of the network interface to be used for the web server, and a port number from which to serve requests. By default, web2py runs its web server on 127.0.0.1:8000 (port 8000 on localhost), but you can run it on any available IP address and port. You can query the IP address of your network interface by opening a command line and typing `ipconfig` on Windows or `ifconfig` on OS X and Linux. From now on we assume web2py is running on localhost (127.0.0.1:8000). Use 0.0.0.0:80 to run web2py publicly on any of your network interfaces.

Welcome to...

web2py Web Framework

Created by Massimo Di Pierro, Copyright 2007-2012
Version 2.4.1-alpha.2+timestamp.2012.12.27.06.44.33

If you do not provide an administrator password, the administration interface is disabled. This is a security measure to prevent publicly exposing the admin interface.

The administrative interface, **admin**, is only accessible from localhost unless you run web2py behind Apache with mod_proxy. If **admin** detects a proxy, the session cookie is set to secure and **admin** login does not work unless the communication between the client and the proxy goes over HTTPS; this is a security measure. All communications between the client and **admin** must always be local or encrypted; otherwise an attacker would be able to perform a man-in-the middle attack or a replay attack and execute arbitrary code on the server.

After the administration password has been set, web2py starts up the web browser at the page:

```
http://127.0.0.1:8000/
```

If the computer does not have a default browser, open a web browser and enter the URL.

Clicking on "administrative interface" takes you to the login page for the administration interface.

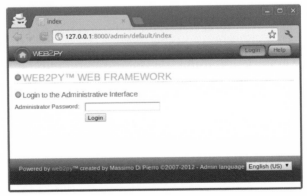

The administrator password is the password you chose at startup. Notice that there is only one administrator, and therefore only one administrator password. For security reasons, the developer is asked to choose a new password every time web2py starts unless the <recycle> option is specified. This is distinct from the authentication mechanism in web2py applications.

After the administrator logs into web2py, the browser is redirected to the "site" page.

This page lists all installed web2py applications and allows the administrator to manage them. web2py comes with three applications:

- An **admin** application, the one you are using right now.

- An **examples** application, with the online interactive documentation and a replica of the web2py official website.

- A **welcome** application. This is the basic template for any other web2py application. It is referred to as the *scaffolding application*. This is also the application that welcomes a user at startup.

Ready-to-use web2py applications are referred to as web2py *appliances*. You can download many freely available appliances from [24]. web2py users are encouraged to submit new appliances, either in open-source or closed-source (compiled and packed) form.

From the **admin** application's *site* page, you can perform the following operations:

- **install** an application by completing the form on the bottom right of the page. Give a name to the application, select the file containing a packaged application or the URL where the application is located, and click "submit".

- **uninstall** an application by clicking the corresponding button. There is a confirmation page.

- **create** a new application by choosing a name and clicking "create".

- **package** an application for distribution by clicking on the corresponding button. A downloaded application is a tar file containing everything, including the database. You should not untar this file; it is automatically unpackaged by web2py when installed with **admin**.

- **clean up** an application's temporary files, such as sessions, errors and cache files.

- **enable/disable** each application. When an application is disabled it cannot be called remotely but it is not disabled form localhost. This means disabled applications can still be accessed behind a proxy. An application is disabled by creating a file called "DISABLED" in the application folder. Users who try to access a disabled application will receive a 503 HTTP error. You can use routes_onerror to customize the error page.

- **EDIT** an application.

  When you create a new application using **admin**, it starts as a clone of the "welcome" scaffolding app with a "models/db.py" that creates a SQLite database, connects to it, instantiates Auth, Crud, and Service, and configures them. It also provides a "controller/default.py" which exposes actions "index", "download", "user" for user management, and "call" for services. In the following, we assume that these files have been removed; we will be creating apps from scratch.

web2py also comes with a **wizard**, described later in this chapter, that can write an alternate scaffolding code for you based on layouts and plugins available on the web and based on high level description of the models.

3.2 Simple examples

3.2.1 Say hello

Here, as an example, we create a simple web app that displays the message "Hello from MyApp" to the user. We will call this application "myapp". We will also add a counter that counts how many times the same user visits the page.

You can create a new application simply by typing its name in the form on the top right of the **site** page in **admin**.

After you press [create], the application is created as a copy of the built-in welcome application.

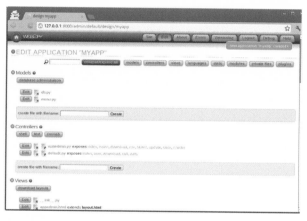

To run the new application, visit:

```
http://127.0.0.1:8000/myapp
```

Now you have a copy of the welcome application.

To edit an application, click on the *edit* button for the newly created application.

The **edit** page tells you what is inside the application. Every web2py application consists of certain files, most of which fall into one of six categories:

- **models**: describe the data representation.
- **controllers**: describe the application logic and workflow.

- **views**: describe the data presentation.

- **languages**: describe how to translate the application presentation to other languages.

- **modules**: Python modules that belong to the application.

- **static files**: static images, CSS files [40, 41, 42], JavaScript files [43, 44], etc.

- **plugins**: groups of files designed to work together.

Everything is neatly organized following the Model-View-Controller design pattern. Each section in the *edit* page corresponds to a subfolder in the application folder.

Notice that clicking on section headings will toggle their content. Folder names under static files are also collapsible.

Each file listed in the section corresponds to a file physically located in the subfolder. Any operation performed on a file via the **admin** interface (create, edit, delete) can be performed directly from the shell using your favorite editor.

The application contains other types of files (database, session files, error files, etc.), but they are not listed on the *edit* page because they are not created or modified by the administrator; they are created and modified by the application itself.

The controllers contain the logic and workflow of the application. Every URL gets mapped into a call to one of the functions in the controllers (actions). There are two default controllers: "appadmin.py" and "default.py". **appadmin** provides the database administrative interface; we do not need it now. "default.py" is the controller that you need to edit, the one that is called by default when no controller is specified in the URL. Edit the "index" function as follows:

```
1  def index():
2      return "Hello from MyApp"
```

Here is what the online editor looks like:

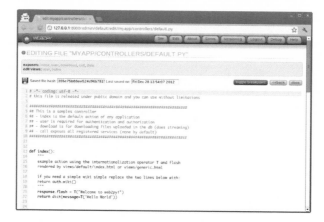

Save it and go back to the *edit* page. Click on the index link to visit the newly created page.

When you visit the URL

```
http://127.0.0.1:8000/myapp/default/index
```

the index action in the default controller of the myapp application is called. It returns a string that the browser displays for us. It should look like this:

Now, edit the "index" function as follows:

```
def index():
    return dict(message="Hello from MyApp")
```

Also from the *edit* page, edit the view "default/index.html" (the view file associated with the action) and completely replace the existing contents of that file with the following:

```
<html>
    <head></head>
    <body>
        <h1>{{=message}}</h1>
```

```
5     </body>
6   </html>
```

Now the action returns a dictionary defining a message. When an action returns a dictionary, web2py looks for a view with the name

```
1   [controller]/[function].[extension]
```

and executes it. Here [extension] is the requested extension. If no extension is specified, it defaults to "html", and that is what we will assume here. Under this assumption, the view is an HTML file that embeds Python code using special {{ }} tags. In particular, in the example, the {{=message}} instructs web2py to replace the tagged code with the value of the message returned by the action. Notice that message here is not a web2py keyword but is defined in the action. So far we have not used any web2py keywords.

If web2py does not find the requested view, it uses the "generic.html" view that comes with every application.

> If an extension other than "html" is specified ("json" for example), and the view file "[controller]/[function].json" is not found, web2py looks for the view "generic.json". web2py comes with generic.html, generic.json, generic.jsonp, generic.xml, generic.rss, generic.ics (for Mac Mail Calendar), generic.map (for embedding Google Maps), and generic.pdf (based on fpdf). These generic views can be modified for each application individually, and additional views can be added easily.

> Generic views are a development tool. In production every action should have its own view. In fact, by default, generic views are only enabled from localhost.

> You can also specify a view with response.view = 'default/something.html'

Read more on this topic in Chapter 10.

If you go back to "EDIT" and click on index, you will now see the following HTML page:

3.2.2   Debugging toolbar

For debugging purposes you can insert

```
{{=response.toolbar()}}
```

to the code in a view and it will show you some useful information, including the request, response and session objects, and list all db queries with their timing.

3.2.3   Let's count

Let's now add a counter to this page that will count how many times the same visitor displays the page. web2py automatically and transparently tracks visitors using sessions and cookies. For each new visitor, it creates a session and assigns a unique "session_id". The session is a container for variables that are stored server-side. The unique id is sent to the browser via a cookie. When the visitor requests another page from the same application, the browser sends the cookie back, it is retrieved by web2py, and the corresponding session is restored.

To use the session, modify the default controller:

```
def index():
    if not session.counter:
        session.counter = 1
    else:
        session.counter += 1
    return dict(message="Hello from MyApp", counter=session.counter)
```

Notice that counter is not a web2py keyword but session is. We are asking web2py to check whether there is a counter variable in the session and, if not, to create one and set it to 1. If the counter is there, we ask web2py to increase the counter by 1. Finally we pass the value of the counter to the view.

A more compact way to code the same function is this:

```
def index():
    session.counter = (session.counter or 0) + 1
    return dict(message="Hello from MyApp", counter=session.counter)
```

Now modify the view to add a line that displays the value of the counter:

```
<html>
  <head></head>
  <body>
    <h1>{{=message}}</h1>
    <h2>Number of visits: {{=counter}}</h2>
  </body>
</html>
```

When you visit the index page again (and again) you should get the following HTML page:

The counter is associated with each visitor, and is incremented each time the visitor reloads the page. Different visitors see different counters.

3.2.4 Say my name

Now create two pages (first and second), where the first page creates a form, asks the visitor's name, and redirects to the second page, which greets the visitor by name.

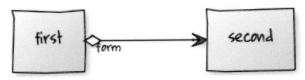

Write the corresponding actions in the default controller:

```
1  def first():
2      return dict()
3
4  def second():
5      return dict()
```

Then create a view "default/first.html" for the first action, and enter:

```
1  {{extend 'layout.html'}}
2  <h1>What is your name?</h1>
3  <form action="second">
4    <input name="visitor_name" />
5    <input type="submit" />
6  </form>
```

Finally, create a view "default/second.html" for the second action:

```
1  {{extend 'layout.html'}}
2  <h1>Hello {{=request.vars.visitor_name}}</h1>
```

In both views we have extended the basic "layout.html" view that comes with web2py. The layout view keeps the look and feel of the two pages consistent. The layout file can be edited and replaced easily, since it mainly contains HTML code.

If you now visit the first page, type your name:

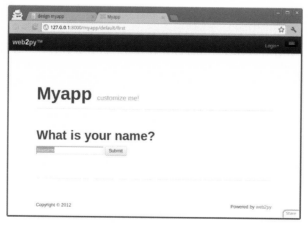

and submit the form, you will receive a greeting:

3.2.5   Postbacks

The mechanism for form submission that we used before is very common, but it is not good programming practice. All input should be validated and, in the above example, the burden of validation would fall on the second action. Thus the action that performs the validation is different from the action that generated the form. This tends to cause redundancy in the code.

A better pattern for form submission is to submit forms to the same action that generated them, in our example the "first". The "first" action should receive the variables, process them, store them server-side, and redirect the visitor to the "second" page, which retrieves the variables. This mechanism is called a *postback*.

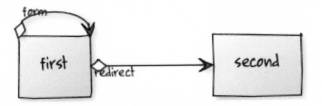

Modify the default controller to implement self-submission:

```
def first():
    if request.vars.visitor_name:
```

```
3        session.visitor_name = request.vars.visitor_name
4        redirect(URL('second'))
5    return dict()
6
7 def second():
8    return dict()
```

Then modify the "default/first.html" view:

```
1 {{extend 'layout.html'}}
2 What is your name?
3 <form>
4   <input name="visitor_name" />
5   <input type="submit" />
6 </form>
```

and the "default/second.html" view needs to retrieve the data from the session instead of from the request.vars:

```
1 {{extend 'layout.html'}}
2 <h1>Hello {{=session.visitor_name or "anonymous"}}</h1>
```

From the point of view of the visitor, the self-submission behaves exactly the same as the previous implementation. We have not added validation yet, but it is now clear that validation should be performed by the first action.

This approach is better also because the name of the visitor stays in the session, and can be accessed by all actions and views in the application without having to be passed around explicitly.

Note that if the "second" action is ever called before a visitor name is set, it will display "Hello anonymous" because session.visitor_name returns None. Alternatively we could have added the following code in the controller (inside the second function):

```
1 if not request.function=='first' and not session.visitor_name:
2    redirect(URL('first'))
```

This is an *ad hoc* mechanism that you can use to enforce authorization on controllers, though see Chapter 9 for a more powerful method.

With web2py we can move one step further and ask web2py to generate the form for us, including validation. web2py provides helpers (FORM, INPUT, TEXTAREA, and SELECT/OPTION) with the same names as the equivalent HTML tags. They can be used to build forms either in the controller or in the view.

For example, here is one possible way to rewrite the first action:

```
def first():
    form = FORM(INPUT(_name='visitor_name', requires=IS_NOT_EMPTY()),
                INPUT(_type='submit'))
    if form.process().accepted:
        session.visitor_name = form.vars.visitor_name
        redirect(URL('second'))
    return dict(form=form)
```

where we are saying that the FORM tag contains two INPUT tags. The attributes of the input tags are specified by the named arguments starting with underscore. The requires argument is not a tag attribute (because it does not start by underscore) but it sets a validator for the value of visitor_name.

Here is yet another better way to create the same form:

```
def first():
    form = SQLFORM.factory(Field('visitor_name',
                                 label='what is your name?',
                                 requires=IS_NOT_EMPTY()))
    if form.process().accepted:
        session.visitor_name = form.vars.visitor_name
        redirect(URL('second'))
    return dict(form=form)
```

The form object can be easily serialized in HTML by embedding it in the "default/first.html" view.

```
{{extend 'layout.html'}}
{{=form}}
```

The form.process() method applies the validators and returns the form itself. The form.accepted variable is set to True if the form was processed and passed validation. If the self-submitted form passes validation, it stores the variables in the session and redirects as before. If the form does not pass validation, error messages are inserted into the form and shown to the user, as below:

In the next section we will show how forms can be generated automatically from a model.

In all our examples we have used the session to pass the user name from the first action to the second. We could have used a different mechanism and passed data as part of a redirect URL:

```
def first():
    form = SQLFORM.factory(Field('visitor_name', requires=IS_NOT_EMPTY()))
    if form.process().accepted:
        name = form.vars.visitor_name
        redirect(URL('second',vars=dict(name=name)))
    return dict(form=form)

def second():
    name = request.vars.visitor_name or redirect(URL('first'))
    return dict(name=name)
```

Mind that in general it is not a good idea to pass data from one action to another using the URL. It makes it harder to secure the application. It is safer to store the data in a session.

3.2.6   Internationalization

Your code is likely to include hardcoded strings such as "What is your name?". You should be able to customize strings without editing the code and in particular insert translations for these strings in different languages.

In this way if a visitor has the language preference of the browser set to "Italian", web2py will use the Italian translation for the strings, if available. This feature of web2py is called "internationalization" and it is described in more detail in the next chapter.

Here we just observe that in order to use this feature you should markup strings that needs translation. This is done by wrapping a quoted string in code such as

```
"What is your name?"
```

with the T operator:

```
T("What is your name?")
```

You can also mark for translations strings hardcoded in views. For example

```
<h1>What is your name?</h1>
```

becomes

```
<h1>{{=T("What is your name?")}}</h1>
```

It is good practice to do this for every string in the code (field labels, flash messages, etc.) except for tables and field names.

Once the strings are identified and marked up, web2py takes care of almost everything else. The admin interface also provides a page where you can translate each string in the languages you desire to support.

> web2py includes a powerful pluralization engine which is described in the next chapter. It is integrated with both the internationalization engine and the markmin renderer.

3.3 An image blog

Here, as another example, we wish to create a web application that allows the administrator to post images and give them a name, and allows the visitors of the web site to view the named images and submit comments (posts).

As before, from the **site** page in **admin**, create a new application called images, and navigate to the *edit* page:

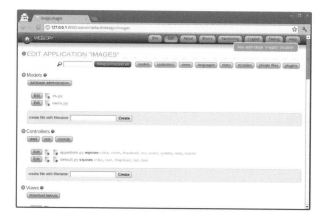

We start by creating a model, a representation of the persistent data in the application (the images to upload, their names, and the comments). First, you need to create/edit a model file which, for lack of imagination, we call "db.py". We assume the code below will replace any existing code in "db.py". Models and controllers must have a .py extension since they are Python code. If the extension is not provided, it is appended by web2py. Views instead have a .html extension since they mainly contain HTML code.

Edit the "db.py" file by clicking the corresponding "edit" button:

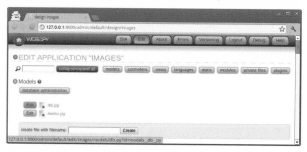

and enter the following:

```
1  db = DAL("sqlite://storage.sqlite")
2
3  db.define_table('image',
4      Field('title', unique=True),
5      Field('file', 'upload'),
6      format = '%(title)s')
7
8  db.define_table('post',
```

```
 9     Field('image_id', 'reference image'),
10     Field('author'),
11     Field('email'),
12     Field('body', 'text'))
13
14   db.image.title.requires = IS_NOT_IN_DB(db, db.image.title)
15   db.post.image_id.requires = IS_IN_DB(db, db.image.id, '%(title)s')
16   db.post.author.requires = IS_NOT_EMPTY()
17   db.post.email.requires = IS_EMAIL()
18   db.post.body.requires = IS_NOT_EMPTY()
19
20   db.post.image_id.writable = db.post.image_id.readable = False
```

Let's analyze this line by line.

Line 1 defines a global variable called db that represents the database connection. In this case it is a connection to a SQLite database stored in the file "applications/images/databases/storage.sqlite". When using SQLite, if the database file does not exist, it is created. You can change the name of the file, as well as the name of the global variable db, but it is convenient to give them the same name, to make it easy to remember.

Lines 3-6 define a table "image". define_table is a method of the db object. The first argument, "image", is the name of the table we are defining. The other arguments are the fields belonging to that table. This table has a field called "title", a field called "file", and a field called "id" that serves as the table primary key ("id" is not explicitly declared because all tables have an id field by default). The field "title" is a string, and the field "file" is of type "upload". "upload" is a special type of field used by the web2py Data Abstraction Layer (DAL) to store the names of uploaded files. web2py knows how to upload files (via streaming if they are large), rename them safely, and store them.

When a table is defined, web2py takes one of several possible actions:

- if the table does not exist, the table is created;

- if the table exists and does not correspond to the definition, the table is altered accordingly, and if a field has a different type, web2py tries to convert its contents;

- if the table exists and corresponds to the definition, web2py does nothing.

This behavior is called "migration". In web2py migrations are automatic, but can be disabled for each table by passing `migrate=False` as the last argument of `define_table`.

Line 6 defines a format string for the table. It determines how a record should be represented as a string. Notice that the `format` argument can also be a function that takes a record and returns a string. For example:

```
format=lambda row: row.title
```

Lines 8-12 define another table called "post". A post has an "author", an "email" (we intend to store the email address of the author of the post), a "body" of type "text" (we intend to use it to store the actual comment posted by the author), and an "image_id" field of type reference that points to `db.image` via the "id" field.

In line 14, `db.image.title` represents the field "title" of table "image". The attribute `requires` allows you to set requirements/constraints that will be enforced by web2py forms. Here we require that the "title" is unique:

```
IS_NOT_IN_DB(db, db.image.title)
```

Notice this is optional because it is set automatically given that `Field('title', unique=True)`.

The objects representing these constraints are called validators. Multiple validators can be grouped in a list. Validators are executed in the order they appear. `IS_NOT_IN_DB(a, b)` is a special validator that checks that the value of a field `b` for a new record is not already in `a`.

Line 15 requires that the field "image_id" of table "post" is in `db.image.id`. As far as the database is concerned, we had already declared this when we defined the table "post". Now we are explicitly telling the model that this condition should be enforced by web2py, too, at the form processing level when a new comment is posted, so that invalid values do not propagate from input forms to the database. We also require that the "image_id" be represented by the "title", `'%(title)s'`, of the corresponding record.

Line 20 indicates that the field "image_id" of table "post" should not be shown in forms, `writable=False` and not even in read-only forms, `readable=False`.

The meaning of the validators in lines 17-18 should be obvious.

Notice that the validator

```
db.post.image_id.requires = IS_IN_DB(db, db.image.id, '%(title)s')
```

can be omitted (and would be automatic) if we specify a format for referenced table:

```
db.define_table('image', ..., format='%(title)s')
```

where the format can be a string or a function that takes a record and returns a string.

Once a model is defined, if there are no errors, web2py creates an application administration interface to manage the database. You access it via the "database administration" link in the *edit* page or directly:

```
http://127.0.0.1:8000/images/appadmin
```

Here is a screenshot of the **appadmin** interface:

This interface is coded in the controller called "appadmin.py" and the corresponding view "appadmin.html". From now on, we will refer to this interface simply as **appadmin**. It allows the administrator to insert new database records, edit and delete existing records, browse tables, and perform database joins.

The first time **appadmin** is accessed, the model is executed and the tables are created. The web2py DAL translates Python code into SQL statements that are specific to the selected database back-end (SQLite in this example). You can see the generated SQL from the *edit* page by clicking on the "sql.log" link under "models". Notice that the link is not present until the tables have been created.

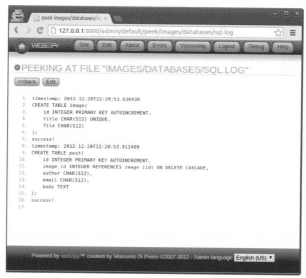

If you were to edit the model and access **appadmin** again, web2py would generate SQL to alter the existing tables. The generated SQL is logged into "sql.log".

Now go back to **appadmin** and try to insert a new image record:

web2py has translated the db.image.file "upload" field into an upload form for the file. When the form is submitted and an image file is uploaded, the file is renamed in a secure way that preserves the extension, it is saved with the new name under the application "uploads" folder, and the new name is stored in the db.image.file field. This process is designed to prevent directory traversal attacks.

Notice that each field type is rendered by a *widget*. Default widgets can be overridden.

When you click on a table name in **appadmin**, web2py performs a select of all records on the current table, identified by the DAL query

```
db.image.id > 0
```

and renders the result.

You can select a different set of records by editing the DAL query and pressing [Submit].

To edit or delete a single record, click on the record id number.

Because of the IS_IN_DB validator, the reference field "image_id" is rendered by a drop-down menu. The items in the drop-down are stored as keys (db.image.id), but are represented by their db.image.title, as specified by the validator.

Validators are powerful objects that know how to represent fields, filter field values, generate errors, and format values extracted from the field.

The following figure shows what happens when you submit a form that does not pass validation:

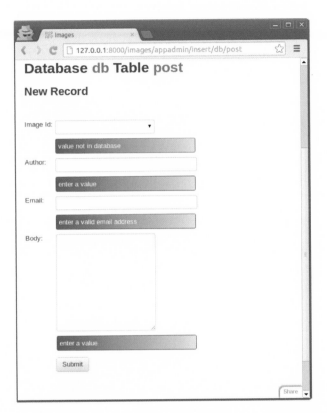

The same forms that are automatically generated by **appadmin** can also be generated programmatically via the SQLFORM helper and embedded in user applications. These forms are CSS-friendly, and can be customized.

Every application has its own **appadmin**; therefore, **appadmin** itself can be modified without affecting other applications.

So far, the application knows how to store data, and we have seen how to access the database via **appadmin**. Access to **appadmin** is restricted to the administrator, and it is not intended as a production web interface for the application; hence the next part of this walk-through. Specifically we want to create:

- An "index" page that lists all available images sorted by title and links to detail pages for the images.

- A "show/[id]" page that shows the visitor the requested image and allows the visitor to view and post comments.

- A "download/[name]" action to download uploaded images.

This is represented schematically here:

Go back to the *edit* page and edit the "default.py" controller, replacing its contents with the following:

```
1 def index():
2     images = db().select(db.image.ALL, orderby=db.image.title)
3     return dict(images=images)
```

This action returns a dictionary. The keys of the items in the dictionary are interpreted as variables passed to the view associated to the action. When developing, if there is no view, the action is rendered by the "generic.html" view that is provided with every web2py application.

The index action performs a select of all fields (db.image.ALL) from table image, ordered by db.image.title. The result of the select is a Rows object containing the records. Assign it to a local variable called images returned by the action to the view. images is iterable and its elements are the selected rows. For each row the columns can be accessed as dictionaries: images[0]['title'] or equivalently as images[0].title.

If you do not write a view, the dictionary is rendered by "views/generic.html" and a call to the index action would look like this:

You have not created a view for this action yet, so web2py renders the set of records in plain tabular form.

Proceed to create a view for the index action. Return to admin, edit "default/index.html" and replace its content with the following:

```
{{extend 'layout.html'}}
<h1>Current Images</h1>
<ul>
{{for image in images:}}
{{=LI(A(image.title, _href=URL("show", args=image.id)))}}
{{pass}}
</ul>
```

The first thing to notice is that a view is pure HTML with special {{...}} tags. The code embedded in {{...}} is pure Python code with one caveat: indentation is irrelevant. Blocks of code start with lines ending in colon (:) and end in lines beginning with the keyword pass. In some cases the end of a block is obvious from context and the use of pass is not required.

Lines 5-7 loop over the image rows and for each row image display:

```
LI(A(image.title, _href=URL('show', args=image.id))
```

This is a <li>...</li> tag that contains an <a href="...">...</a> tag which contains the image.title. The value of the hypertext reference (href attribute) is:

```
URL('show', args=image.id)
```

i.e., the URL within the same application and controller as the current request that calls the function called "show", passing a single argument to the function, args=image.id. LI, A, etc. are web2py helpers that map to the corresponding HTML tags. Their unnamed arguments are interpreted as objects to be serialized and inserted in the tag's innerHTML. Named arguments starting with an underscore (for example _href) are interpreted as tag attributes but without the underscore. For example _href is the href attribute, _class is the class attribute, etc.

As an example, the following statement:

```
{{=LI(A('something', _href=URL('show', args=123)))}}
```

is rendered as:

```
<li><a href="/images/default/show/123">something</a></li>
```

A handful of helpers (INPUT, TEXTAREA, OPTION and SELECT) also support some special named attributes not starting with underscore (value, and requires). They are important for building custom forms and will be discussed later.

Go back to the *edit* page. It now indicates that "default.py exposes index". By clicking on "index", you can visit the newly created page:

```
http://127.0.0.1:8000/images/default/index
```

which looks like:

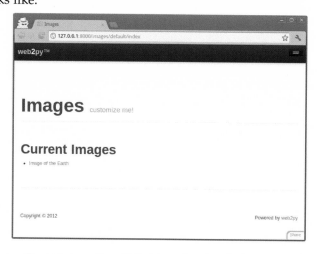

If you click on the image name link, you are directed to:

```
1 http://127.0.0.1:8000/images/default/show/1
```

and this results in an error, since you have not yet created an action called "show" in controller "default.py".

Let's edit the "default.py" controller and replace its content with:

```
1  def index():
2      images = db().select(db.image.ALL, orderby=db.image.title)
3      return dict(images=images)
4
5  def show():
6      image = db.image(request.args(0,cast=int)) or redirect(URL('index'))
7      db.post.image_id.default = image.id
8      form = SQLFORM(db.post)
9      if form.process().accepted:
10         response.flash = 'your comment is posted'
11     comments = db(db.post.image_id==image.id).select()
12     return dict(image=image, comments=comments, form=form)
13
14 def download():
15     return response.download(request, db)
```

The controller contains two actions: "show" and "download". The "show" action selects the image with the id parsed from the request args and all comments related to the image. "show" then passes everything to the view "default/show.html".

The image id referenced by:

```
1 URL('show', args=image.id)
```

in "default/index.html", can be accessed as:

request.args(0,cast=int) from the "show" action. The cast=int argument is optional but very important. It attempts to cast the string value passed in the PATH_INFO into an int. On failure it raises a proper exception instead of causing a ticket. One can also specify a redirect in case of failure to cast:

request.args(0,cast=int,otherwise=URL('error'))

Moreover db.image(...) is a shortcut for

```
1 db(db.image.id==...).select().first()
```

The "download" action expects a filename in request.args(0), builds a path to the location where that file is supposed to be, and sends it back to the client. If the file is too large, it streams the file without incurring any memory overhead.

Notice the following statements:

- Line 7 creates an insert form SQLFORM for the db.post table using only the specified fields.

- Line 8 sets the value for the reference field, which is not part of the input form because it is not in the list of fields specified above.

- Line 9 processes the submitted form (the submitted form variables are in request.vars) within the current session (the session is used to prevent double submissions, and to enforce navigation). If the submitted form variables are validated, the new comment is inserted in the db.post table; otherwise the form is modified to include error messages (for example, if the author's email address is invalid). This is all done in line 9!.

- Line 10 is only executed if the form is accepted, after the record is inserted into the database table. response.flash is a web2py variable that is displayed in the views and used to notify the visitor that something happened.

- Line 11 selects all comments that reference the current image.
  The "download" action is already defined in the "default.py" controller of the scaffolding application.

The "download" action does not return a dictionary, so it does not need a view. The "show" action, though, should have a view, so return to **admin** and create a new view called "default/show.html".

Edit this new file and replace its content with the following:

```
{{extend 'layout.html'}}
<h1>Image: {{=image.title}}</h1>
<center>
<img width="200px"
    src="{{=URL('download', args=image.file)}}" />
</center>
{{if len(comments):}}
  <h2>Comments</h2><br /><p>
  {{for post in comments:}}
    <p>{{=post.author}} says <i>{{=post.body}}</i></p>
  {{pass}}</p>
```

```
12  {{else:}}
13    <h2>No comments posted yet</h2>
14  {{pass}}
15  <h2>Post a comment</h2>
16  {{=form}}
```

This view displays the **image.file** by calling the "download" action inside an `<img ... />` tag. If there are comments, it loops over them and displays each one.

Here is how everything will appear to a visitor.

When a visitor submits a comment via this page, the comment is stored in the database and appended at the bottom of the page.

3.3.1 Adding authentication

The web2py API for Role-Based Access Control is quite sophisticated, but for now we will limit ourselves to restricting access to the show action to authenticated users, deferring a more detailed discussion to Chapter 9.

To limit access to authenticated users, we need to complete three steps. In a model, for example "db.py", we need to add:

```
1  from gluon.tools import Auth
```

```
2  auth = Auth(db)
3  auth.define_tables(username=True)
```

In our controller, we need to add one action:

```
1  def user():
2      return dict(form=auth())
```

This is sufficient to enable login, register, logout, etc. pages. The default
layout will also show options to the corresponding pages in the top right
corner.

We can now decorate the functions that we want to restrict, for example:

```
1  @auth.requires_login()
2  def show():
3      ...
```

Any attempt to access

```
1  http://127.0.0.1:8000/images/default/show/[image_id]
```

will require login. If the user is not logged it, the user will be redirected to

```
1  http://127.0.0.1:8000/images/default/user/login
```

The user function also exposes, among others, the following actions:

```
1  http://127.0.0.1:8000/images/default/user/logout
2  http://127.0.0.1:8000/images/default/user/register
3  http://127.0.0.1:8000/images/default/user/profile
4  http://127.0.0.1:8000/images/default/user/change_password
5  http://127.0.0.1:8000/images/default/user/request_reset_password
6  http://127.0.0.1:8000/images/default/user/retrieve_username
7  http://127.0.0.1:8000/images/default/user/retrieve_password
8  http://127.0.0.1:8000/images/default/user/verify_email
9  http://127.0.0.1:8000/images/default/user/impersonate
10 http://127.0.0.1:8000/images/default/user/not_authorized
```

Now, a first-time user needs to register in order to be able to log in and read or post comments.

> Both the auth object and the user function are already defined in the scaffolding application. The auth object is highly customizable and can deal with email verification, registration approvals, CAPTCHA, and alternate login methods via plugins.

3.3.2   Adding grids

We can improve this further using the SQLFORM.grid and SQLFORM.smartgrid gadgets to create a management interface for our application:

```
1  @auth.requires_membership('manager')
2  def manage():
3      grid = SQLFORM.smartgrid(db.image,linked_tables=['post'])
```

```
4    return dict(grid=grid)
```

with associated "views/default/manage.html"

```
1  {{extend 'layout.html'}}
2  <h2>Management Interface</h2>
3  {{=grid}}
```

Using appadmin create a group "manager" and make some users members of the group. They will not be able to access

```
1  http://127.0.0.1:8000/images/default/manage
```

and browse, search:

create, update and delete images and their comments:

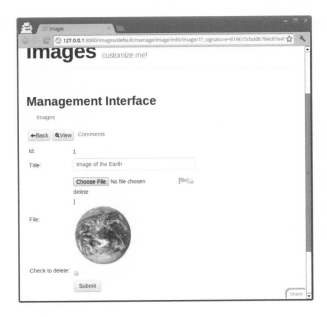

3.3.3   Configuring the layout

You can configure the default layout by editing "views/layout.html" but you can also configure it without editing the HTML. In fact, the "static/base.css" stylesheet is well documented and described in Chapter 5. You can change color, columns, size, borders and background without editing the HTML. If you want to edit the menu, the title or the subtitle, you can do so in any model file. The scaffolding app, sets default values of these parameters in the file "models/menu.py":

```
1  response.title = request.application
2  response.subtitle = 'customize me!'
3  response.meta.author = 'you'
4  response.meta.description = 'describe your app'
5  response.meta.keywords = 'bla bla bla'
6  response.menu = [ [ 'Index', False, URL('index') ] ]
```

3.4   A simple wiki

In this section, we build a simple wiki from scratch using only low level APIs (as opposed to using the built-in wiki capabilities of web2py demonstrated in the next section). The visitor will be able to create pages, search them (by title), and edit them. The visitor will also be able to post comments (exactly as in the previous applications), and also post documents (as attachments to the pages) and link them from the pages. As a convention, we adopt the Markmin syntax for our wiki syntax. We will also implement a search page with Ajax, an RSS feed for the pages, and a handler to search the pages via XML-RPC [45]. The following diagram lists the actions that we need to implement and the links we intend to build among them.

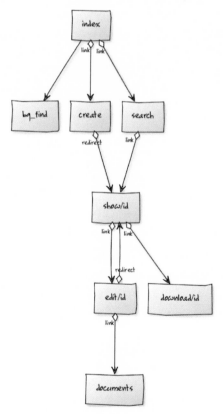

Start by creating a new scaffolding app, naming it "mywiki".

The model must contain three tables: page, comment, and document. Both comment and document reference page because they belong to page. A document contains a file field of type upload as in the previous images application.

Here is the complete model:

```
1  db = DAL('sqlite://storage.sqlite')
2
3  from gluon.tools import *
4  auth = Auth(db)
5  auth.define_tables()
6  crud = Crud(db)
7
8  db.define_table('page',
9      Field('title'),
10     Field('body', 'text'),
11     Field('created_on', 'datetime', default=request.now),
12     Field('created_by', 'reference auth_user', default=auth.user_id),
13     format='%(title)s')
14
15 db.define_table('post',
16     Field('page_id', 'reference page'),
17     Field('body', 'text'),
18     Field('created_on', 'datetime', default=request.now),
19     Field('created_by', 'reference auth_user', default=auth.user_id))
20
21 db.define_table('document',
22     Field('page_id', 'reference page'),
23     Field('name'),
24     Field('file', 'upload'),
25     Field('created_on', 'datetime', default=request.now),
26     Field('created_by', 'reference auth_user', default=auth.user_id),
27     format='%(name)s')
28
29 db.page.title.requires = IS_NOT_IN_DB(db, 'page.title')
30 db.page.body.requires = IS_NOT_EMPTY()
31 db.page.created_by.readable = db.page.created_by.writable = False
32 db.page.created_on.readable = db.page.created_on.writable = False
33
34 db.post.body.requires = IS_NOT_EMPTY()
35 db.post.page_id.readable = db.post.page_id.writable = False
36 db.post.created_by.readable = db.post.created_by.writable = False
37 db.post.created_on.readable = db.post.created_on.writable = False
38
39 db.document.name.requires = IS_NOT_IN_DB(db, 'document.name')
```

```
40 db.document.page_id.readable = db.document.page_id.writable = False
41 db.document.created_by.readable = db.document.created_by.writable = False
42 db.document.created_on.readable = db.document.created_on.writable = False
```

Edit the controller "default.py" and create the following actions:

- index: list all wiki pages

- create: add a new wiki page

- show: show a wiki page and its comments, and add new comments

- edit: edit an existing page

- documents: manage the documents attached to a page

- download: download a document (as in the images example)

- search: display a search box and, via an Ajax callback, return all matching titles as the visitor types

- callback: the Ajax callback function. It returns the HTML that gets embedded in the search page while the visitor types.

Here is the "default.py" controller:

```
 1 def index():
 2     """ this controller returns a dictionary rendered by the view
 3         it lists all wiki pages
 4     >>> index().has_key('pages')
 5     True
 6     """
 7     pages = db().select(db.page.id,db.page.title,orderby=db.page.title)
 8     return dict(pages=pages)
 9
10 @auth.requires_login()
11 def create():
12     """creates a new empty wiki page"""
13     form = SQLFORM(db.page).process(next=URL('index'))
14     return dict(form=form)
15
16 def show():
17     """shows a wiki page"""
18     this_page = db.page(request.args(0,cast=int)) or redirect(URL('index'))
19     db.post.page_id.default = this_page.id
20     form = SQLFORM(db.post).process() if auth.user else None
21     pagecomments = db(db.post.page_id==this_page.id).select()
22     return dict(page=this_page, comments=pagecomments, form=form)
23
```

```
24  @auth.requires_login()
25  def edit():
26      """edit an existing wiki page"""
27      this_page = db.page(request.args(0,cast=int)) or redirect(URL('index'))
28      form = SQLFORM(db.page, this_page).process(
29          next = URL('show',args=request.args))
30      return dict(form=form)
31
32  @auth.requires_login()
33  def documents():
34      """browser, edit all documents attached to a certain page"""
35      page = db.page(request.args(0,cast=int)) or redirect(URL('index'))
36      db.document.page_id.default = page.id
37      db.document.page_id.writable = False
38      grid = SQLFORM.grid(db.document.page_id==page.id,args=[page.id])
39      return dict(page=page, grid=grid)
40
41  def user():
42      return dict(form=auth())
43
44  def download():
45      """allows downloading of documents"""
46      return response.download(request, db)
47
48  def search():
49      """an ajax wiki search page"""
50      return dict(form=FORM(INPUT(_id='keyword',_name='keyword',
51          _onkeyup="ajax('callback', ['keyword'], 'target');")),
52          target_div=DIV(_id='target'))
53
54  def callback():
55      """an ajax callback that returns a <ul> of links to wiki pages"""
56      query = db.page.title.contains(request.vars.keyword)
57      pages = db(query).select(orderby=db.page.title)
58      links = [A(p.title, _href=URL('show',args=p.id)) for p in pages]
59      return UL(*links)
```

Lines 2-6 constitute a comment for the index action. Lines 4-5 inside the comment are interpreted by python as test code (doctest). Tests can be run via the admin interface. In this case the tests verify that the index action runs without errors.

Lines 18, 27, and 35 try to fetch a page record with the id in request.args(0).

Lines 13, 20 define and process create forms for a new page and a new comment and

Line 28 defines and processes an update form for a wiki page.

Line 38 creates a grid object that allows to view, add and update the comments linked to a page.

Some magic happens in line 51. The onkeyup attribute of the INPUT tag "keyword" is set. Every time the visitor releases a key, the JavaScript code inside the onkeyup attribute is executed, client-side. Here is the JavaScript code:

```
ajax('callback', ['keyword'], 'target');
```

ajax is a JavaScript function defined in the file "web2py.js" which is included by the default "layout.html". It takes three parameters: the URL of the action that performs the synchronous callback, a list of the IDs of variables to be sent to the callback (["keyword"]), and the ID where the response has to be inserted ("target").

As soon as you type something in the search box and release a key, the client calls the server and sends the content of the 'keyword' field, and, when the sever responds, the response is embedded in the page itself as the innerHTML of the 'target' tag.

The 'target' tag is a DIV defined in line 52. It could have been defined in the view as well.

Here is the code for the view "default/create.html":

```
{{extend 'layout.html'}}
<h1>Create new wiki page</h1>
{{=form}}
```

Assuming you are registered and logged in, if you visit the **create** page, you see the following:

Here is the code for the view "default/index.html":

```
1 {{extend 'layout.html'}}
2 <h1>Available wiki pages</h1>
3 [ {{=A('search', _href=URL('search'))}} ]<br />
4 <ul>{{for page in pages:}}
5     {{=LI(A(page.title, _href=URL('show', args=page.id)))}}
6 {{pass}}</ul>
7 [ {{=A('create page', _href=URL('create'))}} ]
```

It generates the following page:

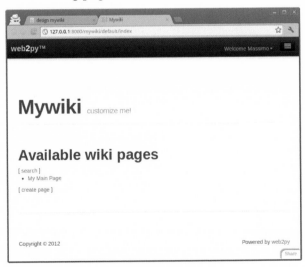

Here is the code for the view "default/show.html":

```
 1   {{extend 'layout.html'}}
 2   <h1>{{=page.title}}</h1>
 3   [ {{=A('edit', _href=URL('edit', args=request.args))}}
 4   | {{=A('documents', _href=URL('documents', args=request.args))}} ]<br />
 5   {{=MARKMIN(page.body)}}
 6   <h2>Comments</h2>
 7   {{for post in comments:}}
 8     <p>{{=db.auth_user[post.created_by].first_name}} on {{=post.created_on}}
 9       says <i>{{=post.body}}</i></p>
10   {{pass}}
11   <h2>Post a comment</h2>
12   {{=form}}
```

If you wish to use markdown syntax instead of markmin syntax:

```
 1   from gluon.contrib.markdown import WIKI as MARKDOWN
```

and use MARKDOWN instead of the MARKMIN helper. Alternatively, you can choose to accept raw HTML instead of markmin syntax. In this case you would replace:

```
 1   {{=MARKMIN(page.body)}}
```

with:

```
 1   {{=XML(page.body)}}
```

(so that the XML does not get escaped, which web2py normally does by default for security reasons).

This can be done better with:

```
 1   {{=XML(page.body, sanitize=True)}}
```

By setting sanitize=True, you tell web2py to escape unsafe XML tags such as "<script>", and thus prevent XSS vulnerabilities.

Now if, from the index page, you click on a page title, you can see the page that you have created:

Here is the code for the view "default/edit.html":

```
1 {{extend 'layout.html'}}
2 <h1>Edit wiki page</h1>
3 [ {{=A('show', _href=URL('show', args=request.args))}} ]<br />
4 {{=form}}
```

It generates a page that looks almost identical to the create page.

Here is the code for the view "default/documents.html":

```
1 {{extend 'layout.html'}}
2 <h1>Documents for page: {{=page.title}}</h1>
3 [ {{=A('show', _href=URL('show', args=request.args))}} ]<br />
4 <h2>Documents</h2>
5 {{=grid}}
```

If, from the "show" page, you click on documents, you can now manage the documents attached to the page.

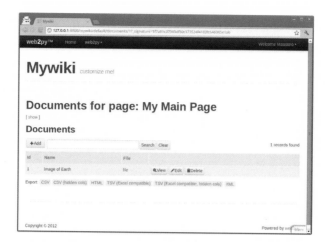

Finally here is the code for the view "default/search.html":

```
1 {{extend 'layout.html'}}
2 <h1>Search wiki pages</h1>
3 [ {{=A('listall', _href=URL('index'))}}]<br />
4 {{=form}}<br />{{=target_div}}
```

which generates the following Ajax search form:

You can also try to call the callback action directly by visiting, for example, the following URL:

```
http://127.0.0.1:8000/mywiki/default/callback?keyword=wiki
```

If you look at the page source you see the HTML returned by the callback:

```
<ul><li><a href="/mywiki/default/show/4">I made a Wiki</a></li></ul>
```

Generating an RSS feed of your wiki pages using web2py is easy because web2py includes gluon.contrib.rss2. Just append the following action to the default controller:

```
def news():
    """generates rss feed form the wiki pages"""
    response.generic_patterns = ['.rss']
    pages = db().select(db.page.ALL, orderby=db.page.title)
    return dict(
        title = 'mywiki rss feed',
        link = 'http://127.0.0.1:8000/mywiki/default/index',
        description = 'mywiki news',
        created_on = request.now,
        items = [
            dict(title = row.title,
                link = URL('show', args=row.id),
                description = MARKMIN(row.body).xml(),
                created_on = row.created_on
                ) for row in pages])
```

and when you visit the page

```
http://127.0.0.1:8000/mywiki/default/news.rss
```

you see the feed (the exact output depends on the feed reader). Notice that the dict is automatically converted to RSS, thanks to the.rss extension in the URL.

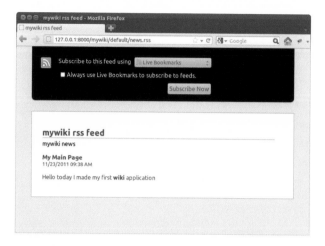

web2py also includes feedparser to read third-party feeds.

Notice that the line:

```
response.generic_patterns = ['.rss']
```

instructs web2py to use generic views (in our case "views/generic.rss") when the URL ends in the glob pattern ".rss". By default generic views are only allowed from localhost for development purposes.

Finally, let's add an XML-RPC handler that allows searching the wiki programmatically:

```
service = Service()

@service.xmlrpc
def find_by(keyword):
    """finds pages that contain keyword for XML-RPC"""
    return db(db.page.title.contains(keyword)).select().as_list()

def call():
    """exposes all registered services, including XML-RPC"""
    return service()
```

Here, the handler action simply publishes (via XML-RPC), the functions specified in the list. In this case, find_by. find_by is not an action (because it takes an argument). It queries the database with .select() and then extracts the records as a list with .response and returns the list.

Here is an example of how to access the XML-RPC handler from an external Python program.

```
1 >>> import xmlrpclib
2 >>> server = xmlrpclib.ServerProxy(
3       'http://127.0.0.1:8000/mywiki/default/call/xmlrpc')
4 >>> for item in server.find_by('wiki'):
5       print item['created_on'], item['title']
```

The handler can be accessed from many other programming languages that understand XML-RPC, including C, C++, C# and Java.

3.4.1   On date, datetime and time format

There are three different representations for each of the field types date, datetime and time:

- the database representation
- the internal web2py representation
- the string representation in forms and tables

The database representation is an internal issue and does not affect the code.   Internally, at the web2py level, they are stored as datetime.date, datetime.datetime and datetime.time object respectively and they can be manipulated as such:

```
1 for page in db(db.page).select():
2     print page.title, page.day, page.month, page.year
```

When dates are converted to strings in forms they are converted using the ISO representation

```
1 %Y-%m-%d %H:%M:%S
```

yet this representation is internationalized and you can use the admin translation page to change the format to an alternate one. For example:

```
1 %m/%b/%Y %H:%M:%S
```

Mind that by default English is not translated because web2py assumes the applications are written in English. If you want internationalization to work for English you need to create the translation file (using admin) and you need to declare that the application's current language is something other than english, for example:

```
T.current_languages = ['null']
```

3.5   The built-in web2py wiki

Now you can forget the code we have built-in the previous section (not what you have learned about web2py APIs, just the code of the specific example) as we are going to provide an example of the built-in web2py wiki.

In fact, web2py comes with wiki capabilities including media attachments, tags, tag cloud, page permissions, and support for oembed [46] and components (chapter 14).   This wiki can be used with any web2py application.

> Notice the API of the built-in wiki is still considered experimental and small changes are still possible.

Here we assume we are starting from scratch from a simple clone of the "welcome" application called "wikidemo". Edit the controller and replace the "index" action with

```
def index(): return auth.wiki()
```

Done! You have a fully working wiki. At this point no page has been created and in order to create pages you must be logged-in and you must be member of a group called "wiki-editor" or "wiki-author".   If you are logged-in as administrator the "wiki-editor" group is created automatically and you are made a member.   The difference between editors and authors is that the editors can create pages, edit and delete any page, while the authors can create pages (with some optional restrictions) and can only edit/delete the pages they have created.

The auth.wiki() function returns in a dictionary with a key content which is understood by the scaffolding "views/default/index.html". You can make your own view for this action:

```
{{extend 'layout.html'}}
{{=content}}
```

and add extra HTML or code as needed. You do not have to use the "index" action to expose the wiki. You can use an action with a different name.

To try the wiki, simply login into admin, visit the page

```
http://127.0.0.1:8000/wikidemo/default/index
```

Then choose a slug (in the publishing business, a slug is a short name given to an article that is in production) and you will be redirected to an empty page where you can edit the content using MARKMIN wiki syntax. A new menu item called "[wiki]" will allow you to create, search, and edit pages. Wiki pages have URLs like:

```
http://127.0.0.1:8000/wikidemo/default/index/[slug]
```

Service pages have names which start by underscore:

```
http://127.0.0.1:8000/wikidemo/default/index/_create
http://127.0.0.1:8000/wikidemo/default/index/_search
http://127.0.0.1:8000/wikidemo/default/index/_could
http://127.0.0.1:8000/wikidemo/default/index/_recent
http://127.0.0.1:8000/wikidemo/default/index/_edit/...
http://127.0.0.1:8000/wikidemo/default/index/_editmedia/...
http://127.0.0.1:8000/wikidemo/default/index/_preview/...
```

Try to create more pages such as "index", "aboutus", and "contactus". Try to edit them.

The `wiki` method has the following signature:

```
def wiki(self, slug=None, env=None, render='markmin',
         manage_permissions=False, force_prefix='',
         restrict_search=False, resolve=True,
         extra=None, menugroups=None)
```

It takes the following arguments:

- `render` which defaults to `'markmin'` but can be set equal to `'html'`. It determines the syntax of the wiki. We will discuss the markmin wiki markup later. If you change it to HTML you can use a wysiwyg javascript editor such as TinyMCE or NicEdit.

- `manage_permissions`. This is set to `False` by default and only recognizes permissions for "wiki-editor" and "wiki-author". If you change it to `True` the create/edit page will give the option to specify by name the group(s) whose members have permission to read and edit the page. There is a group "everybody" which includes all users.

- `force_prefix`. If set to something like `'%(id)s-'` it will restrict authors (not editors) to creating pages with a prefix like "[user id]-[page name]". The prefix can contain the id ("%(id)s") or the username ("%(username)s") or any other field from the auth_user table, as long as the corresponding column contains a valid string that would pass URL validation.

- restrict_search. This defaults to False and any logged-in user can search all wiki pages (but not necessary read or edit them). If set to True, authors can search only their own pages, editors can search everything, other users cannot search anything.

- menu_groups. This defaults to None and it indicates that wiki management menu (search, create, edit, etc.) is always displayed. You can set it to a list of group names whose members only can see this menu, for example ['wiki-editor','wiki-author']. Notice that even if the menu is exposed to everybody that does not mean everybody is allowed to perform actions listed in the menu since they are regulated by the access control system.

The wiki method has some additional parameters which will be explained later: slug, env, and extra.

3.5.1 MARKMIN basics

The MARKMIN syntax allows you to markup **bold** text using **bold**, *italic* text with "italic", and code text should be delimited by double inverted quotes. Titles must be prefixed by a #, sections by ##, and sub-sections by ###. Use a minus(-) to prefix an un-ordered item and plus(+) to prefix an ordered item. URLs are automatically converted into links. Here is an example of markmin text:

```
1  # This is a title
2  ## this is a section title
3  ### this is a subsection title
4
5  Text can be **bold**, ''italic'', ``code`` etc.
6  Learn more at:
7
8  http://web2py.com
```

You can use the extra parameter of auth.wiki to pass extra rendering rules to the MARKMIN helper.

You can find more information about the MARKMIN syntax in chapter 5.

`auth.wiki` is more powerful than the barebones MARKMIN helpers, supporting oembed and components.

You can use the `env` parameter of `auth.wiki` to expose functions to your wiki. For example:

```
auth.wiki(env=dict(join=lambda a,b,c:"%s-%s-%s" % (a,b,c)))
```

allows you to use the markup syntax:

```
@(join:1,2,3)
```

This calls the join function passed as extra with parameters a,b,c=1,2,3 and will be rendered as 1-2-3.

3.5.2   Oembed protocol

You can type in (or cut-and-paste) any URL into a wiki page and it is rendered as a link to the URL. There are exceptions:

- If the URL has an image extension, the link is embedded as an image, `<img/>`.

- If the URL has an audio extension, the link is embedded as HTML5 audio `<audio/>`.

- If the URL has a video extension, the link is embedded as HTML5 video `<video/>`.

- If the URL has a MS Office or PDF extension, Google Doc Viewer is embedded, showing the content of the document (only works for public documents).

- If the URL points to a YouTube page, a Vimeo page, or a Flickr page, web2py contacts the corresponding web service and queries it about the proper way to embed the content. This is done using the oembed protocol.

Here is a complete list of supported formats:

```
Image (.PNG, .GIF, .JPG, .JPEG)
Audio (.WAV, .OGG, .MP3)
Video (.MOV, .MPE, .MP4, .MPG, .MPG2, .MPEG, .MPEG4, .MOVIE)
```

Supported via Google Doc Viewer:

```
 1  Microsoft Excel (.XLS and .XLSX)
 2  Microsoft PowerPoint 2007 / 2010 (.PPTX)
 3  Apple Pages (.PAGES)
 4  Adobe PDF (.PDF)
 5  Adobe Illustrator (.AI)
 6  Adobe Photoshop (.PSD)
 7  Autodesk AutoCad (.DXF)
 8  Scalable Vector Graphics (.SVG)
 9  PostScript (.EPS, .PS)
10  TrueType (.TTF)
11  xml Paper Specification (.XPS)
```

Supported by oembed:

```
 1  flickr.com
 2  youtube.com
 3  hulu.com
 4  vimeo.com
 5  slideshare.net
 6  qik.com
 7  polleverywhere.com
 8  wordpress.com
 9  revision3.com
10  viddler.com
```

This is implemented in the web2py file `gluon.contrib.autolinks` and specifically in the function `expand_one`. You can extend oembed support by registering more services. This is done by appending an entry to the `EMBED_MAPS` list:

```
1  from gluon.contrib.autolinks import EMBED_MAPS
2  EMBED_MAPS.append((re.compile('http://vimeo.com/\S*'),
3                     'http://vimeo.com/api/oembed.json'))
```

3.5.3   Referencing wiki content

If you create a wiki page with slug "contactus" you can refer to this page as

```
1  @////contactus
```

Here @//// stands for

```
1  @/app/controller/function/
```

but "app", "controller", and "function" are omitted thus assuming default.

Similarly you can use the wiki menu to upload a media file (for example an image) linked to the page. The "manage media" page will show all files you have uploaded and will show the proper expression to link the media file. If, for example you upload a file "test.jpg" with title "beach", the link expression will something like:

```
@////15/beach.jpg
```

@//// is the same prefix described before. 15 is the id of the record storing the media file. beach is the title. .jpg is the extension of the original file.

If you cut and paste @////15/beach.jpg into wiki pages you embed the image.

Mind that media files are linked to pages and inherit access permission from the pages.

3.5.4   Wiki menus

If you create a page with slug "wiki-menu" page it will be interpreted as a description of the menu. Here is an example:

```
- Home > @////index
- Info > @////info
- web2py > http://google.com
- - About us > @////aboutus
- - Contact us > @////contactus
```

Each line a menu item. We used double dash for nested menu items. The > symbols separates the menu item title from the menu item link.

Mind that the menu is appended to response.menu. It does not replace it. The [wiki] menu item with service functions is added automatically.

3.5.5   Service functions

If, for example, you want to use the wiki to create an editable sidebar you could create a page with slug="sidebar" and then embed it in your layout.html with

```
{{=auth.wiki(slug='sidebar')}}
```

Notice that there is nothing special with the word "sidebar". Any wiki page can be retrieved and embedded at any point in your code. This allows you mix and match wiki functionalities with regular web2py functionalities.

> Also note that auth.wiki('sidebar') is the same as
> auth.wiki(slug='sidebar'), since the slug kwarg is the first in
> the method signature. The former gives a slightly simpler syntax.

You can also embed special wiki functions such as the search by tags:

```
{{=auth.wiki('_search')}}
```

or the tag cloud:

```
{{=auth.wiki('_cloud')}}
```

3.5.6   Extending the auth.wiki feature

When your wiki-enabled app gets more complicated, perhaps you might
need to customize the wiki db records managed by the Auth interface or
expose customized forms for wiki CRUD tasks. For example, you might want
to customize a wiki table record representation or add a new field validator.
This is not allowed by default, since the wiki model is defined only after the
wiki interface is requested with the auth.wiki() method. To allow access to
the wiki specific db setup within the model of your app you must add the
following sentence to your model file (i.e. db.py)

```
# Make sure this is called after the auth instance is created
# and before any change to the wiki tables
auth.wiki(resolve=False)
```

By using the line above in your model, the wiki tables will be accessible (i.e.
wiki_page) for custom CRUD or other db tasks.

> Note that you still have to call auth.wiki() in the controller or view in
> order to expose the wiki interface, since the resolve=False parameter
> instructs the auth object to just build the wiki model without any
> other interface setup.

Also, by setting resolve to False in the method call, the wiki tables will be
now accessible through the app's default db interface at <app>/appadmin for
managing wiki records.

Another customization possible is adding extra fields to the standard wiki
tables (in the same way as with the auth_user table, as described in Chapter
9). Here is how:

```
1  # Place this after auth object initialization
2  auth.settings.extra_fields["wiki_page"] = [Field("ablob", "blob"),]
```

The line above adds a blob field to the wiki_page table. There is no need to call auth.wiki(resolve=False) for this option, unless you need access to the wiki model for other customizations.

3.5.7 Components

One of the most powerful functions of the new web2py consists in the ability of embedding an action inside another action. We call this a component.

Consider the following model:

```
1  db.define_table('thing',Field('name',requires=IS_NOT_EMPTY()))
```

and the following action:

```
1  @auth.requires_login()
2  def manage_things():
3      return SQLFORM.grid(db.thing)
```

This action is special because it returns a widget/helper not a dict of objects. Now we can embed this manage_things action into any view, with

```
1  {{=LOAD('default','manage_things',ajax=True)}}
```

This allows the visitor interact with the component via Ajax without reloading the host page that embeds the widget. The action is called via Ajax, inherits the style of the host page, and captures all form submissions and flash messages so that they are handled within the current page. On top of this the SQLFORM.grid widget uses digitally signed URLs to restrict access. More information about components can be found in chapter 13.

Components like the one above can be embedded into wiki pages using the MARKMIN syntax:

```
1  @{component:default/manage_things}
```

This simply tells web2py that we want to include the "manage_things" action defined in the "default" controller as an Ajax "component".

> Most users will be able to build relatively complex applications simply by using auth.wiki to create pages and menus and embedded custom components into wiki pages. Wikis can be thought of as a

mechanism to allow members of the group to create pages, but they can also be thought of as a way to develop applications in a modular way.

3.6   More on admin

The administrative interface provides additional functionality that we briefly review here.

3.6.1   Site

This page is the main administrative interface of web2py. It lists all installed applications on the left, while on the right side there are some special action forms.

The first of them shows the web2py version and proposes to upgrade it if new versions are available. Of course, before upgrading be sure to have a full working backup! Then there are two other forms that allow the creation of a new application (simple or by using an online wizard) by specifying its name.

The following form allows uploading an existing application from either a local file or a remote URL. When you upload an application, you need to specify a name for it (using different names allows you to install multiple copies of the same application). You can try, for example, to upload the Movuca Social Networking application app created by Bruno Rocha:

```
https://github.com/rochacbruno/Movuca
```

or Instant Press CMS created by Martin Mulone:

```
http://code.google.com/p/instant-press/
```

or one of the many example applications available at:

```
http://web2py.com/appliances
```

Web2py files are packages as .w2p files. These are tar gzipped files. Web2py uses the .w2p extension instead of the .tgz extension to prevent the browser from unzipping on download. They can be uncompressed manually with `tar zxvf [filename]` although this is never necessary.

Upon successful upload, web2py displays the MD5 checksum of the uploaded file. You can use it to verify that the file was not corrupted during upload. The InstantPress name will appear in the list of installed applications.

If you run web2py from source and you have `gitpython` installed (if necessary, set it up with 'easy_install gitpython'), you can install applications directly from git repositories using the `.git` URL in the upload form. In this case you will also be enabled to use the admin interface to push changes back into the repository, but this is an experimental feature.

For example, you can locally install the application that shows this book on the web2py site with the URL:

```
https://github.com/mdipierro/web2py-book.git
```

That repository hosts the current, updated version of this book (which could be different from the stable version you can see on the web site). You are warmly invited to use it for submitting improvements, fixes and corrections in the form of pull requests.

For each application installed you can use the *site* page to:

• Go directly to the application by clicking on its name.

• Uninstall the application.

• Jump to the *about* page (read below).

• Jump to the *edit* page (read below).

• Jump to the *errors* page (read below).

- Clean up temporary files (sessions, errors, and cache.disk files).

- Pack all. This returns a tar file containing a complete copy of the application. We suggest that you clean up temporary files before packing an application.

- Compile the application. If there are no errors, this option will bytecode-compiles all models, controllers and views. Because views can extend and include other views in a tree, before bytecode compilation, the view tree for every controller is collapsed into a single file. The net effect is that a bytecode-compiled application is faster, because there is no more parsing of templates or string substitutions occurring at runtime.

- Pack compiled. This option is only present for bytecode-compiled applications. It allows packing the application without source code for distribution as closed source. Note that Python (as any other programming language) can technically be decompiled; therefore compilation does not provide complete protection of the source code. Nevertheless, de-compilation can be difficult and can be illegal.

- Remove compiled. It simply removes the byte-code compiled models, views and controllers from the application. If the application was packaged with source code or edited locally, there is no harm in removing the bytecode-compiled files, and the application will continue to work. If the application was installed form a packed compiled file, then this is not safe, because there is no source code to revert to, and the application will no longer work.

> All the functionality available from the web2py admin site page is also accessible programmatically via the API defined in the module gluon/admin.py. Simply open a python shell and import this module.

If the Google App Engine SDK is installer the admin *site* page shows a button to push your applications to GAE. If python-git is installed, there is also a button to push your application to Open Shift. To install applications on Heroku or other hosting system you should look into the "scripts" folder for the appropriate script.

3.6.2   About

The *about* tab allows editing the description of the application and its license. These are written respectively in the ABOUT and LICENSE files in the application folder.

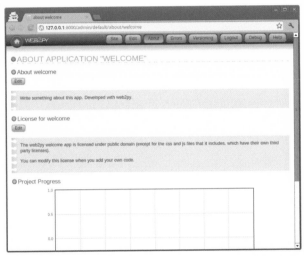

You can use MARKMIN, or gluon.contrib.markdown.WIKI syntax for these files as described in ref. [34].

3.6.3   Design

You have used the *edit* page already in this chapter. Here we want to point out a few more functionalities of the *edit* page.

- If you click on any file name, you can see the contents of the file with syntax highlighting.

- If you click on edit, you can edit the file via a web interface.

- If you click on delete, you can delete the file (permanently).

- If you click on test, web2py will run tests. Tests are written by the developer using Python doctests, and each function should have its own tests.

- You can add language files, scan the app to discover all strings, and edit string translations via the web interface.
- If the static files are organized in folders and subfolders, the folder hierarchy can be toggled by clicking on a folder name.

The image below shows the output of the test page for the welcome application.

The image below show the languages tab for the welcome application.

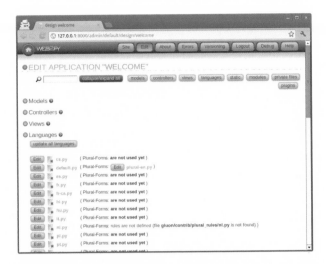

The image below shows how to edit a language file, in this case the "it" (Italian) language for the welcome application.

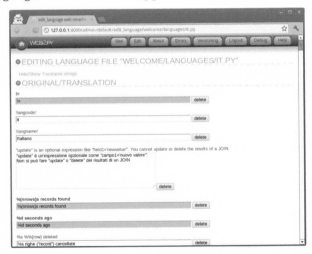

Integrated debugger

(requires Python 2.6 or later)

The web2py admin includes a web based debugger. Using the provided web-based editor you can add breakpoints to the Python code and, from the associated debugger console, you can inspect the system variables at those breakpoints and resume execution. This is illustrated in the following screenshot:

This functionality is based on the Qdb debugger created by Mariano Reingart. It uses multiprocessing.connection to communicate between the backend and frontend, with a JSON-RPC-like stream protocol. [47]

Shell

If you click on the "shell" link under the controllers tab in *edit*, web2py will open a web based Python shell and will execute the models for the current application. This allows you to interactively talk to your application.

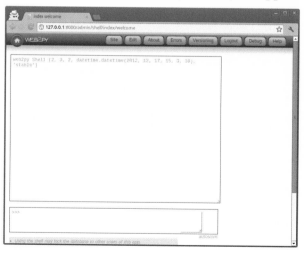

> Be careful using the web based shell - because different shell requests will be executed in different threads.   This easily gives errors, especially if you play with databases creation and connections. For activities like these (i.e. if you need persistence) it's much better to use the python command line.

Crontab

Also under the controllers tab in *edit* there is a "crontab" link. By clicking on this link you will be able to edit the web2py crontab file. This follows the same syntax as the Unix crontab but does not rely on Unix. In fact, it only requires web2py, and it works on Windows. It allows you to register actions that need to be executed in background at scheduled times. For more information about this, see the next chapter.

3.6.4   Errors

When programming web2py, you will inevitably make mistakes and introduce bugs. web2py helps in two ways: 1) it allows you to create tests for every function that can be run in the browser from the *edit* page; and 2) when an error manifests itself, a ticket is issued to the visitor and the error is logged.

Intentionally introduce an error in the images application as shown below:

```
1  def index():
2      images = db().select(db.image.ALL,orderby=db.image.title)
3      1/0
4      return dict(images=images)
```

When you access the index action, you get the following ticket:

Only the administrator can access the ticket:

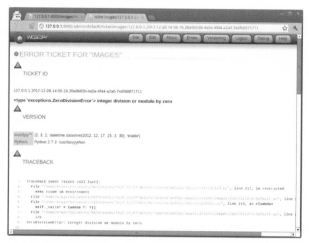

The ticket shows the traceback, and the content of the file that caused the problem, and the complete state of system (variables, request, session, etc.) If the error occurs in a view, web2py shows the view converted from HTML into Python code. This allows to easily identify the logical structure of the file.

By default tickets are stored on filesystem and displayed grouped by traceback. The administrative interface provides an aggregate views (type of traceback and number of occurrence) and a detailed view (all tickets are listed by ticket id). The administrator can switch between the two views.

Notice that everywhere **admin** shows syntax-highlighted code (for example, in error reports, web2py keywords are shown in orange). If you click on a web2py keyword, you are redirected to a documentation page about the keyword.

If you fix the divide-by-zero bug in the index action and introduce one in the index view:

```
1  {{extend 'layout.html'}}
2
3  <h1>Current Images</h1>
4  <ul>
5  {{for image in images:}}
6  {{1/0}}
```

```
7 {{=LI(A(image.title, _href=URL("show", args=image.id)))}}
8 {{pass}}
9 </ul>
```

you get the following ticket:

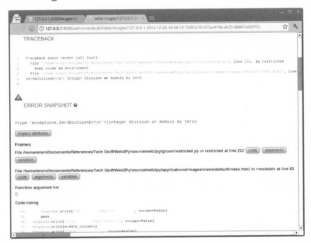

Note that web2py has converted the view from HTML into a Python file, and the error described in the ticket refers to the generated Python code and NOT to the original view file:

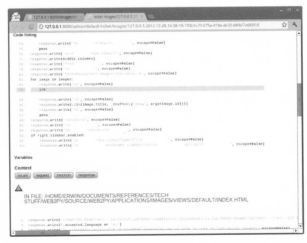

This may seem confusing at first, but in practice it makes debugging easier, because the Python indentation highlights the logical structure of the code that you embedded in the views.

The code is shown at the bottom of the same page.

All tickets are listed under admin in the *errors* page for each application:

3.6.5   Mercurial

If you are running from source, the administrative interface shows one more menu item called "Versioning".

Entering a comment and pressing the "commit" button in the resulting page will commit the current application. With the first commit, a local Mercurial repository for the specific application will be created.   Under the hood, Mercurial stores information about changes you make in your code into a hidden folder ".hg" in your app subfolder. Every app has its own ".hg" folder and its own ".hgignore" file (tells Mercurial which files to ignore). In order to use this feature, you must have the Mercurial version control libraries installed (at least version 1.9):

```
easy_install mercurial
```

The Mercurial web interface does allow you to browse previous commit and diff files but we do recommend you use Mercurial directly from the shell or one of the many GUI-based Mercurial clients since they are more powerful. For example they will allow you sync your app with a remote source repository:

You can read more about Mercurial here:

```
http://mercurial.selenic.com/
```

3.6.6 Application Wizard (experimental)

The **admin** interface includes a Wizard that can help you create a new applications. You can access the wizard from the "sites" page as shown in the image below.

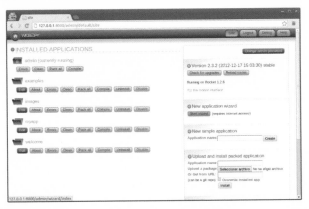

The wizard will guide you through a series of steps involved in creating a new application:

- Chose a name for the application

- Configure the application and choose required plugins

- Build required models (it will create CRUD pages for each model)

- Allow you to edit the views of those pages using MARKMIN syntax

The image below shows the second step of the process.

You can see a dropdown to select a layout plugin (from `web2py.com/layouts`), a multiple choice dropdown to check other plugins (from `web2py.com/plugins`) and a "login config" field where to put the Janrain "domain:key".

The other steps are pretty much self-explanatory.

The Wizard works well for what it does but it is considered an *experimental feature* for two reasons:

- Applications created with the wizard and edited manually, cannot later be modified by the wizard.

- The interface of the wizard will change over time to include support for more features and easier visual development.

In any case the wizard is a handy tool for fast prototyping and it can be used to bootstrap a new application with an alternate layout and optional plugins.

3.6.7   Configuring admin

Normally there is no need to perform any configuration of **admin** but a few customizations are possible. After you login into admin you can edit the admin configuration file via the URL:

```
http://127.0.0.1:8000/admin/default/edit/admin/models/0.py
```

Notice that **admin** can be used to edit itself. In fact **admin** is an app as any other one.

The file "o.py" is more or less self documented, anyway, here are some of the most important possible customizations:

```
1 GAE_APPCFG = os.path.abspath(os.path.join('/usr/local/bin/appcfg.py'))
```

This should point to the location of the "appcfg.py" file that comes with the Google App Engine SDK. If you have the SDK you may want to change these config parameters to the correct value. It will allow you to deploy to GAE from the admin interface.

You can also set web2py admin in demo mode:

```
1 DEMO_MODE = True
2 FILTER_APPS = ['welcome']
```

And only the apps listed in FILTER_APPS will be accessible and they will be only accessible in read-only mode.

If you are a teacher and want to expose the administrative interface to students so that students can share one administrative interface for their projects (think of a virtual lab), can do it by setting:

```
1 MULTI_USER_MODE = True
```

In this way students will be required to login and will only be able to access their own apps via admin. You, as first user/teacher, will be able to access them all.

In multi user mode, you can register students using the "bulk register" link in admin and manage them using the "manage students" link. The system also keeps track of when students login and how many lines of code they add/remove to/from their code. This data is presented to the administrator as charts under the application "about" page.

Mind that this mechanism still assumes all users are trusted. All the apps created under admin run under the same credentials on the same filesystem. It is possible for an app created by a student to access the data and the source of an app created by another student. It is also possible for a student to create an app that locks the server.

3.6.8   Mobile admin

Notice that the admin application includes "plugin_jqmobile" which packages jQuery Mobile. When admin is accessed from a mobile device; this is detected by web2py and the interface is displayed using a mobile-friendly layout:

3.7   More on appadmin

appadmin is not intended to be exposed to the public. It is designed to help you by providing an easy access to the database. It consists of only two files: a controller "appadmin.py" and a view "appadmin.html" which are used by all actions in the controller.

The **appadmin** controller is relatively small and readable; it provides an example of designing a database interface.

appadmin shows which databases are available and which tables exist in each database. You can insert records and list all records for each table individually. **appadmin** paginates output 100 records at a time.

Once a set of records is selected, the header of the pages changes, allowing you to update or delete the selected records.

To update the records, enter an SQL assignment in the Query string field:

```
title = 'test'
```

where string values must be enclosed in single quotes. Multiple fields can be separated by commas.

To delete a record, click the corresponding checkbox to confirm that you are sure.

appadmin can also perform joins if the SQL FILTER contains a SQL condition that involves two or more tables. For example, try:

```
db.image.id == db.post.image_id
```

web2py passes this along to the DAL, and it understands that the query links two tables; hence, both tables are selected with an INNER JOIN. Here is the output:

If you click on the number of an id field, you get an edit page for the record with the corresponding id.

If you click on the number of a reference field, you get an edit page for the referenced record.

You cannot update or delete rows selected by a join, because they involve records from multiple tables and this would be ambiguous.

In addition to its database administration capabilities, **appadmin** also enables you to view details about the contents of the application's cache (at /yourapp/appadmin/cache) as well as the contents of the current request, response, and session objects (at /yourapp/appadmin/state).

appadmin replaces response.menu with its own menu, which provides links to the application's **edit** page in **admin**, the **db** (database administration) page, the **state** page, and the **cache** page. If your application's layout does not generate a menu using response.menu, then you will not see the **appadmin** menu. In that case, you can modify the appadmin.html file and add {{=MENU(response.menu)}} to display the menu.

4
The core

4.1 Command line options

It is possible to skip the GUI and start web2py directly from the command line by typing something like:

```
1 python web2py.py -a 'your password' -i 127.0.0.1 -p 8000
```

When web2py starts, it creates a file called "parameters_8000.py" where it stores the hashed password. If you use "<ask>" as the password, web2py prompts you for it.

For additional security, you can start web2py with:

```
1 python web2py.py -a '<recycle>' -i 127.0.0.1 -p 8000
```

In this case web2py reuses the previously stored hashed password. If no password is provided, or if the "parameters_8000.py" file is deleted, the web-based administrative interface is disabled.

On some Unix/Linux systems, if the password is

```
1 <pam_user:some_user>
```

web2py uses the PAM password of the Operating System account of some_user to authenticate the administrator, unless blocked by the PAM configuration.

web2py normally runs with CPython (the C implementation of the Python interpreter created by Guido van Rossum), but it can also run with PyPy and Jython. The latter possibility allows the use of web2py in the context of a J2EE infrastructure. To use Jython, simply replace "python web2py.py..." with "jython web2py.py". Details about installing Jython, zxJDBC modules required to access the databases can be found in Chapter 14.

The "web2py.py" script can take many command-line arguments specifying the maximum number of threads, enabling of SSL, etc. For a complete list type:

```
>>> python web2py.py -h
Usage: python web2py.py

web2py Web Framework startup script. ATTENTION: unless a password
is specified (-a 'passwd'), web2py will attempt to run a GUI.
In this case command line options are ignored.

Options:
  --version             show program's version number and exit
  -h, --help            show this help message and exit
  -i IP, --ip=IP        IP address of the server (e.g., 127.0.0.1 or ::1);
                        Note: This value is ignored when using the
                        'interfaces' option.
  -p PORT, --port=PORT  port of server (8000)
  -a PASSWORD, --password=PASSWORD
                        password to be used for administration (use -a
                        "<recycle>" to reuse the last password))
  -c SSL_CERTIFICATE, --ssl_certificate=SSL_CERTIFICATE
                        file that contains ssl certificate
  -k SSL_PRIVATE_KEY, --ssl_private_key=SSL_PRIVATE_KEY
                        file that contains ssl private key
  --ca-cert=SSL_CA_CERTIFICATE
                        Use this file containing the CA certificate to
                        validate X509 certificates from clients
  -d PID_FILENAME, --pid_filename=PID_FILENAME
                        file to store the pid of the server
  -l LOG_FILENAME, --log_filename=LOG_FILENAME
                        file to log connections
  -n NUMTHREADS, --numthreads=NUMTHREADS
                        number of threads (deprecated)
  --minthreads=MINTHREADS
                        minimum number of server threads
  --maxthreads=MAXTHREADS
                        maximum number of server threads
```

```
 35   -s SERVER_NAME, --server_name=SERVER_NAME
 36                         server name for the web server
 37   -q REQUEST_QUEUE_SIZE, --request_queue_size=REQUEST_QUEUE_SIZE
 38                         max number of queued requests when server unavailable
 39   -o TIMEOUT, --timeout=TIMEOUT
 40                         timeout for individual request (10 seconds)
 41   -z SHUTDOWN_TIMEOUT, --shutdown_timeout=SHUTDOWN_TIMEOUT
 42                         timeout on shutdown of server (5 seconds)
 43   --socket-timeout=SOCKET_TIMEOUT
 44                         timeout for socket (5 second)
 45   -f FOLDER, --folder=FOLDER
 46                         folder from which to run web2py
 47   -v, --verbose         increase --test verbosity
 48   -Q, --quiet           disable all output
 49   -D DEBUGLEVEL, --debug=DEBUGLEVEL
 50                         set debug output level (0-100, 0 means all, 100 means
 51                         none; default is 30)
 52   -S APPNAME, --shell=APPNAME
 53                         run web2py in interactive shell or IPython (if
 54                         installed) with specified appname (if app does not
 55                         exist it will be created). APPNAME like a/c/f (c,f
 56                         optional)
 57   -B, --bpython         run web2py in interactive shell or bpython (if
 58                         installed) with specified appname (if app does not
 59                         exist it will be created). Use combined with --shell
 60   -P, --plain           only use plain python shell; should be used with
 61                         --shell option
 62   -M, --import_models   auto import model files; default is False; should be
 63                         used with --shell option
 64   -R PYTHON_FILE, --run=PYTHON_FILE
 65                         run PYTHON_FILE in web2py environment; should be used
 66                         with --shell option
 67   -K SCHEDULER, --scheduler=SCHEDULER
 68                         run scheduled tasks for the specified apps: expects a
 69                         list of app names as -K app1,app2,app3 or a list of
 70                         app:groups as -K app1:group1:group2,app2:group1 to
 71                         override specific group_names. (only strings, no
 72                         spaces allowed. Requires a scheduler defined in the
 73                         models
 74   -X, --with-scheduler  run schedulers alongside webserver
 75   -T TEST_PATH, --test=TEST_PATH
 76                         run doctests in web2py environment; TEST_PATH like
 77                         a/c/f (c,f optional)
 78   -W WINSERVICE, --winservice=WINSERVICE
 79                         -W install|start|stop as Windows service
 80   -C, --cron            trigger a cron run manually; usually invoked from a
 81                         system crontab
 82   --softcron            triggers the use of softcron
 83   -Y, --run-cron        start the background cron process
```

```
84   -J, --cronjob            identify cron-initiated command
85   -L CONFIG, --config=CONFIG
86                            config file
87   -F PROFILER_FILENAME, --profiler=PROFILER_FILENAME
88                            profiler filename
89   -t, --taskbar            use web2py gui and run in taskbar (system tray)
90   --nogui                  text-only, no GUI
91   -A ARGS, --args=ARGS     should be followed by a list of arguments to be passed
92                            to script, to be used with -S, -A must be the last
93                            option
94   --no-banner              Do not print header banner
95   --interfaces=INTERFACES
96                            listen on multiple addresses: "ip1:port1:key1:cert1:ca
97                            _cert1;ip2:port2:key2:cert2:ca_cert2;..."
98                            (:key:cert:ca_cert optional; no spaces; IPv6 addresses
99                            must be in square [] brackets)
100  --run_system_tests       runs web2py tests
```

Lower-case options are used to configure the web server. The -L option tells web2py to read configuration options from a file, -W installs web2py as a windows service, while -S, -P and -M options start an interactive Python shell. The -T option finds and runs controller doctests in a web2py execution environment. For example, the following example runs doctests from all controllers in the "welcome" application:

```
1  python web2py.py -vT welcome
```

if you run web2py as Windows Service, -W, it is not convenient to pass the configuration using command line arguments. For this reason, in the web2py folder there is a sample "options_std.py" configuration file for the internal web server:

```
1   import socket
2   import os
3
4   ip = '0.0.0.0'
5   port = 80
6   interfaces = [('0.0.0.0', 80)]
7                #,('0.0.0.0',443,'ssl_private_key.pem','ssl_certificate.pem')]
8   password = '<recycle>'  # ## <recycle> means use the previous password
9   pid_filename = 'httpserver.pid'
10  log_filename = 'httpserver.log'
11  profiler_filename = None
12  ssl_certificate = None  # 'ssl_certificate.pem'  # ## path to certificate file
13  ssl_private_key = None  # 'ssl_private_key.pem'  # ## path to private key file
14  #numthreads = 50 # ## deprecated; remove
15  minthreads = None
```

```
16  maxthreads = None
17  server_name = socket.gethostname()
18  request_queue_size = 5
19  timeout = 30
20  shutdown_timeout = 5
21  folder = os.getcwd()
22  extcron = None
23  nocron = None
```

This file contains the web2py defaults. If you edit this file, you need to import it explicitly with the -L command-line option. It only works if you run web2py as a Windows Service.

4.2 Workflow

The web2py workflow is the following:

- An HTTP requests arrives to the web server (the built-in Rocket server or a different server connected to web2py via WSGI or another adapter). The web server handles each request in its own thread, in parallel.

- The HTTP request header is parsed and passed to the dispatcher (explained later in this chapter).

- The dispatcher decides which of the installed application will handle the request and maps the PATH_INFO in the URL into a function call. Each URL corresponds to one function call.

- Requests for files in the static folder are handled directly, and large files are automatically streamed to the client.

- Requests for anything but a static file are mapped into an action (i.e. a function in a controller file, in the requested application).

- Before calling the action, a few things happen: if the request header contains a session cookie for the app, the session object is retrieved; if not, a session id is created (but the session file is not saved until later); an execution environment for the request is created; models are executed in this environment.

- Finally the controller action is executed in the pre-built environment.

- If the action returns a string, this is returned to the client (or if the action returns a web2py HTML helper object, it is serialized and returned to the client).

- If the action returns an iterable, this is used to loop and stream the data to the client.

- If the action returns a dictionary, web2py tries to locate a view to render the dictionary. The view must have the same name as the action (unless specified otherwise) and the same extension as the requested page (defaults to.html); on failure, web2py may pick up a generic view (if available and if enabled). The view sees every variable defined in the models as well as those in the dictionary returned by the action, but does not see global variables defined in the controller.

- The entire user code is executed in a single database transaction unless specified otherwise.

- If the user code succeeds, the transaction is committed.

- If the user code fails, the traceback is stored in a ticket, and a ticket ID is issued to the client. Only the system administrator can search and read the tracebacks in tickets.

There are some caveats to keep in mind:

- Models in the same folder/subfolder are executed in alphabetical order.

- Any variable defined in a model will be visible to other models following alphabetically, to the controllers, and to the views.

- Models in subfolders are executed conditionally. For example, if the user has requested "/a/c/f" where "a" is the application, "c" is the controller, and "f" is the function (action), then the following models are executed:

```
1  applications/a/models/*.py
2  applications/a/models/c/*.py
3  applications/a/models/c/f/*.py
```

- The requested controller is executed and the requested function is called. This means all top-level code in the controller is also executed at every request for that controller.

- The view is only called if the action returns a dictionary.

- If a view is not found, web2py tries to use a generic view. By default, generic views are disabled, although the 'welcome' app includes a line in /models/db.py to enable them on localhost only. They can be enabled per extension type and per action (using response.generic_patterns). In general, generic views are a development tool and typically should not be used in production. If you want some actions to use a generic view, list those actions in response.generic_patterns (discussed in more detail in the chapter on Services).

The possible behaviors of an action are the following:

Return a string

```
def index(): return 'data'
```

Return a dictionary for a view:

```
def index(): return dict(key='value')
```

Return all local variables:

```
def index(): return locals()
```

Redirect the user to another page:

```
def index(): redirect(URL('other_action'))
```

Return an HTTP page other than "200 OK":

```
def index(): raise HTTP(404)
```

Return a helper (for example, a FORM):

```
def index(): return FORM(INPUT(_name='test'))
```

(this is mostly used for Ajax callbacks and components, see chapter 12)

When an action returns a dictionary, it may contain code generated by helpers, including forms based on database tables or forms from a factory, for example:

```
def index(): return dict(form=SQLFORM.factory(Field('name')).process())
```

(all forms generated by web2py use postbacks, see chapter 3)

4.3   Dispatching

web2py maps a URL of the form:

```
http://127.0.0.1:8000/a/c/f.html
```

to the function f() in controller "c.py" in application "a". If f is not present, web2py defaults to the index controller function. If c is not present, web2py defaults to the "default.py" controller, and if a is not present, web2py defaults to the init application. If there is no init application, web2py tries to run the welcome application. This is shown schematically in the image below:

By default, any new request also creates a new session. In addition, a session cookie is returned to the client browser to keep track of the session.

The extension .html is optional; .html is assumed as default. The extension determines the extension of the view that renders the output of the controller function f(). It allows the same content to be served in multiple formats (html, xml, json, rss, etc.).

> Functions that take arguments or start with a double underscore are not publicly exposed and can only be called by other functions.

There is an exception made for URLs of the form:

```
http://127.0.0.1:8000/a/static/filename
```

There is no controller called "static". web2py interprets this as a request for the file called "filename" in the subfolder "static" of the application "a".

When static files are downloaded, web2py does not create a session, nor does it issue a cookie or execute the models. web2py always streams static files in chunks of 1MB, and sends PARTIAL CONTENT when the client sends a RANGE request for a subset of the file. web2py also supports the IF_MODIFIED_SINCE protocol, and does not send the file if it is already stored in the browser's cache and if the file has not changed since that version.

When linking to an audio or video file in the static folder, if you want to force the browser to download the file instead of streaming the audio/video via a media player, add ?attachment to the URL. This tells web2py to set the Content-Disposition header of the HTTP response to "attachment". For example:

```
<a href="/app/static/my_audio_file.mp3?attachment">Download</a>
```

When the above link is clicked, the browser will prompt the user to download the MP3 file rather than immediately streaming the audio. (As discussed below, you can also set HTTP response headers directly by assigning a dict of header names and their values to response.headers.)

web2py maps GET/POST requests of the form:

```
http://127.0.0.1:8000/a/c/f.html/x/y/z?p=1&q=2
```

to function f in controller "c.py" in application a, and it stores the URL parameters in the request variable as follows:

```
request.args = ['x', 'y', 'z']
```

and:

```
request.vars = {'p':1, 'q':2}
```

and:

```
request.application = 'a'
request.controller = 'c'
request.function = 'f'
```

In the above example, both request.args[i] and request.args(i) can be used to retrieve the i-th element of the request.args, but while the former raises an exception if the list does not have such an index, the latter returns None in this case.

```
request.url
```

stores the full URL of the current request (not including GET variables).

```
request.ajax
```

defaults False but it is True if web2py determines that the action was called by an Ajax request.

If the request is an Ajax request and it is initiated by a web2py component, the name of the component can be found in:

```
request.cid
```

Components are discussed in more detail in Chapter 12.

If the HTTP request is a GET, then request.env.request_method is set to "GET"; if it is a POST, request.env.request_method is set to "POST". URL query variables are stored in the request.vars Storage dictionary; they are also stored in request.get_vars (following a GET request) or request.post_vars (following a POST request). web2py stores WSGI and web2py environment variables in request.env, for example:

```
request.env.path_info = 'a/c/f'
```

and HTTP headers into environment variables, for example:

```
request.env.http_host = '127.0.0.1:8000'
```

> Notice that web2py validates all URLs to prevent directory traversal attacks.

URLs are only allowed to contain alphanumeric characters, underscores, and slashes; the args may contain non-consecutive dots. Spaces are replaced by underscores before validation. If the URL syntax is invalid, web2py returns an HTTP 400 error message [48] [49].

If the URL corresponds to a request for a static file, web2py simply reads and returns (streams) the requested file.

If the URL does not request a static file, web2py processes the request in the following order:

- Parses cookies.

- Creates an environment in which to execute the function.

- Initializes request, response, cache.

- Opens the existing session or creates a new one.

- Executes the models belonging to the requested application.

- Executes the requested controller action function.
- If the function returns a dictionary, executes the associated view.
- On success, commits all open transactions.
- Saves the session.
- Returns an HTTP response.

Notice that the controller and the view are executed in different copies of the same environment; therefore, the view does not see the controller, but it sees the models and it sees the variables returned by the controller action function.

If an exception (other than HTTP) is raised, web2py does the following:

- Stores the traceback in an error file and assigns a ticket number to it.
- Rolls back all open database transactions.
- Returns an error page reporting the ticket number.

If the exception is an HTTP exception, this is assumed to be the intended behavior (for example, an HTTP redirect), and all open database transactions are committed. The behavior after that is specified by the HTTP exception itself. The HTTP exception class is not a standard Python exception; it is defined by web2py.

4.4 Libraries

The web2py libraries are exposed to the user applications as global objects. For example (request, response, session, cache), classes (helpers, validators, DAL API), and functions (T and redirect).

These objects are defined in the following core files:

```
1  web2py.py
2  gluon/__init__.py        gluon/highlight.py      gluon/restricted.py  gluon/streamer.py
3  gluon/admin.py           gluon/html.py           gluon/rewrite.py     gluon/template.py
4  gluon/cache.py           gluon/http.py           gluon/rocket.py      gluon/storage.py
5  gluon/cfs.py             gluon/import_all.py      gluon/sanitizer.py   gluon/tools.py
6  gluon/compileapp.py      gluon/languages.py       gluon/serializers.py gluon/utils.py
```

```
7  gluon/contenttype.py  gluon/main.py              gluon/settings.py    gluon/validators.py
8  gluon/dal.py          gluon/myregex.py           gluon/shell.py       gluon/widget.py
9  gluon/decoder.py      gluon/newcron.py           gluon/sql.py         gluon/winservice.py
10 gluon/fileutils.py    gluon/portalocker.py       gluon/sqlhtml.py     gluon/xmlrpc.py
11 gluon/globals.py      gluon/reserved_sql_keywords.py
```

> Notice that many of these modules, specifically dal (the Database Abstraction Layer), template (the template language), rocket (the web server), and html (the helpers) have no dependencies and can be used outside of web2py.

The tar gzipped scaffolding app that ship with web2py is

```
1  welcome.w2p
```

This is created upon installation and overwritten on upgrade.

> The first time you start web2py, two new folders are created: deposit and applications. The deposit folder is used as temporary storage for installing and uninstalling applications.
>
> The first time you start web2py and after an upgrade, the "welcome" app is zipped into a "welcome.w2p" file to be used as a scaffolding app.

When web2py is upgraded it comes with a file called "NEWINSTALL". If web2py finds this file, it understands an upgrade was performed, hence it removed the file and creates a new "welcome.w2p".

The current web2py version is stored in the field "VERSION" and it follows standard semantic versioning notation where the build id is the build timestamp. web2py unit-tests are in

```
1  gluon/tests/
```

There are handlers for connecting with various web servers:

```
1  cgihandler.py        # discouraged
2  gaehandler.py        # for Google App Engine
3  fcgihandler.py       # for FastCGI
4  wsgihandler.py       # for WSGI
5  isapiwsgihandler.py  # for IIS
6  modpythonhandler.py  # deprecated
```

("fcgihandler" calls "gluon/contrib/gateways/fcgi.py" developed by Allan Saddi) and

```
1  anyserver.py
```

which is a script to interface with many different web servers, described in Chapter 13.

There are three example files:

```
1 options_std.py
2 routes.example.py
3 router.example.py
```

The former is an optional configuration file that can be passed to web2py.py with the -L option. The second is an example of a URL mapping file. It is loaded automatically when renamed "routes.py". The third is an alternative syntax for URL mapping, and can also be renamed (or copied to) "routes.py".

The files

```
1 app.example.yaml
2 queue.example.yaml
```

are example configuration files used for deployment on the Google App Engine. You can read more about them in the Deployment Recipes chapter and on the Google Documentation pages.

There are also additional libraries, some developed by a third party:

feedparser [33] by Mark Pilgrim for reading RSS and Atom feeds:

```
1 gluon/contrib/__init__.py
2 gluon/contrib/feedparser.py
```

markdown2 [34] by Trent Mick for wiki markup:

```
1 gluon/contrib/markdown/__init__.py
2 gluon/contrib/markdown/markdown2.py
```

markmin markup:

```
1 gluon/contrib/markmin
```

fpdf created my Mariano Reingart for generating PDF documents:

```
1 gluon/contrib/fpdf
```

This is not documented in this book but it is hosted and documented here:

```
1 http://code.google.com/p/pyfpdf/
```

pysimplesoap is a lightweight SOAP server implementation created by Mariano Reingart:

```
1 gluon/contrib/pysimplesoap/
```

simplejsonrpc is a lightweight JSON-RPC client also created by Mariano Reingart:

```
1  gluon/contrib/simplejsonrpc.py
```

memcache [35] Python API by Evan Martin:

```
1  gluon/contrib/memcache/__init__.py
2  gluon/contrib/memcache/memcache.py
```

redis_cache is a module to store cache in the redis database:

```
1  gluon/contrib/redis_cache.py
```

gql, a port of the DAL to the Google App Engine:

```
1  gluon/contrib/gql.py
```

memdb, a port of the DAL on top of memcache:

```
1  gluon/contrib/memdb.py
```

gae_memcache is an API to use memcache on the Google App Engine:

```
1  gluon/contrib/gae_memcache.py
```

pyrtf [31] for generating Rich Text Format (RTF) documents, developed by Simon Cusack and revised by Grant Edwards:

```
1  gluon/contrib/pyrtf/
```

PyRSS2Gen [32] developed by Dalke Scientific Software, to generate RSS feeds:

```
1  gluon/contrib/rss2.py
```

simplejson [30] by Bob Ippolito, the standard library for parsing and writing JSON objects:

```
1  gluon/contrib/simplejson/
```

Google Wallet [50] provides "pay now" buttons which link Google as payment processor:

```
1  gluon/contrib/google_wallet.py
```

Stripe.com [51] provides a simple API for accepting credit card payments:

```
1  gluon/contrib/stripe.py
```

AuthorizeNet [52] provides API to accept credit card payments via Authorize.net network

```
1  gluon/contrib/AuthorizeNet.py
```

Dowcommerce [53] credit card processing API:

```
1  gluon/contrib/DowCommerce.py
```

PaymentTech credit card processing API:

```
1  gluon/contrib/paymentech.py
```

PAM [54] authentication API created by Chris AtLee:

```
1  gluon/contrib/pam.py
```

A Bayesian classifier to populate the database with dummy data for testing purposes:

```
1  gluon/contrib/populate.py
```

A file with API for running on Heroku.com :

```
1  gluon/contrib/heroku.py
```

A file that allows interaction with the taskbar in windows, when web2py is running as a service:

```
1  gluon/contrib/taskbar_widget.py
```

Optional **login_methods** and login_forms to be used for authentication:

```
1   gluon/contrib/login_methods/__init__.py
2   gluon/contrib/login_methods/basic_auth.py
3   gluon/contrib/login_methods/browserid_account.py
4   gluon/contrib/login_methods/cas_auth.py
5   gluon/contrib/login_methods/dropbox_account.py
6   gluon/contrib/login_methods/email_auth.py
7   gluon/contrib/login_methods/extended_login_form.py
8   gluon/contrib/login_methods/gae_google_account.py
9   gluon/contrib/login_methods/ldap_auth.py
10  gluon/contrib/login_methods/linkedin_account.py
11  gluon/contrib/login_methods/loginza.py
12  gluon/contrib/login_methods/oauth10a_account.py
13  gluon/contrib/login_methods/oauth20_account.py
14  gluon/contrib/login_methods/oneall_account.py
15  gluon/contrib/login_methods/openid_auth.py
16  gluon/contrib/login_methods/pam_auth.py
17  gluon/contrib/login_methods/rpx_account.py
18  gluon/contrib/login_methods/x509_auth.py
```

web2py also contains a folder with useful scripts including

```
1  scripts/setup-web2py-fedora.sh
2  scripts/setup-web2py-ubuntu.sh
3  scripts/setup-web2py-nginx-uwsgi-ubuntu.sh
4  scripts/setup-web2py-heroku.sh
5  scripts/update-web2py.sh
6  scripts/make_min_web2py.py
```

```
 7 ...
 8 scripts/sessions2trash.py
 9 scripts/sync_languages.py
10 scripts/tickets2db.py
11 scripts/tickets2email.py
12 ...
13 scripts/extract_mysql_models.py
14 scripts/extract_pgsql_models.py
15 ...
16 scripts/access.wsgi
17 scripts/cpdb.py
```

The `setup-web2py-*` are particularly useful because they attempt a complete installation and setup of a web2py production environment from scratch. Some of these are discussed in Chapter 14, but all of them contain a documentation string inside that explains their purpose and usage.

Finally web2py includes these files required to build the binary distributions.

```
1 Makefile
2 setup_exe.py
3 setup_app.py
```

These are setup scripts for **py2exe** and **py2app**, respectively, and they are only required to build the binary distributions of web2py. YOU SHOULD NEVER NEED TO RUN THEM. web2py applications contain additional files, particularly third-party JavaScript libraries, such as jQuery, calendar, and Codemirror. Their authors are acknowledged in the files themselves.

4.5   Applications

Applications developed in web2py are composed of the following parts:

- **models** describe a representation of the data as database tables and relations between tables.

- **controllers** describe the application logic and workflow.

- **views** describe how data should be presented to the user using HTML and JavaScript.

- **languages** describe how to translate strings in the application into various supported languages.

- **static files** do not require processing (e.g. images, CSS stylesheets, etc).

- **ABOUT** and **README** documents are self-explanatory.

- **errors** store error reports generated by the application.

- **sessions** store information related to each particular user.

- **databases** store SQLite databases and additional table information.

- **cache** store cached application items.

- **modules** are other optional Python modules.

- **private** files are accessed by the controllers but not directly by the developer.

- **uploads** files are accessed by the models but not directly by the developer (e.g., files uploaded by users of the application).

- **tests** is a directory for storing test scripts, fixtures and mocks.

Models, views, controllers, languages, and static files are accessible via the web administration [design] interface. ABOUT, README, and errors are also accessible via the administration interface through the corresponding menu items. Sessions, cache, modules and private files are accessible to the applications but not via the administration interface.

Everything is neatly organized in a clear directory structure that is replicated for every installed web2py application, although the user never needs to access the filesystem directly:

```
1  __init__.py   ABOUT     LICENSE    models    views
2  controllers   modules   private    tests     cron
3  cache         errors    upload     sessions  static
```

"__init__.py" is an empty file which is required in order to allow Python (and web2py) to import the modules in the `modules` directory.

Notice that the **admin** application simply provides a web interface to web2py applications on the server file system. web2py applications can also be created and developed from the command-line or your preferred text editor/IDE; you don't have to use the browser **admin** interface. A new application can be created manually by replicating the above directory structure under,e.g., "applications/newapp/" (or simply untar the welcome.w2p file into your new application directory). Application files can also be created and edited from the command-line without having to use the web **admin** interface.

4.6 API

Models, controllers, and views are executed in an environment where the following objects are already imported for us:

Global Objects:

```
1  request, response, session, cache
```

Internationalization:

```
1  T
```

Navigation:

```
1  redirect, HTTP
```

Helpers:

```
1   XML, URL, BEAUTIFY
2
3   A, B, BODY, BR, CENTER, CODE, COL, COLGROUP,
4   DIV, EM, EMBED, FIELDSET, FORM, H1, H2, H3, H4, H5, H6,
5   HEAD, HR, HTML, I, IFRAME, IMG, INPUT, LABEL, LEGEND,
6   LI, LINK, OL, UL, META, OBJECT, OPTION, P, PRE,
7   SCRIPT, OPTGROUP, SELECT, SPAN, STYLE,
8   TABLE, TAG, TD, TEXTAREA, TH, THEAD, TBODY, TFOOT,
9   TITLE, TR, TT, URL, XHTML, xmlescape, embed64
10
11  CAT, MARKMIN, MENU, ON
```

Forms and tables

```
1  SQLFORM (SQLFORM.factory, SQLFORM.grid, SQLFORM.smartgrid)
```

Validators:

```
1  CLEANUP, CRYPT, IS_ALPHANUMERIC, IS_DATE_IN_RANGE, IS_DATE,
2  IS_DATETIME_IN_RANGE, IS_DATETIME, IS_DECIMAL_IN_RANGE,
3  IS_EMAIL, IS_EMPTY_OR, IS_EXPR, IS_FLOAT_IN_RANGE, IS_IMAGE,
4  IS_IN_DB, IS_IN_SET, IS_INT_IN_RANGE, IS_IPV4, IS_LENGTH,
5  IS_LIST_OF, IS_LOWER, IS_MATCH, IS_EQUAL_TO, IS_NOT_EMPTY,
6  IS_NOT_IN_DB, IS_NULL_OR, IS_SLUG, IS_STRONG, IS_TIME,
7  IS_UPLOAD_FILENAME, IS_UPPER, IS_URL
```

Database:

```
DAL, Field
```

For backward compatibility SQLDB=DAL and SQLField=Field. We encourage you to use the new syntax DAL and Field, instead of the old syntax.

Other objects and modules are defined in the libraries, but they are not automatically imported since they are not used as often.

The core API entities in the web2py execution environment are request, response, session, cache, URL, HTTP, redirect and T and are discussed below.

A few objects and functions, including **Auth**, **Crud** and **Service**, are defined in "gluon/tools.py" and they need to be imported as necessary:

```
from gluon.tools import Auth, Crud, Service
```

4.6.1 Accessing the API from Python modules

Your models or controller may import python modules, and these may need to use some of the web2py API. The way to do it is by importing them:

```
from gluon import *
```

In fact, any Python module, even if not imported by a web2py application, can import the web2py API as long as web2py is in the sys.path.

There is one caveat, though. Web2py defines some global objects (request, response, session, cache, T) that can only exist when an HTTP request is present (or is faked). Therefore, modules can access them only if they are called from an application. For this reasons they are placed into a container caller current, which is a thread local object. Here is an example.

Create a module "/myapp/modules/test.py" that contains:

```
from gluon import *
def ip(): return current.request.client
```

Now from a controller in "myapp" you can do

```
import test
def index():
    return "Your ip is " + test.ip()
```

Notice a few things:

- `import test` looks for the module first in the current app's modules folder, then in the folders listed in `sys.path`. Therefore, app-level modules always take precedence over Python modules. This allows different apps to ship with different versions of their modules, without conflicts.

- Different users can call the same action `index` concurrently, which calls the function in the module, and yet there is no conflict because `current.request` is a different object in different threads. Just be careful not to access `current.request` outside of functions or classes (i.e., at the top level) in the module.

- `import test` is a shortcut for `from applications.appname.modules import test`. Using the longer syntax, it is possible to import modules from other applications.

For uniformity with normal Python behavior, by default web2py does not reload modules when changes are made. Yet this can be changed. To turn on the auto-reload feature for modules, use the `track_changes` function as follows (typically in a model file, before any imports):

```
from gluon.custom_import import track_changes; track_changes(True)
```

From now on, every time a module is imported, the importer will check if the Python source file (.py) has changed. If it has changed, the module will be reloaded.

> Do not call track_changes in the modules themselves.

Track changes only tracks changes for modules that are stored in the application. Modules that import `current` can access:

- `current.request`

- `current.response`

- `current.session`

- `current.cache`

- `current.T`

and any other variable your application chooses to store in current. For example a model could do

```
1 auth = Auth(db)
2 from gluon import current
3 current.auth = auth
```

and now all modules imported can access current.auth.

current and import create a powerful mechanism to build extensible and reusable modules for your applications.

> Beware! Given from gluon import current, it is correct to use current.request and any of the other thread local objects but one should never assign them to global variables in the module, such as in
>
> ```
> 1 request = current.request # WRONG! DANGER!
> ```
>
> nor one should use it assign class attributes
>
> ```
> 1 class MyClass:
> 2     request = current.request # WRONG! DANGER!
> ```
>
> This is because the thread local object must be extracted at runtime. Global variables instead are defined only once when the model is imported for the first time.

Another caveat has to do with cache. You cannot use the cache object to decorate functions in modules, that is because it would not behave as expected. In order to cache a function f in a module you must use lazy_cache:

```
1 from gluon.cache import lazy_cache
2
3 lazy_cache('key', time_expire=60, cache_model='ram')
4 def f(a,b,c,): ....
```

Mind that the key is user defined but must be uniquely associated to the function. If omitted web2py will automatically determine a key.

4.7   request

The request object is an instance of the ubiquitous web2py class that is called gluon.storage.Storage, which extends the Python dict class. It is basically a dictionary, but the item values can also be accessed as attributes:

```
1 request.vars
```

is the same as:

```
1  request['vars']
```

Unlike a dictionary, if an attribute (or key) does not exist, it does not raise an exception. Instead, it returns None.

It is sometimes useful to create your own Storage objects. You can do so as follows:

```
1  from gluon.storage import Storage
2  my_storage = Storage() # empty storage object
3  my_other_storage = Storage(dict(a=1, b=2)) # convert dictionary to Storage
```

request has the following items/attributes, some of which are also an instance of the Storage class:

- request.cookies: a Cookie.SimpleCookie() object containing the cookies passed with the HTTP request. It acts like a dictionary of cookies. Each cookie is a Morsel object [55].

- request.env: a Storage object containing the environment variables passed to the controller, including HTTP header variables from the HTTP request and standard WSGI parameters. The environment variables are all converted to lower case, and dots are converted to underscores for easier memorization.

- request.application: the name of the requested application.

- request.controller: the name of the requested controller.

- request.function: the name of the requested function.

- request.extension: the extension of the requested action. It defaults to "html". If the controller function returns a dictionary and does not specify a view, this is used to determine the extension of the view file that will render the dictionary (parsed from the request.env.path_info).

- request.folder: the application directory. For example if the application is "welcome", request.folder is set to the absolute path "/path/to/welcome". In your programs, you should always use this variable and the os.path.join function to build paths to the files you need to access. Although web2py always uses absolute paths, it is a good rule never to explicitly change the current working folder (whatever that is) since this is not a thread-safe practice.

- `request.now`: a `datetime.datetime` object storing the datetime of the current request.

- `request.utcnow`: a `datetime.datetime` object storing the UTC datetime of the current request.

- `request.args`: A list of the URL path components following the controller function name; equivalent to `request.env.path_info.split('/')[3:]`

- `request.vars`: a `gluon.storage.Storage` object containing both the HTTP GET and HTTP POST query variables.

- `request.get_vars`: a `gluon.storage.Storage` object containing only the HTTP GET query variables.

- `request.post_vars`: a `gluon.storage.Storage` object containing only the HTTP POST query variables.

- `request.client`: The ip address of the client as determined by, if present, `request.env.http_x_forwarded_for` or by `request.env.remote_addr` otherwise. While this is useful it should not be trusted because the `http_x_forwarded_for` can be spoofed.

- `request.is_local`: `True` if the client is localhost, `False` otherwise. Should work behind a proxy if the proxy supports `http_x_forwarded_for`.

- `request.is_https`: `True` if the request is using the HTTPS protocol, `False` otherwise.

- `request.body`: a read-only file stream that contains the body of the HTTP request. This is automatically parsed to get the `request.post_vars` and then rewinded. It can be read with `request.body.read()`.

- `request.ajax` is True if the function is being called via an Ajax request.

- `request.cid` is the `id` of the component that generated the Ajax request (if any). You can read more about components in Chapter 12.

- `request.requires_https()` prevents further code execution if the request is not over HTTPS and redirects the visitor to the current page over HTTPS.

- `request.restful` this is a new and very useful decorator that can be used to change the default behavior of web2py actions by separating GET/POST/PUSH/DELETE requests. It will be discussed in some detail in Chapter 10.

- `request.user_agent()` parses the user_agent field from the client and returns the information in the form of a dictionary. It is useful to detect mobile devices. It uses "gluon/contrib/user_agent_parser.py" created by Ross Peoples. To see what it does, try to embed the following code in a view:

```
{{=BEAUTIFY(request.user_agent())}}
```

- `request.global_settings` contains web2py system wide settings. They are set automatically and you should not change them. For example `request.global_settings.gluon_parent` contains the full path to the web2py folder, `request.global_settings.is_pypy` determines if web2py is running on PyPy.

- `request.wsgi` is a hook that allows you to call third party WSGI applications from inside actions

The latter includes:

- `request.wsgi.environ`

- `request.wsgi.start_response`

- `request.wsgi.middleware`

their usage is discussed at the end of this Chapter.

As an example, the following call on a typical system:

```
http://127.0.0.1:8000/examples/default/status/x/y/z?p=1&q=2
```

results in the following `request` object:

variable	value
request.application	examples
request.controller	default
request.function	index
request.extension	html
request.view	status
request.folder	applications/examples/
request.args	['x', 'y', 'z']
request.vars	<Storage {'p': 1, 'q': 2}>
request.get_vars	<Storage {'p': 1, 'q': 2}>
request.post_vars	<Storage {}>
request.is_local	False
request.is_https	False
request.ajax	False
request.cid	None
request.wsgi	<hook>
request.env.content_length	0
request.env.content_type	
request.env.http_accept	text/xml,text/html;
request.env.http_accept_encoding	gzip, deflate
request.env.http_accept_language	en
request.env.http_cookie	session_id_examples=127.0.0.1.119725
request.env.http_host	127.0.0.1:8000
request.env.http_referer	http://web2py.com/
request.env.http_user_agent	Mozilla/5.0
request.env.path_info	/examples/simple_examples/status
request.env.query_string	remote_addr:127.0.0.1
request.env.request_method	GET
request.env.script_name	
request.env.server_name	127.0.0.1
request.env.server_port	8000
request.env.server_protocol	HTTP/1.1
request.env.server_software	Rocket 1.2.6
request.env.web2py_path	/Users/mdipierro/web2py
request.env.web2py_version	Version 2.4.1
request.env.wsgi_errors	<open file, mode 'w' at >
request.env.wsgi_input	
request.env.wsgi_url_scheme	http

Which environment variables are actually defined depends on the web server. Here we are assuming the built-in Rocket wsgi server. The set of variables is not much different when using the Apache web server.

The request.env.http_* variables are parsed from the request HTTP header.

The request.env.web2py_* variables are not parsed from the web server environment, but are created by web2py in case your applications need to know about the web2py location and version, and whether it is running on the Google App Engine (because specific optimizations may be necessary).

Also notice the request.env.wsgi_* variables. They are specific to the wsgi adapter.

4.8   response

response is another instance of the Storage class. It contains the following:

- response.body: a StringIO object into which web2py writes the output page body. NEVER CHANGE THIS VARIABLE.

- response.cookies: similar to request.cookies, but while the latter contains the cookies sent from the client to the server, the former contains cookies sent by the server to the client. The session cookie is handled automatically.

- response.download(request, db):   a method used to implement the controller function that allows downloading of uploaded files. request.download expects the last arg in request.args to be the encoded filename (i.e., the filename generated at upload time and stored in the upload field). It extracts the upload field name and table name as well as the original filename from the encoded filename. response.download takes two optional arguments: chunk_size sets the size in bytes for chunked streaming (defaults to 64K), and attachments determines whether the downloaded file should be treated as an attachment or not (default to True). Note, response.download is specifically for downloading files associated with db upload fields. Use response.stream (see below) for other types of file downloads and streaming. Also, note that it is not necessary to use `response.download` to access files uploaded to the /static folder – static files can (and generally should) be accessed directly via URL (e.g., /app/static/files/myfile.pdf).

- `response.files`: a list of `.css`, `.js`, `coffee`, and `.less` files required by the page. They will automatically be linked in the head of the standard "layout.html" via the included "web2py_ajax.html". To include a new CSS, JS, COFFEE, or LESS file, just append it to this list. It will handle duplicates. The order is important.

- `response.include_files()` generates html head tags to include all `response.files` (used in "views/web2py_ajax.html").

- `response.flash`: optional parameter that may be included in the views. Normally used to notify the user about something that happened.

- `response.headers`: a `dict` for HTTP response headers. Web2py sets some headers by default, including "Content-Length", "Content-Type", and "X-Powered-By" (set equal to web2py). Web2py also sets the "Cache-Control", "Expires", and "Pragma" headers to prevent client-side caching, except for static file requests, for which client-side caching is enabled. The headers that web2py sets can be overwritten or removed, and new headers can be added (e.g., `response.headers['Cache-Control'] = 'private'`). You can remove a header by removing its key from the response.headers dict, e.g.`del response.headers['Custom-Header']`, however web2py's default headers will be re-added just before returning the response. To avoid this behavior, just set the header value to None, e.g. to remove the default Content-Type header, `response.headers['Content-Type'] = None`

- `response.menu`: optional parameter that may be included in the views, normally used to pass a navigation menu tree to the view. It can be rendered by the MENU helper.

- `response.meta`: a Storage object that contains optional <meta> information like `response.meta.author`, `.description`, and/or `.keywords`. The content of each meta variable is automatically placed in the proper META tag by the code in "views/web2py_ajax.html", which is included by default in "views/layout.html".

- `response.include_meta()` generates a string that includes all `response.meta` headers serialized (used in "views/web2py_ajax.html").

- `response.postprocessing`: this is a list of functions, empty by default. These functions are used to filter the response object at the output of an action, before the output is rendered by the view. It can be used to implement support for other template languages.

- `response.render(view, vars)`: a method used to call the view explicitly inside the controller. `view` is an optional parameter which is the name of the view file, `vars` is a dictionary of named values passed to the view.

- `response.session_file`: file stream containing the session.

- `response.session_file_name`: name of the file where the session will be saved.

- `response.session_id`: the id of the current session. It is determined automatically. NEVER CHANGE THIS VARIABLE.

- `response.session_id_name`: the name of the session cookie for this application. NEVER CHANGE THIS VARIABLE.

- `response.status`: the HTTP status code integer to be passed to the response. Default is 200 (OK).

- `response.stream(file, chunk_size, request=request, attachment=False, filename=None, headers=None)`: when a controller returns it, web2py streams the file content back to the client in blocks of size `chunk_size`. The `request` parameter is required to use the chunk start in the HTTP header. `file` should be a file path (for backward compatibility, it can also be an open file object, but this is not recommended). As noted above, `response.download` should be used to retrieve files stored via an upload field. `response.stream` can be used in other cases, such as returning a temporary file or StringIO object created by the controller. If `attachment` is True, the Content-Disposition header will be set to "attachment", and if `filename` is also provided, it will be added to the Content-Disposition header as well (but only when `attachment` is True). If not already included in `response.headers`, the following response headers will be set automatically: Content-Type, Content-Length, Cache-Control, Pragma, and Last-Modified (the latter three are set to allow browser caching of the file). To override any of these automatic header settings, simply set them in `response.headers` before calling `response.stream`.

- `response.subtitle`: optional parameter that may be included in the views. It should contain the subtitle of the page.

- `response.title`: optional parameter that may be included in the views. It should contain the title of the page and should be rendered by the HTML title TAG in the header.

- `response.toolbar`: a function that allows you to embed a toolbar into page for debugging purposes `{{=response.toolbar()}}`. The toolbar displays request, response, session variables and database access time for each query.

- `response._vars`: this variable is accessible only in a view, not in the action. It contains the value returned by the action to the view.

- `response._caller`: this is a function that wraps all action calls. It defaults to the identity function, but it can be modified in order to catch special types of exception to do extra logging;

```
response._caller = lambda f: f()
```

- `response.optimize_css`: if can be set to "concat,minify,inline" to concatenate, minify and inline the CSS files included by web2py.

- `response.optimize_js`: if can be set to "concat,minify,inline" to concatenate, minify and inline the JavaScript files included by web2py.

- `response.view`: the name of the view template that must render the page. This is set by default to:

```
"%s/%s.%s" % (request.controller, request.function, request.extension)
```

or, if the above file cannot be located, to

```
"generic.%s" % (request.extension)
```

Change the value of this variable to modify the view file associated with a particular action.

- `response.delimiters` defaults to `('{{','}}')`. It allows you to change the delimiter of code embedded in views.

- `response.xmlrpc(request, methods)`: when a controller returns it, this function exposes the methods via XML-RPC [45]. This function is deprecated since a better mechanism is available and described in Chapter 10.

- `response.write(text)`: a method to write text into the output page body.

- `response.js` can contain Javascript code. This code will be executed if and only if the response is received by a web2py component as discussed in Chapter 12.

Since `response` is a `gluon.storage.Storage` object, it can be used to store other attributes that you may want to pass to the view. While there is no technical restriction, our recommendation is to store only variables that are to be rendered by all pages in the overall layout ("layout.html").

Anyway, we strongly suggest to stick to the variables listed here:

```
1  response.title
2  response.subtitle
3  response.flash
4  response.menu
5  response.meta.author
6  response.meta.description
7  response.meta.keywords
8  response.meta.*
```

because this will make it easier for you to replace the standard "layout.html" file that comes with web2py with another layout file, one that uses the same set of variables.

Old versions of web2py used `response.author` instead of `response.meta.author` and similar for the other meta attributes.

4.9 session

`session` is another instance of the `Storage` class. Whatever is stored into `session` for example:

```
1  session.myvariable = "hello"
```

can be retrieved at a later time:

```
1 a = session.myvariable
```

as long as the code is executed within the same session by the same user (provided the user has not deleted session cookies and the session has not expired). Because session is a Storage object, trying to access an attribute/key that has not been set does not raise an exception; it returns None instead.

The session object has three important methods. One is forget:

```
1 session.forget(response)
```

It tells web2py not to save the session. This should be used in those controllers whose actions are called often and do not need to track user activity. session.forget() prevents the session file from being written, regardless of whether it has been modified. session.forget(response) additionally unlocks and closes the session file. You rarely need to call this method since sessions are not saved when they are not changed. However, if the page makes multiple simultaneous Ajax requests, it is a good idea for the actions called via Ajax to call session.forget(response) (assuming the session is not needed by the action). Otherwise, each Ajax action will have to wait for the previous one to complete (and unlock the session file) before proceeding, which will slow down the page loading. Notice that sessions are not locked when stored in the database.

Another method is:

```
1 session.secure()
```

which tells web2py to set the session cookie to be a secure cookie. This should be set if the app is going over https. By setting the session cookie to be secure, the server is asking the browser not to send the session cookie back to the server unless over an https connection.

The other method is connect. By default sessions are stored on the filesystem and a session cookie is used to store and retrieve the session.id. Using the connect method it is possible to tell web2py to store sessions in the database or in the cookies thus eliminating need to access the filesystem for session management.

For example to **store sessions in the database**:

```
1 session.connect(request, response, db, masterapp=None)
```

where db is the name of an open database connection (as returned by the DAL). It tells web2py that you want to store the sessions in the database and not on the filesystem. session.connect must come after db=DAL(...), but before any other logic that requires session, for example, setting up Auth. web2py creates a table:

```
db.define_table('web2py_session',
                Field('locked', 'boolean', default=False),
                Field('client_ip'),
                Field('created_datetime', 'datetime', default=now),
                Field('modified_datetime', 'datetime'),
                Field('unique_key'),
                Field('session_data', 'text'))
```

and stores cPickled sessions in the session_data field.

The option masterapp=None, by default, tells web2py to try to retrieve an existing session for the application with name in request.application, in the running application.

If you want two or more applications to share sessions, set masterapp to the name of the master application.

To **store sessions in cookies** instead you can do:

```
session.connect(request,response,cookie_key='yoursecret',compression_level=None)
```

Here cookie_key is a symmetric encryption key. compression_level is an optional zlib encryption level.

While sessions in cookie are often recommended for scalability reason they are limited in size. Large sessions will result in broken cookies.

You can check the state of your application at any time by printing the request, session and response system variables. One way to do it is to create a dedicated action:

```
def status():
    return dict(request=request, session=session, response=response)
```

In the "generic.html" view this is done using {{=response.toolbar()}}.

4.9.1   Separate sessions

If you are storing sessions on filesystems and you have lots of them, the file system access may become a bottle-neck. One solution is the following: If you are storing sessions on filesystem and you have lots of them, the file system access may become a bottle-neck. One solution is the following:

```
session.connect(request, response, separate=True)
```

By setting separate=True web2py will store sessions not in the "sessions/" folder but in subfolders of the "sessions/" folder. The subfolder will be created automatically. Sessions with the same prefix will be in the same subfolder. Again, note that the above must be called before any logic that might require the session.

4.10   cache

cache a global object also available in the web2py execution environment. It has two attributes:

- cache.ram: the application cache in main memory.

- cache.disk: the application cache on disk.

cache is callable, this allows it to be used as a decorator for caching actions and views.

The following example caches the time.ctime() function in RAM:

```
def cache_in_ram():
    import time
    t = cache.ram('time', lambda: time.ctime(), time_expire=5)
    return dict(time=t, link=A('click me', _href=request.url))
```

The output of lambda: time.ctime() is cached in RAM for 5 seconds. The string 'time' is used as cache key.

The following example caches the time.ctime() function on disk:

```
def cache_on_disk():
    import time
    t = cache.disk('time', lambda: time.ctime(), time_expire=5)
    return dict(time=t, link=A('click me', _href=request.url))
```

The output of lambda: time.ctime() is cached on disk (using the shelve module) for 5 seconds.

Note, the second argument to cache.ram and cache.disk must be a function or callable object. If you want to cache an existing object rather than the output of a function, you can simply return it via a lambda function:

```
cache.ram('myobject', lambda: myobject, time_expire=60*60*24)
```

The next example caches the time.ctime() function to both RAM and disk:

```
def cache_in_ram_and_disk():
    import time
    t = cache.ram('time', lambda: cache.disk('time',
                    lambda: time.ctime(), time_expire=5),
                    time_expire=5)
    return dict(time=t, link=A('click me', _href=request.url))
```

The output of lambda: time.ctime() is cached on disk (using the shelve module) and then in RAM for 5 seconds. web2py looks in RAM first and if not there it looks on disk. If it is not in RAM or on disk, lambda: time.ctime() is executed and the cache is updated. This technique is useful in a multiprocessor environment. The two times do not have to be the same.

The following example is caching in RAM the output of the controller function (but not the view):

```
@cache(request.env.path_info, time_expire=5, cache_model=cache.ram)
def cache_controller_in_ram():
    import time
    t = time.ctime()
    return dict(time=t, link=A('click me', _href=request.url))
```

The dictionary returned by cache_controller_in_ram is cached in RAM for 5 seconds. Note that the result of a database select cannot be cached without first being serialized. A better way is to cache the database select directly using the select method's cache argument.

The following example is caching the output of the controller function on disk (but not the view):

```
@cache(request.env.path_info, time_expire=5, cache_model=cache.disk)
def cache_controller_on_disk():
    import time
    t = time.ctime()
    return dict(time=t, link=A('click to reload',
                    _href=request.url))
```

The dictionary returned by cache_controller_on_disk is cached on disk for 5 seconds. Remember that web2py cannot cache a dictionary that contains un-pickleable objects.

It is also possible to cache the view. The trick is to render the view in the controller function, so that the controller returns a string. This is done by returning response.render(d) where d is the dictionary we intended to pass to the view. The following example caches the output of the controller function in RAM (including the rendered view):

```
1  @cache(request.env.path_info, time_expire=5, cache_model=cache.ram)
2  def cache_controller_and_view():
3      import time
4      t = time.ctime()
5      d = dict(time=t, link=A('click to reload', _href=request.url))
6      return response.render(d)
```

response.render(d) returns the rendered view as a string, which is now cached for 5 seconds. This is the best and fastest way of caching.

Note, time_expire is used to compare the current time with the time the requested object was last saved in the cache. It does not affect future requests. This enables time_expire to be set dynamically when an object is requested rather than being fixed when the object is saved. For example:

```
1  message = cache.ram('message', lambda: 'Hello', time_expire=5)
```

Now, suppose the following call is made 10 seconds after the above call:

```
1  message = cache.ram('message', lambda: 'Goodbye', time_expire=20)
```

Because time_expire is set to 20 seconds in the second call and only 10 seconds has elapsed since the message was first saved, the value "Hello" will be retrieved from the cache, and it will not be updated with "Goodbye". The time_expire value of 5 seconds in the first call has no impact on the second call.

Setting time_expire=0 (or a negative value) forces the cached item to be refreshed (because the elapsed time since the last save will always be > 0), and setting time_expire=None forces retrieval of the cached value, regardless of the time elapsed since it was saved (if time_expire is always None, the cached item will effectively never expire).

You can clear one or more cache variables with

```
cache.ram.clear(regex='...')
```

where `regex` is a regular expression matching all the keys you want removed from the cache. You can also clear a single item with:

```
cache.ram(key, None)
```

where `key` is the key of the cached item.

It is also possible to define other caching mechanisms such as memcache. Memcache is available via `gluon.contrib.memcache` and is discussed in more details in Chapter 14.

> Be careful when caching to remeber that caching is usually at the app-level not at the user level. If you need, for example, to cache user specific content, choose a key that includes the user id.

4.11 URL

The `URL` function is one of the most important functions in web2py. It generates internal URL paths for the actions and the static files.

Here is an example:

```
URL('f')
```

is mapped into

```
/[application]/[controller]/f
```

Notice that the output of the `URL` function depends on the name of the current application, the calling controller, and other parameters. web2py supports URL mapping and reverse URL mapping. URL mapping allows you to redefine the format of external URLs. If you use the `URL` function to generate all the internal URLs, then additions or changes to URL mappings will prevent broken links within the web2py application.

You can pass additional parameters to the `URL` function, i.e., extra terms in the URL path (args) and URL query variables (vars):

```
URL('f', args=['x', 'y'], vars=dict(z='t'))
```

is mapped into

```
/[application]/[controller]/f/x/y?z=t
```

The args attributes are automatically parsed, decoded, and finally stored in request.args by web2py. Similarly, the vars are parsed, decoded, and then stored in request.vars. args and vars provide the basic mechanism by which web2py exchanges information with the client's browser.

If args contains only one element, there is no need to pass it in a list.

You can also use the URL function to generate URLs to actions in other controllers and other applications:

```
URL('a', 'c', 'f', args=['x', 'y'], vars=dict(z='t'))
```

is mapped into

```
/a/c/f/x/y?z=t
```

It is also possible to specify application, controller and function using named arguments:

```
URL(a='a', c='c', f='f')
```

If the application name a is missing the current app is assumed.

```
URL('c', 'f')
```

If the controller name is missing, the current one is assumed.

```
URL('f')
```

Instead of passing the name of a controller function it is also possible to pass the function itself

```
URL(f)
```

For the reasons mentioned above, you should always use the URL function to generate URLs of static files for your applications. Static files are stored in the application's static subfolder (that's where they go when uploaded using the administrative interface). web2py provides a virtual 'static' controller whose job is to retrieve files from the static subfolder, determine their content-type, and stream the file to the client. The following example generates the URL for the static file "image.png":

```
URL('static', 'image.png')
```

is mapped into

```
/[application]/static/image.png
```

If the static file is in a subfolder within the static folder, you can include the subfolder(s) as part of the filename. For example, to generate:

```
/[application]/static/images/icons/arrow.png
```

one should use:

```
URL('static', 'images/icons/arrow.png')
```

You do not need to encode/escape the args and vars arguments; this is done automatically for you.

By default, the extension corresponding to the current request (which can be found in request.extension) is appended to the function, unless request.extension is html, the default. This can be overridden by explicitly including an extension as part of the function name URL(f='name.ext') or with the extension argument:

```
URL(..., extension='css')
```

The current extension can be explicitly suppressed:

```
URL(..., extension=False)
```

4.11.1 Absolute urls

By default, URL generates relative URLs. However, you can also generate absolute URLs by specifying the scheme and host arguments (this is useful, for example, when inserting URLs in email messages):

```
URL(..., scheme='http', host='www.mysite.com')
```

You can automatically include the scheme and host of the current request by simply setting the arguments to True.

```
URL(..., scheme=True, host=True)
```

The URL function also accepts a port argument to specify the server port if necessary.

4.11.2 Digitally signed urls

When generating a URL, you have the option to digitally sign it. This will append a _signature GET variable that can be verified by the server. This can be done in two ways.

You can pass to the URL function the following arguments:

- hmac_key: the key for signing the URL (a string)

- salt: an optional string to salt the data before signing

- hash_vars: an optional list of names of variables from the URL query string (i.e., GET variables) to be included in the signature. It can also be set to True (the default) to include all variables, or False to include none of the variables.

Here is an example of usage:

```
1  KEY = 'mykey'
2
3  def one():
4      return dict(link=URL('two', vars=dict(a=123), hmac_key=KEY))
5
6  def two():
7      if not URL.verify(request, hmac_key=KEY): raise HTTP(403)
8      # do something
9      return locals()
```

This makes the action two accessible only via a digitally signed URL. A digitally signed URL looks like this:

```
1  '/welcome/default/two?a=123&_signature=4981bc70e13866bb60e52a09073560ae822224e9'
```

Note, the digital signature is verified via the URL.verify function. URL.verify also takes the hmac_key, salt, and hash_vars arguments described above, and their values must match the values that were passed to the URL function when the digital signature was created in order to verify the URL.

A second and more sophisticated but more common use of digitally signed URLs is in conjunction with Auth. This is best explained with an example:

```
1  @auth.requires_login()
2  def one():
3      return dict(link=URL('two', vars=dict(a=123), user_signature=True)
4
5  @auth.requires_signature()
6  def two():
7      # do something
8      return locals()
```

In this case the hmac_key is automatically generated and shared within the session. This allows action two to delegate any access control to action one. If the link is generated and signed, it is valid; else it is not. If the link is stolen by another user, the link will be invalid.

It is good practice to always digitally sign Ajax callbacks. If you use the web2py LOAD function, it has a user_signature argument too that can be used for this purpose:

```
{{=LOAD('default', 'two', vars=dict(a=123), ajax=True, user_signature=True)}}
```

4.12 HTTP **and** redirect

web2py defines only one new exception called HTTP. This exception can be raised anywhere in a model, a controller, or a view with the command:

```
raise HTTP(400, "my message")
```

It causes the control flow to jump away from the user's code, back to web2py, and return an HTTP response like:

```
HTTP/1.1 400 BAD REQUEST
Date: Sat, 05 Jul 2008 19:36:22 GMT
Server: Rocket WSGI Server
Content-Type: text/html
Via: 1.1 127.0.0.1:8000
Connection: close
Transfer-Encoding: chunked

my message
```

The first argument of HTTP is the HTTP status code. The second argument is the string that will be returned as the body of the response. Additional optional named arguments are used to build the response HTTP header. For example:

```
raise HTTP(400, 'my message', test='hello')
```

generates:

```
HTTP/1.1 400 BAD REQUEST
Date: Sat, 05 Jul 2008 19:36:22 GMT
Server: Rocket WSGI Server
Content-Type: text/html
Via: 1.1 127.0.0.1:8000
Connection: close
Transfer-Encoding: chunked
test: hello

my message
```

If you do not want to commit the open database transaction, rollback before raising the exception.

Any exception other than HTTP causes web2py to roll back any open database transaction, log the error traceback, issue a ticket to the visitor, and return a standard error page.

This means that only HTTP can be used for cross-page control flow. Other exceptions must be caught by the application, otherwise they are ticketed by web2py.

The command:

```
1  redirect('http://www.web2py.com')
```

is simply a shortcut for:

```
1  raise HTTP(303,
2         'You are being redirected <a href="%s">here</a>' % location,
3         Location='http://www.web2py.com')
```

The named arguments of the HTTP initializer method are translated into HTTP header directives, in this case, the redirection target location. redirect takes an optional second argument, which is the HTTP status code for the redirection (303 by default). Change this number to 307 for a temporary redirect or to 301 for a permanent redirect.

The most common way to use redirect is to redirect to other pages in the same app and (optionally) pass parameters:

```
1  redirect(URL('index', args=(1,2,3), vars=dict(a='b')))
```

In chapter 12 we discuss web2py components. They make Ajax requests to web2py actions. If the called action performs a redirect, you may want the Ajax request to follow the redirect or you may want the entire page performing the Ajax request redirecting. In this latter case you can set:

```
1  redirect(...,type='auto')
```

4.13   Internationalization, and Pluralization with T

The object T is the language translator. It constitutes a single global instance of the web2py class gluon.language.translator. All string constants (and only string constants) should be marked by T, for example:

```
1 a = T("hello world")
```

Strings that are marked with T are identified by web2py as needing language translation and they will be translated when the code (in the model, controller, or view) is executed. If the string to be translated is not a constant but a variable, it will be added to the translation file at runtime (except on GAE) to be translated later.

The T object can also contain interpolated variables and supports multiple equivalent syntaxes:

```
1 a = T("hello %s", ('Tim',))
2 a = T("hello %(name)s", dict(name='Tim'))
3 a = T("hello %s") % ('Tim',)
4 a = T("hello %(name)s") % dict(name='Tim')
```

The latter syntax is recommended because it makes translation easier. The first string is translated according to the requested language file and the name variable is replaced independently of the language.

You can concatenating translated strings and normal strings:

```
1 T("blah ") + name + T(" blah")
```

The following code is also allowed and often preferable:

```
1 T("blah %(name)s blah", dict(name='Tim'))
```

or the alternative syntax

```
1 T("blah %(name)s blah") % dict(name='Tim')
```

In both cases the translation occurs before the variable name is substituted in the "%(name)s" slot. The following alternative should NOT BE USED:

```
1 T("blah %(name)s blah" % dict(name='Tim'))
```

because translation would occur after substitution.

4.13.1   Determining the language

The requested language is determined by the "Accept-Language" field in the HTTP header, but this selection can be overwritten programmatically by requesting a specific file, for example:

```
1 T.force('it-it')
```

which reads the "languages/it-it.py" language file. Language files can be created and edited via the administrative interface.

You can also force a per-string language:

```
T("Hello World", language="it-it")
```

In the case multiple languages are requested, for example "it-it, fr-ft", web2py tries to locate "it-it.py" and "fr-fr.py" translation files. If none of the requested files is present, it tries to fall back on "it.py" and "fr.py". If these files are not present it defaults to "default.py". If this is not present either, it default to no-translation. The more general rule is that web2py tries "xx-xy-yy.py", "xx-xy.py", "xx.py", "default.py" for each of the "xx-xy-yy" accepted languages trying to find the closest match to the visitor's preferences.

You can turn off translations completely via

```
T.force(None)
```

Normally, string translation is evaluated lazily when the view is rendered; hence, the translator force method should not be called inside a view.

It is possible to disable lazy evaluation via

```
T.lazy = False
```

In this way, strings are translated immediately by the T operator based on the currently accepted or forced language.

It is also possible to disable lazy evaluation for individual strings:

```
T("Hello World", lazy=False)
```

A common issue is the following. The original application is in English. Suppose that there is a translation file (for example Italian, "it-it.py") and the HTTP client declares that it accepts both English (en) and Italian (it-it) in that order. The following unwanted situation occurs: web2py does not know the default is written in English (en). Therefore, it prefers translating everything into Italian (it-it) because it only found the Italian translation file. If it had not found the "it-it.py" file, it would have used the default language strings (English).

There are two solutions for this problem: create a translation language for English, which would be redundant and unnecessary, or better, tell web2py which languages should use the default language strings (the strings coded into the application). This can be done with:

```
T.set_current_languages('en', 'en-en')
```

It stores in T.current_languages a list of languages that do not require translation and forces a reload of the language files.

Notice that "it" and "it-it" are different languages from the point of view of web2py. To support both of them, one would need two translation files, always lower case. The same is true for all other languages.

The currently accepted language is stored in

```
T.accepted_language
```

4.13.2   Translating variables

T(...) does not only translate strings but it can also transate values stored in variables:

```
>>> a="test"
>>> print T(a)
```

In this case the word "test" is translated but, if not found and if the filesystem is writable, it will add it to the list of words to be translated in the language file.

Notice that this can result in lots of file IO and you may want to disable it:

```
T.is_writable = False
```

prevents T from dynamically updating language files.

4.13.3   Comments and multiple translations

It is possible that the same string appears in different contexts in the application and needs different translations based on context. In order to do this, one can add comments to the original string. The comments will not be rendered but will be used by web2py to determine the most appropriate translation. For example:

```
T("hello world ## first occurrence")
T("hello world ## second occurrence")
```

The text following the ##, including the double ##, are comments.

4.13.4   Pluralization engine

Since version 2.0, web2py includes a powerful pluralization system (PS). This means that when text marked for translation depends on a numeric variable, it may be translated differently based on the numeric value. For example in English we may render:

```
1 x book(s)
```

with

```
1 a book (x==1)
2 5 books (x==5)
```

English has one singular form and one plural form. The plural form is constructed by adding a "-s" or "-es" or using an exceptional form. web2py provides a way to define pluralization rules for each languages, as well as exceptions to the default rules. In fact web2py already knows pluralization rules for many languages. It knows, for example, that Slovenian has one singular form and 3 plural forms (for x==1, x==3 or x==4 and x>4). These rules are encoded in "gluon/contrib/plural_rules/*.py" files and new files can be created. Explicit pluralizations for words are created by editing pluralization files using the administrative interface.

By default the PS is not activated. It is triggered by the symbol argument of the T function. For example:

```
1 T("You have %s %%{book}", symbols=10)
```

Now the PS is activated for the word "book" and for the number 10. The result in English will be: "You have 10 books". Notice that "book" has been pluralized into "books".

The PS consists of 3 parts:

- placeholders %%{} to mark words in T-messages
- rule to give a decision which word form to use ("rules/plural_rules/*.py")
- dictionary with word plural forms ("app/languages/plural-*.py")

The value of symbols can be a single variable, a list/tuple of variables, or a dictionary.

The placeholder %%{} consists of 3 parts:

```
%%{[<modifier>]<world>[<parameter>]},
```

where:

```
<modifier>::= ! | !! | !!!
<word> ::= any word or phrase in singular in lower case (!)
<parameter> ::= [index] | (key) | (number)
```

For example:

- %%{word} is equivalent to %%{word[0]} (if no modifiers are used).

- %%{word[index]} is used when symbols is a tuple. symbols[index] gives us a number used to make a decision on which word form to choose.

- %%{word(key)} is used to get the numeric parameter from symbols[key]

- %%{word(number)} allows to set a number directly (e.g.: %%{word(%i)})

- %%{?word?number} returns "word" if number==1, returns the number otherwise

- %%{?number} or %%{??number} returns number if number!=1, return nothing otherwise

T("blabla %s %%{word}", symbols=var)

%%{word} by default means %%{word[0]}, where [0] is an item index in symbols tuple.

T("blabla %s %s %%{word[1]}", (var1, var2)) PS is used for "word" and var2 respectively.

You can use several %%{} placeholders with one index:

T("%%{this} %%{is} %s %%{book}", var) or

T("%%{this[0]} %%{is[0]} %s %%{book[0]}", var)

They generate:

```
var  output
----------------
1    this is 1 book
2    these are 2 books
```

```
5   3    these are 2 books
```

Similarly you can pass a dictionary to symbols:

```
1   T("blabla %(var1)s %(wordcnt)s %%{word(wordcnt)}",
2     dict(var1="tututu", wordcnt=20))
```

which produces

```
1   blabla tututu 20 words
```

You can replace "1" with any word you wish by this placeholder %%{?word?number}. For example

T("%%{this} %%{is} %%{?a?%s} %%{book}", var) produces:

```
1   var   output
2   -----------------
3   1     this is a book
4   2     these are 2 books
5   3     these are 3 books
6   ...
```

Inside %%{...} you can also use the following modifiers:

- ! to capitalize the text (equivalent to string.capitalize)

- !! to capitalize every word (equivalent to string.title)

- !!! to capitalize every character (equivalent to string.upper)

Notice you can use \ to escape ! and ?.

4.13.5 Translations, pluralization, and MARKMIN

You can also use the powerful MARKMIN syntax inside translation strings by replacing

```
1   T("hello world")
```

with

```
1   T.M("hello world")
```

Now the string accepts MARKMIN markup as described later in the book. You can also use the pluralization system inside MARKMIN.

4.14   Cookies

web2py uses the Python cookies modules for handling cookies.

Cookies from the browser are in `request.cookies` and cookies sent by the server are in `response.cookies`.

You can set a cookie as follows:

```
response.cookies['mycookie'] = 'somevalue'
response.cookies['mycookie']['expires'] = 24 * 3600
response.cookies['mycookie']['path'] = '/'
```

The second line tells the browser to keep the cookie for 24 hours. The third line tells the browser to send the cookie back to any application (URL path) at the current domain. Note, if you do not specify a path for the cookie, the browser will assume the path of the URL that was requested, so the cookie will only be returned to the server when that same URL path is requested.

The cookie can be made secure with:

```
response.cookies['mycookie']['secure'] = True
```

This tells the browser only to send the cookie back over HTTPS and not over HTTP.

The cookie can be retrieved with:

```
if request.cookies.has_key('mycookie'):
    value = request.cookies['mycookie'].value
```

Unless sessions are disabled, web2py, under the hood, sets the following cookie and uses it to handle sessions:

```
response.cookies[response.session_id_name] = response.session_id
response.cookies[response.session_id_name]['path'] = "/"
```

Note, if a single application includes multiple subdomains, and you want to share the session across those subdomains (e.g., sub1.yourdomain.com, sub2.yourdomain.com, etc.), you must explicitly set the domain of the session cookie as follows:

```
if not request.env.remote_addr in ['127.0.0.1', 'localhost']:
    response.cookies[response.session_id_name]['domain'] = ".yourdomain.com"
```

The above can be useful if, for example, you want to allow the user to remain logged in across subdomains.

4.15 Application init

When you deploy web2py, you will want to set a default application, i.e., the application that starts when there is an empty path in the URL, as in:

```
http://127.0.0.1:8000
```

By default, when confronted with an empty path, web2py looks for an application called **init**. If there is no init application it looks for an application called **welcome**.

The name of the default application can be changed from **init** to another name by setting default_application in routes.py:

```
default_application = "myapp"
```

Note: default_application first appeared in web2py version 1.83.

Here are four ways to set the default application:

- Call your default application "init".
- Set default_application to your application's name in routes.py
- Make a symbolic link from "applications/init" to your application's folder.
- Use URL rewrite as discussed in the next section.

4.16 URL rewrite

web2py has the ability to rewrite the URL path of incoming requests prior to calling the controller action (URL mapping), and conversely, web2py can rewrite the URL path generated by the URL function (reverse URL mapping). One reason to do this is for handling legacy URLs, another is to simplify paths and make them shorter. web2py includes two distinct URL rewrite systems: an easy-to-use *parameter-based* system for most use cases, and a flexible *pattern-based* system for more complex cases. To specify the URL rewrite rules, create a new file in the "web2py" folder called routes.py (the contents of routes.py will depend on which of the two rewrite systems you choose, as described in the next two sections). The two systems cannot be mixed.

> Notice that if you edit routes.py, you must reload it. This can be done in two ways: by restarting the web server or by clicking on the routes reload button in admin. If there is a bug in routes, they will not reload.

4.16.1 Parameter-based system

The parameter-based (parametric) router provides easy access to several "canned" URL-rewrite methods. Its capabilities include:

- Omitting default application, controller and function names from externally-visible URLs (those created by the URL() function)

- Mapping domains (and/or ports) to applications or controllers

- Embedding a language selector in the URL

- Removing a fixed prefix from incoming URLs and adding it back to outgoing URLs

- Mapping root files such as /robots.txt to an applications static directory

The parametric router also provides somewhat more flexible validation of incoming URLs.

Suppose you've written an application called myapp and wish to make it the default, so that the application name is no longer part of the URL as seen by the user. Your default controller is still default, and you want to remove its name from user-visible URLs as well. Here's what you put in routes.py:

```
1 routers = dict(
2   BASE  = dict(default_application='myapp'),
3 )
```

That's it. The parametric router is smart enough to know how to do the right thing with URLs such as:

```
1 http://domain.com/myapp/default/myapp
```

or

```
1 http://domain.com/myapp/myapp/index
```

where normal shortening would be ambiguous. If you have two applications, myapp and myapp2, you'll get the same effect, and additionally myapp2's default controller will be stripped from the URL whenever it's safe (which is mostly all the time).

Here is another case: suppose you want to support URL-based languages, where your URLs look like this:

```
http://myapp/en/some/path
```

or (rewritten)

```
http://en/some/path
```

Here's how:

```
routers = dict(
    BASE  = dict(default_application='myapp'),
    myapp = dict(languages=['en', 'it', 'jp'], default_language='en'),
)
```

Now an incoming URL like this:

```
http:/domain.com/it/some/path
```

will be routed to /myapp/some/path, and request.uri_language will be set to 'it', so you can force the translation. You can also have language-specific static files.

```
http://domain.com/it/static/filename
```

will be mapped to:

```
applications/myapp/static/it/filename
```

if that file exists. If it doesn't, then URLs like:

```
http://domain.com/it/static/base.css
```

will still map to:

```
applications/myapp/static/base.css
```

(because there is no static/it/base.css).

So you can now have language-specific static files, including images, if you need to. Domain mapping is supported as well:

```
routers = dict(
    BASE  = dict(
        domains = {
            'domain1.com' : 'app1',
            'domain2.com' : 'app2',
```

```
6        }
7     ),
8 )
```

does what you'd expect.

```
1 routers = dict(
2   BASE  = dict(
3       domains = {
4           'domain.com:80'  : 'app/insecure',
5           'domain.com:443' : 'app/secure',
6       }
7   ),
8 )
```

maps `http://domain.com` accesses to the controller named `insecure`, while HTTPS accesses go to the `secure` controller. Alternatively, you can map different ports to different apps, in the obvious way.

For further information, please consult the file `router.example.py` provided in the base folder of the standard web2py distribution.

Note: The *parameter-based* system first appeared in web2py version 1.92.1.

4.16.2 Pattern-based system

Although the *parameter-based* system just described should be sufficient for most use cases, the alternative *pattern-based* system provides some additional flexibility for more complex cases. To use the pattern-based system, instead of defining routers as dictionaries of routing parameters, you define two lists (or tuples) of 2-tuples, `routes_in` and `routes_out`. Each tuple contains two elements: the pattern to be replaced and the string that replaces it. For example:

```
1 routes_in = (
2   ('/testme', '/examples/default/index'),
3 )
4 routes_out = (
5   ('/examples/default/index', '/testme'),
6 )
```

With these routes, the URL:

```
1 http://127.0.0.1:8000/testme
```

is mapped into:

```
http://127.0.0.1:8000/examples/default/index
```

To the visitor, all links to the page URL looks like /testme.

The patterns have the same syntax as Python regular expressions. For example:

```
('.*\.php', '/init/default/index'),
```

maps all URLs ending in ".php" to the index page.

The second term of a rule can also be a redirection to another page:

```
('.*\.php', '303->http://example.com/newpage'),
```

Here 303 is the HTTP code for the redirect response.

Sometimes you want to get rid of the application prefix from the URLs because you plan to expose only one application. This can be achieved with:

```
routes_in = (
  ('/(?P<any>.*)', '/init/\g<any>'),
)
routes_out = (
  ('/init/(?P<any>.*)', '/\g<any>'),
)
```

There is also an alternative syntax that can be mixed with the regular expression notation above. It consists of using $name instead of (?P<name>\w+) or \g<name>. For example:

```
routes_in = (
  ('/$c/$f', '/init/$c/$f'),
)

routes_out = (
  ('/init/$c/$f', '/$c/$f'),
)
```

would also eliminate the "/example" application prefix in all URLs.

Using the $name notation, you can automatically map routes_in to routes_out, provided you don't use any regular expressions. For example:

```
routes_in = (
  ('/$c/$f', '/init/$c/$f'),
)

routes_out = [(x, y) for (y, x) in routes_in]
```

If there are multiple routes, the first to match the URL is executed. If no pattern matches, the path is left unchanged.

You can use $anything to match anything (.*) until the end of the line.

Here is a minimal "routes.py" for handling favicon and robots requests:

```
routes_in = (
  ('/favicon.ico', '/examples/static/favicon.ico'),
  ('/robots.txt', '/examples/static/robots.txt'),
)
routes_out = ()
```

Here is a more complex example that exposes a single app "myapp" without unnecessary prefixes but also exposes **admin, appadmin** and static:

```
routes_in = (
  ('/admin/$anything', '/admin/$anything'),
  ('/static/$anything', '/myapp/static/$anything'),
  ('/appadmin/$anything', '/myapp/appadmin/$anything'),
  ('/favicon.ico', '/myapp/static/favicon.ico'),
  ('/robots.txt', '/myapp/static/robots.txt'),
)
routes_out = [(x, y) for (y, x) in routes_in[:-2]]
```

The general syntax for routes is more complex than the simple examples we have seen so far. Here is a more general and representative example:

```
routes_in = (
  ('140\.191\.\d+\.\d+:https?://www.web2py.com:post /(?P<any>.*)\.php',
   '/test/default/index?vars=\g<any>'),
)
```

It maps http or https POST requests (note lower case "post") to host www.web2py.com from a remote IP matching the regular expression

```
'140\.191\.\d+\.\d+'
```

requesting a page matching the regular expression

```
'/(?P<any>.*)\.php'
```

into

```
'/test/default/index?vars=\g<any>'
```

where \g<any> is replaced by the matching regular expression.

The general syntax is

```
'[remote address]:[protocol]://[host]:[method] [path]'
```

If the first section of the pattern (all but [path]) is missing, web2py provides a default:

```
'.*?:https?://[^:/]+:[a-z]+'
```

The entire expression is matched as a regular expression, so "." must be escaped and any matching subexpression can be captured using (?P<...>...) using Python regex syntax. The request method (typically GET or POST) must be lower case. The URL being matched has had any %xx escapes unquoted.

This allows to reroute requests based on the client IP address or domain, based on the type of the request, on the method, and the path. It also allows web2py to map different virtual hosts into different applications. Any matched subexpression can be used to build the target URL and, eventually, passed as a GET variable.

All major web servers, such as Apache and lighttpd, also have the ability to rewrite URLs. In a production environment that may be an option instead of routes.py. Whatever you decide to do we strongly suggest that you do not hardcode internal URLs in your app and use the URL function to generate them. This will make your application more portable in case routes should change.

Application-Specific URL rewrite

When using the pattern-based system, an application can set its own routes in an application-specific routes.py file located in the applications base folder. This is enabled by configuring routes_app in the base routes.py to determine from an incoming URL the name of the application to be selected. When this happens, the application-specific routes.py is used in place of the base routes.py.

The format of routes_app is identical to routes_in, except that the replacement pattern is simply the application name. If applying routes_app to the incoming URL does not result in an application name, or the resulting application-specific routes.py is not found, the base routes.py is used as usual.

Note: routes_app first appeared in web2py version 1.83.

Default application, controller, and function

When using the pattern-based system, the name of the default application, controller, and function can be changed from **init**, **default**, and **index** respectively to another name by setting the appropriate value in routes.py:

```
1 default_application = "myapp"
2 default_controller = "admin"
3 default_function = "start"
```

Note: These items first appeared in web2py version 1.83.

4.16.3   Routes on error

You can also use routes.py to re-route requests to special actions in case there is an error on the server. You can specify this mapping globally, for each app, for each error code, or for each app and error code. Here is an example:

```
1 routes_onerror = [
2   ('init/400', '/init/default/login'),
3   ('init/*', '/init/static/fail.html'),
4   ('*/404', '/init/static/cantfind.html'),
5   ('*/*', '/init/error/index')
6 ]
```

For each tuple, the first string is matched against "[app name]/[error code]". If a match is found, the failed request is re-routed to the URL in the second string of the matching tuple. If the error handling URL is a not a static file, the following GET variables will be passed to the error action:

- code: the HTTP status code (e.g., 404, 500)

- ticket: in the form of "[app name]/[ticket number]" (or "None" if no ticket)

- requested_uri: equivalent to request.env.request_uri

- request_url: equivalent to request.url

These variables will be accessible to the error handling action via request.vars and can be used in generating the error response. In particular, it is a good idea for the error action to return the original HTTP error code instead of the default 200 (OK) status code. This can be done by setting response.status = request.vars.code. It is also possible to have the error action send (or queue) an email to an administrator, including a link to the ticket in admin.

Unmatched errors display a default error page. This default error page can also be customized here (see router.example.py and routes.example.py in the root web2py folder):

```
1  error_message = '<html><body><h1>%s</h1></body></html>'
2  error_message_ticket = '''<html><body><h1>Internal error</h1>
3      Ticket issued: <a href="/admin/default/ticket/%(ticket)s"
4      target="_blank">%(ticket)s</a></body></html>'''
```

The first variable contains the error message when an invalid application or function is requested. The second variable contains the error message when a ticket is issued.

routes_onerror work with both routing mechanisms.

In "routes.py" you can also specify an action in charge of error handling:

```
1  error_handler = dict(application='error',
2                       controller='default',
3                       function='index')
```

If the error_handler is specified the action is called without user redirection and the handler action will be in charge of dealing with the error. In the event that the error-handling page itself returns an error, web2py will fall back to its old static responses.

4.16.4   Static asset management

Since version 2.1.0, web2py has the ability to manage static assets.

When an application is in development, static file can change often, therefore web2py sends static files with no cache headers. This has the side-effect of "forcing" the browser to request static files at every request. This results in low performance when loading the page.

In a "production" site, you may want to serve static files with cache headers to prevent un-necessary downloads since static files do not change.

cache headers allow the browser to fetch each file only once, thus saving bandwidth and reducing loading time.

Yet there is a problem: What should the cache headers declare? When should the files expire? When the files are first served, the server cannot forecast when they will be changed.

A manual approach consists of creating subfolders for different versions of static files. For example an early version of "layout.css" can be made available at the URL "/myapp/static/css/1.2.3/layout.css". When you change the file, you create a new subfolder and you link it as "/myapp/static/css/1.2.4/layout.css".

This procedure works but it is pedantic since every time you update the css file, you must remember to move it to another folder, change the URL of the file in your layout.html and deploy.

Static asset management solves the problem by allowing the developer to declare a version for a group of static files and they will be requested again only when the version number changes. The version number of made part of the file url as in the previous example. The difference from the previous approach is that the version number only appears in the URL, not in the file system.

If you want to serve "/myapp/static/layout.css" with the cache headers, you just need to include the file with a modified URL that includes a version number:

```
/myapp/static/_1.2.3/layout.css
```

(notice the URL defines a version number, it does not appear anywhere else).

Notice that the URL starts with "/myapp/static/", followed by a version number composed by an underscore and 3 integers separated by a period (as described in SemVer), then followed by the filename. Also notice that you do not have to create a "_1.2.3/" folder.

Every time the static file is requested with a version in the url, it will be served with "far in the future" cache headers, specifically:

```
Cache-Control : max-age=315360000
Expires: Thu, 31 Dec 2037 23:59:59 GMT
```

This means that the browser will fetch those files only once, and they will be saved "forever" in the browser's cache.

Every time the "_1.2.3/filename" is requested, web2py will remove the version part from the path and serve your file with far in the future headers so they will be cached forever. If you changed the version number in the URL, this tricks the browser into thinking it is requesting a different file, and the file is fetched again.

You can use "_1.2.3", "_0.0.0", "_999.888.888", as long as the version starts with underscore followed by three numbers separated by period.

When in development, you can use response.files.append(...) to link the static URLs of static files. In this case you can include the "_1.2.3/" part manually, or you take advantage of a new parameter of the response object: response.static_version. Just include the files the way you used to, for example

```
{{response.files.append(URL('static','layout.css'))}}
```

and in models set

```
response.static_version = '1.2.3'
```

This will rewrite automatically every "/myapp/static/layout.css" url as "/myapp/static/_1.2.3/layout.css", for every file included in response.files.

Often in production you let the webserver (apache, nginx, etc.) serve the static files. You need to adjust your configuration in such a way that it will "skip" the "_1.2.3/" part.

For example, in Apache, change this:

```
AliasMatch ^/([^/]+)/static/(.*) \
    /home/www-data/web2py/applications/$1/static/$2
```

into this:

```
AliasMatch ^/([^/]+)/static/(?:/_[\d]+\.[\d]+\.[\d]+)?(.*) \
    /home/www-data/web2py/applications/$1/static/$2
```

Similarly, in Nginx change this:

```
location ~* /(\w+)/static/ {
    root /home/www-data/web2py/applications/;
    expires max;
}
```

into this:

```
location ~* /(\w+)/static(?:/_[\d]+\.[\d]+\.[\d]+)?/(.*)$ {
    alias /home/www-data/web2py/applications/$1/static/$2;
    expires max;
}
```

4.17   Running tasks in the background

In web2py, every HTTP request is served in its own thread. Threads are recycled for efficiency and managed by the web server. For security, the web server sets a time-out on each request. This means that actions should not run tasks that take too long, should not create new threads, and should not fork processes (it is possible but not recommended).

The proper way to run time-consuming tasks is doing it in the background. There is not a single way of doing it, but here we describe three mechanisms that are built into web2py: **cron, homemade task queues**, and **scheduler.**

By **cron** we refer to a web2py functionality not to the Unix Cron mechanism. The web2py cron works on windows too. web2py cron is the way to go if you need tasks in the background at scheduled times and these tasks take a relatively short time compared to the time interval between two calls. Each task runs in its own process, and multiple tasks can run concurrently, but you have no control over how many tasks run. If accidentally one task overlaps with itself, it can cause a database lock and a spike in memory usage. web2py scheduler takes a different approach. The number of running processes is fixed, and they can run on different machines. Each process is called a worker. Each worker picks a task when available and executes it as soon as possible after the time when it is scheduled to run, but not necessarily at that exact time. There cannot be more processes running than the number of scheduled tasks and therefore no memory spikes. Scheduler tasks can be defined in models and are stored in the database. The web2py scheduler does not implement a distributed queue since it assumes that the time to distribute tasks is negligible compared with the time to run the tasks. Workers pick up the task from the database.

Homemade tasks queues can be a simpler alternative to the web2py scheduler in some cases.

4.17.1   Cron

The web2py cron provides the ability for applications to execute tasks at preset times, in a platform-independent manner.

For each application, cron functionality is defined by a crontab file:

```
app/cron/crontab
```

It follows the syntax defined in ref. [56] (with some extensions that are specific to web2py).

> Before web2py 2.1.1, cron was enabled by default and could be disabled with the -N command line option, Since 2.1.1, cron is disabled by default and can be enabled by the -Y option. This change was motivated by the desire to push users toward using the new scheduler (which is superior to the cron mechanism) and also because cron may impact on performance.

This means that every application can have a separate cron configuration and that cron config can be changed from within web2py without affecting the host OS itself.

Here is an example:

```
1 0-59/1  *  *  *  *  root python /path/to/python/script.py
2 30      3  *  *  *  root *applications/admin/cron/db_vacuum.py
3 */30    *  *  *  *  root **applications/admin/cron/something.py
4 @reboot root    *mycontroller/myfunction
5 @hourly root    *applications/admin/cron/expire_sessions.py
```

The last two lines in this example use extensions to regular cron syntax to provide additional web2py functionality.

> The file "applications/admin/cron/expire_sessions.py" actually exists and ships with the **admin** app. It checks for expired sessions and deletes them. "applications/admin/cron/crontab" runs this task hourly.

If the task/script is prefixed with an asterisk (*) and ends with .py, it will be executed in the web2py environment. This means you will have all the controllers and models at your disposal. If you use two asterisks (**), the MODELs will not be executed. This is the recommended way of calling, as it has less overhead and avoids potential locking problems.

Notice that scripts/functions executed in the web2py environment require a manual db.commit() at the end of the function or the transaction will be reverted. web2py does not generate tickets or meaningful tracebacks in shell mode, which is how cron is run, so make sure that your web2py code runs without errors before you set it up as a cron task as you will likely not be able to see those errors when run from cron. Moreover, be careful how you use models: while the execution happens in a separate process, database locks have to be taken into account in order to avoid pages waiting for cron tasks that may be blocking the database. Use the ** syntax if you don't need to use the database in your cron task.

You can also call a controller function, in which case there is no need to specify a path. The controller and function will be that of the invoking application. Take special care about the caveats listed above. Example:

```
*/30  *  *  *  *  root *mycontroller/myfunction
```

If you specify @reboot in the first field in the crontab file, the given task will be executed only once, at web2py startup. You can use this feature if you want to pre-cache, check, or initialize data for an application on web2py startup. Note that cron tasks are executed in parallel with the application — if the application is not ready to serve requests until the cron task is finished, you should implement checks to reflect this. Example:

```
@reboot  *  *  *  *  root *mycontroller/myfunction
```

Depending on how you are invoking web2py, there are four modes of operation for web2py cron.

- *soft cron*: available under all execution modes
- *hard cron*: available if using the built-in web server (either directly or via Apache mod_proxy)
- *external cron*: available if you have access to the system's own cron service
- No cron

The default is hard cron if you are using the built-in web server; in all other cases, the default is soft cron. Soft cron is the default method if you are using CGI, FASTCGI or WSGI (but note that soft cron is not enabled by default in the standard `wsgihandler.py` file provided with web2py).

Your tasks will be executed on the first call (page load) to web2py after the time specified in crontab; but only after processing the page, so no delay will be observed by the user. Obviously, there is some uncertainty regarding precisely when the task will be executed, depending on the traffic the site receives. Also, the cron task may get interrupted if the web server has a page load timeout set. If these limitations are not acceptable, see *external cron*. Soft cron is a reasonable last resort, but if your web server allows other cron methods, they should be preferred over soft cron.

Hard cron is the default if you are using the built-in web server (either directly or via Apache mod_proxy). Hard cron is executed in a parallel thread, so unlike soft cron, there are no limitations with regard to run time or execution time precision.

External cron is not default in any scenario, but requires you to have access to the system cron facilities. It runs in a parallel process, so none of the limitations of soft cron apply. This is the recommended way of using cron under WSGI or FASTCGI.

Example of line to add to the system crontab, (usually /etc/crontab):

```
0-59/1 * * * * web2py cd /var/www/web2py/ && python web2py.py -J -C -D 1 >> /tmp/
    cron.output 2>&1
```

With external `cron`, make sure to add either `-J` (or `-cronjob`, which is the same) as indicated above so that web2py knows that task is executed by cron. Web2py sets this internally with soft and hard `cron`.

4.17.2   Homemade task queues

While cron is useful to run tasks at regular time intervals, it is not always the best solution to run a background task. For this purpose web2py provides the ability to run any python script as if it were inside a controller:

```
python web2py.py -S app -M -R applications/app/private/myscript.py -A a b c
```

where `-S app` tells web2py to run "myscript.py" as "app", `-M` tells web2py to execute models, and `-A a b c` passes optional command line arguments `sys.args=['a','b','c']` to "myscript.py".

This type of background process should not be executed via cron (except perhaps for cron @reboot) because you need to be sure that no more than one instance is running at the same time. With cron it is possible that a process starts at cron iteration 1 and is not completed by cron iteration 2, so cron starts it again, and again, and again - thus jamming the mail server.

In chapter 8, we will provide an example of how to use the above method to send emails.

4.17.3   Scheduler (experimental)

The web2py scheduler works very much like the task queue described in the previous sub-section with some differences:

- It provides a standard mechanism for creating, scheduling, and monitoring tasks.

- There is not a single background process but a set of workers processes.

- The job of worker nodes can be monitored because their state, as well as the state of the tasks, is stored in the database.

- It works without web2py but that is not documented here.

The scheduler does not use cron, although one can use cron @reboot to start the worker nodes.

More information about deploying the scheduler under Linux and Windows is in the Deployment recipes chapter.

In the scheduler, a task is simply a function defined in a model (or in a module and imported by a model). For example:

```
def task_add(a,b):
    return a+b
```

Tasks will always be called in the same environment seen by controllers and therefore they see all the global variables defined in models, including database connections (db). Tasks differ from a controller action because they are not associated with an HTTP request and therefore there is no request.env.

> Remember to call db.commit() at the end of every task if it involves inserts/updates to the database. web2py commits by default at the end of a successful action but the scheduler tasks are not actions.

To enable the scheduler you must instantiate the Scheduler class in a model. The recommended way to enable the scheduler to your app is to create a model file named scheduler.py and define your function there. After the functions, you can put the following code into the model:

```
from gluon.scheduler import Scheduler
scheduler = Scheduler(db)
```

If your tasks are defined in a module (as opposed to a model) you may have to restart the workers.

The task is scheduled with

```
scheduler.queue_task(task_add,pvars=dict(a=1,b=2))
```

Parameters

The first argument of the Scheduler class must be the database to be used by the scheduler to communicate with the workers. This can be the db of the app or another dedicated db, perhaps one shared by multiple apps. If you use SQLite it's recommended to use a separate db from the one used by your app in order to keep the app responsive. Once the tasks are defined and the Scheduler is instantiated, all that is needed to do is to start the workers. You can do that in several ways:

```
python web2py.py -K myapp
```

starts a worker for the app myapp. If you want start multiple workers for the same app, you can do so just passing myapp,myapp. You can pass also the group_names (overriding the one set in your model) with

```
python web2py.py -K myapp:group1:group2,myotherapp:group1
```

If you have a model called scheduler.py you can start/stop the workers from web2py's default window (the one you use to set the ip address and the port).

One last nice addition: if you use the embedded webserver, you can start the webserver and the scheduler with just one line of code (this assumes you don't want the web2py window popping up, else you can use the "Schedulers" menu instead)

```
1  python web2py.py -a yourpass -K myapp -X
```

You can pass the usual parameters (-i, -p, here -a prevents the window from showing up), pass whatever app in the -K parameter and append a -X. The scheduler will run alongside the webserver!

Scheduler's complete signature is:

```
1  Scheduler(
2      db,
3      tasks=None,
4      migrate=True,
5      worker_name=None,
6      group_names=None,
7      heartbeat=HEARTBEAT,
8      max_empty_runs=0,
9      discard_results=False,
10     utc_time=False
11 )
```

Let's see them in order:

- db is the database DAL instance where you want the scheduler tables be placed.

- tasks is a dictionary that maps task names into functions. If you do not pass this parameter, function will be searched in the app environment.

- worker_name is None by default. As soon as the worker is started, a worker name is generated as hostname-uuid. If you want to specify that, be sure that it's unique.

- group_names is by default set to [main]. All tasks have a group_name parameter, set to **main** by default. Workers can only pick up tasks of their assigned group.

  NB: This is useful if you have different workers instances (e.g. on different machines) and you want to assign tasks to a specific worker.

  NB2: It's possible to assign a worker more groups, and they can be also all the same, as

['mygroup','mygroup']. Tasks will be distributed taking into consideration that a worker with group_names ['mygroup','mygroup'] is able to process the double of the tasks a worker with group_names ['mygroup'] is.

- `heartbeat` is by default set to 3 seconds. This parameter is the one controlling how often a scheduler will check its status on the `scheduler_worker` table and see if there are any **ASSIGNED** tasks to itself to process.

- `max_empty_runs` is 0 by default, that means that the worker will continue to process tasks as soon as they are **ASSIGNED**. If you set this to a value of, let's say, 10, a worker will die automatically if it's **ACTIVE** and no tasks are **ASSIGNED** to it for 10 loops. A loop is when a worker searches for tasks, every 3 seconds (or the set `heartbeat`)

- `discard_results` is False by default. If set to True, no scheduler_run records will be created.

  NB: scheduler_run records will be created as before for **FAILED**, **TIMEOUT** and **STOPPED** tasks's statuses.

- `utc_time` is False by default. If you need to coordinate with workers living in different timezones, or don't have problems with solar/DST times, supplying datetimes from different countries, etc, you can set this to True. The scheduler will honor the UTC time and work leaving the local time aside. Caveat: you need to schedule tasks with UTC times (for start_time, stop_time, and so on.)

Now we have the infrastructure in place: defined the tasks, told the scheduler about them, started the worker(s). What remains is to actually schedule the tasks

Tasks

Tasks can be scheduled programmatically or via appadmin. In fact, a task is scheduled simply by adding an entry in the table "scheduler_task", which you can access via appadmin:

```
http://127.0.0.1:8000/myapp/appadmin/insert/db/scheduler_task
```

The meaning of the fields in this table is obvious. The "args" and "vars"" fields are the values to be passed to the task in JSON format. In the case of the "task_add" above, an example of "args" and "vars" could be:

```
args = [3, 4]
vars = {}
```

or

```
1 args = []
2 vars = {'a':3, 'b':4}
```

The scheduler_task table is the one where tasks are organized.

All tasks follow a lifecycle

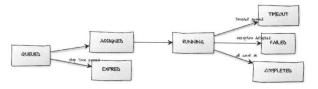

By default, when you send a task to the scheduler, it is in the **QUEUED** status. If you need it to be executed later, use the start_time parameter (default = now). If for some reason you need to be sure that the task does not get executed after a certain point in time (maybe a request to a web service that shuts down at 1AM, a mail that needs to be sent not after the working hours, etc...) you can set a stop_time (default = None) for it. If your task is NOT picked up by a worker before stop_time, it will be set as **EXPIRED**. Tasks with no stop_time set or picked up **BEFORE** stop_time are **ASSIGNED** to a worker. When a workers picks up a task, its status is set to **RUNNING**.

RUNNING tasks may end up:

- **TIMEOUT** when more than n seconds passed with timeout parameter (default = 60 seconds).

- **FAILED** when an exception is detected,

- **COMPLETED** when they successfully complete.

Values for start_time and stop_time should be datetime objects. To schedule "mytask" to run at 30 seconds from the current time, for example, you would do the following:

```
1 from datetime import timedelta as timed
2 scheduler.queue_task('mytask',
3     start_time=request.now + timed(seconds=30))
```

Additionally, you can control how many times a task should be repeated (i.e. you need to aggregate some data at specified intervals). To do so, set the repeats parameter (default = 1 time only, 0 = unlimited). You can influence how many seconds should pass between executions with the period parameter (default = 60 seconds).

> The time period is not calculated between the END of the first round and the START of the next, but from the START time of the first round to the START time of the next cycle)

You can also set how many times the function can raise an exception (i.e. requesting data from a slow web service) and be queued again instead of stopping in **FAILED** status using the parameter retry_failed (default = 0, -1 = unlimited).

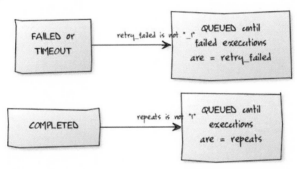

Summary: you have

- period and repeats to get an automatically rescheduled function

- timeout to be sure that a function doesn't exceed a certain amount of time

- retry_failed to control how many times the task can "fail"

- start_time and stop_time to schedule a function in a restricted timeframe

queue_task **and** task_status

The method:

```
scheduler.queue_task(function, pargs=[], pvars={}, **kwargs)
```

allows you to queue tasks to be executed by workers. It takes the following parameters:

- function (required): It can be a task name or a reference to an actual function.

- pargs: are the arguments to be passed to the task, stored as a Python list.

- pvars : are the named arguments to be passed to the task, stored as a Python dictionary.

- kwargs : all other scheduler_task columns can be passed as keywords arguments (for example repeats, period, timeout).

For example:

```
scheduler.queue_task('demo1', [1,2])
```

does the exact same thing as

```
scheduler.queue_task('demo1', pvars={'a':1, 'b':2})
```

as

```
st.validate_and_insert(function_name='demo1', args=json.dumps([1,2]))
```

and as:

```
st.validate_and_insert(function_name='demo1', vars=json.dumps({'a':1,'b':2}))
```

Here is a more complex complete example:

```
def task_add(a,b):
    return a+b

secheduler = Scheduler(db, tasks=dict(demo1=task_add))

scheduler.queue_task('demo1', pvars=dict(a=1,b=2),
                repeats = 0, period = 180)
```

Since version 2.4.1 if you pass an additional parameter immediate=True it will force the main worker to reassign tasks. Until 2.4.1, the worker checks for new tasks every 5 cycles (so, 5*heartbeats seconds). If you had an app that needed to check frequently for new tasks, to get a *snappy* behaviour you were forced to lower the heartbeat parameter, putting the db under pressure for no reason. With immediate=True you can force the check for new tasks: it will happen at most as heartbeat seconds are passed

A call to scheduler.queue_task returns the task id and uuid of the task you queued (can be the one you passed or the auto-generated one), and possible errors:

```
<Row {'errors': {}, 'id': 1, 'uuid': '08e6433a-cf07-4cea-a4cb-01f16ae5f414'}>
```

If there are errors (usually syntax error os input validation errors), you get the result of the validation, and id and uuid will be None

```
<Row {'errors': {'period': 'enter an integer greater than or equal to 0'}, 'id':
    None, 'uuid': None}>
```

Results and output

The table "scheduler_run" stores the status of all running tasks. Each record references a task that has been picked up by a worker. One task can have multiple runs. For example, a task scheduled to repeat 10 times an hour will probably have 10 runs (unless one fails or they take longer than 1 hour). Beware that if the task has no return values, it is removed from the scheduler_run table as soon as it is finished.

Possible run statuses are:

```
RUNNING, COMPLETED, FAILED, TIMEOUT
```

If the run is completed, no exceptions are thrown, and there is no task timeout, the run is marked as COMPLETED and the task is marked as QUEUED or COMPLETED depending on whether it is supposed to run again at a later time. The output of the task is serialized in JSON and stored in the run record.

When a RUNNING task throws an exception, the run is mark as FAILED and the task is marked as FAILED. The traceback is stored in the run record.

Similarly, when a run exceeds the timeout, it is stopped and marked as TIMEOUT, and the task is marked as TIMEOUT.

In any case, the stdout is captured and also logged into the run record.

Using appadmin, one can check all RUNNING tasks, the output of COMPLETED tasks, the error of FAILED tasks, etc.

The scheduler also creates one more table called "scheduler_worker", which stores the workers' heartbeat and their status. Possible worker statuses are:

Managing processes

Worker fine management is hard. This module tries not to leave behind any platform (Mac, Win, Linux).

When you start a worker, you may later want to:

- kill it "no matter what it's doing"
- kill it only if it is not processing tasks

- put it to sleep

Maybe you have yet some tasks queued, and you want to save some resources. You know you want them processed every hour, so, you'll want to:

- process all queued tasks and die automatically

All of these things are possible managing `Scheduler` parameters or the `scheduler_worker` table. To be more precise, for started workers you can change the `status` value of any worker to influence its behavior. As for tasks, workers can be in one of the following statuses: ACTIVE, DISABLED, TERMINATE or KILLED.

ACTIVE and **DISABLED** are "persistent", while **TERMINATE** or **KILL**, as statuses name suggest, are more "commands" than real statuses. Hitting ctrl+c is equal to set a worker to **KILL**

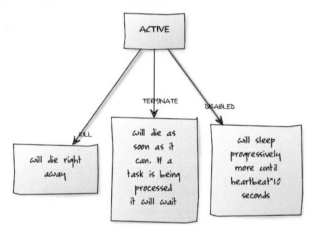

There are a few commodity functions since version 2.4.1 (self-explanatory)

```
1  scheduler.disable()
2  scheduler.resume()
3  scheduler.terminate()
4  scheduler.kill()
```

each function take an optional parameter, that can be a string or a list, to manage workers based on their `group_names`. It defaults to the `group_names` defined in the scheduler istantiation.

An example is better than a thousand words: scheduler.terminate('high_prio') will TERMINATE all the workers that are processing the high_prio tasks, while scheduler.terminate(['high_prio', 'low_prio']) will terminate all high_prio and low_prio workers.

> Watch out: if you have a worker processing high_prio and low_prio, scheduler.terminate('high_prio') will terminate the worker alltogether, even if you didn't want to terminate low_prio too.

Everything that one can do via appadmin one can do programmatically by inserting and updating records in these tables.

Anyway, one should not update records relative to RUNNING tasks as this may create an un-expected behavior. The best practice is to queue tasks using the "queue_task" method.

For example:

```
scheduler.queue_task(
    function_name='task_add',
    pargs=[],
    pvars={'a':3,'b':4},
    repeats = 10, # run 10 times
    period = 3600, # every 1h
    timeout = 120, # should take less than 120 seconds
    )
```

Notice that fields "times_run", "last_run_time" and "assigned_worker_name" are not provided at schedule time but are filled automatically by the workers.

You can also retrieve the output of completed tasks:

```
completed_runs = db(db.scheduler_run.run_status='COMPLETED').select()
```

> The scheduler is considered experimental because it needs more extensive testing and because the table structure may change as more features are added.

Reporting percentages

A special "word" encountered in the print statements of your functions clear all the previous output. That word is !clear!. This, coupled with the sync_output parameter, allows to report percentages a breeze.

Here is an example:

```
1  def reporting_percentages():
2      time.sleep(5)
3      print '50%'
4      time.sleep(5)
5      print '!clear!100%'
6      return 1
```

The function reporting_percentages sleeps for 5 seconds, outputs 50%. Then, it sleeps other 5 seconds and outputs 100%. Note that the output in the scheduler_run table is synced every 2 seconds and that the second print statement that contains !clear!100% gets the 50% output cleared and replaced by 100% only.

```
1  scheduler.queue_task(reporting_percentages,
2                       sync_output=2)
```

4.18   Third party modules

web2py is written in Python, so it can import and use any Python module, including third party modules. It just needs to be able to find them. As with any Python application, modules can be installed in the official Python "site-packages" directory, and they can then be imported from anywhere inside your code.

Modules in the "site-packages" directory are, as the name suggests, site-level packages. Applications requiring site-packages are not portable unless these modules are installed separately. The advantage of having modules in "site-packages" is that multiple applications can share them. Let's consider, for example, the plotting package called "matplotlib". You can install it from the shell using the PEAK easy_install command [57] (or its modern replacement pip [58]):

```
1  easy_install py-matplotlib
```

and then you can import it into any model/controller/view with:

```
1  import matplotlib
```

The web2py source distribution, and the Windows binary distribution has a site-packages in the top-level folder. The Mac binary distribution has a site-packages folder in the folder:

```
web2py.app/Contents/Resources/site-packages
```

The problem with using site-packages is that it becomes difficult to use different versions of a single module at the same time, for example there could be two applications but each one uses a different version of the same file. In this example, sys.path cannot be altered because it would affect both applications.

For this kind of situation, web2py provides another way to import modules in such a way that the global sys.path is not altered: by placing them in the "modules" folder of an application. One side benefit is that the module will be automatically copied and distributed with the application.

> Once a module "mymodule.py" is placed into an app "modules/" folder, it can be imported from anywhere inside a web2py application (without need to alter sys.path with):

```
import mymodule
```

4.19   Execution environment

> While everything discussed here works fine, we recommend instead building your application using components, as described in chapter 12.

web2py model and controller files are not Python modules in that they cannot be imported using the Python import statement. The reason for this is that models and controllers are designed to be executed in a prepared environment that has been pre-populated with web2py global objects (request, response, session, cache and T) and helper functions. This is necessary because Python is a statically (lexically) scoped language, whereas the web2py environment is created dynamically. web2py provides the exec_environment function to allow you to access models and controllers directly. exec_environment creates a web2py execution environment, loads the file into it and then returns a Storage object containing the environment. The Storage object also serves as a namespace mechanism. Any Python file designed to be executed in the execution environment can be loaded using exec_environment. Uses for exec_environment include:

- Accessing data (models) from other applications.

- Accessing global objects from other models or controllers.

- Executing controller functions from other controllers.

- Loading site-wide helper libraries.

This example reads rows from the user table in the cas application:

```
1 from gluon.shell import exec_environment
2 cas = exec_environment('applications/cas/models/db.py')
3 rows = cas.db().select(cas.db.user.ALL)
```

Another example: suppose you have a controller "other.py" that contains:

```
1 def some_action():
2     return dict(remote_addr=request.env.remote_addr)
```

Here is how you can call this action from another controller (or from the web2py shell):

```
1 from gluon.shell import exec_environment
2 other = exec_environment('applications/app/controllers/other.py', request=request)
3 result = other.some_action()
```

In line 2, request=request is optional. It has the effect of passing the current request to the environment of "other". Without this argument, the environment would contain a new and empty (apart from request.folder) request object. It is also possible to pass a response and a session object to exec_environment. Be careful when passing request, response and session objects — modification by the called action or coding dependencies in the called action could lead to unexpected side effects.

The function call in line 3 does not execute the view; it simply returns the dictionary unless response.render is called explicitly by "some_action".

One final caution: don't use exec_environment inappropriately. If you want the results of actions in another application, you probably should implement an XML-RPC API (implementing an XML-RPC API with web2py is almost trivial). Don't use exec_environment as a redirection mechanism; use the redirect helper.

4.20 Cooperation

There are many ways applications can cooperate:

- Applications can connect to the same database and thus share tables. It is not necessary that all tables in the database are defined by all applications, but they must be defined by those that use them. All applications that use the same table, but one, must define the table with migrate=False.

- Applications can embed components from other applications using the LOAD helper (described in Chapter 12).

- Applications can share sessions.

- Applications can call each other's actions remotely via XML-RPC.

- Applications can access each other's files via the filesystem (assuming they share the same filesystem).

- Applications can call each other's actions locally using exec_environment as discussed above.

- Applications can import each other's modules using the syntax:

```
1 from applications.appname.modules import mymodule
```

- Applications can import any module in the PYTHONPATH search path, sys.path.

One app can load the session of another app using the command:

```
1 session.connect(request, response, masterapp='appname', db=db)
```

Here "appname" is the name of the master application, the one that sets the initial session_id in the cookie. db is a database connection to the database that contains the session table (web2py_session). All apps that share sessions must use the same database for session storage.

One application can load a module from another app using

```
1 import applications.otherapp.modules.othermodule
```

4.21 Logging

Python provides logging APIs. Web2py provides a mechanism to configure it so that apps can use it.

In your application, you can create a logger, for example in a model:

```
import logging
logger = logging.getLogger("web2py.app.myapp")
logger.setLevel(logging.DEBUG)
```

and you can use it to log messages of various importance

```
logger.debug("Just checking that %s" % details)
logger.info("You ought to know that %s" % details)
logger.warn("Mind that %s" % details)
logger.error("Oops, something bad happened %s" % details)
```

logging is a standard python module described here:

```
http://docs.python.org/library/logging.html
```

The string "web2py.app.myapp" defines an app-level logger.

For this to work properly, you need a configuration file for the logger. One is provided by web2py in the root web2py folder "logging.example.conf". You need to rename the file "logging.conf" and customize it as necessary.

This file is self documenting, so you should open it and read it.

To create a configurable logger for application "myapp", you must add myapp to the [loggers] keys list:

```
[loggers]
keys=root,rocket,markdown,web2py,rewrite,app,welcome,myapp
```

and you must add a [logger_myapp] section, using [logger_welcome] as a starting point.

```
[logger_myapp]
level=WARNING
qualname=web2py.app.myapp
handlers=consoleHandler
propagate=0
```

The "handlers" directive specifies the type of logging and here it is logging "myapp" to the console.

4.22   WSGI

web2py and WSGI have a love-hate relationship. Our perspective is that WSGI was developed as a protocol to connect web servers to web applications in a portable way, and we use it for that purpose. web2py at its core is a WSGI application: `gluon.main.wsgibase`. Some developers have pushed WSGI to its limits as a protocol for middleware communications and develop web applications as an onion with many layers (each layer being a WSGI middleware developed independently of the entire framework). web2py does not adopt this structure internally. This is because we feel the core functionality of a frameworks (handling cookies, session, errors, transactions, dispatching) can be better optimized for speed and security if they are handled by a single comprehensive layer.

Yet web2py allows you to use third party WSGI applications and middleware in three ways (and their combinations):

- You can edit the file "wsgihandler.py" and include any third party WSGI middleware.

- You can connect third party WSGI middleware to any specific action in your apps.

- You can call a third party WSGI app from your actions.

The only limitation is that you cannot use third party middleware to replace core web2py functions.

4.22.1   External middleware

Consider the file "wsgibase.py":

```
1  #...
2  LOGGING = False
3  #...
4  if LOGGING:
5      application = gluon.main.appfactory(wsgiapp=gluon.main.wsgibase,
6                                          logfilename='httpserver.log',
7                                          profilerfilename=None)
8  else:
```

```
9    application = gluon.main.wsgibase
```

When LOGGING is set to True, gluon.main.wsgibase is wrapped by the middleware function gluon.main.appfactory. It provides logging to the "httpserver.log" file. In a similar fashion you can add any third party middleware. We refer to the official WSGI documentation for more details.

4.22.2 Internal middleware

Given any action in your controllers (for example index) and any third party middleware application (for example MyMiddleware, which converts output to upper case), you can use a web2py decorator to apply the middleware to that action. Here is an example:

```
1    class MyMiddleware:
2        """converts output to upper case"""
3        def __init__(self,app):
4            self.app = app
5        def __call__(self, environ, start_response):
6            items = self.app(environ, start_response)
7            return [item.upper() for item in items]
8
9    @request.wsgi.middleware(MyMiddleware)
10   def index():
11       return 'hello world'
```

We cannot promise that all third party middleware will work with this mechanism.

4.22.3 Calling *WSGI* applications

It is easy to call WSGI app from a web2py action. Here is an example:

```
1    def test_wsgi_app(environ, start_response):
2        """this is a test WSGI app"""
3        status = '200 OK'
4        response_headers = [('Content-type','text/plain'),
5                            ('Content-Length','13')]
6        start_response(status, response_headers)
7        return ['hello world!\n']
8
9    def index():
10       """a test action that calls the previous app and escapes output"""
```

```
11    items = test_wsgi_app(request.wsgi.environ,
12                          request.wsgi.start_response)
13    for item in items:
14        response.write(item,escape=False)
15    return response.body.getvalue()
```

In this case, the index action calls test_wsgi_app and escapes the returned value before returning it. Notice that index is not itself a WSGI app and it must use the normal web2py API (such as response.write to write to the socket).

5
The views

web2py uses Python for its models, controllers, and views, although it uses a slightly modified Python syntax in the views to allow more readable code without imposing any restrictions on proper Python usage.

The purpose of a view is to embed code (Python) in an HTML document. In general, this poses some problems:

- How should embedded code be escaped?

- Should indenting be based on Python or HTML rules?

web2py uses {{ ... }} to escape Python code embedded in HTML. The advantage of using curly brackets instead of angle brackets is that it's transparent to all common HTML editors. This allows the developer to use those editors to create web2py views. These delimiters can be changed for example with

```
response.delimiters = ('<?','?>')
```

If this line is in a model it will be applied everywhere, if in a controller only to views for the controller actions, if inside an action only to the view for that action.

Since the developer is embedding Python code into HTML, the document should be indented according to HTML rules, and not Python rules. Therefore, we allow unindented Python inside the {{ ... }} tags. Since

Python normally uses indentation to delimit blocks of code, we need a different way to delimit them; this is why the web2py template language makes use of the Python keyword pass.

> A code block starts with a line ending with a colon and ends with a line beginning with pass. The keyword pass is not necessary when the end of the block is obvious from the context.

Here is an example:

```
1 {{
2 if i == 0:
3 response.write('i is 0')
4 else:
5 response.write('i is not 0')
6 pass
7 }}
```

Note that pass is a Python keyword, not a web2py keyword. Some Python editors, such as Emacs, use the keyword pass to signify the division of blocks and use it to re-indent code automatically.

The web2py template language does exactly the same. When it finds something like:

```
1 <html><body>
2 {{for x in range(10):}}{{=x}}hello<br />{{pass}}
3 </body></html>
```

it translates it into a program:

```
1 response.write("""<html><body>""", escape=False)
2 for x in range(10):
3     response.write(x)
4     response.write("""hello<br />""", escape=False)
5 response.write("""</body></html>""", escape=False)
```

response.write writes to the response.body.

When there is an error in a web2py view, the error report shows the generated view code, not the actual view as written by the developer. This helps the developer debug the code by highlighting the actual code that is executed (which is something that can be debugged with an HTML editor or the DOM inspector of the browser).

Also note that:

```
1 {{=x}}
```

generates

```
response.write(x)
```

Variables injected into the HTML in this way are escaped by default. The escaping is ignored if x is an XML object, even if escape is set to True.

Here is an example that introduces the H1 helper:

```
{{=H1(i)}}
```

which is translated to:

```
response.write(H1(i))
```

upon evaluation, the H1 object and its components are recursively serialized, escaped and written to the response body. The tags generated by H1 and inner HTML are not escaped. This mechanism guarantees that all text — and only text — displayed on the web page is always escaped, thus preventing XSS vulnerabilities. At the same time, the code is simple and easy to debug.

The method response.write(obj, escape=True) takes two arguments, the object to be written and whether it has to be escaped (set to True by default). If obj has an .xml() method, it is called and the result written to the response body (the escape argument is ignored). Otherwise it uses the object's __str__ method to serialize it and, if the escape argument is True, escapes it. All built-in helper objects (H1 in the example) are objects that know how to serialize themselves via the .xml() method.

This is all done transparently. You never need to (and never should) call the response.write method explicitly.

5.1 Basic syntax

The web2py template language supports all Python control structures. Here we provide some examples of each of them. They can be nested according to usual programming practice.

5.1.1   for...in

In templates you can loop over any iterable object:

```
1 {{items = ['a', 'b', 'c']}}
2 <ul>
3 {{for item in items:}}<li>{{=item}}</li>{{pass}}
4 </ul>
```

which produces:

```
1 <ul>
2 <li>a</li>
3 <li>b</li>
4 <li>c</li>
5 </ul>
```

Here item is any iterable object such as a Python list, Python tuple, or Rows object, or any object that is implemented as an iterator. The elements displayed are first serialized and escaped.

5.1.2 while

You can create a loop using the while keyword:

```
1 {{k = 3}}
2 <ul>
3 {{while k > 0:}}<li>{{=k}}{{k = k - 1}}</li>{{pass}}
4 </ul>
```

which produces:

```
1 <ul>
2 <li>3</li>
3 <li>2</li>
4 <li>1</li>
5 </ul>
```

5.1.3 if...elif...else

You can use conditional clauses:

```
1 {{
2 import random
3 k = random.randint(0, 100)
4 }}
5 <h2>
6 {{=k}}
7 {{if k % 2:}}is odd{{else:}}is even{{pass}}
8 </h2>
```

which produces:

```
1  <h2>
2  45 is odd
3  </h2>
```

Since it is obvious that else closes the first if block, there is no need for a pass statement, and using one would be incorrect. However, you must explicitly close the else block with a pass.

Recall that in Python "else if" is written elif as in the following example:

```
1  {{
2  import random
3  k = random.randint(0, 100)
4  }}
5  <h2>
6  {{=k}}
7  {{if k % 4 == 0:}}is divisible by 4
8  {{elif k % 2 == 0:}}is even
9  {{else:}}is odd
10 {{pass}}
11 </h2>
```

It produces:

```
1  <h2>
2  64 is divisible by 4
3  </h2>
```

5.1.4   try...except...else...finally

It is also possible to use try...except statements in views with one caveat. Consider the following example:

```
1  {{try:}}
2  Hello {{= 1 / 0}}
3  {{except:}}
4  division by zero
5  {{else:}}
6  no division by zero
7  {{finally}}
8  <br />
9  {{pass}}
```

It will produce the following output:

```
1  Hello
2  division by zero
```

```
3  <br />
```

This example illustrates that all output generated before an exception occurs is rendered (including output that preceded the exception) inside the try block. "Hello" is written because it precedes the exception.

5.1.5   def...return

The web2py template language allows the developer to define and implement functions that can return any Python object or a text/html string. Here we consider two examples:

```
1  {{def itemize1(link): return LI(A(link, _href="http://" + link))}}
2  <ul>
3  {{=itemize1('www.google.com')}}
4  </ul>
```

produces the following output:

```
1  <ul>
2  <li><a href="http:/www.google.com">www.google.com</a></li>
3  </ul>
```

The function `itemize1` returns a helper object that is inserted at the location where the function is called.

Consider now the following code:

```
1  {{def itemize2(link):}}
2  <li><a href="http://{{=link}}">{{=link}}</a></li>
3  {{return}}
4  <ul>
5  {{itemize2('www.google.com')}}
6  </ul>
```

It produces exactly the same output as above. In this case, the function `itemize2` represents a piece of HTML that is going to replace the web2py tag where the function is called. Notice that there is no '=' in front of the call to `itemize2`, since the function does not return the text, but it writes it directly into the response.

There is one caveat: functions defined inside a view must terminate with a return statement, or the automatic indentation will fail.

5.2   HTML helpers

Consider the following code in a view:

```
{{=DIV('this', 'is', 'a', 'test', _id='123', _class='myclass')}}
```

it is rendered as:

```
<div id="123" class="myclass">thisisatest</div>
```

DIV is a helper class, i.e., something that can be used to build HTML programmatically. It corresponds to the HTML <div> tag.

Positional arguments are interpreted as objects contained between the open and close tags. Named arguments that start with an underscore are interpreted as HTML tag attributes (without the underscore). Some helpers also have named arguments that do not start with underscore; these arguments are tag-specific.

Instead of a set of unnamed arguments, a helper can also take a single list or tuple as its set of components using the * notation and it can take a single dictionary as its set of attributes using the **, for example:

```
{{
contents = ['this','is','a','test']
attributes = {'_id':'123', '_class':'myclass'}
=DIV(*contents,**attributes)
}}
```

(produces the same output as before).

The following set of helpers:

A, B, BEAUTIFY, BODY, BR, CAT, CENTER, CODE, COL, COLGROUP, DIV, EM, EMBED, FIELDSET, FORM, H1, H2, H3, H4, H5, H6, HEAD, HR, HTML, I, IFRAME, IMG, INPUT, LABEL, LEGEND, LI, LINK, MARKMIN, MENU, META, OBJECT, ON, OL, OPTGROUP, OPTION, P, PRE, SCRIPT, SELECT, SPAN, STYLE, TABLE, TAG, TBODY, TD, TEXTAREA, TFOOT, TH, THEAD, TITLE, TR, TT, UL, URL, XHTML, XML, embed64, xmlescape can be used to build complex expressions that can then be serialized to XML [59] [60]. For example:

```
{{=DIV(B(I("hello ", "<world>"))), _class="myclass")}}
```

is rendered:

```
<div class="myclass"><b><i>hello &lt;world&gt;</i></b></div>
```

Helpers can also be serialized into strings, equivalently, with the __str__ and the xml methods:

```
>>> print str(DIV("hello world"))
<div>hello world</div>
>>> print DIV("hello world").xml()
<div>hello world</div>
```

The helpers mechanism in web2py is more than a system to generate HTML without concatenating strings. It provides a server-side representation of the Document Object Model (DOM).

Components of helpers can be referenced via their position, and helpers act as lists with respect to their components:

```
>>> a = DIV(SPAN('a', 'b'), 'c')
>>> print a
<div><span>ab</span>c</div>
>>> del a[1]
>>> a.append(B('x'))
>>> a[0][0] = 'y'
>>> print a
<div><span>yb</span><b>x</b></div>
```

Attributes of helpers can be referenced by name, and helpers act as dictionaries with respect to their attributes:

```
>>> a = DIV(SPAN('a', 'b'), 'c')
>>> a['_class'] = 's'
>>> a[0]['_class'] = 't'
>>> print a
<div class="s"><span class="t">ab</span>c</div>
```

Note, the complete set of components can be accessed via a list called a.components, and the complete set of attributes can be accessed via a dictionary called a.attributes. So, a[i] is equivalent to a.components[i] when i is an integer, and a[s] is equivalent to a.attributes[s] when s is a string.

Notice that helper attributes are passed as keyword arguments to the helper. In some cases, however, attribute names include special characters that are not allowed in Python identifiers (e.g., hyphens) and therefore cannot be used as keyword argument names. For example:

```
DIV('text', _data-role='collapsible')
```

will not work because "_data-role" includes a hyphen, which will produce a Python syntax error.

In such cases, you can instead pass the attributes as a dictionary and make use of Python's ** function arguments notation, which map a dictionary of (key:value) pairs into a set of keyword arguments:

```
>>> print DIV('text', **{'_data-role': 'collapsible'})
<div data-role="collapsible">text</div>
```

You can also dynamically create special TAGs:

```
>>> print TAG['soap:Body']('whatever',**{'_xmlns:m':'http://www.example.org'})
<soap:Body xmlns:m="http://www.example.org">whatever</soap:Body>
```

5.2.1 XML

XML is an object used to encapsulate text that should not be escaped. The text may or may not contain valid XML. For example, it could contain JavaScript.

The text in this example is escaped:

```
>>> print DIV("<b>hello</b>")
&lt;b&gt;hello&lt;/b&gt;
```

by using XML you can prevent escaping:

```
>>> print DIV(XML("<b>hello</b>"))
<b>hello</b>
```

Sometimes you want to render HTML stored in a variable, but the HTML may contain unsafe tags such as scripts:

```
>>> print XML('<script>alert("unsafe!")</script>')
<script>alert("unsafe!")</script>
```

Un-escaped executable input such as this (for example, entered in the body of a comment in a blog) is unsafe, because it can be used to generate Cross Site Scripting (XSS) attacks against other visitors to the page.

The web2py XML helper can sanitize our text to prevent injections and escape all tags except those that you explicitly allow. Here is an example:

```
>>> print XML('<script>alert("unsafe!")</script>', sanitize=True)
&lt;script&gt;alert(&quot;unsafe!&quot;)&lt;/script&gt;
```

The XML constructors, by default, consider the content of some tags and some of their attributes safe. You can override the defaults using the optional permitted_tags and allowed_attributes arguments. Here are the default values of the optional arguments of the XML helper.

```
1  XML(text, sanitize=False,
2      permitted_tags=['a', 'b', 'blockquote', 'br/', 'i', 'li',
3          'ol', 'ul', 'p', 'cite', 'code', 'pre', 'img/'],
4      allowed_attributes={'a':['href', 'title'],
5          'img':['src', 'alt'], 'blockquote':['type']})
```

5.2.2 Built-in helpers

A

This helper is used to build links.

```
1  >>> print A('<click>', XML('<b>me</b>'),
2          _href='http://www.web2py.com')
3  <a href='http://www.web2py.com'>&lt;click&gt;<b>me/b></a>
```

Instead of _href you can pass the URL using the callback argument. For example in a view:

```
1  {{=A('click me', callback=URL('myaction'))}}
```

and the effect of pressing the link will be an ajax call to "myaction" instead of a redirection. In this case, optionally you can specify two more arguments: target and delete:

```
1  {{=A('click me', callback=URL('myaction'), target="t")}}
2  <div id="t"><div>
```

and the response of the ajax callback will be stored in the DIV with id equal to "t".

```
1  <div id="b">{{=A('click me', callback=URL('myaction'), delete='div#b")}}</div>
```

and upon response, the closest tag matching "div#b" will be deleted. In this case, the button will be deleted. A typical application is:

```
1  {{=A('click me', callback=URL('myaction'), delete='tr")}}
```

in a table. Pressing the button will perform the callback and delete the table row.

callback and delete can be combined.

The A helper takes a special argument called cid. It works as follows:

```
1  {{=A('linked page', _href='http://example.com', cid='myid')}}
2  <div id="myid"></div>
```

and a click on the link causes the content to be loaded in the div. This is similar but more powerful than the above syntax since it is designed to refresh page components. We discuss applications of cid in more detail in Chapter 12, in the context of components.

These ajax features require jQuery and "static/js/web2py_ajax.js", which are automatically included by placing {{include 'web2py_ajax.html'}} in the layout head. "views/web2py_ajax.html" defines some variables based on request and includes all necessary js and css files.

B

This helper makes its contents bold.

```
1  >>> print B('<hello>', XML('<i>world</i>'), _class='test', _id=0)
2  <b id="0" class="test">&lt;hello&gt;<i>world</i></b>
```

BODY

This helper makes the body of a page.

```
1  >>> print BODY('<hello>', XML('<b>world</b>'), _bgcolor='red')
2  <body bgcolor="red">&lt;hello&gt;<b>world</b></body>
```

BR

This helper creates a line break.

```
1  >>> print BR()
2  <br />
```

Notice that helpers can be repeated using the multiplication operator:

```
1  >>> print BR()*5
2  <br /><br /><br /><br /><br />
```

CAT

This helper concatenates other helpers, same as TAG[''].

```
1  >>> print CAT('Here is a ', A('link',_href=URL()), ', and here is some ', B('bold
       text'), '.')
2  Here is a <a href="/app/default/index">link</a>, and here is some <b>bold text</b>.
```

CENTER

This helper centers its content.

```
1  >>> print CENTER('<hello>', XML('<b>world</b>'),
2  >>>              _class='test', _id=0)
3  <center id="0" class="test">&lt;hello&gt;<b>world</b></center>
```

CODE

This helper performs syntax highlighting for Python, C, C++, HTML and web2py code, and is preferable to PRE for code listings. CODE also has the ability to create links to the web2py API documentation.

Here is an example of highlighting sections of Python code.

```
>>> print CODE('print "hello"', language='python').xml()
<table><tr valign="top"><td style="width:40px; text-align: right;"><pre style="
        font-size: 11px;
        font-family: Bitstream Vera Sans Mono,monospace;
        background-color: transparent;
            margin: 0;
            padding: 5px;
            border: none;
        background-color: #E0E0E0;
        color: #A0A0A0;
    ">1.</pre></td><td><pre style="
        font-size: 11px;
        font-family: Bitstream Vera Sans Mono,monospace;
        background-color: transparent;
            margin: 0;
            padding: 5px;
            border: none;
            overflow: auto;
    "><span style="color:#185369; font-weight: bold">print </span>
    <span style="color: #FF9966">"hello"</span></pre></td></tr>
</table>
```

Here is a similar example for HTML

```
>>> print CODE(
>>>     '<html><body>{{=request.env.remote_add}}</body></html>',
>>>     language='html')
```

```
<table>...<code>...
<html><body>{{=request.env.remote_add}}</body></html>
...</code>...</table>
```

These are the default arguments for the CODE helper:

```
CODE("print 'hello world'", language='python', link=None, counter=1, styles={})
```

Supported values for the language argument are "python", "html_plain", "c", "cpp", "web2py", and "html". The "html" language interprets {{ and }} tags as "web2py" code, while "html_plain" doesn't.

If a link value is specified, for example "/examples/global/vars/", web2py API references in the code are linked to documentation at the link URL.

For example "request" would be linked to "/examples/global/vars/request". In the above example, the link URL is handled by the "vars" action in the "global.py" controller that is distributed as part of the web2py "examples" application.

The `counter` argument is used for line numbering. It can be set to any of three different values. It can be `None` for no line numbers, a numerical value specifying the start number, or a string. If the counter is set to a string, it is interpreted as a prompt, and there are no line numbers.

The `styles` argument is a bit tricky. If you look at the generated HTML above, it contains a table with two columns, and each column has its own style declared inline using CSS. The `styles` attributes allows you to override those two CSS styles. For example:

```
{{=CODE(...,styles={'CODE':'margin: 0;padding: 5px;border: none;'})}}
```

The `styles` attribute must be a dictionary, and it allows two possible keys: `CODE` for the style of the actual code, and `LINENUMBERS` for the style of the left column, which contains the line numbers. Mind that these styles completely replace the default styles and are not simply added to them.

COL

```
>>> print COL('a','b')
<col>ab</col>
```

COLGROUP

```
>>> print COLGROUP('a','b')
<colgroup>ab</colgroup>
```

DIV

All helpers apart from XML are derived from DIV and inherit its basic methods.

```
>>> print DIV('<hello>', XML('<b>world</b>'), _class='test', _id=0)
<div id="0" class="test">&lt;hello&gt;<b>world</b></div>
```

EM

Emphasizes its content.

```
>>> print EM('<hello>', XML('<b>world</b>'), _class='test', _id=0)
<em id="0" class="test">&lt;hello&gt;<b>world</b></em>
```

FIELDSET

This is used to create an input field together with its label.

```
1  >>> print FIELDSET('Height:', INPUT(_name='height'), _class='test')
2  <fieldset class="test">Height:<input name="height" /></fieldset>
```

FORM

This is one of the most important helpers. In its simple form, it just makes a <form>...</form> tag, but because helpers are objects and have knowledge of what they contain, they can process submitted forms (for example, perform validation of the fields). This will be discussed in detail in Chapter 7.

```
1  >>> print FORM(INPUT(_type='submit'), _action='', _method='post')
2  <form enctype="multipart/form-data" action="" method="post">
3  <input type="submit" /></form>
```

The "enctype" is "multipart/form-data" by default.

The constructor of a FORM, and of SQLFORM, can also take a special argument called hidden. When a dictionary is passed as hidden, its items are translated into "hidden" INPUT fields. For example:

```
1  >>> print FORM(hidden=dict(a='b'))
2  <form enctype="multipart/form-data" action="" method="post">
3  <input value="b" type="hidden" name="a" /></form>
```

H1, H2, H3, H4, H5, H6

These helpers are for paragraph headings and subheadings:

```
1  >>> print H1('<hello>', XML('<b>world</b>'), _class='test', _id=0)
2  <h1 id="0" class="test">&lt;hello&gt;<b>world</b></h1>
```

HEAD

For tagging the HEAD of an HTML page.

```
1  >>> print HEAD(TITLE('<hello>', XML('<b>world</b>')))
2  <head><title>&lt;hello&gt;<b>world</b></title></head>
```

HTML

This helper is a little different. In addition to making the <html> tags, it prepends the tag with a doctype string [61, 62, 63].

```
1  >>> print HTML(BODY('<hello>', XML('<b>world</b>')))
2  <!DOCTYPE HTML PUBLIC "-//W3C//DTD HTML 4.01 Transitional//EN"
3                        "http://www.w3.org/TR/html4/loose.dtd">
4  <html><body>&lt;hello&gt;<b>world</b></body></html>
```

The HTML helper also takes some additional optional arguments that have the following default:

```
1  HTML(..., lang='en', doctype='transitional')
```

where doctype can be 'strict', 'transitional', 'frameset', 'html5', or a full doctype string.

XHTML

XHTML is similar to HTML but it creates an XHTML doctype instead.

```
1  XHTML(..., lang='en', doctype='transitional', xmlns='http://www.w3.org/1999/xhtml')
```

where doctype can be 'strict', 'transitional', 'frameset', or a full doctype string.

HR

This helper creates a horizontal line in an HTML page

```
1  >>> print HR()
2  <hr />
```

I

This helper makes its contents italic.

```
1  >>> print I('<hello>', XML('<b>world</b>'), _class='test', _id=0)
2  <i id="0" class="test">&lt;hello&gt;<b>world</b></i>
```

INPUT

Creates an <input.../> tag. An input tag may not contain other tags, and is closed by /> instead of >. The input tag has an optional attribute _type that can be set to "text" (the default), "submit", "checkbox", or "radio".

```
1  >>> print INPUT(_name='test', _value='a')
2  <input value="a" name="test" />
```

It also takes an optional special argument called "value", distinct from "_value". The latter sets the default value for the input field; the former sets its current value. For an input of type "text", the former overrides the latter:

```
1  >>> print INPUT(_name='test', _value='a', value='b')
2  <input value="b" name="test" />
```

For radio buttons, INPUT selectively sets the "checked" attribute:

```
1  >>> for v in ['a', 'b', 'c']:
2  >>>     print INPUT(_type='radio', _name='test', _value=v, value='b'), v
3  <input value="a" type="radio" name="test" /> a
4  <input value="b" type="radio" checked="checked" name="test" /> b
```

```
5 <input value="c" type="radio" name="test" /> c
```

and similarly for checkboxes:

```
1 >>> print INPUT(_type='checkbox', _name='test', _value='a', value=True)
2 <input value="a" type="checkbox" checked="checked" name="test" />
3 >>> print INPUT(_type='checkbox', _name='test', _value='a', value=False)
4 <input value="a" type="checkbox" name="test" />
```

IFRAME

This helper includes another web page in the current page. The url of the other page is specified via the "_src" attribute.

```
1 >>> print IFRAME(_src='http://www.web2py.com')
2 <iframe src="http://www.web2py.com"></iframe>
```

IMG

It can be used to embed images into HTML:

```
1 >>> IMG(_src='http://example.com/image.png',_alt='test')
2 <img src="http://example.com/image.ong" alt="rest" />
```

Here is a combination of A, IMG, and URL helpers for including a static image with a link:

```
1 >>> A(IMG(_src=URL('static','logo.png'), _alt="My Logo"),
2     _href=URL('default','index'))
3 <a href="/myapp/default/index">
4   <img src="/myapp/static/logo.png" alt="My Logo" />
5 </a>
```

LABEL

It is used to create a LABEL tag for an INPUT field.

```
1 >>> print LABEL('<hello>', XML('<b>world</b>'), _class='test', _id=0)
2 <label id="0" class="test">&lt;hello&gt;<b>world</b></label>
```

LEGEND

It is used to create a legend tag for a field in a form.

```
1 >>> print LEGEND('Name', _for='myfield')
2 <legend for="myfield">Name</legend>
```

LI

It makes a list item and should be contained in a UL or OL tag.

```
1 >>> print LI('<hello>', XML('<b>world</b>'), _class='test', _id=0)
2 <li id="0" class="test">&lt;hello&gt;<b>world</b></li>
```

META

To be used for building META tags in the HTML head. For example:

```
1  >>> print META(_name='security', _content='high')
2  <meta name="security" content="high" />
```

MARKMIN

Implements the markmin wiki syntax. It converts the input text into output html according to the markmin rules described in the example below:

```
1  >>> print MARKMIN("this is **bold** or ''italic'' and this [[a link http://web2py.
       com]]")
2  <p>this is <b>bold</b> or <i>italic</i> and
3  this <a href="http://web2py.com">a link</a></p>
```

The markmin syntax is described in this file that ships with web2py:

```
1  http://127.0.0.1:8000/examples/static/markmin.html
```

You can use markmin to generate HTML, LaTeX and PDF documents:

```
1  m = "Hello **world** [[link http://web2py.com]]"
2  from gluon.contrib.markmin.markmin2html import markmin2html
3  print markmin2html(m)
4  from gluon.contrib.markmin.markmin2latex import markmin2latex
5  print markmin2latex(m)
6  from gluon.contrib.markmin.markmin2pdf import markmin2pdf
7  print markmin2pdf(m) # requires pdflatex
```

(the MARKMIN helper is a shortcut for markmin2html)

Here is a basic syntax primer:

SOURCE	OUTPUT
# title	**title**
## section	**section**
### subsection	**subsection**
bold	**bold**
''italic''	*italic*
``verbatim``	verbatim
http://google.com	http://google.com
http://...	`<a href="http://...">http:...</a>`
http://...png	`<img src="http://...png" />`
http://...mp3	`<audio src="http://...mp3"></audio>`
http://...mp4	`<video src="http://...mp4"></video>`
qr:http://...	`<a href="http://..."><img src="qr code"/></a>`
embed:http://...	`<iframe src="http://..."></iframe>`
[[click me #myanchor]]	click me
$$\int_a^b sin(x)dx$$	$\int_a^b sin(x)dx$

Simply including a link to an image, a videos or an audio files without markup result in the corresponding image, video or audio file being included automatically (for audio and video it uses html <audio> and <video> tags).

Adding a link with the qr: prefix such as

```
qr:http://web2py.com
```

results in the corresponding QR code being embedded and linking the said URL.

Adding a link with the embed: prefix such as

```
embed:http://www.youtube.com/embed/x1w8hKTJ2Co
```

results in the page being embedded, in this case a youtube video is embedded.

Images can also be embedded with the following syntax:

```
[[image-description http://.../image.png right 200px]]
```

Unordered lists with:

```
- one
- two
- three
```

Ordered lists with:

```
1  + one
2  + two
3  + three
```

and tables with:

```
1  ----------
2  X | 0 | 0
3  0 | X | 0
4  0 | 0 | 1
5  ----------
```

The MARKMIN syntax also supports blockquotes, HTML5 audio and video tags, image alignment, custom css, and it can be extended:

```
1  MARKMIN("``abab``:custom", extra=dict(custom=lambda text: text.replace('a','c')))
```

generates

```
'cbcb'
```

Custom blocks are delimited by "...":<key> and they are rendered by the function passed as value for the corresponding key in the extra dictionary argument of MARKMIN. Mind that the function may need to escape the output to prevent XSS.

OBJECT

Used to embed objects (for example, a flash player) in the HTML.

```
1  >>> print OBJECT('<hello>', XML('<b>world</b>'),
2  >>>              _src='http://www.web2py.com')
3  <object src="http://www.web2py.com">&lt;hello&gt;<b>world</b></object>
```

OL

It stands for Ordered List. The list should contain LI tags. OL arguments that are not LI objects are automatically enclosed in <li>...</li> tags.

```
1  >>> print OL('<hello>', XML('<b>world</b>'), _class='test', _id=0)
2  <ol id="0" class="test"><li>&lt;hello&gt;</li><li><b>world</b></li></ol>
```

ON

This is here for backward compatibility and it is simply an alias for True. It is used exclusively for checkboxes and deprecated since True is more Pythonic.

```
1  >>> print INPUT(_type='checkbox', _name='test', _checked=ON)
2  <input checked="checked" type="checkbox" name="test" />
```

OPTGROUP

Allows you to group multiple options in a SELECT and it is useful to customize the fields using CSS.

```
1  >>> print SELECT('a', OPTGROUP('b', 'c'))
2  <select>
3    <option value="a">a</option>
4    <optgroup>
5      <option value="b">b</option>
6      <option value="c">c</option>
7    </optgroup>
8  </select>
```

OPTION

This should only be used as part of a SELECT/OPTION combination.

```
1  >>> print OPTION('<hello>', XML('<b>world</b>'), _value='a')
2  <option value="a">&lt;hello&gt;<b>world</b></option>
```

As in the case of INPUT, web2py make a distinction between "_value" (the value of the OPTION), and "value" (the current value of the enclosing select). If they are equal, the option is "selected".

```
1  >>> print SELECT('a', 'b', value='b'):
2  <select>
3  <option value="a">a</option>
4  <option value="b" selected="selected">b</option>
5  </select>
```

P

This is for tagging a paragraph.

```
1  >>> print P('<hello>', XML('<b>world</b>'), _class='test', _id=0)
2  <p id="0" class="test">&lt;hello&gt;<b>world</b></p>
```

PRE

Generates a <pre>...</pre> tag for displaying pre-formatted text. The CODE helper is generally preferable for code listings.

```
1  >>> print PRE('<hello>', XML('<b>world</b>'), _class='test', _id=0)
2  <pre id="0" class="test">&lt;hello&gt;<b>world</b></pre>
```

SCRIPT

This is include or link a script, such as JavaScript. The content between the tags is rendered as an HTML comment, for the benefit of really old browsers.

```
1 >>> print SCRIPT('alert("hello world");', _type='text/javascript')
2 <script type="text/javascript"><!--
3 alert("hello world");
4 //--></script>
```

SELECT

Makes a `<select>...</select>` tag. This is used with the OPTION helper. Those SELECT arguments that are not OPTION objects are automatically converted to options.

```
1 >>> print SELECT('<hello>', XML('<b>world</b>'), _class='test', _id=0)
2 <select id="0" class="test">
3   <option value="&lt;hello&gt;">&lt;hello&gt;</option>
4   <option value="&lt;b&gt;world&lt;/b&gt;"><b>world</b></option>
5 </select>
```

SPAN

Similar to DIV but used to tag inline (rather than block) content.

```
1 >>> print SPAN('<hello>', XML('<b>world</b>'), _class='test', _id=0)
2 <span id="0" class="test">&lt;hello&gt;<b>world</b></span>
```

STYLE

Similar to script, but used to either include or link CSS code. Here the CSS is included:

```
1 >>> print STYLE(XML('body {color: white}'))
2 <style><!--
3 body { color: white }
4 //--></style>
```

and here it is linked:

```
1 >>> print STYLE(_src='style.css')
2 <style src="style.css"><!--
3 //--></style>
```

TABLE, TR, TD

These tags (along with the optional THEAD, TBODY and TFOOTER helpers) are used to build HTML tables.

```
1 >>> print TABLE(TR(TD('a'), TD('b')), TR(TD('c'), TD('d')))
2 <table><tr><td>a</td><td>b</td></tr><tr><td>c</td><td>d</td></tr></table>
```

TR expects TD content; arguments that are not TD objects are converted automatically.

```
1 >>> print TABLE(TR('a', 'b'), TR('c', 'd'))
2 <table><tr><td>a</td><td>b</td></tr><tr><td>c</td><td>d</td></tr></table>
```

It is easy to convert a Python array into an HTML table using Python's *
function arguments notation, which maps list elements to positional function
arguments.

Here, we will do it line by line:

```
1 >>> table = [['a', 'b'], ['c', 'd']]
2 >>> print TABLE(TR(*table[0]), TR(*table[1]))
3 <table><tr><td>a</td><td>b</td></tr><tr><td>c</td><td>d</td></tr></table>
```

Here we do all lines at once:

```
1 >>> table = [['a', 'b'], ['c', 'd']]
2 >>> print TABLE(*[TR(*rows) for rows in table])
3 <table><tr><td>a</td><td>b</td></tr><tr><td>c</td><td>d</td></tr></table>
```

TBODY

This is used to tag rows contained in the table body, as opposed to header or
footer rows. It is optional.

```
1 >>> print TBODY(TR('<hello>'), _class='test', _id=0)
2 <tbody id="0" class="test"><tr><td>&lt;hello&gt;</td></tr></tbody>
```

TEXTAREA

This helper makes a <textarea>...</textarea> tag.

```
1 >>> print TEXTAREA('<hello>', XML('<b>world</b>'), _class='test')
2 <textarea class="test" cols="40" rows="10">&lt;hello&gt;<b>world</b></textarea>
```

The only caveat is that its optional "value" overrides its content (inner HTML)

```
1 >>> print TEXTAREA(value="<hello world>", _class="test")
2 <textarea class="test" cols="40" rows="10">&lt;hello world&gt;</textarea>
```

TFOOT

This is used to tag table footer rows.

```
1 >>> print TFOOT(TR(TD('<hello>')), _class='test', _id=0)
2 <tfoot id="0" class="test"><tr><td>&lt;hello&gt;</td></tr></tfoot>
```

TH

This is used instead of TD in table headers.

```
1 >>> print TH('<hello>', XML('<b>world</b>'), _class='test', _id=0)
2 <th id="0" class="test">&lt;hello&gt;<b>world</b></th>
```

THEAD

This is used to tag table header rows.

```
1 >>> print THEAD(TR(TH('<hello>'))), _class='test', _id=0)
2 <thead id="0" class="test"><tr><th>&lt;hello&gt;</th></tr></thead>
```

TITLE

This is used to tag the title of a page in an HTML header.

```
1 >>> print TITLE('<hello>', XML('<b>world</b>'))
2 <title>&lt;hello&gt;<b>world</b></title>
```

TR

Tags a table row. It should be rendered inside a table and contain <td>...</td> tags. TR arguments that are not TD objects will be automatically converted.

```
1 >>> print TR('<hello>', XML('<b>world</b>'), _class='test', _id=0)
2 <tr id="0" class="test"><td>&lt;hello&gt;</td><td><b>world</b></td></tr>
```

TT

Tags text as typewriter (monospaced) text.

```
1 >>> print TT('<hello>', XML('<b>world</b>'), _class='test', _id=0)
2 <tt id="0" class="test">&lt;hello&gt;<b>world</b></tt>
```

UL

Signifies an Unordered List and should contain LI items. If its content is not tagged as LI, UL does it automatically.

```
1 >>> print UL('<hello>', XML('<b>world</b>'), _class='test', _id=0)
2 <ul id="0" class="test"><li>&lt;hello&gt;</li><li><b>world</b></li></ul>
```

embed64

embed64(filename=None, file=None, data=None, extension='image/gif')
encodes the provided (binary) data into base64. filename: if provided, opens and reads this file in 'rb' mode. file: if provided, reads this file. data: if provided, uses the provided data.

xmlescape

xmlescape(data, quote=True) returns an escaped string of the provided data.

```
1 >>> print xmlescape('<hello>')
2 &lt;hello&gt;
```

5.2.3 Custom helpers

TAG

Sometimes you need to generate custom XML tags. web2py provides TAG, a universal tag generator.

```
{{=TAG.name('a', 'b', _c='d')}}
```

generates the following XML

```
<name c="d">ab</name>
```

Arguments "a", "b", and "d" are automatically escaped; use the XML helper to suppress this behavior. Using TAG you can generate HTML/XML tags not already provided by the API. TAGs can be nested, and are serialized with str(). An equivalent syntax is:

```
{{=TAG['name']('a', 'b', c='d')}}
```

If the TAG object is created with an empty name, it can be used to concatenate multiple strings and HTML helpers together without inserting them into a surrounding tag, but this use is deprecated. Use the CAT helper instead.

Notice that TAG is an object, and TAG.name or TAG['name'] is a function that returns a temporary helper class.

MENU

The MENU helper takes a list of lists or of tuples of the form of response.menu (as described in Chapter 4) and generates a tree-like structure using unordered lists representing the menu. For example:

```
>>> print MENU([['One', False, 'link1'], ['Two', False, 'link2']])
<ul class="web2py-menu web2py-menu-vertical">
  <li><a href="link1">One</a></li>
  <li><a href="link2">Two</a></li>
</ul>
```

> The third item in each list/tuple can be an HTML helper (which could include nested helpers), and the MENU helper will simply render that helper rather than creating its own <a> tag.

Each menu item can have a fourth argument that is a nested submenu (and so on recursively):

```
>>> print MENU([['One', False, 'link1', [['Two', False, 'link2']]]])
```

```
 2   <ul class="web2py-menu web2py-menu-vertical">
 3     <li class="web2py-menu-expand">
 4        <a href="link1">One</a>
 5        <ul class="web2py-menu-vertical">
 6           <li><a href="link2">Two</a></li>
 7        </ul>
 8     </li>
 9   </ul>
```

A menu item can also have an optional 5th element, which is a boolean. When false, the menu item is ignored by the MENU helper.

The MENU helper takes the following optional arguments:

- _class: defaults to "web2py-menu web2py-menu-vertical" and sets the class of the outer UL elements.

- ul_class: defaults to "web2py-menu-vertical" and sets the class of the inner UL elements.

- li_class: defaults to "web2py-menu-expand" and sets the class of the inner LI elements.

- li_first: allows to add a class to the first list element.

- li_last: allows to add a class to the last list element.

MENU takes an optional argument mobile. When set to True instead of building a recursive UL menu structure it returns a SELECT dropdown with all the menu options and a onchange attribute that redirects to the page corresponding to the selected option. This is designed an an alternative menu representation that increases usability on small mobile devices such as phones.

Normally the menu is used in a layout with the following syntax:

```
 1   {{=MENU(response.menu, mobile=request.user_agent().is_mobile)}}
```

In this way a mobile device is automatically detected and the menu is rendered accordingly.

5.3   BEAUTIFY

BEAUTIFY is used to build HTML representations of compound objects, including lists, tuples and dictionaries:

```
{{=BEAUTIFY({"a": ["hello", XML("world")], "b": (1, 2)})}}
```

BEAUTIFY returns an XML-like object serializable to XML, with a nice looking representation of its constructor argument. In this case, the XML representation of:

```
{"a": ["hello", XML("world")], "b": (1, 2)}
```

will render as:

```
<table>
<tr><td>a</td><td>:</td><td>hello<br />world</td></tr>
<tr><td>b</td><td>:</td><td>1<br />2</td></tr>
</table>
```

5.4   Server-side *DOM* and parsing

5.4.1   elements

The DIV helper and all derived helpers provide the search methods element and elements.

element returns the first child element matching a specified condition (or None if no match).

elements returns a list of all matching children.

element and **elements** use the same syntax to specify the matching condition, which allows for three possibilities that can be mixed and matched: jQuery-like expressions, match by exact attribute value, match using regular expressions.

Here is a simple example:

```
>>> a = DIV(DIV(DIV('a', _id='target',_class='abc')))
>>> d = a.elements('div#target')
>>> d[0][0] = 'changed'
>>> print a
<div><div><div id="target" class="abc">changed</div></div></div>
```

The un-named argument of elements is a string, which may contain: the name of a tag, the id of a tag preceded by a pound symbol, the class preceded by a dot, the explicit value of an attribute in square brackets.

Here are 4 equivalent ways to search the previous tag by id:

```
1 >>> d = a.elements('#target')
2 >>> d = a.elements('div#target')
3 >>> d = a.elements('div[id=target]')
4 >>> d = a.elements('div',_id='target')
```

Here are 4 equivalent ways to search the previous tag by class:

```
1 >>> d = a.elements('.abc')
2 >>> d = a.elements('div.abc')
3 >>> d = a.elements('div[class=abc]')
4 >>> d = a.elements('div',_class='abc')
```

Any attribute can be used to locate an element (not just id and class), including multiple attributes (the function element can take multiple named arguments), but only the first matching element will be returned.

Using the jQuery syntax "div#target" it is possible to specify multiple search criteria separated by a space:

```
1 >>> a = DIV(SPAN('a', _id='t1'), DIV('b', _class='c2'))
2 >>> d = a.elements('span#t1, div.c2')
```

or equivalently

```
1 >>> a = DIV(SPAN('a', _id='t1'), DIV('b', _class='c2'))
2 >>> d = a.elements('span#t1', 'div.c2')
```

If the value of an attribute is specified using a name argument, it can be a string or a regular expression:

```
1 >>> a = DIV(SPAN('a', _id='test123'), DIV('b', _class='c2'))
2 >>> d = a.elements('span', _id=re.compile('test\d{3}')
```

A special named argument of the DIV (and derived) helpers is find. It can be used to specify a search value or a search regular expression in the text content of the tag. For example:

```
1 >>> a = DIV(SPAN('abcde'), DIV('fghij'))
2 >>> d = a.elements(find='bcd')
3 >>> print d[0]
4 <span>abcde</span>
```

or

```
1 >>> a = DIV(SPAN('abcde'), DIV('fghij'))
2 >>> d = a.elements(find=re.compile('fg\w{3}'))
3 >>> print d[0]
4 <div>fghij</div>
```

5.4.2 components

Here's an example of listing all elements in an html string:

```
1 html = TAG('<a>xxx</a><b>yyy</b>')
2 for item in html.components: print item
```

5.4.3 parent **and** siblings

parent returns the parent of the current element.

```
1 >>> a = DIV(SPAN('a'),DIV('b'))
2 >>> s = a.element('span')
3 >>> d = s.parent
4 >>> d['_class']='abc'
5 >>> print a
6 <div class="abc"><span>a</span><div>b</div></div>
7 >>> for e in s.siblings(): print e
8 <div>b</div>
```

5.4.4 Replacing elements

Elements that are matched can also be replaced or removed by specifying the replace argument. Notice that a list of the original matching elements is still returned as usual.

```
1 >>> a = DIV(SPAN('x'), DIV(SPAN('y'))
2 >>> b = a.elements('span', replace=P('z')
3 >>> print a
4 <div><p>z</p><div><p>z</p></div>
```

replace can be a callable. In this case it will be passed the original element and it is expected to return the replacement element:

```
1 >>> a = DIV(SPAN('x'), DIV(SPAN('y'))
2 >>> b = a.elements('span', replace=lambda t: P(t[0])
3 >>> print a
4 <div><p>x</p><div><p>y</p></div>
```

If replace=None, matching elements will be removed completely.

```
1 >>> a = DIV(SPAN('x'), DIV(SPAN('y'))
2 >>> b = a.elements('span', replace=None)
3 >>> print a
4 <div></div>
```

5.4.5 flatten

The flatten method recursively serializes the content of the children of a given element into regular text (without tags):

```
>>> a = DIV(SPAN('this', DIV('is', B('a'))), SPAN('test'))
>>> print a.flatten()
thisisatest
```

Flatten can be passed an optional argument, render, i.e. a function that renders/flattens the content using a different protocol. Here is an example to serialize some tags into Markmin wiki syntax:

```
>>> a = DIV(H1('title'), P('example of a ', A('link', _href='#test')))
>>> from gluon.html import markmin_serializer
>>> print a.flatten(render=markmin_serializer)
## titles

example of [[a link #test]]
```

At the time of writing we provide markmin_serializer and markdown_serializer.

5.4.6 Parsing

The TAG object is also an XML/HTML parser. It can read text and convert into a tree structure of helpers. This allows manipulation using the API above:

```
>>> html = '<h1>Title</h1><p>this is a <span>test</span></p>'
>>> parsed_html = TAG(html)
>>> parsed_html.element('span')[0]='TEST'
>>> print parsed_html
<h1>Title</h1><p>this is a <span>TEST</span></p>
```

5.5 Page layout

Views can extend and include other views in a tree-like structure.

For example, we can think of a view "index.html" that extends "layout.html" and includes "body.html". At the same time, "layout.html" may include "header.html" and "footer.html".

The root of the tree is what we call a layout view. Just like any other HTML template file, you can edit it using the web2py administrative interface. The file name "layout.html" is just a convention.

Here is a minimalist page that extends the "layout.html" view and includes the "page.html" view:

```
1 {{extend 'layout.html'}}
2 <h1>Hello World</h1>
3 {{include 'page.html'}}
```

The extended layout file must contain an {{include}} directive, something like:

```
1 <html>
2   <head>
3     <title>Page Title</title>
4   </head>
5   <body>
6     {{include}}
7   </body>
8 </html>
```

When the view is called, the extended (layout) view is loaded, and the calling view replaces the {{include}} directive inside the layout. Processing continues recursively until all extend and include directives have been processed. The resulting template is then translated into Python code. Note, when an application is bytecode compiled, it is this Python code that is compiled, not the original view files themselves. So, the bytecode compiled version of a given view is a single.pyc file that includes the Python code not just for the original view file, but for its entire tree of extended and included views.

> extend, include, block and super are special template directives, not Python commands.

Any content or code that precedes the {{extend ...}} directive will be inserted (and therefore executed) before the beginning of the extended view's content/code. Although this is not typically used to insert actual HTML content before the extended view's content, it can be useful as a means to define variables or functions that you want to make available to the extended view. For example, consider a view "index.html":

```
1 {{sidebar_enabled=True}}
```

```
2 {{extend 'layout.html'}}
3 <h1>Home Page</h1>
```

and an excerpt from "layout.html":

```
1 {{if sidebar_enabled:}}
2     <div id="sidebar">
3         Sidebar Content
4     </div>
5 {{pass}}
```

Because the `sidebar_enabled` assignment in "index.html" comes before the extend, that line gets inserted before the beginning of "layout.html", making `sidebar_enabled` available anywhere within the "layout.html" code (a somewhat more sophisticated version of this is used in the **welcome** app).

It is also worth pointing out that the variables returned by the controller function are available not only in the function's main view, but in all of its extended and included views as well.

The argument of an `extend` or `include` (i.e., the extended or included view name) can be a python variable (though not a python expression). However, this imposes a limitation – views that use variables in `extend` or `include` statements cannot be bytecode compiled. As noted above, bytecode-compiled views include the entire tree of extended and included views, so the specific extended and included views must be known at compile time, which is not possible if the view names are variables (whose values are not determined until run time). Because bytecode compiling views can provide a significant speed boost, using variables in `extend` and `include` should generally be avoided if possible.

In some cases, an alternative to using a variable in an `include` is simply to place regular {{include ...}} directives inside an `if...else` block.

```
1 {{if some_condition:}}
2 {{include 'this_view.html'}}
3 {{else:}}
4 {{include 'that_view.html'}}
5 {{pass}}
```

The above code does not present any problem for bytecode compilation because no variables are involved. Note, however, that the bytecode compiled view will actually include the Python code for both "this_view.html" and "that_view.html", though only the code for one of those views will be executed, depending on the value of some_condition.

Keep in mind, this only works for include – you cannot place {{extend ...}} directives inside if...else blocks.

Layouts are used to encapsulate page commonality (headers, footers, menus), and though they are not mandatory, they will make your application easier to write and maintain. In particular, we suggest writing layouts that take advantage of the following variables that can be set in the controller. Using these well known variables will help make your layouts interchangeable:

```
1 response.title
2 response.subtitle
3 response.meta.author
4 response.meta.keywords
5 response.meta.description
6 response.flash
7 response.menu
8 response.files
```

Except for menu and files, these are all strings and their meaning should be obvious.

response.menu menu is a list of 3-tuples or 4-tuples. The three elements are: the link name, a boolean representing whether the link is active (is the current link), and the URL of the linked page. For example:

```
1 response.menu = [('Google', False, 'http://www.google.com',[]),
2                  ('Index', True, URL('index'), [])]
```

The fourth tuple element is an optional sub-menu.

response.files is a list of CSS and JS files that are needed by your page.

We also recommend that you use:

```
1 {{include 'web2py_ajax.html'}}
```

in the HTML head, since this will include the jQuery libraries and define some backward-compatible JavaScript functions for special effects and Ajax. "web2py_ajax.html" includes the response.meta tags in the view, jQuery base, the calendar datepicker, and all required CSS and JS response.files.

5.5.1   Default page layout

The "views/layout.html" that ships with the web2py scaffolding application
welcome (stripped down of some optional parts) is quite complex but it has
the following structure:

```
1  <!DOCTYPE html>
2  <head>
3    <meta charset="utf-8" />
4    <title>{{=response.title or request.application}}</title>
5    ...
6    <script src="{{=URL('static','js/modernizr.custom.js')}}"></script>
7
8    {{
9    response.files.append(URL('static','css/web2py.css'))
10   response.files.append(URL('static','css/bootstrap.min.css'))
11   response.files.append(URL('static','css/bootstrap-responsive.min.css'))
12   response.files.append(URL('static','css/web2py_bootstrap.css'))
13   }}
14
15   {{include 'web2py_ajax.html'}}
16
17   {{
18   # using sidebars need to know what sidebar you want to use
19   left_sidebar_enabled = globals().get('left_sidebar_enabled',False)
20   right_sidebar_enabled = globals().get('right_sidebar_enabled',False)
21   middle_columns = {0:'span12',1:'span9',2:'span6'}[
22     (left_sidebar_enabled and 1 or 0)+(right_sidebar_enabled and 1 or 0)]
23   }}
24
25   {{block head}}{{end}}
26   </head>
27
28   <body>
29     <!-- Navbar ================================================== -->
30     <div class="navbar navbar-inverse navbar-fixed-top">
31       <div class="flash">{{=response.flash or ''}}</div>
32       <div class="navbar-inner">
33         <div class="container">
34           {{=response.logo or ''}}
35           <ul id="navbar" class="nav pull-right">
36             {{='auth' in globals() and auth.navbar(mode="dropdown") or ''}}
37           </ul>
38           <div class="nav-collapse">
39             {{if response.menu:}}
40             {{=MENU(response.menu)}}
41             {{pass}}
42           </div><!--/.nav-collapse -->
```

```
43        </div>
44      </div>
45    </div><!--/top navbar -->
46
47    <div class="container">
48      <!-- Masthead ================================================== -->
49      <header class="mastheader row" id="header">
50          <div class="span12">
51              <div class="page-header">
52                  <h1>
53                      {{=response.title or request.application}}
54                      <small>{{=response.subtitle or ''}}</small>
55                  </h1>
56              </div>
57          </div>
58      </header>
59
60      <section id="main" class="main row">
61          {{if left_sidebar_enabled:}}
62          <div class="span3 left-sidebar">
63              {{block left_sidebar}}
64              <h3>Left Sidebar</h3>
65              <p></p>
66              {{end}}
67          </div>
68          {{pass}}
69
70          <div class="{{=middle_columns}}">
71              {{block center}}
72              {{include}}
73              {{end}}
74          </div>
75
76          {{if right_sidebar_enabled:}}
77          <div class="span3">
78              {{block right_sidebar}}
79              <h3>Right Sidebar</h3>
80              <p></p>
81              {{end}}
82          </div>
83          {{pass}}
84      </section><!--/main-->
85
86      <!-- Footer ==================================================== -->
87      <div class="row">
88          <footer class="footer span12" id="footer">
89              <div class="footer-content">
90                  {{block footer}} <!-- this is default footer -->
91                  ...
```

```
92              {{end}}
93            </div>
94          </footer>
95        </div>
96
97      </div> <!-- /container -->
98
99      <!-- The javascript ===========================================
100         (Placed at the end of the document so the pages load faster) -->
101     <script src="{{=URL('static','js/bootstrap.min.js')}}"></script>
102     <script src="{{=URL('static','js/web2py_bootstrap.js')}}"></script>
103     {{if response.google_analytics_id:}}
104       <script src="{{=URL('static','js/analytics.js')}}"></script>
105       <script type="text/javascript">
106       analytics.initialize({
107         'Google Analytics':{trackingId:'{{=response.google_analytics_id}}'}
108       });</script>
109     {{pass}}
110     </body>
111     </html>
```

There are a few features of this default layout that make it very easy to use and customize:

- It is written in HTML5 and uses the "modernizr" [64] library for backward compatibility. The actual layout include some extra conditional statements required by IE and they are omitted for brevity.

- It displays both response.title and response.subtitle which can be set in a model. If they are not set, it adopts the application name as title

- It includes the web2py_ajax.html file in the header which generated all the link and script import statements.

- It uses a modified version of Twitter Bootstrap for flexible layouts which works on mobile devices and re-arranges columns to fit small screens.

- It uses "analytics.js" to connect to Google Analytics.

- The {{=auth.navbar(...)}} displays a welcome to the current user and links to the auth functions like login, logout, register, change password, etc. depending on context. It is a helper factory and its output can be manipulated as any other helper. It is placed in a {{try:}}...{{except:pass}} in case auth is undefined.

- The `{{=MENU(response.menu)}}` displays the menu structure as `<ul>...</ul>`.

- `{{include}}` is replaced by the content of the extending view when the page is rendered.

- By default it uses a conditional three column (the left and right sidebars can be turned off by the extending views)

- It uses the following classes: header, main, footer

- It contains the following blocks: statusbar, left_sidebar, center, right_sidebar, footer.

In viewsm, you can turn on and customize sidebars as follows:

```
1 {{left_sidebar_enable=True}}
2 {{extend 'layout.html'}}
3
4 This text goes in center
5
6 {{block left_sidebar}}
7 This text goes in sidebar
8 {{end}}
```

5.5.2 Customizing the default layout

Customizing the default layout without editing is easy because the welcome application is based on Twitter Bootstrap which is well documented and supports themes. In web2py four static files which are relevant to style:

- "css/web2py.css" contains web2py specific styles

- "css/bootstrap.min.css" contains the Twitter Bootstrap CSS style [65]

- "css/web2py_bootstrap.css" contains with overrides some Bootstrap styles to conform to web2py needs.

- "js/bootstrap.min.js" which includes the libraries for menu effects, modals, panels.

To change colors and background images, try append the following code to layout.html header:

```
1 <style>
2 body { background: url('images/background.png') repeat-x #3A3A3A; }
```

```
3  a { color: #349C01; }
4  .header h1 { color: #349C01; }
5  .header h2 { color: white; font-style: italic; font-size: 14px;}
6  .statusbar { background: #333333; border-bottom: 5px #349C01 solid; }
7  .statusbar a { color: white; }
8  .footer { border-top: 5px #349C01 solid; }
9  </style>
```

Of course you can also completely replace the "layout.html" and "web2py.css" files with your own.

5.5.3 Mobile development

The default layout.html is designed to be friendly to mobile devices but that is not enough. One may need to use different views when a page is visited by a mobile device.

To make developing for desktop and mobile devices easier, web2py includes the @mobilize decorator. This decorator is applied to actions that should have a normal view and a mobile view. This is demonstrated here:

```
1  from gluon.contrib.user_agent_parser import mobilize
2  @mobilize
3  def index():
4      return dict()
```

Notice that the decorator must be imported before using it in a controller. When the "index" function is called from a regular browser (desktop computer), web2py will render the returned dictionary using the view "[controller]/index.html". However, when it is called by a mobile device, the dictionary will be rendered by "[controller]/index.mobile.html". Notice that mobile views have the "mobile.html" extension.

Alternatively you can apply the following logic to make all views mobile friendly:

```
1  if request.user_agent().is_mobile:
2      response.view.replace('.html','.mobile.html')
```

The task of creating the "*.mobile.html" views is left to the developer but we strongly suggest using the "jQuery Mobile" plugin which makes the task very easy.

5.6 Functions in views

Consider this "layout.html":

```
1  <html>
2    <body>
3      {{include}}
4      <div class="sidebar">
5        {{if 'mysidebar' in globals():}}{{mysidebar()}}{{else:}}
6          my default sidebar
7        {{pass}}
8      </div>
9    </body>
10 </html>
```

and this extending view

```
1  {{def mysidebar():}}
2  my new sidebar!!!
3  {{return}}
4  {{extend 'layout.html'}}
5  Hello World!!!
```

Notice the function is defined before the `{{extend...}}` statement – this results in the function being created before the "layout.html" code is executed, so the function can be called anywhere within "layout.html", even before the `{{include}}`. Also notice the function is included in the extended view without the = prefix.

The code generates the following output:

```
1  <html>
2    <body>
3      Hello World!!!
4      <div class="sidebar">
5          my new sidebar!!!
6      </div>
7    </body>
8  </html>
```

Notice that the function is defined in HTML (although it could also contain Python code) so that `response.write` is used to write its content (the function does not return the content). This is why the layout calls the view function using `{{mysidebar()}}` rather than `{{=mysidebar()}}`. Functions defined in this way can take arguments.

5.7   Blocks in views

The main way to make a view more modular is by using {{block...}}s and this mechanism is an alternative to the mechanism discussed in the previous section.

Consider this "layout.html":

```
1  <html>
2    <body>
3      {{include}}
4      <div class="sidebar">
5        {{block mysidebar}}
6          my default sidebar
7        {{end}}
8      </div>
9    </body>
10 </html>
```

and this extending view

```
1  {{extend 'layout.html'}}
2  Hello World!!!
3  {{block mysidebar}}
4  my new sidebar!!!
5  {{end}}
```

It generates the following output:

```
1  <html>
2    <body>
3      Hello World!!!
4      <div class="sidebar">
5          my new sidebar!!!
6      </div>
7    </body>
8  </html>
```

You can have many blocks, and if a block is present in the extended view but not in the extending view, the content of the extended view is used. Also, notice that unlike with functions, it is not necessary to define blocks before the {{extend ...}} – even if defined after the extend, they can be used to make substitutions anywhere in the extended view.

Inside a block, you can use the expression {{super}} to include the content of the parent. For example, if we replace the above extending view with:

```
1  {{extend 'layout.html'}}
```

```
2  Hello World!!!
3  {{block mysidebar}}
4  {{super}}
5  my new sidebar!!!
6  {{end}}
```

we get:

```
1  <html>
2    <body>
3      Hello World!!!
4      <div class="sidebar">
5          my default sidebar
6          my new sidebar!!!
7      </div>
8    </body>
9  </html>
```

6

The database abstraction layer

6.1 Dependencies

web2py comes with a Database Abstraction Layer (DAL), an API that maps Python objects into database objects such as queries, tables, and records. The DAL dynamically generates the SQL in real time using the specified dialect for the database back end, so that you do not have to write SQL code or learn different SQL dialects (the term SQL is used generically), and the application will be portable among different types of databases. A partial list of supported databases is show in the table below. Please check on the web2py web site and mailing list for more recent adapters. Google NoSQL is treated as a particular case in Chapter 13.

The Windows binary distribution works out of the box with SQLite and MySQL. The Mac binary distribution works out of the box with SQLite. To use any other database back-end, run from the source distribution and install the appropriate driver for the required back end.

Once the proper driver is installed, start web2py from source, and it will find the driver. Here is a list of drivers:

database	drivers (source)
SQLite	sqlite3 or pysqlite2 or zxJDBC [66] (on Jython)
PostgreSQL	psycopg2 [67] or pg8000 [68] or zxJDBC [66] (on Jython)
MySQL	pymysql [69] or MySQLdb [70]
Oracle	cx_Oracle [71]
MSSQL	pyodbc [72]
FireBird	kinterbasdb [73] or fdb or pyodbc
DB2	pyodbc [72]
Informix	informixdb [74]
Ingres	ingresdbi [75]
Cubrid	cubriddb [76] [76]
Sybase	Sybase [77]
Teradata	pyodbc [78]
SAPDB	sapdb [79]
MongoDB	pymongo [80]
IMAP	imaplib [81]

sqlite3, pymysql, pg8000, and imaplib ship with web2py. Support of MongoDB is experimental. The IMAP option allows to use DAL to access IMAP. web2py defines the following classes that make up the DAL:

The **DAL** object represents a database connection. For example:

```
db = DAL('sqlite://storage.db')
```

Table represents a database table. You do not directly instantiate Table; instead, DAL.define_table instantiates it.

```
db.define_table('mytable', Field('myfield'))
```

The most important methods of a Table are: .insert, .truncate, .drop, and .import_from_csv_file.

Field represents a database field. It can be instantiated and passed as an argument to DAL.define_table.

DAL Rows is the object returned by a database select. It can be thought of as a list of Row rows:

```
rows = db(db.mytable.myfield!=None).select()
```

Row contains field values.

```
1 for row in rows:
2     print row.myfield
```

Query is an object that represents a SQL "where" clause:

```
1 myquery = (db.mytable.myfield != None) | (db.mytable.myfield > 'A')
```

Set is an object that represents a set of records. Its most important methods are count, select, update, and delete. For example:

```
1 myset = db(myquery)
2 rows = myset.select()
3 myset.update(myfield='somevalue')
4 myset.delete()
```

Expression is something like an orderby or groupby expression. The Field class is derived from the Expression. Here is an example.

```
1 myorder = db.mytable.myfield.upper() | db.mytable.id
2 db().select(db.table.ALL, orderby=myorder)
```

6.2   Connection strings

A connection with the database is established by creating an instance of the DAL object:

```
1 >>> db = DAL('sqlite://storage.db', pool_size=0)
```

db is not a keyword; it is a local variable that stores the connection object DAL. You are free to give it a different name. The constructor of DAL requires a single argument, the connection string. The connection string is the only web2py code that depends on a specific back-end database. Here are examples of connection strings for specific types of supported back-end databases (in all cases, we assume the database is running from localhost on its default port and is named "test"):

SQLite	`sqlite://storage.db`
MySQL	`mysql://username:password@localhost/test`
PostgreSQL	`postgres://username:password@localhost/test`
MSSQL	`mssql://username:password@localhost/test`
FireBird	`firebird://username:password@localhost/test`
Oracle	`oracle://username/password@test`
DB2	`db2://username:password@test`
Ingres	`ingres://username:password@localhost/test`
Sybase	`sybase://username:password@localhost/test`
Informix	`informix://username:password@test`
Teradata	`teradata://DSN=dsn;UID=user;PWD=pass;DATABASE=name`
Cubrid	`cubrid://username:password@localhost/test`
SAPDB	`sapdb://username:password@localhost/test`
IMAP	`imap://user:password@server:port`
MongoDB	`mongodb://username:password@localhost/test`
Google/SQL	`google:sql`
Google/NoSQL	`google:datastore`

Notice that in SQLite the database consists of a single file. If it does not exist, it is created. This file is locked every time it is accessed. In the case of MySQL, PostgreSQL, MSSQL, FireBird, Oracle, DB2, Ingres and Informix the database "test" must be created outside web2py. Once the connection is established, web2py will create, alter, and drop tables appropriately.

It is also possible to set the connection string to None. In this case DAL will not connect to any back-end database, but the API can still be accessed for testing. Examples of this will be discussed in Chapter 7.

Some times you may need to generate SQL as if you had a connection but without actually connecting to the database. This can be done with

```
db = DAL('...', do_connect=False)
```

In this case you will be able to call _select, _insert, _update, and _delete to generate SQL but not call select, insert, update, and delete. In most of the cases you can use do_connect=False even without having the required database drivers.

Notice that by default web2py uses utf8 character encoding for databases. If you work with existing databases that behave differently, you have to change it with the optional parameter db_codec like

```
1 db = DAL('...', db_codec='latin1')
```

otherwise you'll get UnicodeDecodeErrors tickets.

6.2.1 Connection pooling

The second argument of the DAL constructor is the pool_size; it defaults to zero.

As it is rather slow to establish a new database connection for each request, web2py implements a mechanism for connection pooling. Once a connection is established and the page has been served and the transaction completed, the connection is not closed but goes into a pool. When the next http request arrives, web2py tries to recycle a connection from the pool and use that for the new transaction. If there are no available connections in the pool, a new connection is established.

When web2py starts, the pool is always empty. The pool grows up to the minimum between the value of pool_size and the max number of concurrent requests. This means that if pool_size=10 but our server never receives more than 5 concurrent requests, then the actual pool size will only grow to 5. If pool_size=0 then connection pooling is not used.

Connections in the pools are shared sequentially among threads, in the sense that they may be used by two different but not simultaneous threads. There is only one pool for each web2py process.

The pool_size parameter is ignored by SQLite and Google App Engine. Connection pooling is ignored for SQLite, since it would not yield any benefit.

6.2.2   Connection failures

If web2py fails to connect to the database it waits 1 seconds and tries again up to 5 times before declaring a failure. In case of connection pooling it is possible that a pooled connection that stays open but unused for some time is closed by the database end. Thanks to the retry feature web2py tries to re-establish these dropped connections.

6.2.3   Replicated databases

The first argument of DAL(...) can be a list of URIs. In this case web2py tries to connect to each of them. The main purpose for this is to deal with multiple database servers and distribute the workload among them). Here is a typical use case:

```
db = DAL(['mysql://...1','mysql://...2','mysql://...3'])
```

In this case the DAL tries to connect to the first and, on failure, it will try the second and the third. This can also be used to distribute load in a database master-slave configuration. We will talk more about this in Chapter 13 in the context of scalability.

6.3   Reserved keywords

check_reserved is yet another argument that can be passed to the DAL constructor. It tells it to check table names and column names against reserved SQL keywords in target back-end databases.

This argument is check_reserved and it defaults to None.

This is a list of strings that contain the database back-end adapter names.

The adapter name is the same as used in the DAL connection string. So if you want to check against PostgreSQL and MSSQL then your connection string would look as follows:

```
db = DAL('sqlite://storage.db',
    check_reserved=['postgres', 'mssql'])
```

The DAL will scan the keywords in the same order as of the list.

There are two extra options "all" and "common". If you specify all, it will check against all known SQL keywords. If you specify common, it will only check against common SQL keywords such as SELECT, INSERT, UPDATE, etc.

For supported back-ends you may also specify if you would like to check against the non-reserved SQL keywords as well. In this case you would append _nonreserved to the name. For example:

```
check_reserved=['postgres', 'postgres_nonreserved']
```

The following database backends support reserved words checking.

PostgreSQL	postgres(_nonreserved)
MySQL	mysql
FireBird	firebird(_nonreserved)
MSSQL	mssql
Oracle	oracle

6.4   DAL, Table, Field

You can experiment with the DAL API using the web2py shell.

Start by creating a connection. For the sake of example, you can use SQLite. Nothing in this discussion changes when you change the back-end engine.

```
>>> db = DAL('sqlite://storage.db')
```

The database is now connected and the connection is stored in the global variable db.

At any time you can retrieve the connection string.

```
>>> print db._uri
sqlite://storage.db
```

and the database name

```
>>> print db._dbname
sqlite
```

The connection string is called a _uri because it is an instance of a Uniform Resource Identifier.

The DAL allows multiple connections with the same database or with different databases, even databases of different types. For now, we will assume the presence of a single database since this is the most common situation.

The most important method of a DAL is define_table:

```
>>> db.define_table('person', Field('name'))
```

It defines, stores and returns a Table object called "person" containing a field (column) "name". This object can also be accessed via db.person, so you do not need to catch the return value.

Do not declare a field called "id", because one is created by web2py anyway. Every table has a field called "id" by default. It is an auto-increment integer field (starting at 1) used for cross-reference and for making every record unique, so "id" is a primary key. (Note: the id's starting at 1 is back-end specific. For example, this does not apply to the Google App Engine NoSQL.)

Optionally you can define a field of type='id' and web2py will use this field as auto-increment id field. This is not recommended except when accessing legacy database tables. With some limitation, you can also use different primary keys and this is discussed in the section on "Legacy databases and keyed tables".

Tables can be defined only once but you can force web2py to redefine an existing table:

```
db.define_table('person', Field('name'))
db.define_table('person', Field('name'), redefine=True)
```

The redefinition may trigger a migration if field content is different.

> Because usually in web2py models are executed before controllers, it is possible that some table are defined even if not needed. It is therefore necessary to speed up the code by making table definitions lazy. This is done by setting the DAL(...,lazy_tables=True) attributes. Tables will be actually created only when accessed.

6.5   Record representation

It is optional but recommended to specify a format representation for records:

```
>>> db.define_table('person', Field('name'), format='%(name)s')
```

or

```
>>> db.define_table('person', Field('name'), format='%(name)s %(id)s')
```

or even more complex ones using a function:

```
>>> db.define_table('person', Field('name'),
        format=lambda r: r.name or 'anonymous')
```

The format attribute will be used for two purposes:

- To represent referenced records in select/option drop-downs.

- To set the db.othertable.person.represent attribute for all fields referencing this table. This means that SQLTABLE will not show references by id but will use the format preferred representation instead.

These are the default values of a Field constructor:

```
Field(name, 'string', length=None, default=None,
      required=False, requires='<default>',
      ondelete='CASCADE', notnull=False, unique=False,
      uploadfield=True, widget=None, label=None, comment=None,
      writable=True, readable=True, update=None, authorize=None,
      autodelete=False, represent=None, compute=None,
      uploadfolder=os.path.join(request.folder,'uploads'),
      uploadseparate=None,uploadfs=None)
```

Not all of them are relevant for every field. "length" is relevant only for fields of type "string". "uploadfield" and "authorize" are relevant only for fields of type "upload". "ondelete" is relevant only for fields of type "reference" and "upload".

- length sets the maximum length of a "string", "password" or "upload" field. If length is not specified a default value is used but the default value is not guaranteed to be backward compatible. *To avoid unwanted migrations on upgrades, we recommend that you always specify the length for string, password and upload fields.*

- default sets the default value for the field. The default value is used when performing an insert if a value is not explicitly specified. It is also used to pre-populate forms built from the table using SQLFORM. Note, rather than being a fixed value, the default can instead be a function (including a lambda function) that returns a value of the appropriate type for the field. In that case, the function is called once for each record inserted, even when multiple records are inserted in a single transaction.

- required tells the DAL that no insert should be allowed on this table if a value for this field is not explicitly specified.

- requires is a validator or a list of validators. This is not used by the DAL, but it is used by SQLFORM. The default validators for the given types are shown in the following table:

field type	default field validators
string	IS_LENGTH(length) default length is 512
text	IS_LENGTH(65536)
blob	None
boolean	None
integer	IS_INT_IN_RANGE(-1e100, 1e100)
double	IS_FLOAT_IN_RANGE(-1e100, 1e100)
decimal(n,m)	IS_DECIMAL_IN_RANGE(-1e100, 1e100)
date	IS_DATE()
time	IS_TIME()
datetime	IS_DATETIME()
password	None
upload	None
reference <table>	IS_IN_DB(db,table.field,format)
list:string	None
list:integer	None
list:reference <table>	IS_IN_DB(db,table.field,format,multiple=True)
json	IS_JSON()
bigint	None
big-id	None
big-reference	None

Decimal requires and returns values as Decimal objects, as defined in the Python decimal module. SQLite does not handle the decimal type so internally we treat it as a double. The (n,m) are the number of digits in total and the number of digits after the decimal point respectively.

The big-id and, big-reference are only supported by some of the database engines and are experimental. They are not normally used as field types unless for legacy tables, however, the DAL constructor has a bigint_id argument that when set to True makes the id fields and reference fields big-id and big-reference respectively.

The list:<type> fields are special because they are designed to take advantage of certain denormalization features on NoSQL (in the case of Google App Engine NoSQL, the field types ListProperty and StringListProperty) and back-port them all the other supported relational databases. On relational databases lists are stored as a text field. The items are separated by a | and each | in string item is escaped as a ||. They are discussed in their own section.

The json field type is pretty much explanatory. It can store any json serializable object. It is designed to work specifically for MongoDB and backported to the other database adapters for portability.

> Notice that requires=... is enforced at the level of forms, required=True is enforced at the level of the DAL (insert), while notnull, unique and ondelete are enforced at the level of the database. While they sometimes may seem redundant, it is important to maintain the distinction when programming with the DAL.

- ondelete translates into the "ON DELETE" SQL statement. By default it is set to "CASCADE". This tells the database that when it deletes a record, it should also delete all records that refer to it. To disable this feature, set ondelete to "NO ACTION" or "SET NULL".

- notnull=True translates into the "NOT NULL" SQL statement. It prevents the database from inserting null values for the field.

- unique=True translates into the "UNIQUE" SQL statement and it makes sure that values of this field are unique within the table. It is enforced at the database level.

- `uploadfield` applies only to fields of type "upload". A field of type "upload" stores the name of a file saved somewhere else, by default on the filesystem under the application "uploads/" folder. If `uploadfield` is set, then the file is stored in a blob field within the same table and the value of `uploadfield` is the name of the blob field. This will be discussed in more detail later in the context of SQLFORM.

- `uploadfolder` defaults to the application's "uploads/" folder. If set to a different path, files will uploaded to a different folder. For example,

```
Field(...,uploadfolder=os.path.join(request.folder,'static/temp'))
```

will upload files to the "web2py/applications/myapp/static/temp" folder.

- `uploadseparate` if set to True will upload files under different subfolders of the *uploadfolder* folder. This is optimized to avoid too many files under the same folder/subfolder. ATTENTION: You cannot change the value of `uploadseparate` from True to False without breaking links to existing uploads. web2py either uses the separate subfolders or it does not. Changing the behavior after files have been uploaded will prevent web2py from being able to retrieve those files. If this happens it is possible to move files and fix the problem but this is not described here.

- `uploadfs` allows you specify a different file system where to upload files, including an Amazon S3 storage or a remote SFTP storage. This option requires PyFileSystem installed. `uploadfs` must point to `PyFileSystem`. `uploadfs`

- `widget` must be one of the available widget objects, including custom widgets, for example: `SQLFORM.widgets.string.widget`. A list of available widgets will be discussed later. Each field type has a default widget.

- `label` is a string (or a helper or something that can be serialized to a string) that contains the label to be used for this field in auto-generated forms.

- `comment` is a string (or a helper or something that can be serialized to a string) that contains a comment associated with this field, and will be displayed to the right of the input field in the autogenerated forms.

- `writable` declares whether a field is writable in forms.

- `readable` declares whether a field is readable in forms. If a field is neither readable nor writable, it will not be displayed in create and update forms.

- `update` contains the default value for this field when the record is updated.

- `compute` is an optional function. If a record is inserted or updated, the compute function will be executed and the field will be populated with the function result. The record is passed to the compute function as a `dict`, and the dict will not include the current value of that, or any other compute field.

- `authorize` can be used to require access control on the corresponding field, for "upload" fields only. It will be discussed more in detail in the context of Authentication and Authorization.

- `autodelete` determines if the corresponding uploaded file should be deleted when the record referencing the file is deleted. For "upload" fields only.

- `represent` can be None or can point to a function that takes a field value and returns an alternate representation for the field value. Examples:

```
1 db.mytable.name.represent = lambda name,row: name.capitalize()
2 db.mytable.other_id.represent = lambda id,row: row.myfield
3 db.mytable.some_uploadfield.represent = lambda value,row: \
4    A('get it', _href=URL('download', args=value))
```

"blob" fields are also special. By default, binary data is encoded in base64 before being stored into the actual database field, and it is decoded when extracted. This has the negative effect of using 25% more storage space than necessary in blob fields, but has two advantages. On average it reduces the amount of data communicated between web2py and the database server, and it makes the communication independent of back-end-specific escaping conventions.

Most attributes of fields and tables can be modified after they are defined:

```
1 db.define_table('person',Field('name',default=''),format='%(name)s')
2 db.person._format = '%(name)s/%(id)s'
3 db.person.name.default = 'anonymous'
```

(notice that attributes of tables are usually prefixed by an underscore to avoid conflict with possible field names).

You can list the tables that have been defined for a given database connection:

```
>>> print db.tables
['person']
```

You can also list the fields that have been defined for a given table:

```
>>> print db.person.fields
['id', 'name']
```

You can query for the type of a table:

```
>>> print type(db.person)
<class 'gluon.sql.Table'>
```

and you can access a table from the DAL connection using:

```
>>> print type(db['person'])
<class 'gluon.sql.Table'>
```

Similarly you can access fields from their name in multiple equivalent ways:

```
>>> print type(db.person.name)
<class 'gluon.sql.Field'>
>>> print type(db.person['name'])
<class 'gluon.sql.Field'>
>>> print type(db['person']['name'])
<class 'gluon.sql.Field'>
```

Given a field, you can access the attributes set in its definition:

```
>>> print db.person.name.type
string
>>> print db.person.name.unique
False
>>> print db.person.name.notnull
False
>>> print db.person.name.length
32
```

including its parent table, tablename, and parent connection:

```
>>> db.person.name._table == db.person
True
>>> db.person.name._tablename == 'person'
True
>>> db.person.name._db == db
True
```

A field also has methods. Some of them are used to build queries and we will see them later. A special method of the field object is validate and it calls the validators for the field.

```
print db.person.name.validate('John')
```

which returns a tuple (value, error). error is None if the input passes validation.

6.6 Migrations

define_table checks whether or not the corresponding table exists. If it does not, it generates the SQL to create it and executes the SQL. If the table does exist but differs from the one being defined, it generates the SQL to alter the table and executes it. If a field has changed type but not name, it will try to convert the data (If you do not want this, you need to redefine the table twice, the first time, letting web2py drop the field by removing it, and the second time adding the newly defined field so that web2py can create it.). If the table exists and matches the current definition, it will leave it alone. In all cases it will create the db.person object that represents the table.

We refer to this behavior as a "migration". web2py logs all migrations and migration attempts in the file "databases/sql.log".

The first argument of define_table is always the table name. The other unnamed arguments are the fields (Field). The function also takes an optional last argument called "migrate" which must be referred to explicitly by name as in:

```
>>> db.define_table('person', Field('name'), migrate='person.table')
```

The value of migrate is the filename (in the "databases" folder for the application) where web2py stores internal migration information for this table. These files are very important and should never be removed while the corresponding tables exist. In cases where a table has been dropped and the corresponding file still exist, it can be removed manually. By default, migrate is set to True. This causes web2py to generate the filename from a hash of the connection string. If migrate is set to False, the migration is not performed, and web2py assumes that the table exists in the datastore and it contains (at least) the fields listed in define_table. The best practice is to give an explicit name to the migrate table.

There may not be two tables in the same application with the same migrate filename.

The DAL class also takes a "migrate" argument, which determines the default value of migrate for calls to define_table. For example,

```
>>> db = DAL('sqlite://storage.db', migrate=False)
```

will set the default value of migrate to False whenever db.define_table is called without a migrate argument.

> Notice that web2py only migrates new columns, removed columns, and changes in column type (except in sqlite). web2py does not migrate changes in attributes such as changes in the values of default, unique, notnull, and ondelete.

Migrations can be disabled for all tables at once:

```
db = DAL(...,migrate_enabled=False)
```

This is the recommended behavior when two apps share the same database. Only one of the two apps should perform migrations, the other should disabled them.

6.7   Fixing broken migrations

There are two common problems with migrations and there are ways to recover from them.

One problem is specific with SQLite. SQLite does not enforce column types and cannot drop columns. This means that if you have a column of type string and you remove it, it is not really removed. If you add the column again with a different type (for example datetime) you end up with a datetime column that contains strings (junk for practical purposes). web2py does not complain about this because it does not know what is in the database, until it tries to retrieve records and fails.

If web2py returns an error in the gluon.sql.parse function when selecting records, this is the problem: corrupted data in a column because of the above issue.

The solution consists in updating all records of the table and updating the values in the column in question with None.

The other problem is more generic but typical with MySQL. MySQL does not allow more than one ALTER TABLE in a transaction. This means that web2py must break complex transactions into smaller ones (one ALTER TABLE at the time) and commit one piece at the time. It is therefore possible that part of a complex transaction gets committed and one part fails, leaving web2py in a corrupted state. Why would part of a transaction fail? Because, for example, it involves altering a table and converting a string column into a datetime column, web2py tries to convert the data, but the data cannot be converted. What happens to web2py? It gets confused about what exactly is the table structure actually stored in the database.

The solution consists of disabling migrations for all tables and enabling fake migrations:

```
1 db.define_table(....,migrate=False,fake_migrate=True)
```

This will rebuild web2py metadata about the table according to the table definition. Try multiple table definitions to see which one works (the one before the failed migration and the one after the failed migration). Once successful remove the fake_migrate=True attribute.

Before attempting to fix migration problems it is prudent to make a copy of "applications/yourapp/databases/*.table" files.

Migration problems can also be fixed for all tables at once:

```
1 db = DAL(...,fake_migrate_all=True)
```

This also fails if the model describes tables that do not exist in the database, but it can help narrowing down the problem.

6.8 insert

Given a table, you can insert records

```
1 >>> db.person.insert(name="Alex")
2 1
3 >>> db.person.insert(name="Bob")
4 2
```

Insert returns the unique "id" value of each record inserted.

You can truncate the table, i.e., delete all records and reset the counter of the id.

```
>>> db.person.truncate()
```

Now, if you insert a record again, the counter starts again at 1 (this is back-end specific and does not apply to Google NoSQL):

```
>>> db.person.insert(name="Alex")
1
```

Notice you can pass parameters to truncate, for example you can tell SQLITE to restart the id counter.

```
db.person.truncate('RESTART IDENTITY CASCADE')
```

The argument is in raw SQL and therefore engine specific.

web2py also provides a bulk_insert method

```
>>> db.person.bulk_insert([{'name':'Alex'}, {'name':'John'}, {'name':'Tim'}])
[3,4,5]
```

It takes a list of dictionaries of fields to be inserted and performs multiple inserts at once. It returns the IDs of the inserted records. On the supported relational databases there is no advantage in using this function as opposed to looping and performing individual inserts but on Google App Engine NoSQL, there is a major speed advantage.

6.9 commit **and** rollback

No create, drop, insert, truncate, delete, or update operation is actually committed until you issue the commit command

```
>>> db.commit()
```

To check it let's insert a new record:

```
>>> db.person.insert(name="Bob")
2
```

and roll back, i.e., ignore all operations since the last commit:

```
>>> db.rollback()
```

If you now insert again, the counter will again be set to 2, since the previous insert was rolled back.

```
1 >>> db.person.insert(name="Bob")
2 2
```

Code in models, views and controllers is enclosed in web2py code that looks like this:

```
1 try:
2     execute models, controller function and view
3 except:
4     rollback all connections
5     log the traceback
6     send a ticket to the visitor
7 else:
8     commit all connections
9     save cookies, sessions and return the page
```

There is no need to ever call commit or rollback explicitly in web2py unless one needs more granular control.

6.10   Raw SQL

6.10.1   Timing queries

All queries are automatically timed by web2py. The variable db._timings is a list of tuples. Each tuple contains the raw SQL query as passed to the database driver and the time it took to execute in seconds. This variable can be displayed in views using the toolbar:

```
1 {{=response.toolbar()}}
```

6.10.2   executesql

The DAL allows you to explicitly issue SQL statements.

```
1 >>> print db.executesql('SELECT * FROM person;')
2 [(1, u'Massimo'), (2, u'Massimo')]
```

In this case, the return values are not parsed or transformed by the DAL, and the format depends on the specific database driver. This usage with selects is normally not needed, but it is more common with indexes. executesql takes four optional arguments: placeholders, as_dict, fields and colnames. placeholders is an optional sequence of values to be substituted in or, if supported by the DB driver, a dictionary with keys matching named placeholders in your SQL.

If as_dict is set to True, and the results cursor returned by the DB driver will be converted to a sequence of dictionaries keyed with the db field names. Results returned with as_dict = True are the same as those returned when applying **.as_list()** to a normal select.

```
[{field1: value1, field2: value2}, {field1: value1b, field2: value2b}]
```

The fields argument is a list of DAL Field objects that match the fields returned from the DB. The Field objects should be part of one or more Table objects defined on the DAL object. The fields list can include one or more DAL Table objects in addition to or instead of including Field objects, or it can be just a single table (not in a list). In that case, the Field objects will be extracted from the table(s).

Instead of specifying the fields argument, the colnames argument can be specified as a list of field names in tablename.fieldname format. Again, these should represent tables and fields defined on the DAL object.

It is also possible to specify both fields and the associated colnames. In that case, fields can also include DAL Expression objects in addition to Field objects. For Field objects in "fields", the associated colnames must still be in tablename.fieldname format. For Expression objects in fields, the associated colnames can be any arbitrary labels.

Notice, the DAL Table objects referred to by fields or colnames can be dummy tables and do not have to represent any real tables in the database. Also, note that the fields and colnames must be in the same order as the fields in the results cursor returned from the DB.

6.10.3 _lastsql

Whether SQL was executed manually using executesql or was SQL generated by the DAL, you can always find the SQL code in db._lastsql. This is useful for debugging purposes:

```
>>> rows = db().select(db.person.ALL)
>>> print db._lastsql
```

```
3 SELECT person.id, person.name FROM person;
```

> web2py never generates queries using the "*" operator. web2py is always explicit when selecting fields.

6.11 drop

Finally, you can drop tables and all data will be lost:

```
1 >>> db.person.drop()
```

6.12 Indexes

Currently the DAL API does not provide a command to create indexes on tables, but this can be done using the `executesql` command. This is because the existence of indexes can make migrations complex, and it is better to deal with them explicitly. Indexes may be needed for those fields that are used in recurrent queries.

Here is an example of how to create an index using SQL in SQLite:

```
1 >>> db = DAL('sqlite://storage.db')
2 >>> db.define_table('person', Field('name'))
3 >>> db.executesql('CREATE INDEX IF NOT EXISTS myidx ON person (name);')
```

Other database dialects have very similar syntaxes but may not support the optional "IF NOT EXISTS" directive.

6.13 Legacy databases and keyed tables

web2py can connect to legacy databases under some conditions.

The easiest way is when these conditions are met:

- Each table must have a unique auto-increment integer field called "id"
- Records must be referenced exclusively using the "id" field.

When accessing an existing table, i.e., a table not created by web2py in the current application, always set `migrate=False`.

If the legacy table has an auto-increment integer field but it is not called "id", web2py can still access it but the table definition must contain explicitly as Field('....','id') where... is the name of the auto-increment integer field.

Finally if the legacy table uses a primary key that is not an auto-increment id field it is possible to use a "keyed table", for example:

```
db.define_table('account',
    Field('accnum','integer'),
    Field('acctype'),
    Field('accdesc'),
    primarykey=['accnum','acctype'],
    migrate=False)
```

- primarykey is a list of the field names that make up the primary key.

- All primarykey fields have a NOT NULL set even if not specified.

- Keyed tables can only reference other keyed tables.

- Referencing fields must use the reference tablename.fieldname format.

- The update_record function is not available for Rows of keyed tables.

Currently keyed tables are only supported for DB2, MS-SQL, Ingres and Informix, but others engines will be added.

At the time of writing, we cannot guarantee that the primarykey attribute works with every existing legacy table and every supported database backend. For simplicity, we recommend, if possible, creating a database view that has an auto-increment id field.

6.14   Distributed transaction

At the time of writing this feature is only supported by PostgreSQL, MySQL and Firebird, since they expose API for two-phase commits.

Assuming you have two (or more) connections to distinct PostgreSQL databases, for example:

```
db_a = DAL('postgres://...')
db_b = DAL('postgres://...')
```

In your models or controllers, you can commit them concurrently with:

```
1 DAL.distributed_transaction_commit(db_a, db_b)
```

On failure, this function rolls back and raises an `Exception`.

In controllers, when one action returns, if you have two distinct connections and you do not call the above function, web2py commits them separately. This means there is a possibility that one of the commits succeeds and one fails. The distributed transaction prevents this from happening.

6.15   More on uploads

Consider the following model:

```
1 >>> db.define_table('myfile',
2     Field('image', 'upload', default='path/'))
```

In the case of an 'upload' field, the default value can optionally be set to a path (an absolute path or a path relative to the current app folder) and the default image will be set to a copy of the file at the path. A new copy is made for each new record that does not specify an image.

Normally an insert is handled automatically via a SQLFORM or a crud form (which is a SQLFORM) but occasionally you already have the file on the filesystem and want to upload it programmatically. This can be done in this way:

```
1 >>> stream = open(filename, 'rb')
2 >>> db.myfile.insert(image=db.myfile.image.store(stream, filename))
```

It is also possible to insert a file in a simpler way and have the insert method call store automatically:

```
1 >>> stream = open(filename, 'rb')
2 >>> db.myfile.insert(image=stream)
```

In this case the filename is obtained from the stream object if available.

The `store` method of the upload field object takes a file stream and a filename. It uses the filename to determine the extension (type) of the file, creates a new temp name for the file (according to web2py upload mechanism) and loads the file content in this new temp file (under the uploads folder unless specified otherwise). It returns the new temp name, which is then stored in the `image` field of the `db.myfile` table.

Note, if the file is to be stored in an associated blob field rather than the file system, the store() method will not insert the file in the blob field (because store() is called before the insert), so the file must be explicitly inserted into the blob field:

```
>>> db.define_table('myfile',
    Field('image', 'upload', uploadfield='image_file'),
    Field('image_file', 'blob'))
>>> stream = open(filename, 'rb')
>>> db.myfile.insert(image=db.myfile.image.store(stream, filename),
    image_file=stream.read())
```

The opposite of .store is .retrieve:

```
>>> row = db(db.myfile).select().first()
>>> (filename, stream) = db.myfile.image.retrieve(row.image)
>>> import shutil
>>> shutil.copyfileobj(stream,open(filename,'wb'))
```

6.16 Query, Set, Rows

Let's consider again the table defined (and dropped) previously and insert three records:

```
>>> db.define_table('person', Field('name'))
>>> db.person.insert(name="Alex")
1
>>> db.person.insert(name="Bob")
2
>>> db.person.insert(name="Carl")
3
```

You can store the table in a variable. For example, with variable person, you could do:

```
>>> person = db.person
```

You can also store a field in a variable such as name. For example, you could also do:

```
>>> name = person.name
```

You can even build a query (using operators like ==, !=, <, >, <=, >=, like, belongs) and store the query in a variable q such as in:

```
>>> q = name=='Alex'
```

When you call db with a query, you define a set of records. You can store it in a variable s and write:

```
>>> s = db(q)
```

Notice that no database query has been performed so far. DAL + Query simply define a set of records in this db that match the query. web2py determines from the query which table (or tables) are involved and, in fact, there is no need to specify that.

6.17   select

Given a Set, s, you can fetch the records with the command select:

```
>>> rows = s.select()
```

It returns an iterable object of class gluon.sql.Rows whose elements are Row objects. gluon.sql.Row objects act like dictionaries, but their elements can also be accessed as attributes, like gluon.storage.Storage.The former differ from the latter because its values are read-only.

The Rows object allows looping over the result of the select and printing the selected field values for each row:

```
>>> for row in rows:
        print row.id, row.name
1 Alex
```

You can do all the steps in one statement:

```
>>> for row in db(db.person.name=='Alex').select():
        print row.name
Alex
```

The select command can take arguments. All unnamed arguments are interpreted as the names of the fields that you want to fetch. For example, you can be explicit on fetching field "id" and field "name":

```
>>> for row in db().select(db.person.id, db.person.name):
        print row.name
Alex
Bob
Carl
```

The table attribute ALL allows you to specify all fields:

```
1 >>> for row in db().select(db.person.ALL):
2        print row.name
3 Alex
4 Bob
5 Carl
```

Notice that there is no query string passed to db. web2py understands that if you want all fields of the table person without additional information then you want all records of the table person.

An equivalent alternative syntax is the following:

```
1 >>> for row in db(db.person.id > 0).select():
2        print row.name
3 Alex
4 Bob
5 Carl
```

and web2py understands that if you ask for all records of the table person (id > 0) without additional information, then you want all the fields of table person.

Given one row

```
1 row = rows[0]
```

you can extract its values using multiple equivalent expressions:

```
1 >>> row.name
2 Alex
3 >>> row['name']
4 Alex
5 >>> row('person.name')
6 Alex
```

The latter syntax is particularly handy when selecting en expression instead of a column. We will show this later.

You can also do

```
1 rows.compact = False
```

to disable the notation

```
1 row[i].name
```

and enable, instead, the less compact notation:

```
1 row[i].person.name
```

Yes this is unusual and rarely needed.

6.17.1   Shortcuts

The DAL supports various code-simplifying shortcuts. In particular:

```
1  myrecord = db.mytable[id]
```

returns the record with the given id if it exists. If the id does not exist, it returns None. The above statement is equivalent to

```
1  myrecord = db(db.mytable.id==id).select().first()
```

You can delete records by id:

```
1  del db.mytable[id]
```

and this is equivalent to

```
1  db(db.mytable.id==id).delete()
```

and deletes the record with the given id, if it exists.

You can insert records:

```
1  db.mytable[0] = dict(myfield='somevalue')
```

It is equivalent to

```
1  db.mytable.insert(myfield='somevalue')
```

and it creates a new record with field values specified by the dictionary on the right hand side.

You can update records:

```
1  db.mytable[id] = dict(myfield='somevalue')
```

which is equivalent to

```
1  db(db.mytable.id==id).update(myfield='somevalue')
```

and it updates an existing record with field values specified by the dictionary on the right hand side.

6.17.2   Fetching a Row

Yet another convenient syntax is the following:

```
1  record = db.mytable(id)
2  record = db.mytable(db.mytable.id==id)
3  record = db.mytable(id,myfield='somevalue')
```

Apparently similar to `db.mytable[id]` the above syntax is more flexible and safer. First of all it checks whether `id` is an int (or `str(id)` is an int) and returns `None` if not (it never raises an exception). It also allows to specify multiple conditions that the record must meet. If they are not met, it also returns `None`.

6.17.3 Recursive `selects`

Consider the previous table person and a new table "thing" referencing a "person":

```
>>> db.define_table('thing',
        Field('name'),
        Field('owner_id','reference person'))
```

and a simple select from this table:

```
>>> things = db(db.thing).select()
```

which is equivalent to

```
>>> things = db(db.thing._id>0).select()
```

where `._id` is a reference to the primary key of the table. Normally `db.thing._id` is the same as `db.thing.id` and we will assume that in most of this book.

For each Row of things it is possible to fetch not just fields from the selected table (thing) but also from linked tables (recursively):

```
>>> for thing in things: print thing.name, thing.owner_id.name
```

Here `thing.owner_id.name` requires one database select for each thing in things and it is therefore inefficient. We suggest using joins whenever possible instead of recursive selects, nevertheless this is convenient and practical when accessing individual records.

You can also do it backwards, by selecting the things referenced by a person:

```
person = db.person(id)
for thing in person.thing.select(orderby=db.thing.name):
    print person.name, 'owns', thing.name
```

In this last expressions `person.thing` is a shortcut for

```
db(db.thing.owner_id==person.id)
```

i.e. the Set of things referenced by the current person. This syntax breaks down if the referencing table has multiple references to the referenced table. In this case one needs to be more explicit and use a full Query.

6.17.4 Serializing Rows in views

Given the following action containing a query

```
def index()
    return dict(rows = db(query).select())
```

The result of a select can be displayed in a view with the following syntax:

```
{{extend 'layout.html'}}
<h1>Records</h1>
{{=rows}}
```

Which is equivalent to:

```
{{extend 'layout.html'}}
<h1>Records</h1>
{{=SQLTABLE(rows)}}
```

SQLTABLE converts the rows into an HTML table with a header containing the column names and one row per record. The rows are marked as alternating class "even" and class "odd". Under the hood, Rows is first converted into a SQLTABLE object (not to be confused with Table) and then serialized. The values extracted from the database are also formatted by the validators associated to the field and then escaped.

Yet it is possible and sometimes convenient to call SQLTABLE explicitly.

The SQLTABLE constructor takes the following optional arguments:

- linkto the URL or an action to be used to link reference fields (default to None)

- upload the URL or the download action to allow downloading of uploaded files (default to None)

- headers a dictionary mapping field names to their labels to be used as headers (default to {}). It can also be an instruction. Currently we support headers='fieldname:capitalize'.

- truncate the number of characters for truncating long values in the table (default is 16)

- columns the list of fieldnames to be shown as columns (in tablename.fieldname format).

Those not listed are not displayed (defaults to all).

- **attributes generic helper attributes to be passed to the most external TABLE object.

Here is an example:

```
{{extend 'layout.html'}}
<h1>Records</h1>
{{=SQLTABLE(rows,
    headers='fieldname:capitalize',
    truncate=100,
    upload=URL('download'))
}}
```

SQLTABLE is useful but there are times when one needs more. SQLFORM.grid is an extension of SQLTABLE that creates a table with search features and pagination, as well as ability to open detailed records, create, edit and delete records. SQLFORM.smartgrid is a further generalization that allows all of the above but also creates buttons to access referencing records.

Here is an example of usage of SQLFORM.grid:

```
def index():
    return dict(grid=SQLFORM.grid(query))
```

and the corresponding view:

```
{{extend 'layout.html'}}
{{=grid}}
```

SQLFORM.grid and SQLFORM.smartgrid should be preferred to SQLTABLE because they are more powerful although higher level and therefore more constraining. They will be explained in more detail in chapter 8.

6.17.5   orderby, groupby, limitby, distinct, having

The select command takes five optional arguments: orderby, groupby, limitby, left and cache. Here we discuss the first three.

You can fetch the records sorted by name:

```
>>> for row in db().select(
        db.person.ALL, orderby=db.person.name):
        print row.name
Alex
Bob
Carl
```

You can fetch the records sorted by name in reverse order (notice the tilde):

```
>>> for row in db().select(
        db.person.ALL, orderby=~db.person.name):
        print row.name
Carl
Bob
Alex
```

You can have the fetched records appear in random order:

```
>>> for row in db().select(
        db.person.ALL, orderby='<random>'):
        print row.name
Carl
Alex
Bob
```

The use of orderby='<random>' is not supported on Google NoSQL.
However, in this situation and likewise in many others where built-ins are insufficient, imports can be used:

```
import random
rows=db(...).select().sort(lambda row: random.random())
```

You can sort the records according to multiple fields by concatenating them with a "|":

```
>>> for row in db().select(
        db.person.ALL, orderby=db.person.name|db.person.id):
        print row.name
Carl
Bob
Alex
```

Using groupby together with orderby, you can group records with the same value for the specified field (this is back-end specific, and is not on the Google NoSQL):

```
>>> for row in db().select(
        db.person.ALL,
        orderby=db.person.name, groupby=db.person.name):
    print row.name
Alex
Bob
Carl
```

You can use `having` in conjunction with `groupby` to group conditionally (only those `having` the condition are grouped.

```
>>> print db(query1).select(db.person.ALL, groupby=db.person.name, having=query2)
```

Notice that query1 filters records to be displayed, query2 filters records to be grouped.

With the argument `distinct=True`, you can specify that you only want to select distinct records. This has the same effect as grouping using all specified fields except that it does not require sorting. When using distinct it is important not to select ALL fields, and in particular not to select the "id" field, else all records will always be distinct.

Here is an example:

```
>>> for row in db().select(db.person.name, distinct=True):
    print row.name
Alex
Bob
Carl
```

Notice that `distinct` can also be an expression for example:

```
>>> for row in db().select(db.person.name,distinct=db.person.name):
    print row.name
Alex
Bob
Carl
```

With limitby=(min, max), you can select a subset of the records from offset=min to but not including offset=max (in this case, the first two starting at zero):

```
>>> for row in db().select(db.person.ALL, limitby=(0, 2)):
    print row.name
Alex
Bob
```

6.17.6 Logical operators

Queries can be combined using the binary AND operator "&":

```
1 >>> rows = db((db.person.name=='Alex') & (db.person.id>3)).select()
2 >>> for row in rows: print row.id, row.name
3 4 Alex
```

and the binary OR operator "|":

```
1 >>> rows = db((db.person.name=='Alex') | (db.person.id>3)).select()
2 >>> for row in rows: print row.id, row.name
3 1 Alex
```

You can negate a query (or sub-query) with the "!=" binary operator:

```
1 >>> rows = db((db.person.name!='Alex') | (db.person.id>3)).select()
2 >>> for row in rows: print row.id, row.name
3 2 Bob
4 3 Carl
```

or by explicit negation with the " " unary operator:

```
1 >>> rows = db((~(db.person.name=='Alex') | (db.person.id>3)).select()
2 >>> for row in rows: print row.id, row.name
3 2 Bob
4 3 Carl
```

> Due to Python restrictions in overloading "and" and "or" operators, these cannot be used in forming queries. The binary operators "&" and "|" must be used instead. Note that these operators (unlike "and" and "or") have higher precedence than comparison operators, so the "extra" parentheses in the above examples are mandatory. Similarly, the unary operator " " has higher precedence than comparison operators, so -negated comparisons must also be parenthesized.

It is also possible to build queries using in-place logical operators:

```
1 >>> query = db.person.name!='Alex'
2 >>> query &= db.person.id>3
3 >>> query |= db.person.name=='John'
```

6.17.7 count, isempty, delete, update

You can count records in a set:

```
1 >>> print db(db.person.id > 0).count()
2 3
```

Notice that `count` takes an optional `distinct` argument which defaults to False, and it works very much like the same argument for `select`. `count` has also a `cache` argument that works very much like the equivalent argument of the `select` method.

Sometimes you may need to check if a table is empty. A more efficient way than counting is using the `isempty` method:

```
>>> print db(db.person.id > 0).isempty()
False
```

or equivalently:

```
>>> print db(db.person).isempty()
False
```

You can delete records in a set:

```
>>> db(db.person.id > 3).delete()
```

And you can update all records in a set by passing named arguments corresponding to the fields that need to be updated:

```
>>> db(db.person.id > 3).update(name='Ken')
```

6.17.8   Expressions

The value assigned an update statement can be an expression. For example consider this model

```
>>> db.define_table('person',
        Field('name'),
        Field('visits', 'integer', default=0))
>>> db(db.person.name == 'Massimo').update(
        visits = db.person.visits + 1)
```

The values used in queries can also be expressions

```
>>> db.define_table('person',
        Field('name'),
        Field('visits', 'integer', default=0),
        Field('clicks', 'integer', default=0))
>>> db(db.person.visits == db.person.clicks + 1).delete()
```

6.17.9   case

An expression can contain a case clause for example:

```
1 >>> db.define_table('person',Field('name'))
2 >>> condition = db.person.name.startswith('M')
3 >>> yes_or_no = condition.case('Yes','No')
4 >>> for row in db().select(db.person.name, yes_or_no):
5 ...     print row.person.name,  row(yes_or_no)
6 Max Yes
7 John No
```

6.17.10 update_record

web2py also allows updating a single record that is already in memory using update_record

```
1 >>> row = db(db.person.id==2).select().first()
2 >>> row.update_record(name='Curt')
```

update_record should not be confused with

```
1 >>> row.update(name='Curt')
```

because for a single row, the method update updates the row object but not the database record, as in the case of update_record.

It is also possible to change the attributes of a row (one at a time) and then call update_record() without arguments to save the changes:

```
1 >>> row = db(db.person.id > 2).select().first()
2 >>> row.name = 'Curt'
3 >>> row.update_record() # saves above change
```

The update_record method is available only if the table's id field is included in the select, and cacheable is not set to True.

6.17.11   Inserting and updating from a dictionary

A common issue consists of needing to insert or update records in a table where the name of the table, the field to be updated, and the value for the field are all stored in variables. For example: tablename, fieldname, and value.

The insert can be done using the following syntax:

```
1 db[tablename].insert(**{fieldname:value})
```

The update of record with given id can be done with:

```
1 db(db[tablename]._id==id).update(**{fieldname:value})
```

Notice we used table._id instead of table.id. In this way the query works even for tables with a field of type "id" which has a name other than "id".

6.17.12   first and last

Given a Rows object containing records:

```
>>> rows = db(query).select()
>>> first_row = rows.first()
>>> last_row = rows.last()
```

are equivalent to

```
>>> first_row = rows[0] if len(rows)>0 else None
>>> last_row = rows[-1] if len(rows)>0 else None
```

6.17.13   as_dict and as_list

A Row object can be serialized into a regular dictionary using the as_dict() method and a Rows object can be serialized into a list of dictionaries using the as_list() method. Here are some examples:

```
>>> rows = db(query).select()
>>> rows_list = rows.as_list()
>>> first_row_dict = rows.first().as_dict()
```

These methods are convenient for passing Rows to generic views and or to store Rows in sessions (since Rows objects themselves cannot be serialized since contain a reference to an open DB connection):

```
>>> rows = db(query).select()
>>> session.rows = rows # not allowed!
>>> session.rows = rows.as_list() # allowed!
```

6.17.14   Combining rows

Row objects can be combined at the Python level. Here we assume:

```
>>> print rows1
person.name
Max
Tim
>>> print rows2
```

```
6 person.name
7 John
8 Tim
```

You can do a union of the records in two set of rows:

```
1 >>> rows3 = rows1 & rows2
2 >>> print rows3
3 name
4 Max
5 Tim
6 John
7 Tim
```

You can do a union of the records removing duplicates:

```
1 >>> rows3 = rows1 | rows2
2 >>> print rows3
3 name
4 Max
5 Tim
6 John
```

6.17.15 find, exclude, sort

Some times you to perform two selects and one contains a subset of a previous select. In this case it is pointless to access the database again. The find, exclude and sort objects allow you to manipulate a Rows objects and generate another one without accessing the database. More specifically:

- find returns a new set of Rows filtered by a condition and leaves the original unchanged.

- exclude returns a new set of Rows filtered by a condition and removes them from the original Rows.

- sort returns a new set of Rows sorted by a condition and leaves the original unchanged.

All these methods take a single argument, a function that acts on each individual row.

Here is an example of usage:

```
1 >>> db.define_table('person',Field('name'))
2 >>> db.person.insert(name='John')
```

```
3  >>> db.person.insert(name='Max')
4  >>> db.person.insert(name='Alex')
5  >>> rows = db(db.person).select()
6  >>> for row in rows.find(lambda row: row.name[0]=='M'):
7          print row.name
8  Max
9  >>> print len(rows)
10 3
11 >>> for row in rows.exclude(lambda row: row.name[0]=='M'):
12         print row.name
13 Max
14 >>> print len(rows)
15 2
16 >>> for row in rows.sort(lambda row: row.name):
17         print row.name
18 Alex
19 John
```

They can be combined:

```
1  >>> rows = db(db.person).select()
2  >>> rows = rows.find(
3          lambda row: 'x' in row.name).sort(
4              lambda row: row.name)
5  >>> for row in rows:
6          print row.name
7  Alex
8  Max
```

Sort takes an optional argument reverse=True with the obvious meaning.

The find method as an optional limitby argument with the same syntax and functionality as the Set select method.

6.18 Other methods

6.18.1 update_or_insert

Some times you need to perform an insert only if there is no record with the same values as those being inserted. This can be done with

```
1  db.define_table('person',Field('name'),Field('birthplace'))
2  db.person.update_or_insert(name='John',birthplace='Chicago')
```

The record will be inserted only of there is no other user called John born in Chicago.

You can specify which values to use as a key to determine if the record exists.
For example:

```
db.person.update_or_insert(db.person.name=='John',
    name='John',birthplace='Chicago')
```

and if there is John his birthplace will be updated else a new record will be
created.

6.18.2   validate_and_insert, validate_and_update

The function

```
ret = db.mytable.validate_and_insert(field='value')
```

works very much like

```
id = db.mytable.insert(field='value')
```

except that it calls the validators for the fields before performing the insert
and bails out if the validation does not pass. If validation does not pass the
errors can be found in ret.error. If it passes, the id of the new record is in
ret.id. Mind that normally validation is done by the form processing logic
so this function is rarely needed.

Similarly

```
ret = db(query).validate_and_update(field='value')
```

works very much the same as

```
num = db(query).update(field='value')
```

except that it calls the validators for the fields before performing the update.
Notice that it only works if query involves a single table. The number of
updated records can be found in res.updated and errors will be ret.errors.

6.18.3   smart_query (experimental)

There are times when you need to parse a query using natural language such
as

```
name contain m and age greater than 18
```

The DAL provides a method to parse this type of queries:

```
1 search = 'name contain m and age greater than 18'
2 rows = db.smart_query([db.person],search).select()
```

The first argument must be a list of tables or fields that should be allowed in the search. It raises a RuntimeError if the search string is invalid. This functionality can be used to build RESTful interfaces (see chapter 10) and it is used internally by the SQLFORM.grid and SQLFORM.smartgrid.

In the smartquery search string, a field can be identified by fieldname only and or by tablename.fieldname. Strings may be delimited by double quotes if they contain spaces.

6.19 Computed fields

DAL fields may have a compute attribute. This must be a function (or lambda) that takes a Row object and returns a value for the field. When a new record is modified, including both insertions and updates, if a value for the field is not provided, web2py tries to compute from the other field values using the compute function. Here is an example:

```
1 >>> db.define_table('item',
2        Field('unit_price','double'),
3        Field('quantity','integer'),
4        Field('total_price',
5            compute=lambda r: r['unit_price']*r['quantity']))
6 >>> r = db.item.insert(unit_price=1.99, quantity=5)
7 >>> print r.total_price
8 9.95
```

Notice that the computed value is stored in the db and it is not computed on retrieval, as in the case of virtual fields, described later. Two typical applications of computed fields are:

- in wiki applications, to store the processed input wiki text as HTML, to avoid re-processing on every request

- for searching, to compute normalized values for a field, to be used for searching.

6.20 Virtual fields

Virtual fields are also computed fields (as in the previous subsection) but they differ from those because they are *virtual* in the sense that they are not stored in the db and they are computed each time records are extracted from the database. They can be used to simplify the user's code without using additional storage but they cannot be used for searching.

6.20.1 New style virtual fields

web2py provides a new and easier way to define virtual fields and lazy virtual fields. This section is marked experimental because they APIs may still change a little from what is described here.

Here we will consider the same example as in the previous subsection. In particular we consider the following model:

```
>>> db.define_table('item',
      Field('unit_price','double'),
      Field('quantity','integer'),
```

One can define a total_price virtual field as

```
>>> db.item.total_price = Field.Virtual(
    lambda row: row.item.unit_price*row.item.quantity)
```

i.e. by simply defining a new field total_price to be a Field.Virtual. The only argument of the constructor is a function that takes a row and returns the computed values.

A virtual field defined as the one above is automatically computed for all records when the records are selected:

```
>>> for row in db(db.item).select(): print row.total_price
```

It is also possible to define method fields which are calculated on-demand, when called. For example:

```
>>> db.item.discounted_total = Field.Method(lambda row, discount=0.0: \
      row.item.unit_price*row.item.quantity*(1.0-discount/100))
```

In this case row.discounted_total is not a value but a function. The function takes the same arguments as the function passed to the Method constructor except for row which is implicit (think of it as self for rows objects).

The lazy field in the example above allows one to compute the total price for each item:

```
>>> for row in db(db.item).select(): print row.discounted_total()
```

And it also allows to pass an optional discount percentage (15%):

```
>>> for row in db(db.item).select(): print row.discounted_total(15)
```

Virtual and Method fields can also be defined in place when a table is defined:

```
>>> db.define_table('item',
        Field('unit_price','double'),
        Field('quantity','integer'),
        Field.Virtual('total_price', lambda row: ...),
        Field.Method('discounted_total', lambda row, discount=0.0: ...))
```

> Mind that virtual fields do not have the same attributes as the other fields (default, readable, requires, etc) and they do not appear in the list of db.table.fields and are not visualized by default in tables (TABLE) and grids (SQLFORM.grid, SQLFORM.smartgrid).

6.20.2   Old style virtual fields

In order to define one or more virtual fields, you can also define a container class, instantiate it and link it to a table or to a select. For example, consider the following table:

```
>>> db.define_table('item',
        Field('unit_price','double'),
        Field('quantity','integer'),
```

One can define a total_price virtual field as

```
>>> class MyVirtualFields(object):
        def total_price(self):
            return self.item.unit_price*self.item.quantity
>>> db.item.virtualfields.append(MyVirtualFields())
```

Notice that each method of the class that takes a single argument (self) is a new virtual field. self refers to each one row of the select. Field values are referred by full path as in self.item.unit_price. The table is linked to the virtual fields by appending an instance of the class to the table's virtualfields attribute.

Virtual fields can also access recursive fields as in

```
1 >>> db.define_table('item',
2       Field('unit_price','double'))
3 >>> db.define_table('order_item',
4       Field('item','reference item'),
5       Field('quantity','integer'))
6 >>> class MyVirtualFields(object):
7       def total_price(self):
8           return self.order_item.item.unit_price \
9               * self.order_item.quantity
10 >>> db.order_item.virtualfields.append(MyVirtualFields())
```

Notice the recursive field access `self.order_item.item.unit_price` where `self` is the looping record.

They can also act on the result of a JOIN

```
1 >>> db.define_table('item',
2       Field('unit_price','double'))
3 >>> db.define_table('order_item',
4       Field('item','reference item'),
5       Field('quantity','integer'))
6 >>> rows = db(db.order_item.item==db.item.id).select()
7 >>> class MyVirtualFields(object):
8       def total_price(self):
9           return self.item.unit_price \
10              * self.order_item.quantity
11 >>> rows.setvirtualfields(order_item=MyVirtualFields())
12 >>> for row in rows: print row.order_item.total_price
```

Notice how in this case the syntax is different. The virtual field accesses both `self.item.unit_price` and `self.order_item.quantity` which belong to the join select. The virtual field is attached to the rows of the table using the `setvirtualfields` method of the rows object. This method takes an arbitrary number of named arguments and can be used to set multiple virtual fields, defined in multiple classes, and attach them to multiple tables:

```
1 >>> class MyVirtualFields1(object):
2       def discounted_unit_price(self):
3           return self.item.unit_price*0.90
4 >>> class MyVirtualFields2(object):
5       def total_price(self):
6           return self.item.unit_price \
7               * self.order_item.quantity
8       def discounted_total_price(self):
9           return self.item.discounted_unit_price \
10              * self.order_item.quantity
11 >>> rows.setvirtualfields(
12      item=MyVirtualFields1(),
```

```
13           order_item=MyVirtualFields2())
14  >>> for row in rows:
15           print row.order_item.discounted_total_price
```

Virtual fields can be *lazy*; all they need to do is return a function and access it by calling the function:

```
1  >>> db.define_table('item',
2         Field('unit_price','double'),
3         Field('quantity','integer'),
4  >>> class MyVirtualFields(object):
5         def lazy_total_price(self):
6             def lazy(self=self):
7                 return self.item.unit_price \
8                     * self.item.quantity
9             return lazy
10  >>> db.item.virtualfields.append(MyVirtualFields())
11  >>> for item in db(db.item).select():
12         print item.lazy_total_price()
```

or shorter using a lambda function:

```
1  >>> class MyVirtualFields(object):
2         def lazy_total_price(self):
3             return lambda self=self: self.item.unit_price \
4                 * self.item.quantity
```

6.21   One to many relation

To illustrate how to implement one to many relations with the web2py DAL, define another table "thing" that refers to the table "person" which we redefine here:

```
1  >>> db.define_table('person',
2                 Field('name'),
3                 format='%(name)s')
4  >>> db.define_table('thing',
5                 Field('name'),
6                 Field('owner_id', 'reference person'),
7                 format='%(name)s')
```

Table "thing" has two fields, the name of the thing and the owner of the thing. The "owner_id" field id a reference field. A reference type can be specified in two equivalent ways:

```
1  Field('owner_id', 'reference person')
2  Field('owner_id', db.person)
```

The latter is always converted to the former. They are equivalent except in the case of lazy tables, self references or other types of cyclic references where the former notation is the only allowed notation.

When a field type is another table, it is intended that the field reference the other table by its id. In fact, you can print the actual type value and get:

```
1 >>> print db.thing.owner_id.type
2 reference person
```

Now, insert three things, two owned by Alex and one by Bob:

```
1 >>> db.thing.insert(name='Boat', owner_id=1)
2 1
3 >>> db.thing.insert(name='Chair', owner_id=1)
4 2
5 >>> db.thing.insert(name='Shoes', owner_id=2)
6 3
```

You can select as you did for any other table:

```
1 >>> for row in db(db.thing.owner_id==1).select():
2         print row.name
3 Boat
4 Chair
```

Because a thing has a reference to a person, a person can have many things, so a record of table person now acquires a new attribute thing, which is a Set, that defines the things of that person. This allows looping over all persons and fetching their things easily:

```
1 >>> for person in db().select(db.person.ALL):
2         print person.name
3         for thing in person.thing.select():
4             print '    ', thing.name
5 Alex
6     Boat
7     Chair
8 Bob
9     Shoes
10 Carl
```

6.21.1   Inner joins

Another way to achieve a similar result is by using a join, specifically an INNER JOIN. web2py performs joins automatically and transparently when the query links two or more tables as in the following example:

```
>>> rows = db(db.person.id==db.thing.owner_id).select()
>>> for row in rows:
        print row.person.name, 'has', row.thing.name
Alex has Boat
Alex has Chair
Bob has Shoes
```

Observe that web2py did a join, so the rows now contain two records, one from each table, linked together. Because the two records may have fields with conflicting names, you need to specify the table when extracting a field value from a row. This means that while before you could do:

```
row.name
```

and it was obvious whether this was the name of a person or a thing, in the result of a join you have to be more explicit and say:

```
row.person.name
```

or:

```
row.thing.name
```

There is an alternative syntax for INNER JOINS:

```
>>> rows = db(db.person).select(join=db.thing.on(db.person.id==db.thing.owner_id))
>>> for row in rows:
    print row.person.name, 'has', row.thing.name
Alex has Boat
Alex has Chair
Bob has Shoes
```

While the output is the same, the generated SQL in the two cases can be different. The latter syntax removes possible ambiguities when the same table is joined twice and aliased:

```
>>> db.define_table('thing',
        Field('name'),
        Field('owner_id1','reference person'),
        Field('owner_id2','reference person'))
>>> rows = db(db.person).select(
    join=[db.person.with_alias('owner_id1').on(db.person.id==db.thing.owner_id1).
        db.person.with_alias('owner_id2').on(db.person.id==db.thing.owner_id2)])
```

The value of join can be list of db.table.on(...) to join.

6.21.2   Left outer join

Notice that Carl did not appear in the list above because he has no things. If you intend to select on persons (whether they have things or not) and their things (if they have any), then you need to perform a LEFT OUTER JOIN. This is done using the argument "left" of the select command. Here is an example:

```
1 >>> rows=db().select(
2        db.person.ALL, db.thing.ALL,
3        left=db.thing.on(db.person.id==db.thing.owner_id))
4 >>> for row in rows:
5        print row.person.name, 'has', row.thing.name
6 Alex has Boat
7 Alex has Chair
8 Bob has Shoes
9 Carl has None
```

where:

```
1 left = db.thing.on(...)
```

does the left join query. Here the argument of db.thing.on is the condition required for the join (the same used above for the inner join). In the case of a left join, it is necessary to be explicit about which fields to select.

Multiple left joins can be combined by passing a list or tuple of db.mytable.on(...) to the left attribute.

6.21.3   Grouping and counting

When doing joins, sometimes you want to group rows according to certain criteria and count them. For example, count the number of things owned by every person. web2py allows this as well. First, you need a count operator. Second, you want to join the person table with the thing table by owner. Third, you want to select all rows (person + thing), group them by person, and count them while grouping:

```
1 >>> count = db.person.id.count()
2 >>> for row in db(db.person.id==db.thing.owner_id).select(
3        db.person.name, count, groupby=db.person.name):
4        print row.person.name, row[count]
5 Alex 2
```

```
6  Bob 1
```

Notice the count operator (which is built-in) is used as a field. The only issue here is in how to retrieve the information. Each row clearly contains a person and the count, but the count is not a field of a person nor is it a table. So where does it go? It goes into the storage object representing the record with a key equal to the query expression itself. The count method of the Field object has an optional `distinct` argument. When set to `True` it specifies that only distinct values of the field in question are to be counted.

6.22   Many to many

In the previous examples, we allowed a thing to have one owner but one person could have many things. What if Boat was owned by Alex and Curt? This requires a many-to-many relation, and it is realized via an intermediate table that links a person to a thing via an ownership relation.

Here is how to do it:

```
1  >>> db.define_table('person',
2                 Field('name'))
3  >>> db.define_table('thing',
4                 Field('name'))
5  >>> db.define_table('ownership',
6                 Field('person', 'reference person'),
7                 Field('thing', 'reference thing'))
```

the existing ownership relationship can now be rewritten as:

```
1  >>> db.ownership.insert(person=1, thing=1) # Alex owns Boat
2  >>> db.ownership.insert(person=1, thing=2) # Alex owns Chair
3  >>> db.ownership.insert(person=2, thing=3) # Bob owns Shoes
```

Now you can add the new relation that Curt co-owns Boat:

```
1  >>> db.ownership.insert(person=3, thing=1) # Curt owns Boat too
```

Because you now have a three-way relation between tables, it may be convenient to define a new set on which to perform operations:

```
1  >>> persons_and_things = db(
2          (db.person.id==db.ownership.person) \
3          & (db.thing.id==db.ownership.thing))
```

Now it is easy to select all persons and their things from the new Set:

```
1 >>> for row in persons_and_things.select():
2     print row.person.name, row.thing.name
3 Alex Boat
4 Alex Chair
5 Bob Shoes
6 Curt Boat
```

Similarly, you can search for all things owned by Alex:

```
1 >>> for row in persons_and_things(db.person.name=='Alex').select():
2     print row.thing.name
3 Boat
4 Chair
```

and all owners of Boat:

```
1 >>> for row in persons_and_things(db.thing.name=='Boat').select():
2     print row.person.name
3 Alex
4 Curt
```

A lighter alternative to Many 2 Many relations is tagging. Tagging is discussed in the context of the IS_IN_DB validator. Tagging works even on database backends that do not support JOINs like the Google App Engine NoSQL.

6.23 list:<type>, and contains

web2py provides the following special field types:

```
1 list:string
2 list:integer
3 list:reference <table>
```

They can contain lists of strings, of integers and of references respectively.

On Google App Engine NoSQL list:string is mapped into StringListProperty, the other two are mapped into ListProperty(int). On relational databases they all mapped into text fields which contain the list of items separated by |. For example [1,2,3] is mapped into |1|2|3|.

For lists of string the items are escaped so that any | in the item is replaced by a ||. Anyway this is an internal representation and it is transparent to the user.

You can use list:string, for example, in the following way:

```
1 >>> db.define_table('product',
2       Field('name'),
3       Field('colors','list:string'))
4 >>> db.product.colors.requires=IS_IN_SET(('red','blue','green'))
5 >>> db.product.insert(name='Toy Car',colors=['red','green'])
6 >>> products = db(db.product.colors.contains('red')).select()
7 >>> for item in products:
8       print item.name, item.colors
9 Toy Car ['red', 'green']
```

list:integer works in the same way but the items must be integers.

As usual the requirements are enforced at the level of forms, not at the level of insert.

> For list:<type> fields the contains(value) operator maps into a non trivial query that checks for lists containing the value. The contains operator also works for regular string and text fields and it maps into a LIKE '%value%'.

The list:reference and the contains(value) operator are particularly useful to de-normalize many-to-many relations. Here is an example:

```
1 >>> db.define_table('tag',Field('name'),format='%(name)s')
2 >>> db.define_table('product',
3       Field('name'),
4       Field('tags','list:reference tag'))
5 >>> a = db.tag.insert(name='red')
6 >>> b = db.tag.insert(name='green')
7 >>> c = db.tag.insert(name='blue')
8 >>> db.product.insert(name='Toy Car',tags=[a, b, c])
9 >>> products = db(db.product.tags.contains(b)).select()
10 >>> for item in products:
11       print item.name, item.tags
12 Toy Car [1, 2, 3]
13 >>> for item in products:
14       print item.name, db.product.tags.represent(item.tags)
15 Toy Car red, green, blue
```

Notice that a list:reference tag field get a default constraint

```
1 requires = IS_IN_DB(db,'tag.id',db.tag._format,multiple=True)
```

that produces a SELECT/OPTION multiple drop-box in forms.

Also notice that this field gets a default represent attribute which represents the list of references as a comma-separated list of formatted references. This is used in read forms and SQLTABLEs.

While list:reference has a default validator and a default representation, list:integer and list:string do not. So these two need an IS_IN_SET or an IS_IN_DB validator if you want to use them in forms.

6.24 Other operators

web2py has other operators that provide an API to access equivalent SQL operators. Let's define another table "log" to store security events, their event_time and severity, where the severity is an integer number.

```
>>> db.define_table('log', Field('event'),
                     Field('event_time', 'datetime'),
                     Field('severity', 'integer'))
```

As before, insert a few events, a "port scan", an "xss injection" and an "unauthorized login". For the sake of the example, you can log events with the same event_time but with different severities (1, 2, and 3 respectively).

```
>>> import datetime
>>> now = datetime.datetime.now()
>>> print db.log.insert(
        event='port scan', event_time=now, severity=1)
1
>>> print db.log.insert(
        event='xss injection', event_time=now, severity=2)
2
>>> print db.log.insert(
        event='unauthorized login', event_time=now, severity=3)
3
```

6.24.1 like, regexp, startswith, contains, upper, lower

Fields have a like operator that you can use to match strings:

```
>>> for row in db(db.log.event.like('port%')).select():
        print row.event
port scan
```

Here "port%" indicates a string starting with "port". The percent sign character, "%", is a wild-card character that means "any sequence of characters".

The like operator is case-insensitive but it can be made case-sensitive with

```
1 db.mytable.myfield.like('value',case_sensitive=True)
```

web2py also provides some shortcuts:

```
1 db.mytable.myfield.startswith('value')
2 db.mytable.myfield.contains('value')
```

which are equivalent respectively to

```
1 db.mytable.myfield.like('value%')
2 db.mytable.myfield.like('%value%')
```

Notice that contains has a special meaning for list:<type> fields and it was discussed in a previous section.

The contains method can also be passed a list of values and an optional boolean argument all to search for records that contain all values:

```
1 db.mytable.myfield.contains(['value1','value2'], all=True)
```

or any value from the list

```
1 db.mytable.myfield.contains(['value1','value2'], all=false)
```

There is a also a regexp method that works like the like method but allows regular expression syntax for the look-up expression. It is only supported by PostgreSQL and SQLite.

The upper and lower methods allow you to convert the value of the field to upper or lower case, and you can also combine them with the like operator:

```
1 >>> for row in db(db.log.event.upper().like('PORT%')).select():
2       print row.event
3 port scan
```

6.24.2   year, month, day, hour, minutes, seconds

The date and datetime fields have day, month and year methods. The datetime and time fields have hour, minutes and seconds methods. Here is an example:

```
1 >>> for row in db(db.log.event_time.year()==2009).select():
2       print row.event
3 port scan
4 xss injection
5 unauthorized login
```

6.24.3 belongs

The SQL IN operator is realized via the belongs method which returns true
when the field value belongs to the specified set (list of tuples):

```
1 >>> for row in db(db.log.severity.belongs((1, 2))).select():
2         print row.event
3 port scan
4 xss injection
```

The DAL also allows a nested select as the argument of the belongs operator.
The only caveat is that the nested select has to be a _select, not a select, and
only one field has to be selected explicitly, the one that defines the set.

```
1 >>> bad_days = db(db.log.severity==3)._select(db.log.event_time)
2 >>> for row in db(db.log.event_time.belongs(bad_days)).select():
3         print row.event
4 port scan
5 xss injection
6 unauthorized login
```

In those cases where a nested select is required and the look-up field is a
reference we can also use a query as argument. For example:

```
1 db.define_table('person',Field('name'))
2 db.define_table('thing,Field('name'), Field('owner_id','reference thing'))
3 db(db.thing.owner_id.belongs(db.person.name=='Jonathan')).select()
```

In this case it is obvious that the next select only needs the field referenced
by the db.thing.owner_id field so we do not need the more verbose _select
notation.

A nested select can also be used as insert/update value but in this case the
syntax is different:

```
1 lazy = db(db.person.name=='Jonathan').nested_select(db.person.id)
2 db(db.thing.id==1).update(owner_id = lazy)
```

In this case lazy is a nested expression that computes the id of person
"Jonathan". The two lines result in one single SQL query.

6.24.4 sum, avg, min, max **and** len

Previously, you have used the count operator to count records. Similarly, you
can use the sum operator to add (sum) the values of a specific field from a

group of records. As in the case of count, the result of a sum is retrieved via the store object:

```
1 >>> sum = db.log.severity.sum()
2 >>> print db().select(sum).first()[sum]
3 6
```

You can also use avg, min, and max to the average, minimum, and maximum value respectively for the selected records. For example:

```
1 >>> max = db.log.severity.max()
2 >>> print db().select(max).first()[max]
3 3
```

.len() computes the length of a string, text or boolean fields.

Expressions can be combined to form more complex expressions. For example here we are computing the sum of the length of all the severity strings in the logs, increased of one:

```
1 >>> sum = (db.log.severity.len()+1).sum()
2 >>> print db().select(sum).first()[sum]
```

6.24.5   Substrings

One can build an expression to refer to a substring. For example, we can group things whose name starts with the same three characters and select only one from each group:

```
1 db(db.thing).select(distinct = db.thing.name[:3])
```

6.24.6   Default values with coalesce and coalesce_zero

There are times when you need to pull a value from database but also need a default values if the value for a record is set to NULL. In SQL there is a keyword, COALESCE, for this. web2py has an equivalent coalesce method:

```
1 >>> db.define_table('sysuser',Field('username'),Field('fullname'))
2 >>> db.sysuser.insert(username='max',fullname='Max Power')
3 >>> db.sysuser.insert(username='tim',fullname=None)
4 print db(db.sysuser).select(db.sysuser.fullname.coalesce(db.sysuser.username))
5 "COALESCE(sysuser.fullname,sysuser.username)"
6 Max Power
7 tim
```

Other times you need to compute a mathematical expression but some fields have a value set to None while it should be zero. coalesce_zero comes to the rescue by defaulting None to zero in the query:

```
1 >>> db.define_table('sysuser',Field('username'),Field('points'))
2 >>> db.sysuser.insert(username='max',points=10)
3 >>> db.sysuser.insert(username='tim',points=None)
4 >>> print db(db.sysuser).select(db.sysuser.points.coalesce_zero().sum())
5 "SUM(COALESCE(sysuser.points,0))"
6 10
```

6.25 Generating raw sql

Sometimes you need to generate the SQL but not execute it. This is easy to do with web2py since every command that performs database IO has an equivalent command that does not, and simply returns the SQL that would have been executed. These commands have the same names and syntax as the functional ones, but they start with an underscore:

Here is _insert

```
1 >>> print db.person._insert(name='Alex')
2 INSERT INTO person(name) VALUES ('Alex');
```

Here is _count

```
1 >>> print db(db.person.name=='Alex')._count()
2 SELECT count(*) FROM person WHERE person.name='Alex';
```

Here is _select

```
1 >>> print db(db.person.name=='Alex')._select()
2 SELECT person.id, person.name FROM person WHERE person.name='Alex';
```

Here is _delete

```
1 >>> print db(db.person.name=='Alex')._delete()
2 DELETE FROM person WHERE person.name='Alex';
```

And finally, here is _update

```
1 >>> print db(db.person.name=='Alex')._update()
2 UPDATE person SET  WHERE person.name='Alex';
```

Moreover you can always use db._lastsql to return the most recent SQL code, whether it was executed manually using executesql or was SQL generated by the DAL.

6.26   Exporting and importing data

6.26.1   CSV (one Table at a time)

When a Rows object is converted to a string it is automatically serialized in CSV:

```
1 >>> rows = db(db.person.id==db.thing.owner_id).select()
2 >>> print rows
3 person.id,person.name,thing.id,thing.name,thing.owner_id
4 1,Alex,1,Boat,1
5 1,Alex,2,Chair,1
6 2,Bob,3,Shoes,2
```

You can serialize a single table in CSV and store it in a file "test.csv":

```
1 >>> open('test.csv', 'wb').write(str(db(db.person.id).select()))
```

This is equivalent to

```
1 >>> rows = db(db.person.id).select()
2 >>> rows.export_to_csv_file(open('test.csv', 'wb'))
```

You can read the CSV file back with:

```
1 >>> db.person.import_from_csv_file(open('test.csv', 'r'))
```

When importing, web2py looks for the field names in the CSV header. In this example, it finds two columns: "person.id" and "person.name". It ignores the "person." prefix, and it ignores the "id" fields. Then all records are appended and assigned new ids. Both of these operations can be performed via the appadmin web interface.

6.26.2   CSV (all tables at once)

In web2py, you can backup/restore an entire database with two commands:

To export:

```
1 >>> db.export_to_csv_file(open('somefile.csv', 'wb'))
```

To import:

```
1 >>> db.import_from_csv_file(open('somefile.csv', 'rb'))
```

This mechanism can be used even if the importing database is of a different type than the exporting database. The data is stored in "somefile.csv" as a

CSV file where each table starts with one line that indicates the tablename, and another line with the fieldnames:

```
1  TABLE tablename
2  field1, field2, field3, ...
```

Two tables are separated \r\n\r\n. The file ends with the line

```
1  END
```

The file does not include uploaded files if these are not stored in the database. In any case it is easy enough to zip the "uploads" folder separately.

When importing, the new records will be appended to the database if it is not empty. In general the new imported records will not have the same record id as the original (saved) records but web2py will restore references so they are not broken, even if the id values may change.

If a table contains a field called "uuid", this field will be used to identify duplicates. Also, if an imported record has the same "uuid" as an existing record, the previous record will be updated.

6.26.3   CSV and remote database synchronization

Consider the following model:

```
1   db = DAL('sqlite:memory:')
2   db.define_table('person',
3       Field('name'),
4       format='%(name)s')
5   db.define_table('thing',
6       Field('owner_id', 'reference person'),
7       Field('name'),
8       format='%(name)s')
9
10  if not db(db.person).count():
11      id = db.person.insert(name="Massimo")
12      db.thing.insert(owner_id=id, name="Chair")
```

Each record is identified by an ID and referenced by that ID. If you have two copies of the database used by distinct web2py installations, the ID is unique only within each database and not across the databases. This is a problem when merging records from different databases.

In order to make a record uniquely identifiable across databases, they must:

- have a unique id (UUID),

- have an event_time (to figure out which one is more recent if multiple copies),

- reference the UUID instead of the id.

This can be achieved without modifying web2py. Here is what to do:

Change the above model into:

```
db.define_table('person',
    Field('uuid', length=64, default=lambda:str(uuid.uuid4())),
    Field('modified_on', 'datetime', default=now),
    Field('name'),
    format='%(name)s')

db.define_table('thing',
    Field('uuid', length=64, default=lambda:str(uuid.uuid4())),
    Field('modified_on', 'datetime', default=now),
    Field('owner_id', length=64),
    Field('name'),
    format='%(name)s')

db.thing.owner_id.requires = IS_IN_DB(db,'person.uuid','%(name)s')

if not db(db.person.id).count():
    id = uuid.uuid4()
    db.person.insert(name="Massimo", uuid=id)
    db.thing.insert(owner_id=id, name="Chair")
```

Notice that in the above table definitions, the default value for the two uuid fields is set to a lambda function, which returns a UUID (converted to a string). The lambda function is called once for each record inserted, ensuring that each record gets a unique UUID, even if multiple records are inserted in a single transaction.

Create a controller action to export the database:

```
def export():
    s = StringIO.StringIO()
    db.export_to_csv_file(s)
    response.headers['Content-Type'] = 'text/csv'
    return s.getvalue()
```

Create a controller action to import a saved copy of the other database and sync records:

```
def import_and_sync():
```

```
 2   form = FORM(INPUT(_type='file', _name='data'), INPUT(_type='submit'))
 3   if form.process().accepted:
 4       db.import_from_csv_file(form.vars.data.file,unique=False)
 5       # for every table
 6       for table in db.tables:
 7           # for every uuid, delete all but the latest
 8           items = db(db[table]).select(db[table].id,
 9                       db[table].uuid,
10                       orderby=db[table].modified_on,
11                       groupby=db[table].uuid)
12           for item in items:
13               db((db[table].uuid==item.uuid)&\
14                   (db[table].id!=item.id)).delete()
15   return dict(form=form)
```

Optionally you should create an index manually to make the search by uuid faster.

Alternatively, you can use XML-RPC to export/import the file.

If the records reference uploaded files, you also need to export/import the content of the uploads folder. Notice that files therein are already labeled by UUIDs so you do not need to worry about naming conflicts and references.

6.26.4   HTML and XML (one Table at a time)

Rows objects also have an xml method (like helpers) that serializes it to XML/HTML:

```
 1  >>> rows = db(db.person.id > 0).select()
 2  >>> print rows.xml()
 3  <table>
 4    <thead>
 5      <tr>
 6        <th>person.id</th>
 7        <th>person.name</th>
 8        <th>thing.id</th>
 9        <th>thing.name</th>
10        <th>thing.owner_id</th>
11      </tr>
12    </thead>
13    <tbody>
14      <tr class="even">
15        <td>1</td>
16        <td>Alex</td>
17        <td>1</td>
```

```
18        <td>Boat</td>
19        <td>1</td>
20      </tr>
21      ...
22    </tbody>
23  </table>
```

If you need to serialize the Rows in any other XML format with custom tags, you can easily do that using the universal TAG helper and the * notation:

```
1  >>> rows = db(db.person.id > 0).select()
2  >>> print TAG.result(*[TAG.row(*[TAG.field(r[f], _name=f) \
3          for f in db.person.fields]) for r in rows])
4  <result>
5    <row>
6      <field name="id">1</field>
7      <field name="name">Alex</field>
8    </row>
9    ...
10  </result>
```

6.26.5 Data representation

The `export_to_csv_file` function accepts a keyword argument named `represent`. When `True` it will use the columns `represent` function while exporting the data instead of the raw data.

The function also accepts a keyword argument named `colnames` that should contain a list of column names one wish to export. It defaults to all columns.

Both `export_to_csv_file` and `import_from_csv_file` accept keyword arguments that tell the csv parser the format to save/load the files:

- `delimiter`: delimiter to separate values (default ',')

- `quotechar`: character to use to quote string values (default to double quotes)

- `quoting`: quote system (default `csv.QUOTE_MINIMAL`)

Here is some example usage:

```
1  >>> import csv
2  >>> rows = db(query).select()
3  >>> rows.export_to_csv_file(open('/tmp/test.txt', 'w'),
4          delimiter='|',
5          quotechar='"',
```

```
6      quoting=csv.QUOTE_NONNUMERIC)
```

Which would render something similar to

```
1  "hello"|35|"this is the text description"|"2009-03-03"
```

For more information consult the official Python documentation [82]

6.27   Caching selects

The select method also takes a cache argument, which defaults to None. For caching purposes, it should be set to a tuple where the first element is the cache model (cache.ram, cache.disk, etc.), and the second element is the expiration time in seconds.

In the following example, you see a controller that caches a select on the previously defined db.log table. The actual select fetches data from the back-end database no more frequently than once every 60 seconds and stores the result in cache.ram. If the next call to this controller occurs in less than 60 seconds since the last database IO, it simply fetches the previous data from cache.ram.

```
1  def cache_db_select():
2      logs = db().select(db.log.ALL, cache=(cache.ram, 60))
3      return dict(logs=logs)
```

The select method has an optional cacheable argument, normally set to False. When cacheable=True the resulting Rows is serializable but The Rows lack update_record and delete_record methods.

If you do not need these methods you can speed up selects a lot by setting the cacheable attribute:

```
1  rows = db(query).select(cacheable=True)
```

When the cache argument is set but cacheable=False (default) only the database results are cached, not the actual Rows object. When the cache argument is used in conjunction with cacheable=True the entire Rows object is cached and this results in much faster caching:

```
1  rows = db(query).select(cache=(cache.ram,3600),cacheable=True)
```

6.28   Self-Reference and aliases

It is possible to define tables with fields that refer to themselves, here is an example:

```
db.define_table('person',
    Field('name'),
    Field('father_id', 'reference person'),
    Field('mother_id', 'reference person'))
```

Notice that the alternative notation of using a table object as field type will fail in this case, because it uses a variable db.person before it is defined:

```
db.define_table('person',
    Field('name'),
    Field('father_id', db.person), # wrong!
    Field('mother_id', db.person)) # wrong!
```

In general db.tablename and "reference tablename" are equivalent field types, but the latter is the only one allowed for self.references.

If the table refers to itself, then it is not possible to perform a JOIN to select a person and its parents without use of the SQL "AS" keyword. This is achieved in web2py using the with_alias. Here is an example:

```
>>> Father = db.person.with_alias('father')
>>> Mother = db.person.with_alias('mother')
>>> db.person.insert(name='Massimo')
1
>>> db.person.insert(name='Claudia')
2
>>> db.person.insert(name='Marco', father_id=1, mother_id=2)
3
>>> rows = db().select(db.person.name, Father.name, Mother.name,
        left=(Father.on(Father.id==db.person.father_id),
            Mother.on(Mother.id==db.person.mother_id)))
>>> for row in rows:
        print row.person.name, row.father.name, row.mother.name
Massimo None None
Claudia None None
Marco Massimo Claudia
```

Notice that we have chosen to make a distinction between:

- "father_id": the field name used in the table "person";

- "father": the alias we want to use for the table referenced by the above field; this is communicated to the database;

- "Father": the variable used by web2py to refer to that alias.

The difference is subtle, and there is nothing wrong in using the same name for the three of them:

```
db.define_table('person',
    Field('name'),
    Field('father', 'reference person'),
    Field('mother', 'reference person'))
>>> father = db.person.with_alias('father')
>>> mother = db.person.with_alias('mother')
>>> db.person.insert(name='Massimo')
1
>>> db.person.insert(name='Claudia')
2
>>> db.person.insert(name='Marco', father=1, mother=2)
3
>>> rows = db().select(db.person.name, father.name, mother.name,
        left=(father.on(father.id==db.person.father),
            mother.on(mother.id==db.person.mother)))
>>> for row in rows:
        print row.person.name, row.father.name, row.mother.name
Massimo None None
Claudia None None
Marco Massimo Claudia
```

But it is important to have the distinction clear in order to build correct queries.

6.29   Advanced features

6.29.1   Table inheritance

It is possible to create a table that contains all the fields from another table. It is sufficient to pass the other table in place of a field to define_table. For example

```
db.define_table('person', Field('name'))
db.define_table('doctor', db.person, Field('specialization'))
```

It is also possible to define a dummy table that is not stored in a database in order to reuse it in multiple other places. For example:

```
signature = db.Table(db, 'signature',
    Field('created_on', 'datetime', default=request.now),
```

```
3    Field('created_by', db.auth_user, default=auth.user_id),
4    Field('updated_on', 'datetime', update=request.now),
5    Field('updated_by', db.auth_user, update=auth.user_id))
6
7  db.define_table('payment', Field('amount', 'double'), signature)
```

This example assumes that standard web2py authentication is enabled.

Notice that if you use Auth web2py already creates one such table for you:

```
1  auth = Auth(db)
2  db.define_table('payment', Field('amount', 'double'), auth.signature)
```

When using table inheritance, if you want the inheriting table to inherit validators, be sure to define the validators of the parent table before defining the inheriting table.

6.29.2   filter_in **and** filter_out

It is possible to define a filter for each field to be called before a value is inserted into the database for that field and after a value is retrieved from the database.

Imagine for example that you want to store a serializable Python data structure in a field in the json format. Here is how it could be accomplished:

```
1  >>> from simplejson import loads, dumps
2  >>> db.define_table('anyobj',Field('name'),Field('data','text'))
3  >>> db.anyobj.data.filter_in = lambda obj, dumps=dumps: dumps(obj)
4  >>> db.anyobj.data.filter_out = lambda txt, loads=loads: loads(txt)
5  >>> myobj = ['hello', 'world', 1, {2: 3}]
6  >>> id = db.anyobj.insert(name='myobjname', data=myobj)
7  >>> row = db.anyobj(id)
8  >>> row.data
9  ['hello', 'world', 1, {2: 3}]
```

Another way to accomplish the same is by using a Field of type SQLCustomType, as discussed later.

6.29.3   before and after callbacks

Web2py provides a mechanism to register callbacks to be called before and/or after insert, update and delete of records.

Each table stores six lists of callbacks:

```
db.mytable._before_insert
db.mytable._after_insert
db.mytable._before_update
db.mytable._after_update
db.mytable._before_delete
db.mytable._after_delete
```

You can register callback function by appending it the corresponding function to one of those lists. The caveat is that depending on the functionality, the callback has different signature.

This is best explained via some examples.

```
>>> db.define_table('person',Field('name'))
>>> def pprint(*args): print args
>>> db.person._before_insert.append(lambda f: pprint(f))
>>> db.person._after_insert.append(lambda f,id: pprint(f,id))
>>> db.person._before_update.append(lambda s,f: pprint(s,f))
>>> db.person._after_update.append(lambda s,f: pprint(s,f))
>>> db.person._before_delete.append(lambda s: pprint(s))
>>> db.person._after_delete.append(lambda s: pprint(s))
```

Here f is a dict of fields passed to insert or update, id is the id of the newly inserted record, s is the Set object used for update or delete.

```
>>> db.person.insert(name='John')
({'name': 'John'},)
({'name': 'John'}, 1)
>>> db(db.person.id==1).update(name='Tim')
(<Set (person.id = 1)>, {'name': 'Tim'})
(<Set (person.id = 1)>, {'name': 'Tim'})
>>> db(db.person.id==1).delete()
(<Set (person.id = 1)>,)
(<Set (person.id = 1)>,)
```

The return values of these callback should be None or False. If any of the _before_* callback returns a True value it will abort the actual insert/update/delete operation.

.

Some times a callback may need to perform an update in the same of a different table and one wants to avoid callbacks calling themselves recursively.

For this purpose there the Set objects have an update_naive method that works like update but ignores before and after callbacks.

6.29.4   Record versioning

It is possible to ask web2py to save every copy of a record when the record is individually modified. There are different ways to do it and it can be done for all tables at once using the syntax:

```
auth.enable_record_versioning(db)
```

this requires Auth and it is discussed in the chapter about authentication. It can also be done for each individual table as discussed below.

Consider the following table:

```
db.define_table('stored_item',
    Field('name'),
    Field('quantity','integer'),
    Field('is_active','boolean',
        writable=False,readable=False,default=True))
```

Notice the hidden boolean field called is_active and defaulting to True.

We can tell web2py to create a new table (in the same or a different database) and store all previous versions of each record in the table, when modified.

This is done in the following way:

```
db.stored_item._enable_record_versioning()
```

or in a more verbose syntax:

```
db.stored_item._enable_record_versioning(
    archive_db = db,
    archive_name = 'stored_item_archive',
    current_record = 'current_record',
    is_active = 'is_active')
```

The archive_db=db tells web2py to store the archive table in the same database as the stored_item table. The archive_name sets the name for the archive table. The archive table has the same fields as the original table stored_item except that unique fields are no longer unique (because it needs to store multiple versions) and has an extra field which name is specified by current_record and which is a reference to the current record in the stored_item table.

When records are deleted, they are not really deleted. A deleted record is copied in the stored_item_archive table (like when it is modified) and the is_active field is set to False. By enabling record versioning web2py sets a custom_filter on this table that hides all fields in table stored_item where the is_active field is set to False. The is_active parameter in the _enable_record_versioning method allows to specify the name of the field used by the custom_filter to determine if the field was deleted or not.

custom_filters are ignored by the appadmin interface.

6.29.5   Common fields and multi-tenancy

db._common_fields is a list of fields that should belong to all the tables. This list can also contain tables and it is understood as all fields from the table. For example occasionally you find yourself in need to add a signature to all your tables but the 'auth tables. In this case, after you db.define_tables() but before defining any other table, insert

```
db._common_fields.append(auth.signature)
```

One field is special: "request_tenant". This field does not exist but you can create it and add it to any of your tables (or them all):

```
db._common_fields.append(Field('request_tenant',
    default=request.env.http_host,writable=False))
```

For every table with a field called db._request_tenant, all records for all queries are always automatically filtered by:

```
db.table.request_tenant == db.table.request_tenant.default
```

and for every record insert, this field is set to the default value. In the example above we have chosen

```
default = request.env.http_host
```

i.e. we have chose to ask our app to filter all tables in all queries with

```
db.table.request_tenant == request.env.http_host
```

This simple trick allow us to turn any application into a multi-tenant application. i.e. even if we run one instance of the app and we use one single database, if the app is accessed under two or more domains (in the example the domain name is retrieved from request.env.http_host) the visitors will see different data depending on the domain. Think of running multiple web stores under different domains with one app and one database.

You can turn off multi tenancy filters using:

```
1 rows = db(query, ignore_common_filters=True).select()
```

6.29.6 Common filters

A common filter is a generalization of the above multi-tenancy idea. It provides an easy way to prevent repeating of the same query. Consider for example the following table:

```
1 db.define_table('blog_post',
2     Field('subject'),
3     Field('post_text', 'text'),
4     Field('is_public', 'boolean'),
5     common_filter = lambda query: db.blog_post.is_public==True
6 )
```

Any select, delete or update in this table, will include only public blog posts. The attribute can also be changed in controllers:

```
1 db.blog_post._common_filter = lambda query: db.blog_post.is_public == True
```

It serves both as a way to avoid repeating the "db.blog_post.is_public==True" phrase in each blog post search, and also as a security enhancement, that prevents you from forgetting to disallow viewing of none public posts.

In case you actually do want items left out by the common filter (for example, allowing the admin to see none public posts), you can either remove the filter:

```
1 db.blog_post._common_filter = None
```

or ignore it:

```
1 db(query, ignore_common_filters=True).select(...)
```

6.29.7 Custom Field types (experimental)

Aside for using filter_in and filter_out, it is possible to define new/custom field types. For example we consider here the example if a field that contains binary data in compressed form:

```
1  from gluon.dal import SQLCustomType
2  import zlib
3
4  compressed = SQLCustomType(
5      type ='text',
6      native='text',
7      encoder =(lambda x: zlib.compress(x or '')),
8      decoder = (lambda x: zlib.decompress(x))
9  )
10
11 db.define_table('example', Field('data',type=compressed))
```

SQLCustomType is a field type factory. Its type argument must be one of the standard web2py types. It tells web2py how to treat the field values at the web2py level. native is the name of the field as far as the database is concerned. Allowed names depend on the database engine. encoder is an optional transformation function applied when the data is stored and decoder is the optional reversed transformation function.

This feature is marked as experimental. In practice it has been in web2py for a long time and it works but it can make the code not portable, for example when the native type is database specific. It does not work on Google App Engine NoSQL.

6.29.8   Using DAL without define tables

The DAL can be used from any Python program simply by doing this:

```
1  from gluon import DAL, Field
2  db = DAL('sqlite://storage.sqlite',folder='path/to/app/databases')
```

i.e. import the DAL, Field, connect and specify the folder which contains the.table files (the app/databases folder).

To access the data and its attributes we still have to define all the tables we are going to access with db.define_tables(...).

If we just need access to the data but not to the web2py table attributes, we get away without re-defining the tables but simply asking web2py to read the necessary info from the metadata in the.table files:

```
1  from gluon import DAL, Field
2  db = DAL('sqlite://storage.sqlite',folder='path/to/app/databases',
```

```
3        auto_import=True))
```

This allows us to access any db.table without need to re-define it.

6.29.9   PostGIS, SpatiaLite, and MS Geo (experimental)

The DAL supports geographical APIs using PostGIS (for PostgreSQL),
spatialite (for SQLite), and MSSQL and Spatial Extensions. This is a feature
that was sponsored by the Sahana project and implemented by Denes
Lengyel.

DAL provides geometry and geography fields types and the following
functions:

```
 1  st_asgeojson (PostGIS only)
 2  st_astext
 3  st_contains
 4  st_distance
 5  st_equals
 6  st_intersects
 7  st_overlaps
 8  st_simplify (PostGIS only)
 9  st_touches
10  st_within
11  st_x
12  st_y
```

Here are some examples:

```
 1  from gluon.dal import DAL, Field, geoPoint, geoLine, geoPolygon
 2  db = DAL("mssql://user:pass@host:db")
 3  sp = db.define_table('spatial', Field('loc','geometry()'))
```

Below we insert a point, a line, and a polygon:

```
 1  sp.insert(loc=geoPoint(1,1))
 2  sp.insert(loc=geoLine((100,100),(20,180),(180,180)))
 3  sp.insert(loc=geoPolygon((0,0),(150,0),(150,150),(0,150),(0,0)))
```

Notice that

```
 1  rows = db(sp.id>0).select()
```

Always returns the geometry data serialized as text. You can also do the
same more explicitly using st_astext():

```
 1  print db(sp.id>0).select(sp.id, sp.loc.st_astext())
 2  spatial.id,spatial.loc.STAsText()
```

```
3  1, "POINT (1 2)"
4  2, "LINESTRING (100 100, 20 180, 180 180)"
5  3, "POLYGON ((0 0, 150 0, 150 150, 0 150, 0 0))"
```

You can ask for the native representation by using st_asgeojson() (in PostGIS only):

```
1  print db(sp.id>0).select(sp.id, sp.loc.st_asgeojson().with_alias('loc'))
2  spatial.id,loc
3  1, [1, 2]
4  2, [[100, 100], [20 180], [180, 180]]
5  3, [[[0, 0], [150, 0], [150, 150], [0, 150], [0, 0]]]
```

(notice an array is a point, an array of arrays is a line, and an array of array of arrays is a polygon).

Here are example of how to use geographical functions:

```
1  query = sp.loc.st_intersects(geoLine((20,120),(60,160)))
2  query = sp.loc.st_overlaps(geoPolygon((1,1),(11,1),(11,11),(11,1),(1,1)))
3  query = sp.loc.st_contains(geoPoint(1,1))
4  print db(query).select(sp.id,sp.loc)
5  spatial.id,spatial.loc
6  3,"POLYGON ((0 0, 150 0, 150 150, 0 150, 0 0))"
```

Computed distances can also be retrieved as floating point numbers:

```
1  dist = sp.loc.st_distance(geoPoint(-1,2)).with_alias('dist')
2  print db(sp.id>0).select(sp.id, dist)
3  spatial.id, dist
4  1 2.0
5  2 140.714249456
6  3 1.0
```

6.29.10 Copy data from one db into another

Consider the situation in which you have been using the following database:

```
1  db = DAL('sqlite://storage.sqlite')
```

and you wish to move to another database using a different connection string:

```
1  db = DAL('postgres://username:password@localhost/mydb')
```

Before you switch, you want to move the data and rebuild all the metadata for the new database. We assume the new database to exist but we also assume it is empty.

Web2py provides a script that does this work for you:

```
 1  cd web2py
 2  python scripts/cpdb.py \
 3     -f applications/app/databases \
 4     -y 'sqlite://storage.sqlite' \
 5     -Y 'postgres://username:password@localhost/mydb'
```

After running the script you can simply switch the connection string in the model and everything should work out of the box. The new data should be there.

This script provides various command line options that allows you to move data from one application to another, move all tables or only some tables, clear the data in the tables. for more info try:

```
 1  python scripts/cpdb.py -h
```

6.29.11   Note on new DAL and adapters

The source code of the Database Abstraction Layer was completely rewritten in 2010. While it stays backward compatible, the rewrite made it more modular and easier to extend. Here we explain the main logic.

The file "gluon/dal.py" defines, among other, the following classes.

```
 1  ConnectionPool
 2  BaseAdapter extends ConnectionPool
 3  Row
 4  DAL
 5  Reference
 6  Table
 7  Expression
 8  Field
 9  Query
10  Set
11  Rows
```

Their use has been explained in the previous sections, except for BaseAdapter. When the methods of a Table or Set object need to communicate with the database they delegate to methods of the adapter the task to generate the SQL and or the function call.

For example:

```
 1  db.mytable.insert(myfield='myvalue')
```

calls

```
1  Table.insert(myfield='myvalue')
```

which delegates the adapter by returning:

```
1  db._adapter.insert(db.mytable,db.mytable._listify(dict(myfield='myvalue')))
```

Here `db.mytable._listify` converts the dict of arguments into a list of (field,value) and calls the `insert` method of the adapter. `db._adapter` does more or less the following:

```
1  query = db._adapter._insert(db.mytable,list_of_fields)
2  db._adapter.execute(query)
```

where the first line builds the query and the second executes it.

`BaseAdapter` defines the interface for all adapters.

"gluon/dal.py" at the moment of writing this book, contains the following adapters:

```
1   SQLiteAdapter extends BaseAdapter
2   JDBCSQLiteAdapter extends SQLiteAdapter
3   MySQLAdapter extends BaseAdapter
4   PostgreSQLAdapter extends BaseAdapter
5   JDBCPostgreSQLAdapter extends PostgreSQLAdapter
6   OracleAdapter extends BaseAdapter
7   MSSQLAdapter extends BaseAdapter
8   MSSQL2Adapter extends MSSQLAdapter
9   FireBirdAdapter extends BaseAdapter
10  FireBirdEmbeddedAdapter extends FireBirdAdapter
11  InformixAdapter extends BaseAdapter
12  DB2Adapter extends BaseAdapter
13  IngresAdapter extends BaseAdapter
14  IngresUnicodeAdapter extends IngresAdapter
15  GoogleSQLAdapter extends MySQLAdapter
16  NoSQLAdapter extends BaseAdapter
17  GoogleDatastoreAdapter extends NoSQLAdapter
18  CubridAdapter extends MySQLAdapter (experimental)
19  TeradataAdapter extends DB2Adapter (experimental)
20  SAPDBAdapter extends BaseAdapter (experimental)
21  CouchDBAdapter extends NoSQLAdapter (experimental)
22  MongoDBAdapter extends NoSQLAdapter (experimental)
```

which override the behavior of the `BaseAdapter`.

Each adapter has more or less this structure:

```
1  class MySQLAdapter(BaseAdapter):
2
3      # specify a diver to use
4      driver = globals().get('pymysql',None)
```

```
5
6      # map web2py types into database types
7      types = {
8          'boolean': 'CHAR(1)',
9          'string': 'VARCHAR(%(length)s)',
10         'text': 'LONGTEXT',
11         ...
12         }
13
14     # connect to the database using driver
15     def __init__(self,db,uri,pool_size=0,folder=None,db_codec ='UTF-8',
16                  credential_decoder=lambda x:x, driver_args={},
17                  adapter_args={}):
18         # parse uri string and store parameters in driver_args
19         ...
20         # define a connection function
21         def connect(driver_args=driver_args):
22             return self.driver.connect(**driver_args)
23         # place it in the pool
24         self.pool_connection(connect)
25         # set optional parameters (after connection)
26         self.execute('SET FOREIGN_KEY_CHECKS=1;')
27         self.execute("SET sql_mode='NO_BACKSLASH_ESCAPES';")
28
29     # override BaseAdapter methods as needed
30     def lastrowid(self,table):
31         self.execute('select last_insert_id();')
32         return int(self.cursor.fetchone()[0])
```

Looking at the various adapters as example should be easy to write new ones.

When db instance is created:

```
1  db = DAL('mysql://...')
```

the prefix in the uri string defines the adapter. The mapping is defined in the following dictionary also in "gluon/dal.py":

```
1   ADAPTERS = {
2       'sqlite': SQLiteAdapter,
3       'sqlite:memory': SQLiteAdapter,
4       'mysql': MySQLAdapter,
5       'postgres': PostgreSQLAdapter,
6       'oracle': OracleAdapter,
7       'mssql': MSSQLAdapter,
8       'mssql2': MSSQL2Adapter,
9       'db2': DB2Adapter,
10      'teradata': TeradataAdapter,
11      'informix': InformixAdapter,
```

```
12    'firebird': FireBirdAdapter,
13    'firebird_embedded': FireBirdAdapter,
14    'ingres': IngresAdapter,
15    'ingresu': IngresUnicodeAdapter,
16    'sapdb': SAPDBAdapter,
17    'cubrid': CubridAdapter,
18    'jdbc:sqlite': JDBCSQLiteAdapter,
19    'jdbc:sqlite:memory': JDBCSQLiteAdapter,
20    'jdbc:postgres': JDBCPostgreSQLAdapter,
21    'gae': GoogleDatastoreAdapter, # discouraged, for backward compatibility
22    'google:datastore': GoogleDatastoreAdapter,
23    'google:sql': GoogleSQLAdapter,
24    'couchdb': CouchDBAdapter,
25    'mongodb': MongoDBAdapter,
26  }
```

the uri string is then parsed in more detail by the adapter itself.

For any adapter you can replace the driver with a different one:

```
1  from gluon.dal import MySQLAdapter
2  MySQLAdapter.driver = mysqldb
```

and you can specify optional driver arguments and adapter arguments:

```
1  db =DAL(..., driver_args={}, adapter_args={})
```

6.29.12   Gotchas

SQLite does not support dropping and altering columns. That means that web2py migrations will work up to a point. If you delete a field from a table, the column will remain in the database but be invisible to web2py. If you decide to reinstate the column, web2py will try re-create it and fail. In this case you must set fake_migrate=True so that metadata is rebuilt without attempting to add the column again. Also, for the same reason, **SQLite** is not aware of any change of column type. If you insert a number in a string field, it will be stored as string. If you later change the model and replace the type "string" with type "integer", SQLite will continue to keep the number as a string and this may cause problem when you try to extract the data.

MySQL does not support multiple ALTER TABLE within a single transaction. This means that any migration process is broken into multiple commits. If something happens that causes a failure it is possible to break a migration (the web2py metadata are no longer in sync with the actual table structure in the database). This is unfortunate but it can be prevented (migrate one table at the time) or it can be fixed a posteriori (revert the web2py model to what corresponds to the table structure in database, set fake_migrate=True and after the metadata has been rebuilt, set fake_migrate=False and migrate the table again).

Google SQL has the same problems as MySQL and more. In particular table metadata itself must be stored in the database in a table that is not migrated by web2py. This is because Google App Engine has a read-only file system. Web2py migrations in Google:SQL combined with the MySQL issue described above can result in metadata corruption. Again, this can be prevented (my migrating the table at once and then setting migrate=False so that the metadata table is not accessed any more) or it can fixed a posteriori (my accessing the database using the Google dashboard and deleting any corrupted entry from the table called web2py_filesystem.

MSSQL does not support the SQL OFFSET keyword. Therefore the database cannot do pagination. When doing a limitby=(a,b) web2py will fetch the first b rows and discard the first a. This may result in a considerable overhead when compared with other database engines.

Oracle also does not support pagination. It does not support neither the OFFSET nor the LIMIT keywords. Web2py achieves pagination by translating a db(...).select(limitby=(a,b)) into a complex three-way nested select (as suggested by official Oracle documentation). This works for simple select but may break for complex selects involving aliased fields and or joins.

MSSQL has problems with circular references in tables that have ONDELETE CASCADE. This is an MSSSQL bug and you work around it by setting the ondelete attribute for all reference fields to "NO ACTION". You can also do it once and for all before you define tables:

```
db = DAL('mssql://....')
for key in ['reference','reference FK']:
    db._adapter.types[key]=db._adapter.types[key].replace(
        '%(on_delete_action)s','NO ACTION')
```

MSSQL also has problems with arguments passed to the DISTINCT keyword and therefore while this works,

```
db(query).select(distinct=True)
```

this does not

```
db(query).select(distinct=db.mytable.myfield)
```

Google NoSQL (Datastore) does not allow joins, left joins, aggregates, expression, OR involving more than one table, the 'like' operator searches in "text" fields. Transactions are limited and not provided automatically by web2py (you need to use the Google API run_in_transaction which you can look up in the Google App Engine documentation online). Google also limits the number of records you can retrieve in each one query (1000 at the time of writing). On the Google datastore record IDs are integer but they are not sequential. While on SQL the "list:string" type is mapped into a "text" type, on the Google Datastore it is mapped into a ListStringProperty. Similarly "list:integer" and "list:reference" are mapped into "ListProperty". This makes searches for content inside these fields types are more efficient on Google NoSQL than on SQL databases.

7

Forms and validators

There are four distinct ways to build forms in web2py:

- FORM provides a low-level implementation in terms of HTML helpers. A FORM object can be serialized into HTML and is aware of the fields it contains. A FORM object knows how to validate submitted form values.

- SQLFORM provides a high-level API for building create, update and delete forms from an existing database table.

- SQLFORM.factory is an abstraction layer on top of SQLFORM in order to take advantage of the form generation features even if there is no database present. It generates a form very similar to SQLFORM from the description of a table but without the need to create the database table.

- CRUD methods. These are functionally equivalent to SQLFORM and are based on SQLFORM, but provide a more compact notation.

All these forms are self-aware and, if the input does not pass validation, they can modify themselves and add error messages. The forms can be queried for the validated variables and for error messages that have been generated by validation.

Arbitrary HTML code can be inserted into or extracted from the form using helpers.

FORM and SQLFORM are helpers and they can be manipulated in a similar way as the DIV. For example you can set a form style:

```
1  form = SQLFORM(..)
2  form['_style']='border:1px solid black'
```

7.1   FORM

Consider as an example a **test** application with the following "default.py" controller:

```
1  def display_form():
2      return dict()
```

and the associated "default/display_form.html" view:

```
1  {{extend 'layout.html'}}
2  <h2>Input form</h2>
3  <form enctype="multipart/form-data"
4        action="{{=URL()}}" method="post">
5  Your name:
6  <input name="name" />
7  <input type="submit" />
8  </form>
9  <h2>Submitted variables</h2>
10 {{=BEAUTIFY(request.vars)}}
```

This is a regular HTML form that asks for the user's name. When you fill the form and click the submit button, the form self-submits, and the variable request.vars.name along with its provided value is displayed at the bottom.

You can generate the same form using helpers. This can be done in the view or in the action. Since web2py processed the form in the action, it is better to define the form in the action itself.

Here is the new controller:

```
1  def display_form():
2      form=FORM('Your name:', INPUT(_name='name'), INPUT(_type='submit'))
3      return dict(form=form)
```

and the associated "default/display_form.html" view:

```
1  {{extend 'layout.html'}}
2  <h2>Input form</h2>
3  {{=form}}
4  <h2>Submitted variables</h2>
```

```
5 {{=BEAUTIFY(request.vars)}}
```

The code so far is equivalent to the previous code, but the form is generated by the statement {{=form}} which serializes the FORM object.

Now we add one level of complexity by adding form validation and processing.

Change the controller as follows:

```
1 def display_form():
2     form=FORM('Your name:',
3              INPUT(_name='name', requires=IS_NOT_EMPTY()),
4              INPUT(_type='submit'))
5     if form.accepts(request,session):
6         response.flash = 'form accepted'
7     elif form.errors:
8         response.flash = 'form has errors'
9     else:
10        response.flash = 'please fill the form'
11    return dict(form=form)
```

and the associated "default/display_form.html" view:

```
1 {{extend 'layout.html'}}
2 <h2>Input form</h2>
3 {{=form}}
4 <h2>Submitted variables</h2>
5 {{=BEAUTIFY(request.vars)}}
6 <h2>Accepted variables</h2>
7 {{=BEAUTIFY(form.vars)}}
8 <h2>Errors in form</h2>
9 {{=BEAUTIFY(form.errors)}}
```

Notice that:

- In the action, we added the requires=IS_NOT_EMPTY() validator for the input field "name".

- In the action, we added a call to form.accepts(..)

- In the view, we are printing form.vars and form.errors as well as the form and request.vars.

All the work is done by the accepts method of the form object. It filters the request.vars according to the declared requirements (expressed by validators). accepts stores those variables that pass validation into form.vars. If a field value does not meet a requirement, the failing validator returns an error and the error is stored in `form.errors`. Both `form.vars` and `form.errors` are `gluon.storage.Storage` objects similar to `request.vars`. The former contains the values that passed validation, for example:

```
form.vars.name = "Max"
```

The latter contains the errors, for example:

```
form.errors.name = "Cannot be empty!"
```

The full signature of the `accepts` method is the following:

```
form.accepts(vars, session=None, formname='default',
             keepvalues=False, onvalidation=None,
             dbio=True, hideerror=False):
```

The meaning of the optional parameters is explained in the next sub-sections.

The first argument can be `request.vars` or `request.get_vars` or `request.post_vars` or simply `request`. The latter is equivalent to accepting as input the `request.post_vars`.

The `accepts` function returns `True` if the form is accepted and `False` otherwise. A form is not accepted if it has errors or when it has not been submitted (for example, the first time it is shown).

Here is how this page looks the first time it is displayed:

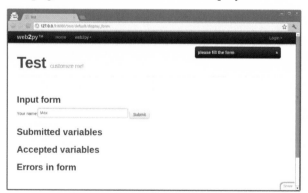

Here is how it looks upon invalid submission:

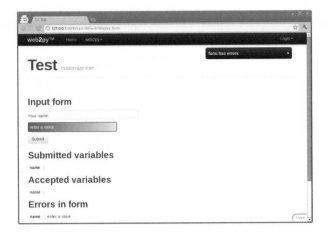

Here is how it looks upon a valid submission:

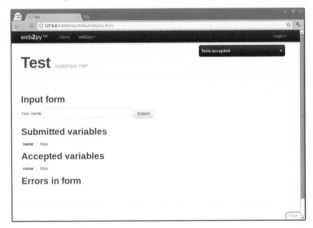

7.1.1   The process and validate methods

A shortcut for

```
form.accepts(request.post_vars,session,...)
```

is

```
form.process(...).accepted
```

the latter does not need the request and session arguments (although you can specify them optionally). it also differs from accepts because it returns the form itself. Internally process calls accepts and passes its arguments to it. The value returned by accepts is stored in form.accepted.

The process function takes some extra argument that accepts does not take:

- message_onsuccess

- onsuccess: if equal to 'flash' (default) and the form is accepted it will flash the above 'message_onsuccess

```
-
```

message_onfailure

```
-
```

onfailure: if equal to 'flash' (default) and the form fails validation, it will flash the above 'message_onfailure

- next the user to redirect after the form is accepted.

onsuccess   and   onfailure   can   be   functions   like   lambda form: do_something(form).

```
form.validate(...)
```

is a shortcut for

```
form.process(...,dbio=False).accepted
```

7.1.2 Hidden fields

When the above form object is serialized by {{=form}}, and because of the previous call to the accepts method, it now looks like this:

```
<form enctype="multipart/form-data" action="" method="post">
your name:
<input name="name" />
<input type="submit" />
<input value="783531473471" type="hidden" name="_formkey" />
<input value="default" type="hidden" name="_formname" />
</form>
```

Notice the presence of two hidden fields: "_formkey" and "_formname". Their presence is triggered by the call to accepts and they play two different and important roles:

- The hidden field called "_formkey" is a one-time token that web2py uses to prevent double submission of forms. The value of this key is generated when the form is serialized and stored in the session. When the form is submitted this value must match, or else accepts returns False without errors as if the form was not submitted at all. This is because web2py cannot determine whether the form was submitted correctly.

- The hidden field called "_formname" is generated by web2py as a name for the form, but the name can be overridden. This field is necessary to allow pages that contain and process multiple forms. web2py distinguishes the different submitted forms by their names.

- Optional hidden fields specified as FORM(..,hidden=dict(...)).

The role of these hidden fields and their usage in custom forms and pages with multiple forms is discussed in more detail later in the chapter.

If the form above is submitted with an empty "name" field, the form does not pass validation. When the form is serialized again it appears as:

```
1  <form enctype="multipart/form-data" action="" method="post">
2  your name:
3  <input value="" name="name" />
4  <div class="error">cannot be empty!</div>
5  <input type="submit" />
6  <input value="783531473471" type="hidden" name="_formkey" />
7  <input value="default" type="hidden" name="_formname" />
8  </form>
```

Notice the presence of a DIV of class "error" in the serialized form. web2py inserts this error message in the form to notify the visitor about the field that did not pass validation. The accepts method, upon submission, determines that the form is submitted, checks whether the field "name" is empty and whether it is required, and eventually inserts the error message from the validator into the form.

The base "layout.html" view is expected to handle DIVs of class "error". The default layout uses jQuery effects to make errors appear and slide down with a red background. See Chapter 11 for more details.

7.1.3 keepvalues

The optional argument keepvalues tells web2py what to do when a form is accepted and there is no redirection, so the same form is displayed again. By default the form is cleared. If keepvalues is set to True, the form is pre-populated with the previously inserted values. This is useful when you have a form that is supposed to be used repeatedly to insert multiple similar records. If the dbio argument is set to False, web2py will not perform any DB insert/update after accepting form. If hideerror is set to True and the form contains errors, these will not be displayed when the form is rendered (it will be up to you to display them from form.errors somehow. The onvalidation argument is explained below.

7.1.4 onvalidation

The onvalidation argument can be None or can be a function that takes the form and returns nothing. Such a function would be called and passed the form, immediately after validation (if validation passes) and before anything else happens. The purpose of this function is multifold. It can be used, for example, to perform additional checks on the form and eventually add errors to the form. It can also be used to compute the values of some fields based on the values of other fields. It can be used to trigger some action (like sending an email) before a record is created/updated.

Here is an example:

```
 1 db.define_table('numbers',
 2     Field('a', 'integer'),
 3     Field('b', 'integer'),
 4     Field('c', 'integer', readable=False, writable=False))
 5
 6 def my_form_processing(form):
 7     c = form.vars.a * form.vars.b
 8     if c < 0:
 9         form.errors.b = 'a*b cannot be negative'
10     else:
11         form.vars.c = c
12
13 def insert_numbers():
14     form = SQLFORM(db.numbers)
```

```
15    if form.process(onvalidation=my_form_processing).accepted:
16        session.flash = 'record inserted'
17        redirect(URL())
18    return dict(form=form)
```

7.1.5   Detect record change

When filling a form to edit a record there is a small probability that another user may concurrently be editing the same record. So when we save the record we want to check for possible conflicts. This can be done:

```
1  db.define_table('dog',Field('name'))
2
3  def edit_dog():
4      dog = db.dog(request.args(0)) or redirect(URL('error'))
5      form=SQLFORM(db.dog,dog)
6      form.process(detect_record_change=True)
7      if form.record_changed:
8          # do something
9      elif form.accepted:
10          # do something else
11      else:
12          # do nothing
13      return dict(form=form)
```

7.1.6   Forms and redirection

The most common way to use forms is via self-submission, so that the submitted field variables are processed by the same action that generated the form. Once the form is accepted, it is unusual to display the current page again (something we are doing here only to keep things simple). It is more common to redirect the visitor to a "next" page.

Here is the new example controller:

```
1  def display_form():
2      form = FORM('Your name:',
3              INPUT(_name='name', requires=IS_NOT_EMPTY()),
4              INPUT(_type='submit'))
5      if form.process().accepted:
6          session.flash = 'form accepted'
7          redirect(URL('next'))
8      elif form.errors:
```

```
 9        response.flash = 'form has errors'
10    else:
11        response.flash = 'please fill the form'
12    return dict(form=form)
13
14 def next():
15    return dict()
```

In order to set a flash on the next page instead of the current page you must use session.flash instead of response.flash. web2py moves the former into the latter after redirection. Note that using session.flash requires that you do not session.forget().

7.1.7 Multiple forms per page

The content of this section applies to both FORM and SQLFORM objects. It is possible to have multiple forms per page, but you must allow web2py to distinguish them. If these are derived by SQLFORM from different tables, then web2py gives them different names automatically; otherwise you need to explicitly give them different form names. Here is an example:

```
 1 def two_forms():
 2     form1 = FORM(INPUT(_name='name', requires=IS_NOT_EMPTY()),
 3                  INPUT(_type='submit'))
 4     form2 = FORM(INPUT(_name='name', requires=IS_NOT_EMPTY()),
 5                  INPUT(_type='submit'))
 6     if form1.process(formname='form_one').accepted:
 7         response.flash = 'form one accepted'
 8     if form2.process(formname='form_two').accepted:
 9         response.flash = 'form two accepted'
10     return dict(form1=form1, form2=form2)
```

and here is the output it produces:

When the visitor submits an empty form1, only form1 displays an error; if the visitor submits an empty form2, only form2 displays an error message.

7.1.8   Sharing forms

The content of this section applies to both FORM and SQLFORM objects. What we discuss here is possible but not recommended, since it is always good practice to have forms that self-submit. Sometimes, though, you don't have a choice, because the action that sends the form and the action that receives it belong to different applications.

It is possible to generate a form that submits to a different action. This is done by specifying the URL of the processing action in the attributes of the FORM or SQLFORM object. For example:

```
form = FORM(INPUT(_name='name', requires=IS_NOT_EMPTY()),
        INPUT(_type='submit'), _action=URL('page_two'))

def page_one():
    return dict(form=form)

def page_two():
    if form.process(session=None, formname=None).accepted:
        response.flash = 'form accepted'
    else:
        response.flash = 'there was an error in the form'
    return dict()
```

Notice that since both "page_one" and "page_two" use the same form, we have defined it only once by placing it outside of all the actions, in order not to repeat ourselves. The common portion of code at the beginning of a controller gets executed every time before giving control to the called action.

Since "page_one" does not call process (nor accepts), the form has no name and no key, so you must pass session=None and set formname=None in process, or the form will not validate when "page_two" receives it.

7.1.9   Adding buttons to FORMs

Usually a form provides a single submit button. It is common to want to add a "back" button that instead of submitting the form, directs the visitor to a different page.

This can be done with the add_button method:

```
form.add_button('Back', URL('other_page'))
```

You can add more than one button to form. The arguments of add_button are the value of the button (its text) and the url where to redirect to.

7.1.10   More about manipulation of FORMs

As discussed in the Views chapter, a FORM is an HTML helper. Helpers can be manipulated as Python lists and as dictionaries, which enables run-time creation and modification.

7.2   SQLFORM

We now move to the next level by providing the application with a model file:

```
db = DAL('sqlite://storage.sqlite')
db.define_table('person', Field('name', requires=IS_NOT_EMPTY()))
```

Modify the controller as follows:

```
def display_form():
```

```
2    form = SQLFORM(db.person)
3    if form.process().accepted:
4        response.flash = 'form accepted'
5    elif form.errors:
6        response.flash = 'form has errors'
7    else:
8        response.flash = 'please fill out the form'
9    return dict(form=form)
```

The view does not need to be changed.

In the new controller, you do not need to build a FORM, since the SQLFORM constructor built one from the table db.person defined in the model. This new form, when serialized, appears as:

```
1    <form enctype="multipart/form-data" action="" method="post">
2      <table>
3        <tr id="person_name__row">
4          <td><label id="person_name__label"
5                      for="person_name">Your name: </label></td>
6          <td><input type="text" class="string"
7                      name="name" value="" id="person_name" /></td>
8          <td></td>
9        </tr>
10       <tr id="submit_record__row">
11         <td></td>
12         <td><input value="Submit" type="submit" /></td>
13         <td></td>
14       </tr>
15     </table>
16     <input value="9038845529" type="hidden" name="_formkey" />
17     <input value="person" type="hidden" name="_formname" />
18   </form>
```

The automatically generated form is more complex than the previous low-level form. First of all, it contains a table of rows, and each row has three columns. The first column contains the field labels (as determined from the db.person), the second column contains the input fields (and eventually error messages), and the third column is optional and therefore empty (it can be populated with the fields in the SQLFORM constructor).

All tags in the form have names derived from the table and field name. This allows easy customization of the form using CSS and JavaScript. This capability is discussed in more detail in Chapter 11.

More important is that now the accepts method does a lot more work for you. As in the previous case, it performs validation of the input, but additionally, if the input passes validation, it also performs a database insert of the new record and stores in form.vars.id the unique "id" of the new record.

A SQLFORM object also deals automatically with "upload" fields by saving uploaded files in the "uploads" folder (after having them renamed safely to avoid conflicts and prevent directory traversal attacks) and stores their names (their new names) into the appropriate field in the database. After the form has been processed, the new filename is available in form.vars.fieldname (i.e., it replaces the cgi.FieldStorage object in request.vars.fieldname), so you can easily reference the new name right after upload.

A SQLFORM displays "boolean" values with checkboxes, "text" values with textareas, values required to be in a definite set or a database with dropboxes, and "upload" fields with links that allow users to download the uploaded files. It hides "blob" fields, since they are supposed to be handled differently, as discussed later.

For example, consider the following model:

```
db.define_table('person',
    Field('name', requires=IS_NOT_EMPTY()),
    Field('married', 'boolean'),
    Field('gender', requires=IS_IN_SET(['Male', 'Female', 'Other'])),
    Field('profile', 'text'),
    Field('image', 'upload'))
```

In this case, SQLFORM(db.person) generates the form shown below:

The SQLFORM constructor allows various customizations, such as displaying only a subset of the fields, changing the labels, adding values to the optional third column, or creating UPDATE and DELETE forms, as opposed to INSERT forms like the current one. SQLFORM is the single biggest time-saver object in web2py.

The class SQLFORM is defined in "gluon/sqlhtml.py". It can be easily extended by overriding its xml method, the method that serializes the objects, to change its output.

The signature for the SQLFORM constructor is the following:

```
SQLFORM(table, record = None,
        deletable = False, linkto = None,
        upload = None, fields = None, labels = None,
        col3 = {}, submit_button = 'Submit',
        delete_label = 'Check to delete:',
        showid = True, readonly = False,
        comments = True, keepopts = [],
        ignore_rw = False, record_id = None,
        formstyle = 'table3cols',
        buttons = ['submit'], separator = ': ',
        **attributes)
```

- The optional second argument turns the INSERT form into an UPDATE form for the specified record (see next subsection).

- If deletable is set to True, the UPDATE form displays a "Check to delete" checkbox. The value of the label if this field is set via the delete_label argument.

- submit_button sets the value of the submit button.

- id_label sets the label of the record "id"

- The "id" of the record is not shown if showid is set to False.

- fields is an optional list of field names that you want to display. If a list is provided, only fields in the list are displayed. For example:

```
fields = ['name']
```

- labels is a dictionary of field labels. The dictionary key is a field name and the corresponding value is what gets displayed as its label. If a label is not provided, web2py derives the label from the field name (it capitalizes the field name and replaces underscores with spaces). For example:

```
labels = {'name':'Your Full Name:'}
```

- col3 is a dictionary of values for the third column. For example:

```
col3 = {'name':A('what is this?',
    _href='http://www.google.com/search?q=define:name')}
```

- linkto and upload are optional URLs to user-defined controllers that allow the form to deal with reference fields. This is discussed in more detail later in the section.

- readonly. If set to True, displays the form as readonly

- comments. If set to False, does not display the col3 comments

- ignore_rw. Normally, for a create/update form, only fields marked as writable=True are shown, and for readonly forms, only fields marked as readable=True are shown. Setting ignore_rw=True causes those constraints to be ignored, and all fields are displayed. This is mostly used in the appadmin interface to display all fields for each table, overriding what the model indicates.

- formstyle determines the style to be used when serializing the form in html. It can be "table3cols" (default), "table2cols" (one row for label and comment, and one row for input), "ul" (makes an unordered list of input fields), "divs" (represents the form using css friendly divs, for arbitrary customization). formstyle can also be a function that takes (record_id, field_label, field_widget, field_comment) as attributes and returns a TR() object.

- is a list of INPUTs or TAG.BUTTONs (though technically could be any combination of helpers) that will be added to a DIV where the submit button would go.

- separator sets the string that separates form labels from form input fields.

- Optional attributes are arguments starting with underscore that you want to pass to the FORM tag that renders the SQLFORM object. Examples are:

```
1 _action = '.'
2 _method = 'POST'
```

There is a special hidden attribute. When a dictionary is passed as hidden, its items are translated into "hidden" INPUT fields (see the example for the FORM helper in Chapter 5).

```
1 form = SQLFORM(....,hidden=...)
```

causes the hidden fields to be passed with the submission, no more, no less. form.accepts(...) is not intended to read the received hidden fields and move them into form.vars. The reason is security. hidden fields can be tampered with. So you have to do explicitly move hidden fields from the request to the form:

```
1 form.vars.a = request.vars.a
2 form = SQLFORM(..., hidden=dict(a='b'))
```

7.2.1 SQLFORM and insert/update/delete

SQLFORM creates a new db record when the form is accepted. Assuming form=SQLFORM(db.test), then the id of the last-created record will be accessible in myform.vars.id.

If you pass a record as the optional second argument to the SQLFORM constructor, the form becomes an UPDATE form for that record. This means that when the form is submitted the existing record is updated and no new record is inserted. If you set the argument deletable=True, the UPDATE form displays a "check to delete" checkbox. If checked, the record is deleted.

> If a form is submitted and the delete checkbox is checked the
> attribute form.deleted is set to True.

You can modify the controller of the previous example so that when we pass
an additional integer argument in the URL path, as in:

```
/test/default/display_form/2
```

and if there is a record with the corresponding id, the SQLFORM generates an
UPDATE/DELETE form for the record:

```
def display_form():
    record = db.person(request.args(0)) or redirect(URL('index'))
    form = SQLFORM(db.person, record)
    if form.process().accepted:
        response.flash = 'form accepted'
    elif form.errors:
        response.flash = 'form has errors'
    return dict(form=form)
```

Line 2 finds the record and line 3 makes an UPDATE/DELETE form. Line 4
does all the corresponding form processing.

> An update form is very similar to a create form except that it is
> pre-populated with the current record and it previews images. By
> default deletable = True which means the update form will display
> a "delete record" option.

Edit forms also contain a hidden INPUT field with name="id" which is used to
identify the record. This id is also stored server-side for additional security
and, if the visitor tampers with the value of this field, the UPDATE is not
performed and web2py raises a SyntaxError, "user is tampering with form".

When a Field is marked with writable=False, the field is not shown in create
forms, and it is shown readonly in update forms. If a field is marked as
writable=False and readable=False, then the field is not shown at all, not even
in update forms.

Forms created with

```
form = SQLFORM(...,ignore_rw=True)
```

ignore the readable and writable attributes and always show all fields. Forms
in appadmin ignore them by default.

Forms created with

```
1  form = SQLFORM(table,record_id,readonly=True)
```

always show all fields in readonly mode, and they cannot be accepted.

7.2.2 SQLFORM in HTML

There are times when you want to use SQLFORM to benefit from its form generation and processing, but you need a level of customization of the form in HTML that you cannot achieve with the parameters of the SQLFORM object, so you have to design the form using HTML.

Now, edit the previous controller and add a new action:

```
1  def display_manual_form():
2      form = SQLFORM(db.person)
3      if form.process(session=None, formname='test').accepted:
4          response.flash = 'form accepted'
5      elif form.errors:
6          response.flash = 'form has errors'
7      else:
8          response.flash = 'please fill the form'
9      # Note: no form instance is passed to the view
10     return dict()
```

and insert the form in the associated "default/display_manual_form.html" view:

```
1  {{extend 'layout.html'}}
2  <form>
3  <ul>
4    <li>Your name is <input name="name" /></li>
5  </ul>
6    <input type="submit" />
7    <input type="hidden" name="_formname" value="test" />
8  </form>
```

Notice that the action does not return the form because it does not need to pass it to the view. The view contains a form created manually in HTML. The form contains a hidden field "_formname" that must be the same formname specified as an argument of accepts in the action. web2py uses the form name in case there are multiple forms on the same page, to determine which one was submitted. If the page contains a single form, you can set formname=None and omit the hidden field in the view.

form.accepts will look inside response.vars for data that matches fields in the

database table db.person. These fields are declared in the HTML in the format
<input name="field_name_goes_here" />

Note that in the example given, the form variables will be passed on the URL as arguments. If this is not desired, the POST protocol will have to be specified. Note furthermore, that if upload fields are specified, the form will have to be set up to allow this. Here, both options are shown:

```
<form enctype="multipart/form-data" method="post">
```

7.2.3   SQLFORM **and uploads**

Fields of type "upload" are special. They are rendered as INPUT fields of type="file". Unless otherwise specified, the uploaded file is streamed in using a buffer, and stored under the "uploads" folder of the application using a new safe name, assigned automatically. The name of this file is then saved into the field of type uploads.

As an example, consider the following model:

```
db.define_table('person',
   Field('name', requires=IS_NOT_EMPTY()),
   Field('image', 'upload'))
```

You can use the same controller action "display_form" shown above.

When you insert a new record, the form allows you to browse for a file. Choose, for example, a jpg image. The file is uploaded and stored as:

```
applications/test/uploads/person.image.XXXXX.jpg
```

"XXXXXX" is a random identifier for the file assigned by web2py.

> Notice that, by default, the original filename of an uploaded file is b16encoded and used to build the new name for the file. This name is retrieved by the default "download" action and used to set the content disposition header to the original filename.

Only its extension is preserved. This is a security requirement since the filename may contain special characters that could allow a visitor to perform directory traversal attacks or other malicious operations.

The new filename is also stored in form.vars.image.

When editing the record using an UPDATE form, it would be nice to display a link to the existing uploaded file, and web2py provides a way to do it.

If you pass a URL to the SQLFORM constructor via the upload argument, web2py uses the action at that URL to download the file. Consider the following actions:

```
1 def display_form():
2     record = db.person(request.args(0)) or redirect(URL('index'))
3     form = SQLFORM(db.person, record, deletable=True,
4                     upload=URL('download'))
5     if form.process().accepted:
6         response.flash = 'form accepted'
7     elif form.errors:
8         response.flash = 'form has errors'
9     return dict(form=form)
10
11 def download():
12     return response.download(request, db)
```

Now, insert a new record at the URL:

```
1 http://127.0.0.1:8000/test/default/display_form
```

Upload an image, submit the form, and then edit the newly created record by visiting:

```
1 http://127.0.0.1:8000/test/default/display_form/3
```

(here we assume the latest record has id=3). The form will display an image preview as shown below:

This form, when serialized, generates the following HTML:

```
1  <td><label id="person_image__label" for="person_image">Image: </label></td>
2  <td><div><input type="file" id="person_image" class="upload" name="image"
3  />[<a href="/test/default/download/person.image.0246683463831.jpg">file</a>|
4  <input type="checkbox" name="image__delete" />delete]</div></td><td></td></tr>
5  <tr id="delete_record__row"><td><label id="delete_record__label" for="delete_record
       "
6  >Check to delete:</label></td><td><input type="checkbox" id="delete_record"
7  class="delete" name="delete_this_record" /></td>
```

which contains a link to allow downloading of the uploaded file, and a checkbox to remove the file from the database record, thus storing NULL in the "image" field.

Why is this mechanism exposed? Why do you need to write the download function? Because you may want to enforce some authorization mechanism in the download function. See Chapter 9 for an example.

Normally uploaded files are stored into "app/uploads" but you can specify an alternate location:

```
1  Field('image', 'upload', uploadfolder='...')
```

In most operating system, accessing the file system can become slow when there are many files in the same folder. If you plan to upload more than 1000 files you can ask web2py to organize the uploads in subfolders:

```
1  Field('image', 'upload', uploadseparate=True)
```

7.2.4   Storing the original filename

web2py automatically stores the original filename inside the new UUID filename and retrieves it when the file is downloaded. Upon download, the original filename is stored in the content-disposition header of the HTTP response. This is all done transparently without the need for programming.

Occasionally you may want to store the original filename in a database field. In this case, you need to modify the model and add a field to store it in:

```
1  db.define_table('person',
2      Field('name', requires=IS_NOT_EMPTY()),
3      Field('image_filename'),
4      Field('image', 'upload'))
```

then you need to modify the controller to handle it:

```
1  def display_form():
2      record = db.person(request.args(0)) or redirect(URL('index'))
3      url = URL('download')
4      form = SQLFORM(db.person, record, deletable=True,
5                     upload=url, fields=['name', 'image'])
6      if request.vars.image!=None:
7          form.vars.image_filename = request.vars.image.filename
8      if form.process().accepted:
9          response.flash = 'form accepted'
10     elif form.errors:
11         response.flash = 'form has errors'
12     return dict(form=form)
```

Notice that the SQLFORM does not display the "image_filename" field. The "display_form" action moves the filename of the request.vars.image into the form.vars.image_filename, so that it gets processed by accepts and stored in the database. The download function, before serving the file, checks in the database for the original filename and uses it in the content-disposition header.

7.2.5 autodelete

The SQLFORM, upon deleting a record, does not delete the physical uploaded file(s) referenced by the record. The reason is that web2py does not know whether the same file is used/linked by other tables or used for other purpose. If you know it is safe to delete the actual file when the corresponding record is deleted, you can do the following:

```
1  db.define_table('image',
2      Field('name', requires=IS_NOT_EMPTY()),
3      Field('source','upload',autodelete=True))
```

The autodelete attribute is False by default. When set to True is makes sure the file is deleted when the record is deleted.

7.2.6 Links to referencing records

Now consider the case of two tables linked by a reference field. For example:

```
1  db.define_table('person',
```

```
2      Field('name', requires=IS_NOT_EMPTY()))
3  db.define_table('dog',
4      Field('owner', 'reference person'),
5      Field('name', requires=IS_NOT_EMPTY()))
6  db.dog.owner.requires = IS_IN_DB(db,db.person.id,'%(name)s')
```

A person has dogs, and each dog belongs to an owner, which is a person. The dog owner is required to reference a valid db.person.id by '%(name)s'.

Let's use the **appadmin** interface for this application to add a few persons and their dogs.

When editing an existing person, the **appadmin** UPDATE form shows a link to a page that lists the dogs that belong to the person. This behavior can be replicated using the linkto argument of the SQLFORM. linkto has to point to the URL of a new action that receives a query string from the SQLFORM and lists the corresponding records. Here is an example:

```
1  def display_form():
2      record = db.person(request.args(0)) or redirect(URL('index'))
3      url = URL('download')
4      link = URL('list_records', args='db')
5      form = SQLFORM(db.person, record, deletable=True,
6                     upload=url, linkto=link)
7      if form.process().accepted:
8          response.flash = 'form accepted'
9      elif form.errors:
10         response.flash = 'form has errors'
11     return dict(form=form)
```

Here is the page:

There is a link called "dog.owner". The name of this link can be changed via the `labels` argument of the SQLFORM, for example:

```
1  labels = {'dog.owner':"This person's dogs"}
```

If you click on the link you get directed to:

```
1  /test/default/list_records/dog?query=db.dog.owner%3D%3D5
```

"list_records" is the specified action, with `request.args(0)` set to the name of the referencing table and `request.vars.query` set to the SQL query string. The query string in the URL contains the value "dog.owner=5" appropriately url-encoded (web2py decodes this automatically when the URL is parsed).

You can easily implement a very general "list_records" action as follows:

```
1  def list_records():
2      REGEX = re.compile('^(\w+)\.(\w+)\.(\w+)\=\=(\d+)$')
3      match = REGEX.match(request.vars.query)
4      if not match:
5          redirect(URL('error'))
6      table, field, id = match.group(2), match.group(3), match.group(4)
7      records = db(db[table][field]==id).select()
8      return dict(records=records)
```

with the associated "default/list_records.html" view:

```
1  {{extend 'layout.html'}}
2  {{=records}}
```

When a set of records is returned by a select and serialized in a view, it is first converted into a SQLTABLE object (not the same as a Table) and then serialized into an HTML table, where each field corresponds to a table column.

7.2.7 Pre-populating the form

It is always possible to pre-populate a form using the syntax:

```
1  form.vars.name = 'fieldvalue'
```

Statements like the one above must be inserted after the form declaration and before the form is accepted, whether or not the field ("name" in the example) is explicitly visualized in the form.

7.2.8 Adding extra form elements to SQLFORM

Sometimes you may wish to add an extra element to your form after it has been created. For example, you may wish to add a checkbox which confirms the user agrees with the terms and conditions of your website:

```
form = SQLFORM(db.yourtable)
my_extra_element = TR(LABEL('I agree to the terms and conditions'), \
                      INPUT(_name='agree',value=True,_type='checkbox'))
form[0].insert(-1,my_extra_element)
```

The variable my_extra_element should be adapted to the formstyle. In this example, the default formstyle='table3cols' has been assumed.

After submission, form.vars.agree will contain the status of the checkbox, which could then be used in an onvalidation function, for instance.

7.2.9 SQLFORM without database IO

There are times when you want to generate a form from a database table using SQLFORM and you want to validate a submitted form accordingly, but you do not want any automatic INSERT/UPDATE/DELETE in the database. This is the case, for example, when one of the fields needs to be computed from the value of other input fields. This is also the case when you need to perform additional validation on the inserted data that cannot be achieved via standard validators.

This can be done easily by breaking:

```
form = SQLFORM(db.person)
if form.process().accepted:
    response.flash = 'record inserted'
```

into:

```
form = SQLFORM(db.person)
if form.validate():
    ### deal with uploads explicitly
    form.vars.id = db.person.insert(**dict(form.vars))
    response.flash = 'record inserted'
```

The same can be done for UPDATE/DELETE forms by breaking:

```
form = SQLFORM(db.person,record)
if form.process().accepted:
```

```
3    response.flash = 'record updated'
```

into:

```
1  form = SQLFORM(db.person,record)
2  if form.validate():
3      if form.deleted:
4          db(db.person.id==record.id).delete()
5      else:
6          record.update_record(**dict(form.vars))
7      response.flash = 'record updated'
```

In the case of a table including an "upload"-type field ("fieldname"), both process(dbio=False) and validate() deal with the storage of the uploaded file as if process(dbio=True), the default behavior.

The name assigned by web2py to the uploaded file can be found in:

```
1  form.vars.fieldname
```

7.3 Other types of Forms

7.3.1 SQLFORM.factory

There are cases when you want to generate forms *as if* you had a database table but you do not want the database table. You simply want to take advantage of the SQLFORM capability to generate a nice looking CSS-friendly form and perhaps perform file upload and renaming.

This can be done via a form_factory. Here is an example where you generate the form, perform validation, upload a file and store everything in the session :

```
1  def form_from_factory():
2      form = SQLFORM.factory(
3          Field('your_name', requires=IS_NOT_EMPTY()),
4          Field('your_image', 'upload'))
5      if form.process().accepted:
6          response.flash = 'form accepted'
7          session.your_name = form.vars.your_name
8          session.your_image = form.vars.your_image
9      elif form.errors:
10         response.flash = 'form has errors'
11     return dict(form=form)
```

The Field object in the SQLFORM.factory() constructor is fully documented in the DAL chapter. A run-time construction technique for SQLFORM.factory() is

```
1 fields = []
2 fields.append(Field(...))
3 form=SQLFORM.factory(*fields)
```

Here is the "default/form_from_factory.html" view:

```
1 {{extend 'layout.html'}}
2 {{=form}}
```

You need to use an underscore instead of a space for field labels, or explicitly pass a dictionary of labels to form_factory, as you would for a SQLFORM. By default SQLFORM.factory generates the form using html "id" attributes generated as if the form was generated from a table called "no_table". To change this dummy table name, use the table_name attribute for the factory:

```
1 form = SQLFORM.factory(...,table_name='other_dummy_name')
```

Changing the table_name is necessary if you need to place two factory generated forms in the same table and want to avoid CSS conflicts.

Uploading files with SQLFORM.factory

7.3.2   One form for multiple tables

It often happens that you have two tables (for example 'client' and 'address' which are linked together by a reference and you want to create a single form that allows to insert info about one client and its default address. Here is how: model:

```
1 db.define_table('client',
2     Field('name'))
3 db.define_table('address',
4    Field('client','reference client',
5          writable=False,readable=False),
6    Field('street'),Field('city'))
```

controller:

```
1 def register():
2     form=SQLFORM.factory(db.client,db.address)
3     if form.process().accepted:
4         id = db.client.insert(**db.client._filter_fields(form.vars))
```

```
5    form.vars.client=id
6    id = db.address.insert(**db.address._filter_fields(form.vars))
7    response.flash='Thanks for filling the form'
8  return dict(form=form)
```

Notice the SQLFORM.factory (it makes ONE form using public fields from both tables and inherits their validators too). On form accepts this does two inserts, some data in one table and some data in the other.

▌ This only works when the tables don't have field names in common.

7.3.3 Confirmation Forms

Often you need a form with a confirmation choice. The form should be accepted if the choice is accepted and none otherwise. The form may have additional options that link other web pages. web2py provides a simple way to do this:

```
1  form = FORM.confirm('Are you sure?')
2  if form.accepted: do_what_needs_to_be_done()
```

Notice that the confirm form does not need and must not call .accepts or .process because this is done internally. You can add buttons with links to the confirmation form in the form of a dictionary of {'value':'link'}:

```
1  form = FORM.confirm('Are you sure?',{'Back':URL('other_page')})
2  if form.accepted: do_what_needs_to_be_done()
```


7.3.4 Form to edit a dictionary

Imagine a system that stores configurations options in a dictionary,

```
1  config = dict(color='black', language='English')
```

and you need a form to allow the visitor to modify this dictionary. This can be done with:

```
1  form = SQLFORM.dictform(config)
2  if form.process().accepted: config.update(form.vars)
```

The form will display one INPUT field for each item in the dictionary. It will use dictionary keys as INPUT names and labels and current values to infer types (string, int, double, date, datetime, boolean).

This works great but leave to you the logic of making the config dictionary persistent. For example you may want to store the config in a session.

```
1  session.config or dict(color='black', language='English')
2  form = SQLFORM.dictform(session.config)
3  if form.process().accepted:
4      session.config.update(form.vars)
```

7.4 CRUD

One of the recent additions to web2py is the Create/Read/Update/Delete (CRUD) API on top of SQLFORM. CRUD creates an SQLFORM, but it simplifies the coding because it incorporates the creation of the form, the processing of the form, the notification, and the redirection, all in one single function.

The first thing to notice is that CRUD differs from the other web2py APIs we have used so far because it is not already exposed. It must be imported. It also must be linked to a specific database. For example:

```
1  from gluon.tools import Crud
2  crud = Crud(db)
```

The crud object defined above provides the following API:

.

- crud.tables() returns a list of tables defined in the database.

- crud.create(db.tablename) returns a create form for table tablename.

- crud.read(db.tablename, id) returns a readonly form for tablename and record id.

- crud.update(db.tablename, id) returns an update form for tablename and record id.

- crud.delete(db.tablename, id) deletes the record.

- crud.select(db.tablename, query) returns a list of records selected from the table.

- crud.search(db.tablename) returns a tuple (form, records) where form is a search form and records is a list of records based on the submitted search form.

- `crud()` returns one of the above based on the `request.args()`.

For example, the following action:

```
def data(): return dict(form=crud())
```

would expose the following URLs:

```
http://.../[app]/[controller]/data/tables
http://.../[app]/[controller]/data/create/[tablename]
http://.../[app]/[controller]/data/read/[tablename]/[id]
http://.../[app]/[controller]/data/update/[tablename]/[id]
http://.../[app]/[controller]/data/delete/[tablename]/[id]
http://.../[app]/[controller]/data/select/[tablename]
http://.../[app]/[controller]/data/search/[tablename]
```

However, the following action:

```
def create_tablename():
    return dict(form=crud.create(db.tablename))
```

would only expose the create method

```
http://.../[app]/[controller]/create_tablename
```

While the following action:

```
def update_tablename():
    return dict(form=crud.update(db.tablename, request.args(0)))
```

would only expose the update method

```
http://.../[app]/[controller]/update_tablename/[id]
```

and so on.

The behavior of CRUD can be customized in two ways: by setting some attributes of the `crud` object or by passing extra parameters to each of its methods.

7.4.1 Settings

Here is a complete list of current CRUD attributes, their default values, and meaning:

To enforce authentication on all crud forms:

```
crud.settings.auth = auth
```

The use is explained in chapter 9.

To specify the controller that defines the data function which returns the crud object

```
crud.settings.controller = 'default'
```

To specify the URL to redirect to after a successful "create" record:

```
crud.settings.create_next = URL('index')
```

To specify the URL to redirect to after a successful "update" record:

```
crud.settings.update_next = URL('index')
```

To specify the URL to redirect to after a successful "delete" record:

```
crud.settings.delete_next = URL('index')
```

To specify the URL to be used for linking uploaded files:

```
crud.settings.download_url = URL('download')
```

To specify extra functions to be executed after standard validation procedures for crud.create forms:

```
crud.settings.create_onvalidation = StorageList()
```

StorageList is the same as a Storage object, they are both defined in the file "gluon/storage.py", but it defaults to [] as opposed to None. It allows the following syntax:

```
crud.settings.create_onvalidation.mytablename.append(lambda form:....)
```

To specify extra functions to be executed after standard validation procedures for crud.update forms:

```
crud.settings.update_onvalidation = StorageList()
```

To specify extra functions to be executed after completion of crud.create forms:

```
crud.settings.create_onaccept = StorageList()
```

To specify extra functions to be executed after completion of crud.update forms:

```
crud.settings.update_onaccept = StorageList()
```

To specify extra functions to be executed after completion of crud.update if record is deleted:

```
1 crud.settings.update_ondelete = StorageList()
```

To specify extra functions to be executed after completion of `crud.delete`:

```
1 crud.settings.delete_onaccept = StorageList()
```

To determine whether the "update" forms should have a "delete" button:

```
1 crud.settings.update_deletable = True
```

To determine whether the "update" forms should show the id of the edited record:

```
1 crud.settings.showid = False
```

To determine whether forms should keep the previously inserted values or reset to default after successful submission:

```
1 crud.settings.keepvalues = False
```

Crud always detects whether a record being edited has been modified by a third party in the time between the time when the form is displayed and the time when it is submitted. This behavior is equivalent to

```
1 form.process(detect_record_change=True)
```

and it is set in:

```
1 crud.settings.detect_record_change = True
```

and it can be changed/disabled by setting the variable to False.

You can change the form style by

```
1 crud.settings.formstyle = 'table3cols' or 'table2cols' or 'divs' or 'ul'
```

You can set the separator in all crud forms:

```
1 crud.settings.label_separator = ':'
```

You can add captcha to forms, using the same convention explained for auth, with:

```
1 crud.settings.create_captcha = None
2 crud.settings.update_captcha = None
3 crud.settings.captcha = None
```

7.4.2 Messages

Here is a list of customizable messages:

```
1 crud.messages.submit_button = 'Submit'
```

sets the text of the "submit" button for both create and update forms.

```
1 crud.messages.delete_label = 'Check to delete:'
```

sets the label of the "delete" button in "update" forms.

```
1 crud.messages.record_created = 'Record Created'
```

sets the flash message on successful record creation.

```
1 crud.messages.record_updated = 'Record Updated'
```

sets the flash message on successful record update.

```
1 crud.messages.record_deleted = 'Record Deleted'
```

sets the flash message on successful record deletion.

```
1 crud.messages.update_log = 'Record %(id)s updated'
```

sets the log message on successful record update.

```
1 crud.messages.create_log = 'Record %(id)s created'
```

sets the log message on successful record creation.

```
1 crud.messages.read_log = 'Record %(id)s read'
```

sets the log message on successful record read access.

```
1 crud.messages.delete_log = 'Record %(id)s deleted'
```

sets the log message on successful record deletion.

> Notice that crud.messages belongs to the class gluon.storage.Message
> which is similar to gluon.storage.Storage but it automatically
> translates its values, without need for the T operator.

Log messages are used if and only if CRUD is connected to Auth as discussed in Chapter 9. The events are logged in the Auth table "auth_events".

7.4.3 Methods

The behavior of CRUD methods can also be customized on a per call basis. Here are their signatures:

```
1 crud.tables()
2 crud.create(table, next, onvalidation, onaccept, log, message)
3 crud.read(table, record)
4 crud.update(table, record, next, onvalidation, onaccept, ondelete, log, message,
       deletable)
5 crud.delete(table, record_id, next, message)
```

```
6  crud.select(table, query, fields, orderby, limitby, headers, **attr)
7  crud.search(table, query, queries, query_labels, fields, field_labels, zero,
       showall, chkall)
```

- `table` is a DAL table or a tablename the method should act on.

- `record` and `record_id` are the id of the record the method should act on.

- `next` is the URL to redirect to after success. If the URL contains the substring "[id]" this will be replaced by the id of the record currently created/updated.

- `onvalidation` has the same function as SQLFORM(..., onvalidation)

- `onaccept` is a function to be called after the form submission is accepted and acted upon, but before redirection.

- `log` is the log message. Log messages in CRUD see variables in the `form.vars` dictionary such as "%(id)s".

- `message` is the flash message upon form acceptance.

- `ondelete` is called in place of `onaccept` when a record is deleted via an "update" form.

- `deletable` determines whether the "update" form should have a delete option.

- `query` is the query to be used to select records.

- `fields` is a list of fields to be selected.

- `orderby` determines the order in which records should be selected (see Chapter 6).

- `limitby` determines the range of selected records that should be displayed (see Chapter 6).

- `headers` is a dictionary with the table header names.

- `queries` a list like `['equals', 'not equal', 'contains']` containing the allowed methods in the search form.

- `query_labels` a dictionary like `query_labels=dict(equals='Equals')` giving names to search methods.

- `fields` a list of fields to be listed in the search widget.

- `field_labels` a dictionary mapping field names into labels.

- `zero` defaults to "choose one" is used as default option for the drop-down in the search widget.

- `showall` set it to True if you want rows returned as per the query in the first call (added after 1.98.2).

- `chkall` set it to True to turn on all the checkboxes in the search form (added after 1.98.2).

Here is an example of usage in a single controller function:

```
## assuming db.define_table('person', Field('name'))
def people():
    form = crud.create(db.person, next=URL('index'),
        message=T("record created"))
    persons = crud.select(db.person, fields=['name'],
        headers={'person.name': 'Name'})
    return dict(form=form, persons=persons)
```

Here is another very generic controller function that lets you search, create and edit any records from any table where the tablename is passed request.args(0):

```
def manage():
    table=db[request.args(0)]
    form = crud.update(table,request.args(1))
    table.id.represent = lambda id, row: \
        A('edit:',id,_href=URL(args=(request.args(0),id)))
    search, rows = crud.search(table)
    return dict(form=form,search=search,rows=rows)
```

Notice the line `table.id.represent=...` that tells web2py to change the representation of the id field and display a link instead to the page itself and passes the id as request.args(1) which turns the create page into an update page.

7.4.4   Record versioning

Both SQLFORM and CRUD provides a utility to version database records:

If you have a table (db.mytable) that needs full revision history you can just do:

```
1  form = SQLFORM(db.mytable, myrecord).process(onsuccess=auth.archive)
1  form = crud.update(db.mytable, myrecord, onaccept=auth.archive)
```

auth.archive defines a new table called **db.mytable_archive** (the name is derived from the name of the table to which it refers) and on updating, it stores a copy of the record (as it was before the update) in the created archive table, including a reference to the current record.

Because the record is actually updated (only its previous state is archived), references are never broken.

This is all done under the hood. Should you wish to access the archive table you should define it in a model:

```
1  db.define_table('mytable_archive',
2      Field('current_record', 'reference mytable'),
3      db.mytable)
```

Notice the table extends db.mytable (including all its fields), and adds a reference to the current_record.

auth.archive does not timestamp the stored record unless your original table has timestamp fields, for example:

```
1  db.define_table('mytable',
2      Field('created_on', 'datetime',
3              default=request.now, update=request.now, writable=False),
4      Field('created_by', 'reference auth_user',
5              default=auth.user_id, update=auth.user_id, writable=False),
```

There is nothing special about these fields and you may give them any name you like. They are filled before the record is archived and are archived with each copy of the record. The archive table name and/or reference field name can be changed like this:

```
1  db.define_table('myhistory',
2      Field('parent_record', 'reference mytable'),
3      db.mytable)
4  ## ...
5  form = SQLFORM(db.mytable,myrecord)
6  form.process(onsuccess = lambda form:auth.archive(form,
7              archive_table=db.myhistory,
8              current_record='parent_record'))
```

7.5   Custom forms

If a form is created with SQLFORM, SQLFORM.factory or CRUD, there are multiple ways it can be embedded in a view allowing multiple degrees of customization. Consider for example the following model:

```
1 db.define_table('image',
2    Field('name', requires=IS_NOT_EMPTY()),
3    Field('source', 'upload'))
```

and upload action

```
1 def upload_image():
2    return dict(form=SQLFORM(db.image).process())
```

The simplest way to embed the form in the view for upload_image is

```
1 {{=form}}
```

This results in a standard table layout. If you wish to use a different layout, you can break the form into components

```
1 {{=form.custom.begin}}
2 Image name: <div>{{=form.custom.widget.name}}</div>
3 Image file: <div>{{=form.custom.widget.source}}</div>
4 Click here to upload: {{=form.custom.submit}}
5 {{=form.custom.end}}
```

where form.custom.widget[fieldname] gets serialized into the proper widget for the field. If the form is submitted and it contains errors, they are appended below the widgets, as usual.

The above sample form is show in the image below.

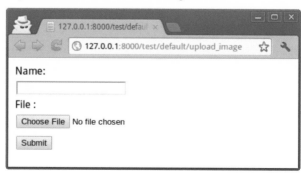

A similar result could have been obtained without using a custom form:

```
1  SQLFORM(...,formstyle='table2cols')
```

or in case of CRUD forms with the following parameter:

```
1  crud.settings.formstyle='table2cols'
```

Other possible formstyles are "table3cols" (the default), "divs" and "ul".

If you do not wish to use the widgets serialized by web2py, you can replace them with HTML. There are some variables that will be useful for this:

- form.custom.label[fieldname] contains the label for the field.

- form.custom.comment[fieldname] contains the comment for the field.

- form.custom.dspval[fieldname] form-type and field-type dependent display representation of the field.

- form.custom.inpval[fieldname] form-type and field-type dependent values to be used in field code.

If you form has deletable=True you should also insert

```
1  {{=form.custom.delete}}
```

to display the delete checkbox.

It is important to follow the conventions described below.

7.5.1   CSS conventions

Tags in forms generated by SQLFORM, SQLFORM.factory and CRUD follow a strict CSS naming convention that can be used to further customize the forms.

Given a table "mytable", and a field "myfield" of type "string", it is rendered by default by a

```
1  SQLFORM.widgets.string.widget
```

that looks like this:

```
1  <input type="text" name="myfield" id="mytable_myfield"
2        class="string" />
```

Notice that:

- the class of the INPUT tag is the same as the type of the field. This is very important for the jQuery code in "web2py_ajax.html" to work. It makes sure that you can only have numbers in "integer" and "double" fields, and that "time", "date" and "datetime" fields display the popup calendar/datepicker.

- the id is the name of the class plus the name of the field, joined by one underscore. This allows you to uniquely refer to the field via, for example, jQuery('#mytable_myfield') and manipulate the stylesheet of the field or bind actions associated to the field events (focus, blur, keyup, etc.).

- the name is, as you would expect, the field name.

7.5.2 Hide errors

Occasionally, you may want to disable the automatic error placement and display form error messages in some place other than the default. That can be done easily.

- In the case of FORM or SQLFORM, pass hideerror=True to the accepts method.

- In the case of CRUD, set crud.settings.hideerror=True

You may also want to modify the views to display the error (since they are no longer displayed automatically).

Here is an example where the errors are displayed above the form and not in the form.

```
1  {{if form.errors:}}
2    Your submitted form contains the following errors:
3    <ul>
4    {{for fieldname in form.errors:}}
5      <li>{{=fieldname}} error: {{=form.errors[fieldname]}}</li>
6    {{pass}}
7    </ul>
8    {{form.errors.clear()}}
9  {{pass}}
10 {{=form}}
```

The errors will displayed as in the image shown below.

This mechanism also works for custom forms.

7.6 Validators

Validators are classes used to validate input fields (including forms generated from database tables).

Here is an example of using a validator with a FORM:

```
INPUT(_name='a', requires=IS_INT_IN_RANGE(0, 10))
```

Here is an example of how to require a validator for a table field:

```
db.define_table('person', Field('name'))
db.person.name.requires = IS_NOT_EMPTY()
```

Validators are always assigned using the requires attribute of a field. A field can have a single validator or multiple validators. Multiple validators are made part of a list:

```
db.person.name.requires = [IS_NOT_EMPTY(),
                           IS_NOT_IN_DB(db, 'person.name')]
```

Normally validators are called automatically by the function accepts and process of a FORM or other HTML helper object that contains a form. They are called in the order in which they are listed.

One can also call validators explicitly for a field:

```
db.person.name.validate(value)
```

which returns a tuple (value,error) and error is None if no the value validates.

Built-in validators have constructors that take an optional argument:

```
IS_NOT_EMPTY(error_message='cannot be empty')
```

error_message allows you to override the default error message for any validator.

Here is an example of a validator on a database table:

```
db.person.name.requires = IS_NOT_EMPTY(error_message='fill this!')
```

where we have used the translation operator T to allow for internationalization. Notice that default error messages are not translated.

Mind that the only validators that can be used with list: type fields are:

- IS_IN_DB(...,multiple=True)

- IS_IN_SET(...,multiple=True)

- IS_NOT_EMPTY()

- IS_LIST_OF(...)

The latter can be used to apply any validator to the individual items in the list.

7.6.1 Validators

IS_ALPHANUMERIC

This validator checks that a field value contains only characters in the ranges a-z, A-Z, or 0-9.

```
requires = IS_ALPHANUMERIC(error_message='must be alphanumeric!')
```

IS_DATE

This validator checks that a field value contains a valid date in the specified format. It is good practice to specify the format using the translation operator, in order to support different formats in different locales.

```
requires = IS_DATE(format=T('%Y-%m-%d'),
                   error_message='must be YYYY-MM-DD!')
```

For the full description on % directives look under the IS_DATETIME validator.

IS_DATE_IN_RANGE

Works very much like the previous validator but allows to specify a range:

```
1  requires = IS_DATE_IN_RANGE(format=T('%Y-%m-%d'),
2                     minimum=datetime.date(2008,1,1),
3                     maximum=datetime.date(2009,12,31),
4                     error_message='must be YYYY-MM-DD!')
```

For the full description on % directives look under the IS_DATETIME validator.

IS_DATETIME

This validator checks that a field value contains a valid datetime in the specified format. It is good practice to specify the format using the translation operator, in order to support different formats in different locales.

```
1  requires = IS_DATETIME(format=T('%Y-%m-%d %H:%M:%S'),
2                     error_message='must be YYYY-MM-DD HH:MM:SS!')
```

The following symbols can be used for the format string (this shows the symbol and an example string):

```
1  %Y  '1963'
2  %y  '63'
3  %d  '28'
4  %m  '08'
5  %b  'Aug'
6  %b  'August'
7  %H  '14'
8  %I  '02'
9  %p  'PM'
10 %M  '30'
11 %S  '59'
```

IS_DATETIME_IN_RANGE

Works very much like the previous validator but allows to specify a range:

```
1  requires = IS_DATETIME_IN_RANGE(format=T('%Y-%m-%d %H:%M:%S'),
2                     minimum=datetime.datetime(2008,1,1,10,30),
3                     maximum=datetime.datetime(2009,12,31,11,45),
4                     error_message='must be YYYY-MM-DD HH:MM::SS!')
```

For the full description on % directives look under the IS_DATETIME validator.

IS_DECIMAL_IN_RANGE

```
1  INPUT(_type='text', _name='name', requires=IS_DECIMAL_IN_RANGE(0, 10, dot="."))
```

It converts the input into a Python Decimal or generates an error if the decimal does not fall within the specified inclusive range. The comparison is made with Python Decimal arithmetic.

The minimum and maximum limits can be None, meaning no lower or upper limit, respectively.

The dot argument is optional and allows you to internationalize the symbol used to separate the decimals.

IS_EMAIL

It checks that the field value looks like an email address. It does not try to send email to confirm.

```
requires = IS_EMAIL(error_message='invalid email!')
```

IS_EQUAL_TO

Checks whether the validated value is equal to a given value (which can be a variable):

```
requires = IS_EQUAL_TO(request.vars.password,
                       error_message='passwords do not match')
```

IS_EXPR

Its first argument is a string containing a logical expression in terms of a variable value. It validates a field value if the expression evaluates to True. For example:

```
requires = IS_EXPR('int(value)%3==0',
                   error_message='not divisible by 3')
```

One should first check that the value is an integer so that an exception will not occur.

```
requires = [IS_INT_IN_RANGE(0, 100), IS_EXPR('value%3==0')]
```

IS_FLOAT_IN_RANGE

Checks that the field value is a floating point number within a definite range, $0 <=$ value $<= 100$ in the following example:

```
requires = IS_FLOAT_IN_RANGE(0, 100, dot=".",
           error_message='too small or too large!')
```

The dot argument is optional and allows you to internationalize the symbol used to separate the decimals.

IS_INT_IN_RANGE

Checks that the field value is an integer number within a definite range, 0 <= value < 100 in the following example:

```
1  requires = IS_INT_IN_RANGE(0, 100,
2          error_message='too small or too large!')
```

IS_IN_SET

Checks that the field values are in a set:

```
1  requires = IS_IN_SET(['a', 'b', 'c'],zero=T('choose one'),
2          error_message='must be a or b or c')
```

The zero argument is optional and it determines the text of the option selected by default, an option which is not accepted by the IS_IN_SET validator itself. If you do not want a "choose one" option, set zero=None.

The zero option was introduced in revision (1.67.1). It did not break backward compatibility in the sense that it did not break applications but it did change their behavior since, before, there was no zero option.

The elements of the set must always be strings unless this validator is preceded by IS_INT_IN_RANGE (which converts the value to int) or IS_FLOAT_IN_RANGE (which converts the value to float). For example:

```
1  requires = [IS_INT_IN_RANGE(0, 8), IS_IN_SET([2, 3, 5, 7],
2          error_message='must be prime and less than 10')]
```

You may also use a dictionary or a list of tuples to make the drop down list more descriptive:

```
1  #### Dictionary example:
2  requires = IS_IN_SET({'A':'Apple','B':'Banana','C':'Cherry'},zero=None)
3  #### List of tuples example:
4  requires = IS_IN_SET([('A','Apple'),('B','Banana'),('C','Cherry')])
```

IS_IN_SET **and Tagging**

The IS_IN_SET validator has an optional attribute multiple=False. If set to True, multiple values can be stored in one field. The field should be of type list:integer or list:string. multiple references are handled automatically in create and update forms, but they are transparent to the DAL. We strongly suggest using the jQuery multiselect plugin to render multiple fields.

Note that when multiple=True, IS_IN_SET will accept zero or more values, i.e. it will accept the field when nothing has been selected. multiple can also be a tuple of the form (a,b) where a and b are the minimum and (exclusive) maximum number of items that can be selected respectively.

IS_LENGTH

Checks if length of field's value fits between given boundaries. Works for both text and file inputs.

Its arguments are:

- maxsize: the maximum allowed length / size (has default = 255)

- minsize: the minimum allowed length / size

Examples: Check if text string is shorter than 33 characters:

```
INPUT(_type='text', _name='name', requires=IS_LENGTH(32))
```

Check if password string is longer than 5 characters:

```
INPUT(_type='password', _name='name', requires=IS_LENGTH(minsize=6))
```

Check if uploaded file has size between 1KB and 1MB:

```
INPUT(_type='file', _name='name', requires=IS_LENGTH(1048576, 1024))
```

For all field types except for files, it checks the length of the value. In the case of files, the value is a cookie.FieldStorage, so it validates the length of the data in the file, which is the behavior one might intuitively expect.

IS_LIST_OF

This is not properly a validator. Its intended use is to allow validations of fields that return multiple values. It is used in those rare cases when a form contains multiple fields with the same name or a multiple selection box. Its only argument is another validator, and all it does is to apply the other validator to each element of the list. For example, the following expression checks that every item in a list is an integer in the range 0-10:

```
requires = IS_LIST_OF(IS_INT_IN_RANGE(0, 10))
```

It never returns an error and does not contain an error message. The inner validator controls the error generation.

IS_LOWER

This validator never returns an error. It just converts the value to lower case.

```
1   requires = IS_LOWER()
```

IS_MATCH

This validator matches the value against a regular expression and returns an error if it does not match. Here is an example of usage to validate a US zip code:

```
1   requires = IS_MATCH('^\d{5}(-\d{4})?$',
2          error_message='not a zip code')
```

Here is an example of usage to validate an IPv4 address (note: the IS_IPV4 validator is more appropriate for this purpose):

```
1   requires = IS_MATCH('^\d{1,3}(\.\d{1,3}){3}$',
2          error_message='not an IP address')
```

Here is an example of usage to validate a US phone number:

```
1   requires = IS_MATCH('^1?((-)\d{3}-?|\(\d{3}\))\d{3}-?\d{4}$',
2          error_message='not a phone number')
```

For more information on Python regular expressions, refer to the official Python documentation.

IS_MATCH takes an optional argument strict which defaults to False. When set to True it only matches the beginning of the string:

```
1   >>> IS_MATCH('a')('ba')
2   ('ba', <lazyT 'invalid expression'>) # no pass
3   >>> IS_MATCH('a',strict=False)('ab')
4   ('a', None)                    # pass!
```

IS_MATCH takes an other optional argument search which defaults to False. When set to True, it uses regex method search instead of method match to validate the string.

IS_MATCH('...', extract=True) filters and extract only the first matching substring rather than the original value.

IS_NOT_EMPTY

This validator checks that the content of the field value is not an empty string.

```
1   requires = IS_NOT_EMPTY(error_message='cannot be empty!')
```

IS_TIME

This validator checks that a field value contains a valid time in the specified format.

```
requires = IS_TIME(error_message='must be HH:MM:SS!')
```

IS_URL

Rejects a URL string if any of the following is true:

- The string is empty or None

- The string uses characters that are not allowed in a URL

- The string breaks any of the HTTP syntactic rules

- The URL scheme specified (if one is specified) is not 'http' or 'https'

- The top-level domain (if a host name is specified) does not exist

(These rules are based on RFC 2616 [83])

This function only checks the URL's syntax. It does not check that the URL points to a real document, for example, or that it otherwise makes semantic sense. This function does automatically prepend 'http://' in front of a URL in the case of an abbreviated URL (e.g. 'google.ca').

If the parameter mode='generic' is used, then this function's behavior changes. It then rejects a URL string if any of the following is true:

- The string is empty or None

- The string uses characters that are not allowed in a URL

- The URL scheme specified (if one is specified) is not valid

(These rules are based on RFC 2396 [84])

The list of allowed schemes is customizable with the allowed_schemes parameter. If you exclude None from the list, then abbreviated URLs (lacking a scheme such as 'http') will be rejected.

The default prepended scheme is customizable with the prepend_scheme parameter. If you set prepend_scheme to None, then prepending will be disabled. URLs that require prepending to parse will still be accepted, but the return value will not be modified.

IS_URL is compatible with the Internationalized Domain Name (IDN) standard specified in RFC 3490 [85]). As a result, URLs can be regular strings or unicode strings. If the URL's domain component (e.g. google.ca) contains non-US-ASCII letters, then the domain will be converted into Punycode (defined in RFC 3492 [86]). IS_URL goes a bit beyond the standards, and allows non-US-ASCII characters to be present in the path and query components of the URL as well. These non-US-ASCII characters will be encoded. For example, space will be encoded as '%20'. The unicode character with hex code 0x4e86 will become '%4e%86'.

Examples:

```
1  requires = IS_URL())
2  requires = IS_URL(mode='generic')
3  requires = IS_URL(allowed_schemes=['https'])
4  requires = IS_URL(prepend_scheme='https')
5  requires = IS_URL(mode='generic',
6               allowed_schemes=['ftps', 'https'],
7               prepend_scheme='https')
```

IS_SLUG

```
1  requires = IS_SLUG(maxlen=80, check=False, error_message='must be slug')
```

If check is set to True it check whether the validated value is a slug (allowing only alphanumeric characters and non-repeated dashes).

If check is set to False (default) it converts the input value to a slug.

IS_STRONG

Enforces complexity requirements on a field (usually a password field)

Example:

```
1  requires = IS_STRONG(min=10, special=2, upper=2)
```

where

- min is minimum length of the value

- special is the minimum number of required special characters special characters are any of the following !@#$%&*(){}[]-+

- upper is the minimum number of upper case characters

IS_IMAGE

This validator checks if a file uploaded through the file input was saved in one of the selected image formats and has dimensions (width and height) within given limits.

It does not check for maximum file size (use IS_LENGTH for that). It returns a validation failure if no data was uploaded. It supports the file formats BMP, GIF, JPEG, PNG, and it does not require the Python Imaging Library.

Code parts taken from ref. [87]

It takes the following arguments:

- extensions: iterable containing allowed image file extensions in lowercase

- maxsize: iterable containing maximum width and height of the image

- minsize: iterable containing minimum width and height of the image

Use (-1, -1) as minsize to bypass the image-size check.

Here are some Examples:

- Check if uploaded file is in any of supported image formats:

```
requires = IS_IMAGE()
```

- Check if uploaded file is either JPEG or PNG:

```
requires = IS_IMAGE(extensions=('jpeg', 'png'))
```

- Check if uploaded file is PNG with maximum size of 200x200 pixels:

```
requires = IS_IMAGE(extensions=('png'), maxsize=(200, 200))
```

- Note: on displaying an edit form for a table including requires = IS_IMAGE(), a delete checkbox will NOT appear because to delete the file would cause the validation to fail. To display the delete checkbox use this validation:

```
requires = IS_EMPTY_OR(IS_IMAGE())
```

IS_UPLOAD_FILENAME

This validator checks if the name and extension of a file uploaded through the file input matches the given criteria.

It does not ensure the file type in any way. Returns validation failure if no data was uploaded.

Its arguments are:

- filename: filename (before dot) regex.

- extension: extension (after dot) regex.

- lastdot: which dot should be used as a filename / extension separator: True indicates last dot (e.g., "file.tar.gz" will be broken in "file.tar" + "gz") while False means first dot (e.g., "file.tar.gz" will be broken into "file" + "tar.gz").

- case: 0 means keep the case; 1 means transform the string into lowercase (default); 2 means transform the string into uppercase.

If there is no dot present, extension checks will be done against an empty string and filename checks will be done against the whole value.

Examples:

Check if file has a pdf extension (case insensitive):

```
requires = IS_UPLOAD_FILENAME(extension='pdf')
```

Check if file has a tar.gz extension and name starting with backup:

```
requires = IS_UPLOAD_FILENAME(filename='backup.*', extension='tar.gz', lastdot=
    False)
```

Check if file has no extension and name matching README (case sensitive):

```
requires = IS_UPLOAD_FILENAME(filename='^README$', extension='^$', case=0)
```

IS_IPV4

This validator checks if a field's value is an IP version 4 address in decimal form. Can be set to force addresses from a certain range.

IPv4 regex taken from ref. [88] Its arguments are:

- minip lowest allowed address; accepts: **str**, e.g., 192.168.0.1; **iterable of numbers**, e.g., [192, 168, 0, 1]; **int**, e.g., 3232235521

- maxip highest allowed address; same as above

All three example values are equal, since addresses are converted to integers for inclusion check with following function:

```
number = 16777216 * IP[0] + 65536 * IP[1] + 256 * IP[2] + IP[3]
```

Examples:

Check for valid IPv4 address:

```
requires = IS_IPV4()
```

Check for valid private network IPv4 address:

```
requires = IS_IPV4(minip='192.168.0.1', maxip='192.168.255.255')
```

IS_UPPER

This validator never returns an error. It converts the value to upper case.

```
requires = IS_UPPER()
```

IS_NULL_OR

Deprecated, an alias for IS_EMPTY_OR described below.

IS_EMPTY_OR

Sometimes you need to allow empty values on a field along with other requirements. For example a field may be a date but it can also be empty. The IS_EMPTY_OR validator allows this:

```
requires = IS_EMPTY_OR(IS_DATE())
```

CLEANUP

This is a filter. It never fails. It just removes all characters whose decimal ASCII codes are not in the list [10, 13, 32-127].

```
requires = CLEANUP()
```

CRYPT

This is also a filter. It performs a secure hash on the input and it is used to prevent passwords from being passed in the clear to the database.

```
requires = CRYPT()
```

By default, CRYPT uses 1000 iterations of the pbkdf2 algorithm combined with SHA512 to produce a 20-byte-long hash. Older versions of web2py used "md5" or HMAC+SHA512 depending on whether a key was was specified or not.

If a key is specified, CRYPT uses the HMAC algorithm. The key may contain a prefix that determines the algorithm to use with HMAC, for example SHA512:

```
1  requires = CRYPT(key='sha512:thisisthekey')
```

This is the recommended syntax. The key must be a unique string associated with the database used. The key can never be changed. If you lose the key, the previously hashed values become useless.

By default, CRYPT uses random salt, such that each result is different. To use a constant salt value, specify its value:

```
1  requires = CRYPT(salt='mysaltvalue')
```

Or, to use no salt:

```
1  requires = CRYPT(salt=False)
```

The CRYPT validator hashes its input, and this makes it somewhat special. If you need to validate a password field before it is hashed, you can use CRYPT in a list of validators, but must make sure it is the last of the list, so that it is called last. For example:

```
1  requires = [IS_STRONG(),CRYPT(key='sha512:thisisthekey')]
```

CRYPT also takes a min_length argument, which defaults to zero.

The resulting hash takes the form alg$salt$hash, where alg is the hash algorithm used, salt is the salt string (which can be empty), and hash is the algorithm's output. Consequently, the hash is self-identifying, allowing, for example, the algorithm to be changed without invalidating previous hashes. The key, however, must remain the same.

7.6.2   Database validators

IS_NOT_IN_DB

Consider the following example:

```
1  db.define_table('person', Field('name'))
2  db.person.name.requires = IS_NOT_IN_DB(db, 'person.name')
```

It requires that when you insert a new person, his/her name is not already in the database, db, in the field person.name. As with all other validators this requirement is enforced at the form processing level, not at the database level. This means that there is a small probability that, if two visitors try to concurrently insert records with the same person.name, this results in a race condition and both records are accepted. It is therefore safer to also inform the database that this field should have a unique value:

```
1  db.define_table('person', Field('name', unique=True))
2  db.person.name.requires = IS_NOT_IN_DB(db, 'person.name')
```

Now if a race condition occurs, the database raises an OperationalError and one of the two inserts is rejected.

The first argument of IS_NOT_IN_DB can be a database connection or a Set. In the latter case, you would be checking only the set defined by the Set.

The following code, for example, does not allow registration of two persons with the same name within 10 days of each other:

```
1  import datetime
2  now = datetime.datetime.today()
3  db.define_table('person',
4      Field('name'),
5      Field('registration_stamp', 'datetime', default=now))
6  recent = db(db.person.registration_stamp>now-datetime.timedelta(10))
7  db.person.name.requires = IS_NOT_IN_DB(recent, 'person.name')
```

IS_IN_DB

Consider the following tables and requirement:

```
1  db.define_table('person', Field('name', unique=True))
2  db.define_table('dog', Field('name'), Field('owner', db.person))
3  db.dog.owner.requires = IS_IN_DB(db, 'person.id', '%(name)s',
4                                   zero=T('choose one'))
```

It is enforced at the level of dog INSERT/UPDATE/DELETE forms. It requires that a dog.owner be a valid id in the field person.id in the database db. Because of this validator, the dog.owner field is represented as a dropbox. The third argument of the validator is a string that describes the elements in the dropbox. In the example you want to see the person %(name)s instead of the person %(id)s. %(...)s is replaced by the value of the field in brackets for each record.

The zero option works very much like for the IS_IN_SET validator.

The first argument of the validator can be a database connection or a DAL Set, as in IS_NOT_IN_DB. This can be useful for example when wishing to limit the records in the drop-down box. In this example, we use IS_IN_DB in a controller to limit the records dynamically each time the controller is called:

```
1  def index():
2      (...)
3      query = (db.table.field == 'xyz') #in practice 'xyz' would be a variable
4      db.table.field.requires=IS_IN_DB(db(query),....)
5      form=SQLFORM(...)
6      if form.process().accepted: ...
7      (...)
```

If you want the field validated, but you do not want a dropbox, you must put
the validator in a list.

```
1  db.dog.owner.requires = [IS_IN_DB(db, 'person.id', '%(name)s')]
```

Occasionally you want the drop-box (so you do not want to use the list
syntax above) yet you want to use additional validators. For this purpose
the IS_IN_DB validator takes an extra argument _and that can point to a list of
other validators applied if the validated value passes the IS_IN_DB validation.
For example to validate all dog owners in db that are not in a subset:

```
1  subset=db(db.person.id>100)
2  db.dog.owner.requires = IS_IN_DB(db, 'person.id', '%(name)s',
3                              _and=IS_NOT_IN_DB(subset,'person.id'))
```

IS_IN_DB has a boolean distinct argument which defaults to False. When set
to True it prevents repeated values in the dropdown.

IS_IN_DB also takes a cache argument that works like the cache argument of
select.

IS_IN_DB and Tagging

The IS_IN_DB validator has an optional attribute multiple=False. If set to True
multiple values can be stored in one field. This field should be of type
list:reference as discussed in Chapter 6. An explicit example of tagging
is discussed there. multiple references are handled automatically in create
and update forms, but they are transparent to the DAL. We strongly suggest
using the jQuery multiselect plugin to render multiple fields.

7.6.3   Custom validators

All validators follow the prototype below:

```
1  class sample_validator:
2      def __init__(self, *a, error_message='error'):
```

```
3         self.a = a
4         self.e = error_message
5     def __call__(self, value):
6         if validate(value):
7             return (parsed(value), None)
8         return (value, self.e)
9     def formatter(self, value):
10        return format(value)
```

i.e., when called to validate a value, a validator returns a tuple (x, y). If y is None, then the value passed validation and x contains a parsed value. For example, if the validator requires the value to be an integer, x is converted to int(value). If the value did not pass validation, then x contains the input value and y contains an error message that explains the failed validation. This error message is used to report the error in forms that do not validate.

The validator may also contain a formatter method. It must perform the opposite conversion to the one the __call__ does. For example, consider the source code for IS_DATE:

```
1  class IS_DATE(object):
2      def __init__(self, format='%Y-%m-%d', error_message='must be YYYY-MM-DD!'):
3          self.format = format
4          self.error_message = error_message
5      def __call__(self, value):
6          try:
7              y, m, d, hh, mm, ss, t0, t1, t2 = time.strptime(value, str(self.format)
                )
8              value = datetime.date(y, m, d)
9              return (value, None)
10         except:
11             return (value, self.error_message)
12     def formatter(self, value):
13         return value.strftime(str(self.format))
```

On success, the __call__ method reads a date string from the form and converts it into a datetime.date object using the format string specified in the constructor. The formatter object takes a datetime.date object and converts it to a string representation using the same format. The formatter is called automatically in forms, but you can also call it explicitly to convert objects into their proper representation. For example:

```
1  >>> db = DAL()
2  >>> db.define_table('atable',
3      Field('birth', 'date', requires=IS_DATE('%m/%d/%Y')))
4  >>> id = db.atable.insert(birth=datetime.date(2008, 1, 1))
```

```
5  >>> row = db.atable[id]
6  >>> print db.atable.formatter(row.birth)
7  01/01/2008
```

When multiple validators are required (and stored in a list), they are executed in order and the output of one is passed as input to the next. The chain breaks when one of the validators fails.

Conversely, when we call the `formatter` method of a field, the formatters of the associated validators are also chained, but in reverse order.

> Notice that as alternative to custom validators, you can also use the `onvalidate` argument of `form.accepts(...)`, `form.process(...)` and `form.validate(...)`.

7.6.4 Validators with dependencies

Usually validators are set once for all in models.

Occasionally, you need to validate a field and the validator depends on the value of another field. This can be done in various ways. It can be done in the model or in the controller.

For example, here is a page that generates a registration form that asks for username and password twice. None of the fields can be empty, and both passwords must match:

```
1  def index():
2      form = SQLFORM.factory(
3          Field('username', requires=IS_NOT_EMPTY()),
4          Field('password', requires=IS_NOT_EMPTY()),
5          Field('password_again',
6              requires=IS_EQUAL_TO(request.vars.password)))
7      if form.process().accepted:
8          pass # or take some action
9      return dict(form=form)
```

The same mechanism can be applied to FORM and SQLFORM objects.

7.7 Widgets

Here is a list of available web2py widgets:

```
 1  SQLFORM.widgets.string.widget
 2  SQLFORM.widgets.text.widget
 3  SQLFORM.widgets.password.widget
 4  SQLFORM.widgets.integer.widget
 5  SQLFORM.widgets.double.widget
 6  SQLFORM.widgets.time.widget
 7  SQLFORM.widgets.date.widget
 8  SQLFORM.widgets.datetime.widget
 9  SQLFORM.widgets.upload.widget
10  SQLFORM.widgets.boolean.widget
11  SQLFORM.widgets.options.widget
12  SQLFORM.widgets.multiple.widget
13  SQLFORM.widgets.radio.widget
14  SQLFORM.widgets.checkboxes.widget
15  SQLFORM.widgets.autocomplete
```

The first ten of them are the defaults for the corresponding field types. The "options" widget is used when a field's requires is IS_IN_SET or IS_IN_DB with multiple=False (default behavior). The "multiple" widget is used when a field's requires is IS_IN_SET or IS_IN_DB with multiple=True. The "radio" and "checkboxes" widgets are never used by default, but can be set manually. The autocomplete widget is special and discussed in its own section.

For example, to have a "string" field represented by a textarea:

```
 1  Field('comment', 'string', widget=SQLFORM.widgets.text.widget)
```

Widgets can also be assigned to fields *a posteriori*:

```
 1  db.mytable.myfield.widget = SQLFORM.widgets.string.widget
```

Sometimes widgets take additional arguments and one needs to specify their values. In this case one can use lambda

```
 1  db.mytable.myfield.widget = lambda field,value: \
 2      SQLFORM.widgets.string.widget(field,value,_style='color:blue')
```

Widgets are helper factories and their first two arguments are always field and value. The other arguments can include normal helper attributes such as _style, _class, etc. Some widgets also take special arguments. In particular SQLFORM.widgets.radio and SQLFORM.widgets.checkboxes take a style argument (not to be confused with _style) which can be set to "table", "ul", or "divs" in order to match the formstyle of the containing form.

You can create new widgets or extend existing widgets.

SQLFORM.widgets[type] is a class and SQLFORM.widgets[type].widget is a static member function of the corresponding class. Each widget function takes two arguments: the field object, and the current value of that field. It returns a representation of the widget. As an example, the string widget could be re-coded as follows:

```
def my_string_widget(field, value):
    return INPUT(_name=field.name,
                 _id="%s_%s" % (field._tablename, field.name),
                 _class=field.type,
                 _value=value,
                 requires=field.requires)

Field('comment', 'string', widget=my_string_widget)
```

The id and class values must follow the convention described later in this chapter. A widget may contain its own validators, but it is good practice to associate the validators to the "requires" attribute of the field and have the widget get them from there.

7.7.1 Autocomplete widget

There are two possible uses for the autocomplete widget: to autocomplete a field that takes a value from a list or to autocomplete a reference field (where the string to be autocompleted is a representation of the reference which is implemented as an id).

The first case is easy:

```
db.define_table('category',Field('name'))
db.define_table('product',Field('name'),Field('category'))
db.product.category.widget = SQLFORM.widgets.autocomplete(
    request, db.category.name, limitby=(0,10), min_length=2)
```

Where limitby instructs the widget to display no more than 10 suggestions at the time, and min_length instructs the widget to perform an Ajax callback to fetch suggestions only after the user has typed at least 2 characters in the search box.

The second case is more complex:

```
db.define_table('category',Field('name'))
db.define_table('product',Field('name'),Field('category'))
```

```
3  db.product.category.widget = SQLFORM.widgets.autocomplete(
4      request, db.category.name, id_field=db.category.id)
```

In this case the value of id_field tells the widget that even if the value to be autocompleted is a db.category.name, the value to be stored is the corresponding db.category.id. An optional parameter is orderby that instructs the widget on how to sort the suggestions (alphabetical by default).

This widget works via Ajax. Where is the Ajax callback? Some magic is going on in this widget. The callback is a method of the widget object itself. How is it exposed? In web2py any piece of code can generate a response by raising an HTTP exception. This widget exploits this possibility in the following way: the widget sends the Ajax call to the same URL that generated the widget in the first place and puts a special token in the request.vars. Should the widget get instantiated again, it finds the token and raises an HTTP exception that responds to the request. All of this is done under the hood and hidden to the developer.

7.8   SQLFORM.grid **and** SQLFORM.smartgrid

Attention: grid and smartgrid were experimental prior web2py version 2.0 and were vulnerable to information leakage. The grid and smartgrid are no longer experimental, but we are still not promising backward compatibility of the presentation layer of the grid, only of its APIs.

These are two high level gadgets that create complex CRUD controls. They provide pagination, the ability to browser, search, sort, create, update and delete records from a single gadgets.

The simplest of the two is SQLFORM.grid. Here is an example of usage:

```
1  @auth.requires_login()
2  def manage_users():
3      grid = SQLFORM.grid(db.auth_user)
4      return locals()
```

which produces the following page:

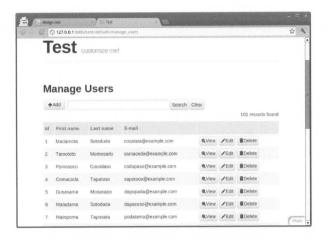

The first argument of SQLFORM.grid can be a table or a query. The grid gadget will provide access to records matching the query.

Before we dive into the long list of arguments of the grid gadget we need to understand how it works. The gadget looks at request.args in order to decide what to do (browse, search, create, update, delete, etc.). Each button created by the gadget links the same function (manage_users in the above case) but passes different request.args. By default all the URL generated by the grid are digitally signed and verified. This means one cannot perform certain actions (create, update, delete) without being logged-in. These restrictions can be relaxed:

```
def manage_users():
    grid = SQLFORM.grid(db.auth_user,user_signature=False)
    return locals()
```

but we do not recommend it.

> Because of the way grid works one can only have one grid per controller function, unless they are embedded as components via LOAD. To make the default search grid work in more than one LOADed grid, please use a different formname for each one.

Because the function that contains the grid may itself manipulate the command line arguments, the grid needs to know which args should be handled by the grid and which not. For example here is an example of code that allows one to manage any table:

```
1 @auth.requires_login()
2 def manage():
3     table = request.args(0)
4     if not table in db.tables(): redirect(URL('error'))
5     grid = SQLFORM.grid(db[table],args=request.args[:1])
6     return locals()
```

the args argument of the grid specifies which request.args should be passed along and ignored by the gadget. In our case request.args[:1] is the name of the table we want to manage and it is handled by the manage function itself, not by the gadget.

The complete signature for the grid is the following:

```
1  SQLFORM.grid(
2     query,
3     fields=None,
4     field_id=None,
5     left=None,
6     headers={},
7     orderby=None,
8     groupby=None,
9     searchable=True,
10    sortable=True,
11    paginate=20,
12    deletable=True,
13    editable=True,
14    details=True,
15    selectable=None,
16    create=True,
17    csv=True,
18    links=None,
19    links_in_grid=True,
20    upload='<default>',
21    args=[],
22    user_signature=True,
23    maxtextlengths={},
24    maxtextlength=20,
25    onvalidation=None,
26    oncreate=None,
27    onupdate=None,
28    ondelete=None,
29    sorter_icons=(XML('&#x2191;'), XML('&#x2193;')),
30    ui = 'web2py',
31    showbuttontext=True,
32    _class="web2py_grid",
33    formname='web2py_grid',
34    search_widget='default',
```

```
35    ignore_rw = False,
36    formstyle = 'table3cols',
37    exportclasses = None,
38    formargs={},
39    createargs={},
40    editargs={},
41    viewargs={},
42    buttons_placement = 'right',
43    links_placement = 'right'
44    )
```

- `fields` is a list of fields to be fetched from the database. It is also used to determine which fields to be shown in the grid view.

- `field_id` must be the field of the table to be used as ID, for example `db.mytable.id`.

- `left` is an optional left join expressions used to build ...`select(left=...)`.

- `headers` is a dictionary that maps 'tablename.fieldname' into the corresponding header label, e.g. `{'auth_user.email'` : `'Email Address'}`

- `orderby` is used as default ordering for the rows.

- `groupby` is used to group the set. Use the same syntax as you were passing in a simple `select(groupby=...)`.

- `searchable`, `sortable`, `deletable`, `editable`, `details`, `create` determine whether one can search, sort, delete, edit, view details, and create new records respectively.

- `selectable` can be used to call a custom function on multiple records (a checkbox will be inserted for every row) e.g.

```
1    selectable = lambda ids : redirect(URL('default', 'mapping_multiple', vars=dict(
         id=ids)))
```

- `paginate` sets the max number of rows per page.

- `csv` if set to true allows to download the grid in various format (more on that later).

- `links` is used to display new columns which can be links to other pages. The `links` argument must be a list of `dict(header='name',body=lambda row: A(...))` where `header` is the header of the new column and `body` is a function that takes a row and returns a value. In the example, the value is a A(...) helper.

- links_in_grid if set to False, links will only be displayed in the "details" and "edit" page (so, not on the main grid)

- upload same as SQLFORM's one. web2py uses the action at that URL to download the file

- maxtextlength sets the maximum length of text to be displayed for each field value, in the grid view. This value can be overwritten for each field using maxtextlengths, a dictionary of 'tablename.fieldname':length e.g. {'auth_user.email' : 50}

- onvalidation, oncreate, onupdate and ondelete are callback functions. All but ondelete take a form object as input.

- sorter_icons is a list of two strings (or helpers) that will be used to represent the up and down sorting options for each field.

- ui can be set equal to 'web2py' and will generate web2py friendly class names, can be set equal to jquery-ui and will generate jquery UI friendly class names, but it can also be its own set of class names for the various grid components:

```
ui = dict(
    widget='',
    header='',
    content='',
    default='',
    cornerall='',
    cornertop='',
    cornerbottom='',
    button='button',
    buttontext='buttontext button',
    buttonadd='icon plus',
    buttonback='icon leftarrow',
    buttonexport='icon downarrow',
    buttondelete='icon trash',
    buttonedit='icon pen',
    buttontable='icon rightarrow',
    buttonview='icon magnifier')
```

- search_widget allows to override the default search widget and we refer the reader the source code in "gluon/sqlhtml.py" for details.

- showbuttontext allows to have buttons without text (there will effectively be only icons)

- _class is the class for the grid container.

- showbutton allows to turn off all buttons.

- exportclasses takes a dictionary of tuples: by default it's defined as

```
1 csv_with_hidden_cols=(ExporterCSV, 'CSV (hidden cols)'),
2 csv=(ExporterCSV, 'CSV'),
3 xml=(ExporterXML, 'XML'),
4 html=(ExporterHTML, 'HTML'),
5 tsv_with_hidden_cols=(ExporterTSV, 'TSV (Excel compatible, hidden cols)'),
6 tsv=(ExporterTSV, 'TSV (Excel compatible)'))
```

ExporterCSV, ExporterXML, ExporterHTML and ExporterTSV are all defined in gluon/sqlhtml.py. Take a look at those for creating your own exporter. If you pass a dict like dict(xml=False, html=False) you will disable the xml and html export formats.

- formargs is passed to all SQLFORM objects used by the grid, while createargs,editargs and viewargs are passed only to the specific create, edit and details SQLFORMs

- formname, ignore_rw and formstyle are passed to the SQLFORM objects used by the grid for create/update forms.

- buttons_placement and links_placement both take a parameter ('right', 'left', 'both') that will affect where on the row the buttons (or the links) will be placed

  deletable, editable and details are usually boolean values but they can be functions which take the row object and decide whether to display the corresponding button or not.

A SQLFORM.smartgrid looks a lot like a grid, in fact it contains a grid but it is designed to take as input not a query but only one table and to browse said table and selected referencing tables.

For example consider the following table structure:

```
1 db.define_table('parent',Field('name'))
2 db.define_table('child',Field('name'),Field('parent','reference parent'))
```

With SQLFORM.grid you can list all parents:

```
1  SQLFORM.grid(db.parent)
```

all children:

```
1  SQLFORM.grid(db.child)
```

and all parents and children in one table:

```
1  SQLFORM.grid(db.parent,left=db.child.on(db.child.parent==db.parent.id))
```

With SQLFORM.smartgrid you can put all the data in one gadget that spawns both tables:

```
1  @auth.requires_login()
2  def manage():
3      grid = SQLFORM.smartgrid(db.parent,linked_tables=['child'])
4      return locals()
```

which looks like this:

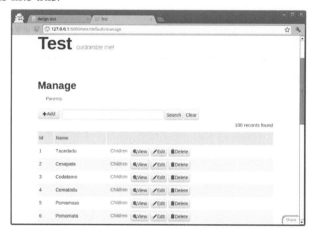

Notice the extra "children" links. One could create the extra links using a regular grid but they would point to a different action. With a smartgrid they are created automatically and handled by the same gadget.

Also notice that when clicking on the "children" link for a given parent one only gets the list of children for that parent (and that is obvious) but also notice that if one now tried to add a new child, the parent value for the new child is automatically set to the selected parent (displayed in the breadcrumbs associated to the gadget). The value of this field can be overwritten. We can prevent this by making it readonly:

```
1  @auth.requires_login():
```

```
2  def manage():
3      db.child.parent.writable = False
4      grid = SQLFORM.smartgrid(db.parent,linked_tables=['child'])
5      return locals()
```

If the linked_tables argument is not specified all referencing tables are automatically linked. Anyway, to avoid accidentally exposing data we recommend explicitly listing tables that should be linked.

The following code creates a very powerful management interface for all tables in the system:

```
1  @auth.requires_membership('managers'):
2  def manage():
3      table = request.args(0) or 'auth_user'
4      if not table in db.tables(): redirect(URL('error'))
5      grid = SQLFORM.smartgrid(db[table],args=request.args[:1])
6      return locals()
```

The smartgrid takes the same arguments as a grid and some more with some caveats:

- The first argument is a table, not a query

- There is a extra argument constraints which is a dictionary of 'tablename':query which can be used to further restrict access to the records displayed in the 'tablename' grid.

- There is a extra argument linked_tables which is a list of tablenames of tables that should be accessible via the smartgrid.

- divider allows to specify a character to use in the breadcrumb navigator, breadcrumbs_class will apply the class to the breadcrumb element

- All the arguments but the table, args, linked_tables and user_signatures can be dictionaries as explained below.

Consider the previous grid:

```
1  grid = SQLFORM.smartgrid(db.parent,linked_tables=['child'])
```

It allows one to access both a db.parent and a db.child. Apart for navigation controls, for each one table, a smarttable is nothing but a grid. This means that, in this case, one smartgrid can create a grid for parent and one grid for child. We may want to pass different sets of parameters to these grids. For example different sets of searchable parameters.

While for a grid we would pass a boolean:

```
grid = SQLFORM.grid(db.parent,searchable=True)
```

for a smartgrid we would pass a dictionary of booleans:

```
grid = SQLFORM.smartgrid(db.parent,linked_tables=['child'],
    searchable= dict(parent=True, child=False))
```

In this way we made parents searchable but children for each parent not searchable (there should not be that many to need the search widget).

> The grid and smartgrid gadgets are here to stay but they are marked experimental because the actual html layout of what they return and the exact set of parameters one can pass to them may be subject to change as new functionalities are added.

grid and smartgrid do not automatically enforce access control like crud does but you can integrate it with auth using explicit permission checking:

```
grid = SQLFORM.grid(db.auth_user,
    editable = auth.has_membership('managers'),
    deletable = auth.has_membership('managers'))
```

or

```
grid = SQLFORM.grid(db.auth_user,
    editable = auth.has_permission('edit','auth_user'),
    deletable = auth.has_permission('delete','auth_user'))
```

The smartgrid is the only gadget in web2py that displays the table name and it need both the singular and the plural. For example one parent can have one "Child" or many "Children". Therefore a table object needs to know its own singular and plural names. web2py normally guesses them but you can set the explicitly:

```
db.define_table('child', ..., singular="Child", plural="Children")
```

or with:

```
db.define_table('child', ...)
db.child._singular = "Child"
db.child._plural = "Children"
```

They should also be internationalized using the T operator.

The plural and singular values are then used by smartgrid to provide correct names for headers and links.

8

Emails and SMS

8.1 Setting up email

Web2py provides the `gluon.tools.Mail` class to make it easy to send emails using web2py. One can define a mailer with

```
from gluon.tools import Mail
mail = Mail()
mail.settings.server = 'smtp.example.com:25'
mail.settings.sender = 'you@example.com'
mail.settings.login = 'username:password'
```

Note, if your application uses `Auth` (discussed in the next chapter), the `auth` object will include its own mailer in `auth.settings.mailer`, so you can use that instead as follows:

```
mail = auth.settings.mailer
mail.settings.server = 'smtp.example.com:25'
mail.settings.sender = 'you@example.com'
mail.settings.login = 'username:password'
```

You need to replace the mail.settings with the proper parameters for your SMTP server. Set `mail.settings.login = None` if the SMTP server does not require authentication. If you don't want to use TLS, set `mail.settings.tls = False`

> For debugging purposes you can set
>
> ```
> mail.settings.server = 'logging'
> ```

| and emails will not be sent but logged to the console instead.

8.1.1 Configuring email for Google App Engine

For sending emails from Google App Engine account:

```
1 mail.settings.server = 'gae'
```

At the time of writing web2py does not support attachments and encrypted emails on Google App Engine. Notice cron and scheduler do not work on GAE.

8.1.2 x509 and PGP Encryption

It is possible to send x509 (SMIME) encrypted emails using the following settings:

```
1 mail.settings.cipher_type = 'x509'
2 mail.settings.sign = True
3 mail.settings.sign_passphrase = 'your passphrase'
4 mail.settings.encrypt = True
5 mail.settings.x509_sign_keyfile = 'filename.key'
6 mail.settings.x509_sign_certfile = 'filename.cert'
7 mail.settings.x509_crypt_certfiles = 'filename.cert'
```

It is possible to send PGP encrypted emails. First of all you need to install the python-pyme package. Then you can use GnuPG (GPG) to create the keyfiles for the sender (take the email-address from mail.settings.sender) and put the files pubring.gpg and secring.gpg in a directory (e.g. "/home/www-data/.gnupg").

Use the following settings:

```
1 mail.settings.gpg_home = '/home/www-data/.gnupg/'
2 mail.settings.cipher_type = 'gpg'
3 mail.settings.sign = True
4 mail.settings.sign_passphrase = 'your passphrase'
5 mail.settings.encrypt = True
```

8.2   Sending emails

Once mail is defined, it can be used to send email via:

```
mail.send(to=['somebody@example.com'],
          subject='hello',
          # If reply_to is omitted, then mail.settings.sender is used
          reply_to='us@example.com',
          message='hi there')
```

Mail returns True if it succeeds in sending the email and False otherwise. A complete argument list for mail.send() is as follows:

```
send(self, to, subject='None', message='None', attachments=1,
     cc=1, bcc=1, reply_to=1, encoding='utf-8',headers={},
     sender=None)
```

Note, to, cc, and bcc each take a list of email addresses.

headers is dictionary of headers to refine the headers just before sending the email. For example:

```
headers = {'Return-Path' : 'bounces@example.org'}
```

sender defaults to None and in this case the sender will be set to mail.settings.sender.

Following are some additional examples demonstrating the use of mail.send().

8.2.1   Simple text email

```
mail.send('you@example.com',
  'Message subject',
  'Plain text body of the message')
```

8.2.2   HTML emails

```
mail.send('you@example.com',
  'Message subject',
  '<html>html body</html>')
```

If the email body starts with <html> and ends with </html>, it will be sent as a HTML email.

8.2.3 Combining text and HTML emails

The email message can be a tuple (text, html):

```
mail.send('you@example.com',
  'Message subject',
  ('Plain text body', '<html>html body</html>'))
```

8.2.4 cc and bcc emails

```
mail.send('you@example.com',
  'Message subject',
  'Plain text body',
  cc=['other1@example.com', 'other2@example.com'],
  bcc=['other3@example.com', 'other4@example.com'])
```

8.2.5 Attachments

```
mail.send('you@example.com',
  'Message subject',
  '<html><img src="cid:photo" /></html>',
  attachments = mail.Attachment('/path/to/photo.jpg', content_id='photo'))
```

8.2.6 Multiple attachments

```
mail.send('you@example.com',
  'Message subject',
  'Message body',
  attachments = [mail.Attachment('/path/to/fist.file'),
                 mail.Attachment('/path/to/second.file')])
```

8.3 Sending SMS messages

Sending SMS messages from a web2py application requires a third party service that can relay the messages to the receiver. Usually this is not a free service, but it differs from country to country. We have tried a few of these services with little success. Phone companies block emails originating from these services since they are eventually used as a source of spam.

A better way is to use the phone companies themselves to relay the SMS. Each phone company has an email address uniquely associated with every cell-phone number, so SMS messages can be sent as emails to the phone number. web2py comes with a module to help in this process:

```
1 from gluon.contrib.sms_utils import SMSCODES, sms_email
2 email = sms_email('1 (111) 111-1111','T-Mobile USA (tmail)')
3 mail.sent(to=email, subject='test', message='test')
```

SMSCODES is a dictionary that maps names of major phone companies to the email address postfix. The `sms_email` function takes a phone number (as a string) and the name of a phone company and returns the email address of the phone.

8.4 Using the template system to generate messages

It is possible to use the template system to generate emails. For example, consider the database table

```
1 db.define_table('person', Field('name'))
```

where you want to send to every person in the database the following message, stored in a view file "message.html":

```
1 Dear {{=person.name}},
2 You have won the second prize, a set of steak knives.
```

You can achieve this in the following way

```
1 for person in db(db.person).select():
2     context = dict(person=person)
3     message = response.render('message.html', context)
4     mail.send(to=['who@example.com'],
5             subject='None',
6             message=message)
```

Most of the work is done in the statement

```
1 response.render('message.html', context)
```

It renders the view "message.html" with the variables defined in the dictionary "context", and it returns a string with the rendered email text. The context is a dictionary that contains variables that will be visible to the template file.

If the message starts with <html> and ends with </html>, the email will be an HTML email.

Note, if you want to include a link back to your website in an HTML email, you can use the URL function. However, by default, the URL function generates a relative URL, which will not work from an email. To generate an absolute URL, you need to specify the scheme and host arguments to the URL function. For example:

```
1  <a href="{{=URL(..., scheme=True, host=True)}}">Click here</a>
```

or

```
1  <a href="{{=URL(..., scheme='http', host='www.site.com')}}">Click here</a>
```

The same mechanism that is used to generate email text can also be used to generate SMS messages or any other type of message based on a template.

8.5   Sending messages using a background task

The operation of sending an email message can take up to several seconds because of the need to log into and communicate with a potentially remote SMTP server. To keep the user from having to wait for the send operation to complete, it is sometimes desirable to queue the email to be sent at a later time via a background task. As described in Chapter 4, this can be done by setting up a homemade task queue or using the web2py scheduler. Here we provide an example using a homemade task queue.

First, in a model file within our application, we set up a database model to store our email queue:

```
1  db.define_table('queue',
2      Field('status'),
3      Field('email'),
4      Field('subject'),
5      Field('message'))
```

From a controller, we can then enqueue messages to be sent by:

```
1  db.queue.insert(status='pending',
2                  email='you@example.com',
3                  subject='test',
4                  message='test')
```

Next, we need a background processing script that reads the queue and sends the emails:

```
1  ## in file /app/private/mail_queue.py
2  import time
3  while True:
```

```
 4    rows = db(db.queue.status=='pending').select()
 5    for row in rows:
 6        if mail.send(to=row.email,
 7            subject=row.subject,
 8            message=row.message):
 9            row.update_record(status='sent')
10        else:
11            row.update_record(status='failed')
12        db.commit()
13    time.sleep(60) # check every minute
```

Finally, as described in Chapter 4, we need to run the mail_queue.py script as if it were inside a controller in our app:

```
1 python web2py.py -S app -M -N -R applications/app/private/mail_queue.py
```

where -S app tells web2py to run "mail_queue.py" as "app", -M tells web2py to execute models, and -N tells web2py not to run cron.

Here we assume that the mail object referenced in "mail_queue.py" is defined in a model file in our app and is therefore available in the "mail_queue.py" script because of the -M option. Also notice that it is important to commit any change as soon as possible in order not to lock the database to other concurrent processes.

As noted in Chapter 4, this type of background process should not be executed via cron (except perhaps for cron @reboot) because you need to be sure that no more than one instance is running at the same time.

Note, one drawback to sending email via a background process is that it makes it difficult to provide feedback to the user in case the email fails. If email is sent directly from the controller action, you can catch any errors and immediately return an error message to the user. With a background process, however, the email is sent asynchronously, after the controller action has already returned its response, so it becomes more complex to notify the user of a failure.

8.6   Reading and managing email boxes (Experimental)

The IMAP adapter is intended as an interface with email IMAP servers to perform simple queries in the web2py DAL query syntax, so email read, search and other related IMAP mail services (as those implemented by brands like Google(r), and Yahoo(r) can be managed from web2py applications.

It creates its table and field names "statically", meaning that the developer should leave the table and field definitions to the DAL instance by calling the adapter .define_tables() method. The tables are defined with the IMAP server mailbox list information.

8.6.1 Connection

For a single mail account, this is the code recommended to start IMAP support at the app's model

```
1  # Replace user, password, server and port in the connection string
2  # Set port as 993 for SSL support
3  imapdb = DAL("imap://user:password@server:port", pool_size=1)
4  imapdb.define_tables()
```

Note that <imapdb>.define_tables() returns a dictionary of strings mapping DAL tablenames to the server mailbox names with the structure {<tablename>: <server mailbox name>, ...}, so you can get the actual mailbox name in the IMAP server.

To handle the different native mailbox names for the user interface, the following attributes give access to the adapter auto mailbox mapped names (which native mailbox has what table name and vice versa):

Attribute	Type	Format
imapdb.mailboxes	dict	{<tablename>: <server native name>, ...}
imapdb.<table>.mailbox	string	"server native name"

The first can be useful to retrieve IMAP query sets by the native email service mailbox

```
1  # mailbox is a string containing the actual mailbox name
2  tablenames = dict([(v,k) for k,v in imapdb.mailboxes.items()])
3  myset = imapdb(imapdb[tablenames[mailbox]])
```

8.6.2   Fetching mail and updating flags

Here's a list of IMAP commands you could use in the controller. For the examples, it's assumed that your IMAP service has a mailbox named INBOX, which is the case for Gmail(r) accounts.

To count today's unseen messages smaller than 6000 octets from the inbox mailbox do

```
1  q = imapdb.INBOX.seen == False
2  q &= imapdb.INBOX.created == datetime.date.today()
3  q &= imapdb.INBOX.size < 6000
4  unread = imapdb(q).count()
```

You can fetch the previous query messages with

```
1  rows = imapdb(q).select()
```

Usual query operators are implemented, including belongs

```
1  messages = imapdb(imapdb.INBOX.uid.belongs(<uid sequence>)).select()
```

Note: It's strongly advised that you keep the query results below a given data size threshold to avoid jamming the server with large select commands. As of now, the messages are retrieved entirely by the adapter before any filter by field can be applied.

It is possible to filter query select results with limitby and sequences of mailbox fields

```
1  # Replace the arguments with actual values
2  myset.select(<fields sequence>, limitby=(<int>, <int>))
```

Say you want to have an app action show a mailbox message. First we retrieve the message (If your IMAP service supports it, fetch messages by uid field to avoid using old sequence references).

```
1  mymessage = imapdb(imapdb.INBOX.uid == <uid>).select().first()
```

Otherwise, you can use the message's id.

```
1  mymessage = imapdb.INBOX[<id>]
```

Note that using the message's id as reference is not recommended, because sequence numbers can change with mailbox maintenance operations as message deletions. If you still want to record references to messages (i.e. in another database's record field), the solution is to use the uid field as reference whenever supported, and retrieve each message with the recorded value.

Finally, add something like the following to show the message content in a view

```
{{=P(T("Message from"), " ", mymessage.sender)}}
{{=P(T("Received on"), " ", mymessage.created)}}
{{=H5(mymessage.subject)}}
{{for text in mymessage.content:}}
  {{=DIV(text)}}
  {{=TR()}}
{{pass}}
```

As expected, we can take advantage of the SQLTABLE helper to build message lists in views

```
{{=SQLTABLE(myset.select(), linkto=URL(...))}}
```

And of course, it's possible to feed a form helper with the appropriate sequence id value

```
{{=SQLFORM(imapdb.INBOX, <message id>, fields=[...])}}
```

The current adapter supported fields available are the following:

Field	Type	Description
uid	string	
answered	boolean	Flag
created	date	
content	list:string	A list of text or html parts
to	string	
cc	string	
bcc	string	
size	integer	the amount of octets of the message*
deleted	boolean	Flag
draft	boolean	Flag
flagged	boolean	Flag
sender	string	
recent	boolean	Flag
seen	boolean	Flag
subject	string	
mime	string	The mime header declaration
email	string	The complete RFC822 message**
attachments	list:string	Each non text decoded part as string

*At the application side it is measured as the length of the RFC822 message string

WARNING: As row id's are mapped to email sequence numbers, make sure your IMAP client web2py app does not delete messages during select or update actions, to prevent updating or deleting different messages.

Standard CRUD database operations are not supported. There's no way of defining custom fields or tables and make inserts with different data types because updating mailboxes with IMAP services is usually reduced to posting flag updates to the server. Still, it's possible to access those flag commands through the DAL IMAP interface

To mark last query messages as seen

```
seen = imapdb(q).update(seen=True)
```

Here we delete messages in the IMAP database that have mails from mr. Gumby

```
1  deleted = 0
2  for tablename in imapdb.tables():
3      deleted += imapdb(imapdb[tablename].sender.contains("gumby")).delete()
```

It is possible also to mark messages for deletion instead of erasing them directly with

```
1  myset.update(deleted=True)
```

9

Access Control

web2py includes a powerful and customizable Role Based Access Control mechanism (RBAC).

Here is a definition from Wikipedia:

"Role-Based Access Control (RBAC) is an approach to restricting system access to authorized users. It is a newer alternative approach to mandatory access control (MAC) and discretionary access control (DAC). RBAC is sometimes referred to as role-based security.

RBAC is a policy neutral and flexible access control technology sufficiently powerful to simulate DAC and MAC. Conversely, MAC can simulate RBAC if the role graph is restricted to a tree rather than a partially ordered set.

Prior to the development of RBAC, MAC and DAC were considered to be the only known models for access control: if a model was not MAC, it was considered to be a DAC model, and vice versa. Research in the late 1990s demonstrated that RBAC falls in neither category.

Within an organization, roles are created for various job functions. The permissions to perform certain operations are assigned to specific roles. Members of staff (or other system users) are assigned particular roles, and through those role assignments acquire the permissions to perform particular system functions. Unlike context-based access control (CBAC), RBAC does not look at the message context (such as a connection's source).

Since users are not assigned permissions directly, but only acquire them through their role (or roles), management of individual user rights becomes a matter of simply assigning appropriate roles to the user; this simplifies common operations, such as adding a user, or changing a user's department.

RBAC differs from access control lists (ACLs) used in traditional discretionary access control systems in that it assigns permissions to specific operations with meaning in the organization, rather than to low level data objects. For example, an access control list could be used to grant or deny write access to a particular system file, but it would not dictate how that file could be changed."

The web2py class that implements RBAC is called **Auth**.

Auth needs (and defines) the following tables:

- auth_user stores users' name, email address, password, and status (registration pending, accepted, blocked)

- auth_group stores groups or roles for users in a many-to-many structure. By default, each user is in its own group, but a user can be in multiple groups, and each group can contain multiple users. A group is identified by a role and a description.

- auth_membership links users and groups in a many-to-many structure.

- auth_permission links groups and permissions. A permission is identified by a name and, optionally, a table and a record. For example, members of a certain group can have "update" permissions on a specific record of a specific table.

- auth_event logs changes in the other tables and successful access via CRUD to objects controlled by the RBAC.

- auth_cas is used for Central Authentication Service (CAS). Every web2py application is a CAS provider and can optionally be a CAS consumer.

The schema is reproduced graphically in the image below:

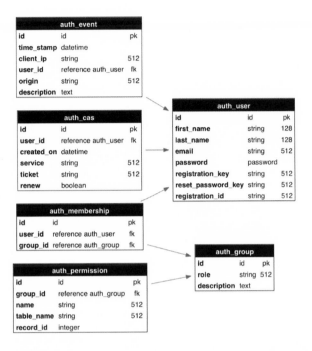

In principle, there is no restriction on the names of the roles and the names of the permissions; the developer can create them to fix the roles and permissions in the organization. Once they have been created, web2py provides an API to check if a user is logged in, if a user is a member of a given group, and/or if the user is a member of any group that has a given required permission. web2py also provides decorators to restrict access to any function based on login, membership and permissions. web2py also understands some specific permissions, i.e., those that have a name that correspond to the CRUD methods (create, read, update, delete) and can enforce them automatically without the need to use decorators.

In this chapter, we are going to discuss different parts of RBAC one by one.

9.1   Authentication

In order to use RBAC, users need to be identified. This means that they need to register (or be registered) and log in.

Auth provides multiple login methods. The default one consists of identifying users based on the local auth_user table. Alternatively, it can log in users against third-party authentication systems and single sign on providers such as Google, PAM, LDAP, Facebook, LinkedIn, Dropbox, OpenID, OAuth, etc..

To start using Auth, you need at least this code in a model file, which is also provided with the web2py "welcome" application and assumes a db connection object:

```
1  from gluon.tools import Auth
2  auth = Auth(db)
3  auth.define_tables()
```

Auth has an optional secure=True argument, which will force authenticated pages to go over HTTPS.

> The password field of the db.auth_user table defaults to a CRYPT validator, which needs and hmac_key. On legacy web2py applications you may see an extra argument passed to the Auth constructor: hmac_key = Auth.get_or_create_key(). The latter is a function that read the HMAC key from a file "private/auth.key" within the application folder. If the file does not exist it creates a random hmac_key. If multiple apps share the same auth database, make sure they also use the same hmac_key. This is no longer necessary for new applications since passwords are salted with an individual random salt.

By default, web2py uses email for login. If instead you want to log in using username set auth.define_tables(username=True)

If multiple apps share the same auth database you may want to disable migrations: auth.define_tables(migrate=False).

To expose **Auth**, you also need the following function in a controller (for example in "default.py"):

```
1  def user(): return dict(form=auth())
```

> The auth object and the user action are already defined in the scaffolding application.

web2py also includes a sample view "welcome/views/default/user.html" to render this function properly that looks like this:

```
1   {{extend 'layout.html'}}
2   <h2>{{=T( request.args(0).replace('_',' ').capitalize() )}}</h2>
3   <div id="web2py_user_form">
4     {{=form}}
5     {{if request.args(0)=='login':}}
6       {{if not 'register' in auth.settings.actions_disabled:}}
7         <br/><a href="{{=URL(args='register')}}">register</a>
8       {{pass}}
9       {{if not 'request_reset_password' in auth.settings.actions_disabled:}}
10        <br/>
11        <a href="{{=URL(args='request_reset_password')}}">lost password</a>
12      {{pass}}
13    {{pass}}
14  </div>
```

Notice that this function simply displays a form and therefore it can be customized using normal custom form syntax. The only caveat is that the form displayed by form=auth() depends on request.args(0); therefore, if you replace the default auth() login form with a custom login form, you may need an if statement like this in the view:

```
1   {{if request.args(0)=='login':}}...custom login form...{{pass}}
```

The controller above exposes multiple actions:

```
1   http://.../[app]/default/user/register
2   http://.../[app]/default/user/login
3   http://.../[app]/default/user/logout
4   http://.../[app]/default/user/profile
5   http://.../[app]/default/user/change_password
6   http://.../[app]/default/user/verify_email
7   http://.../[app]/default/user/retrieve_username
8   http://.../[app]/default/user/request_reset_password
9   http://.../[app]/default/user/reset_password
10  http://.../[app]/default/user/impersonate
11  http://.../[app]/default/user/groups
12  http://.../[app]/default/user/not_authorized
```

- **register** allows users to register. It is integrated with CAPTCHA, although this is disabled by default. This is also integrated with a client-side entropy calculator defined in "web2py.js". The calculator indicates the strength of the new password. You can use the IS_STRONG validator to prevent web2py from accepting weak passwords.

- **login** allows users who are registered to log in (if the registration is verified or does not require verification, if it has been approved or does not require approval, and if it has not been blocked).

- **logout** does what you would expect but also, as the other methods, logs the event and can be used to trigger some event.

- **profile** allows users to edit their profile, i.e. the content of the auth_user table. Notice that this table does not have a fixed structure and can be customized.

- **change_password** allows users to change their password in a fail-safe way.

- **verify_email**. If email verification is turned on, then visitors, upon registration, receive an email with a link to verify their email information. The link points to this action.

- **retrieve_username**. By default, **Auth** uses email and password for login, but it can, optionally, use username instead of email. In this latter case, if a user forgets his/her username, the retrieve_username method allows the user to type the email address and retrieve the username by email.

- **request_reset_password**. Allows users who forgot their password to request a new password. They will get a confirmation email pointing to **reset_password**.

- **impersonate** allows a user to "impersonate" another user. This is important for debugging and for support purposes. request.args[0] is the id of the user to be impersonated. This is only allowed if the logged in user has_permission('impersonate', db.auth_user, user_id). You can use auth.is_impersonating() to check is the current user is impersonating somebody else.

- **groups** lists the groups of which the current logged in user is a member.

- **not_authorized** displays an error message when the visitor tried to do something that he/she is not authorized to do

- **navbar** is a helper that generates a bar with login/register/etc. links.

Logout, profile, change_password, impersonate, and groups require login.

By default they are all exposed, but it is possible to restrict access to only some of these actions.

All of the methods above can be extended or replaced by subclassing **Auth**.

All of the methods above can be used in separate actions. For example:

```
1 def mylogin(): return dict(form=auth.login())
2 def myregister(): return dict(form=auth.register())
3 def myprofile(): return dict(form=auth.profile())
4 ...
```

To restrict access to functions to only logged in visitors, decorate the function as in the following example

```
1 @auth.requires_login()
2 def hello():
3     return dict(message='hello %(first_name)s' % auth.user)
```

Any function can be decorated, not just exposed actions. Of course this is still only a very simple example of access control. More complex examples will be discussed later.   auth.user_groups.

> auth.user contains a copy of the db.auth_user records for the current logged in user or None otherwise. There is also a auth.user_id which is the same as auth.user.id (i.e. the id of the current logger in user) or None. Similarly, auth.user_groups contains a dictionary where each key is the id of a group of with the current logged in user is member of, the value is the corresponding group role.

The auth.requires_login() decorator as well as the other auth.requires_* decorators take an optional otherwise argument. It can be set to a string where to redirect the user if registration files or to a callable object. It is called if registration fails.

9.1.1   Restrictions on registration

If you want to allow visitors to register but not to log in until registration has been approved by the administrator:

```
1 auth.settings.registration_requires_approval = True
```

You can approve a registration via the appadmin interface. Look into the table auth_user. Pending registrations have a registration_key field set to "pending". A registration is approved when this field is set to blank.

Via the appadmin interface, you can also block a user from logging in. Locate the user in the table auth_user and set the registration_key to "blocked". "blocked" users are not allowed to log in. Notice that this will prevent a visitor from logging in but it will not force a visitor who is already logged in to log out. The word "disabled" may be used instead of "blocked" if preferred, with exactly the same behavior.

You can also block access to the "register" page completely with this statement:

```
1 auth.settings.actions_disabled.append('register')
```

If you want to allow people to register and automatically log them in after registration but still want to send an email for verification so that they cannot login again after logout, unless they completed the instructions in the email, you can accomplish it as follows:

```
1 auth.settings.registration_requires_approval = True
2 auth.settings.login_after_registration = True
```

Other methods of **Auth** can be restricted in the same way.

9.1.2   Integration with OpenID, Facebook, etc.

You can use the web2py Role Base Access Control and authenticate with other services like OpenID, Facebook, LinkedIn, Google, Dropbox, MySpace, Flickr, etc. The easiest way is to use Janrain Engage (formerly RPX) (Janrain.com).

Dropbox is discussed as a special case in Chapter 14 since it allows more than just login, it also provides storage services for the logged in users.

Janrain Engage is a service that provides middleware authentication. You can register with Janrain.com, register a domain (the name of your app) and set of URLs you will be using, and they will provide you with an API key.

Now edit the model of your web2py application and place the following lines somewhere after the definition of the auth object :

```
1 from gluon.contrib.login_methods.rpx_account import RPXAccount
2 auth.settings.actions_disabled=['register','change_password','
      request_reset_password']
3 auth.settings.login_form = RPXAccount(request,
4    api_key='...',
5    domain='...',
6    url = "http://your-external-address/%s/default/user/login" % request.
         application)
```

The first line imports the new login method, the second line disables local registration, and the third line asks web2py to use the RPX login method. You must insert your own api_key provided by Janrain.com, the domain you choose upon registration and the external url of your login page. To obtain then login at janrain.com, then go to [Deployment][Application Settings]. On the right side there is the "Application Info", The api_key is called "API Key (Secret)".

The domain is the "Application Domain" without leading "https://" and without the trailing ".rpxnow.com/" For example: if you have registered a website as "secure.mywebsite.org", Janrain turns it to the Application Domain "https://secure-mywebsite.rpxnow.com".

When a new user logins for the first time, web2py creates a new db.auth_user record associated to the user. It will use the registration_id field to store a unique id for the user. Most authentication methods will also provide a username, email, first_name and last_name but that is not guaranteed. Which fields are provided depends on the login method selected by the user. If the same user logs in twice using different authentication mechanisms (for example once with OpenID and once with Facebook), Janrain may not recognize his/her as the same user and issue different registration_id.

You can customize the mapping between the data provided by Janrain and the data stored in db.auth_user. Here is an example for Facebook:

```
auth.settings.login_form.mappings.Facebook = lambda profile:\
    dict(registration_id = profile["identifier"],
         username = profile["preferredUsername"],
         email = profile["email"],
         first_name = profile["name"]["givenName"],
         last_name = profile["name"]["familyName"])
```

The keys in the dictionary are fields in db.auth_user and the values are data entries in the profile object provided by Janrain. Look at the online Janrain documentation for details on the latter.

Janrain will also keep statistics about your users' login.

This login form is fully integrated with web2py Role Based Access Control and you can still create groups, make users members of groups, assign permissions, block users, etc.

Janrain's free Basic service allows up to 2500 unique registered users to sign in annually. Accommodating more users requires an upgrade to one of their paid service tiers.

If you prefer not to use Janrain and want to use a different login method (LDAP, PAM, Google, OpenID, OAuth/Facebook, LinkedIn, etc.) you can do so. The API to do so is described later in the chapter.

9.1.3 CAPTCHA and reCAPTCHA

To prevent spammers and bots registering on your site, you may require a registration CAPTCHA. web2py supports reCAPTCHA [89] out of the box. This is because reCAPTCHA is very well designed, free, accessible (it can read the words to the visitors), easy to set up, and does not require installing any third-party libraries.

This is what you need to do to use reCAPTCHA:

- Register with reCAPTCHA [89] and obtain a (PUBLIC_KEY, PRIVATE_KEY) couple for your account. These are just two strings.

- Append the following code to your model after the auth object is defined:

```
from gluon.tools import Recaptcha
auth.settings.captcha = Recaptcha(request,
  'PUBLIC_KEY', 'PRIVATE_KEY')
```

reCAPTCHA may not work if you access the web site as 'localhost' or '127.0.0.1', because it is registered to work with publicly visible web sites only.

The Recaptcha constructor takes some optional arguments:

```
Recaptcha(..., use_ssl=True, error_message='invalid', label='Verify:', options='')
```

Notice that use_ssl=False by default.

options may be a configuration string, e.g. options="theme:'white', lang:'fr'"

More details: reCAPTCHA [90] and customizing.

If you do not want to use reCAPTCHA, look into the definition of the Recaptcha class in "gluon/tools.py", since it is easy to use other CAPTCHA systems.

Notice that Recaptcha is just a helper that extends DIV. It generates a dummy field that validates using the reCaptcha service and, therefore, it can be used in any form, including used defined FORMs:

```
form = FORM(INPUT(...),Recaptcha(...),INPUT(_type='submit'))
```

You can use it in all types of SQLFORM by injection:

```
form = SQLFORM(...) or SQLFORM.factory(...)
form.element('table').insert(-1,TR('',Recaptcha(...),''))
```

9.1.4 Customizing Auth

The call to

```
1 auth.define_tables()
```

defines all **Auth** tables that have not been defined already. This means that if you wish to do so, you can define your own auth_user table.

There are a number of ways to customize auth. The simplest way is to add extra fields:

```
1 ## after auth = Auth(db)
2 auth.settings.extra_fields['auth_user']= [
3   Field('address'),
4   Field('city'),
5   Field('zip'),
6   Field('phone')]
7 ## before auth.define_tables(username=True)
```

You can declare extra fields not just for table "auth_user" but also for other "auth_" tables. Using extra_fields is the recommended way as it will not break any internal mechanism.

Another way to do this, although not really recommended, consists of defining your auth tables yourself. If a table is declared before auth.define_tables() it is used instead of the default one. Here is how to do it:

```
1  ## after auth = Auth(db)
2  db.define_table(
3      auth.settings.table_user_name,
4      Field('first_name', length=128, default=''),
5      Field('last_name', length=128, default=''),
6      Field('email', length=128, default='', unique=True), # required
7      Field('password', 'password', length=512,          # required
8          readable=False, label='Password'),
9      Field('address'),
10     Field('city'),
11     Field('zip'),
12     Field('phone'),
13     Field('registration_key', length=512,              # required
14         writable=False, readable=False, default=''),
15     Field('reset_password_key', length=512,            # required
16         writable=False, readable=False, default=''),
17     Field('registration_id', length=512,               # required
18         writable=False, readable=False, default=''))
19
20 ## do not forget validators
21 custom_auth_table = db[auth.settings.table_user_name] # get the custom_auth_table
22 custom_auth_table.first_name.requires = \
23   IS_NOT_EMPTY(error_message=auth.messages.is_empty)
```

```
24 custom_auth_table.last_name.requires = \
25   IS_NOT_EMPTY(error_message=auth.messages.is_empty)
26 custom_auth_table.password.requires = [IS_STRONG(), CRYPT()]
27 custom_auth_table.email.requires = [
28   IS_EMAIL(error_message=auth.messages.invalid_email),
29   IS_NOT_IN_DB(db, custom_auth_table.email)]
30
31 auth.settings.table_user = custom_auth_table # tell auth to use custom_auth_table
32
33 ## before auth.define_tables()
```

You can add any field you wish, and you can change validators but you cannot remove the fields marked as "required" in this example.

It is important to make "password", "registration_key", "reset_password_key" and "registration_id" fields readable=False and writable=False, since a visitor must not be allowed to tamper with them.

If you add a field called "username", it will be used in place of "email" for login. If you do, you will need to add a validator as well:

```
1 auth_table.username.requires = IS_NOT_IN_DB(db, auth_table.username)
```

9.1.5   Renaming Auth tables

The actual names of the Auth tables are stored in

```
1 auth.settings.table_user_name = 'auth_user'
2 auth.settings.table_group_name = 'auth_group'
3 auth.settings.table_membership_name = 'auth_membership'
4 auth.settings.table_permission_name = 'auth_permission'
5 auth.settings.table_event_name = 'auth_event'
```

The names of the table can be changed by reassigning the above variables after the auth object is defined and before the Auth tables are defined. For example:

```
1 auth = Auth(db)
2 auth.settings.table_user_name = 'person'
3 #...
4 auth.define_tables()
```

The actual tables can also be referenced, independently of their actual names, by

```
1 auth.settings.table_user
2 auth.settings.table_group
```

```
3  auth.settings.table_membership
4  auth.settings.table_permission
5  auth.settings.table_event
```

9.1.6   Other login methods and login forms

Auth provides multiple login methods and hooks to create new login methods. Each supported login method corresponds to a file in the folder

```
1  gluon/contrib/login_methods/
```

Refer to the documentation in the files themselves for each login method, but here are some examples.

First of all, we need to make a distinction between two types of alternate login methods:

- login methods that use a web2py login form (although the credentials are verified outside web2py). An example is LDAP.

- login methods that require an external single-sign-on form (an example is Google and Facebook).

In the latter case, web2py never gets the login credentials, only a login token issued by the service provider.   The token is stored in db.auth_user.registration_id.

Let's consider examples of the first case:

Basic

Let's say you have an authentication service, for example at the url

```
1  https://basic.example.com
```

that accepts basic access authentication. That means the server accepts HTTP requests with a header of the form:

```
1  GET /index.html HTTP/1.0
2  Host: basic.example.com
3  Authorization: Basic QWxhZGRpbjpvcGVuIHNlc2FtZQ==
```

where the latter string is the base64 encoding of the string username:password. The service responds 200 OK if the user is authorized and 400, 401, 402, 403 or 404 otherwise.

You want to enter username and password using the standard Auth login form and verify the credentials against such a service. All you need to do is add the following code to your application

```
1  from gluon.contrib.login_methods.basic_auth import basic_auth
2  auth.settings.login_methods.append(
3      basic_auth('https://basic.example.com'))
```

Notice that auth.settings.login_methods is a list of authentication methods that are executed sequentially. By default it is set to

```
1  auth.settings.login_methods = [auth]
```

When an alternate method is appended, for example basic_auth, **Auth** first tries to log in the visitor based on the content of auth_user, and when this fails, it tries the next method in the list. If a method succeeds in logging in the visitor, and if auth.settings.login_methods[0]==auth, Auth takes the following actions:

- if the user does not exist in auth_user, a new user is created and the username/email and passwords are stored.

- if the user does exist in auth_user but the new accepted password does not match the old stored password, the old password is replaced with the new one (notice that passwords are always stored hashed unless specified otherwise).

If you do not wish to store the new password in auth_user, then it is sufficient to change the order of login methods, or remove auth from the list. For example:

```
1  from gluon.contrib.login_methods.basic_auth import basic_auth
2  auth.settings.login_methods = \
3      [basic_auth('https://basic.example.com')]
```

The same applies for any other login method described here.

SMTP and Gmail

You can verify login credentials using a remote SMTP server, for example Gmail; i.e., you log the user in if the email and password they provide are valid credentials to access the Gmail SMTP server (smtp.gmail.com:587). All that is needed is the following code:

```
1  from gluon.contrib.login_methods.email_auth import email_auth
```

```
2  auth.settings.login_methods.append(
3      email_auth("smtp.gmail.com:587", "@gmail.com"))
```

The first argument of email_auth is the address:port of the SMTP server. The second argument is the email domain.

This works with any SMTP server that requires TLS authentication.

PAM

Authentication using Pluggable Authentication Modules (PAM) works as in the previous cases. It allows web2py to authenticate users using the operating system accounts:

```
1  from gluon.contrib.login_methods.pam_auth import pam_auth
2  auth.settings.login_methods.append(pam_auth())
```

LDAP

Authentication using LDAP works very much as in the previous cases.

To use LDAP login with MS Active Directory:

```
1  from gluon.contrib.login_methods.ldap_auth import ldap_auth
2  auth.settings.login_methods.append(ldap_auth(mode='ad',
3      server='my.domain.controller',
4      base_dn='ou=Users,dc=domain,dc=com'))
```

To use LDAP login with Lotus Notes and Domino:

```
1  auth.settings.login_methods.append(ldap_auth(mode='domino',
2      server='my.domino.server'))
```

To use LDAP login with OpenLDAP (with UID):

```
1  auth.settings.login_methods.append(ldap_auth(server='my.ldap.server',
2      base_dn='ou=Users,dc=domain,dc=com'))
```

To use LDAP login with OpenLDAP (with CN):

```
1  auth.settings.login_methods.append(ldap_auth(mode='cn',
2      server='my.ldap.server', base_dn='ou=Users,dc=domain,dc=com'))
```

Google App Engine

Authentication using Google when running on Google App Engine requires skipping the web2py login form, being redirected to the Google login page, and back upon success. Because the behavior is different than in the previous examples, the API is a little different.

```
1  from gluon.contrib.login_methods.gae_google_login import GaeGoogleAccount
2  auth.settings.login_form = GaeGoogleAccount()
```

OpenID

We have previously discussed integration with Janrain (which has OpenID support) and that is the easiest way to use OpenID. Yet sometimes you do not want to rely on a third party service and you want to access the OpenID provider directly from the consumer (your app).

Here is an example:

```
1 from gluon.contrib.login_methods.openid_auth import OpenIDAuth
2 auth.settings.login_form = OpenIDAuth(auth)
```

OpenIDAuth requires the *python-openid* module to be installed separately. Under the hood, this login method defines the following table:

```
1 db.define_table('alt_logins',
2     Field('username', length=512, default=''),
3     Field('type', length =128, default='openid', readable=False),
4     Field('user', self.table_user, readable=False))
```

which stores the openid usernames for each user. If you want to display the openids for the current logged in user:

```
1 {{=auth.settings.login_form.list_user_openids()}}
```

OAuth2.0 and Facebook

We have previously discussed integration with Janrain (which has Facebook support), yet sometimes you do not want to rely on a third party service and you want to access a OAuth2.0 provider directly; for example, Facebook. Here is how:

```
1 from gluon.contrib.login_methods.oauth20_account import OAuthAccount
2 auth.settings.login_form=OAuthAccount(YOUR_CLIENT_ID,YOUR_CLIENT_SECRET)
```

Things get a little more complex if you want to use Facebook OAuth2.0 to login into a specific Facebook app to access its API, instead of your own app. Here is an example for accessing the Facebook Graph API.

First of all you must install the Facebook Python SDK.

Second, you need the following code in your model:

```
1 ## import required modules
2 from facebook import GraphAPI
3 from gluon.contrib.login_methods.oauth20_account import OAuthAccount
4 ## extend the OAUthAccount class
5 class FaceBookAccount(OAuthAccount):
```

```
6    """OAuth impl for Facebook"""
7    AUTH_URL="https://graph.facebook.com/oauth/authorize"
8    TOKEN_URL="https://graph.facebook.com/oauth/access_token"
9    def __init__(self, g):
10       OAuthAccount.__init__(self, g,
11                             YOUR_CLIENT_ID,
12                             YOUR_CLIENT_SECRET,
13                             self.AUTH_URL,
14                             self.TOKEN_URL)
15       self.graph = None
16   # override function that fetches user info
17   def get_user(self):
18       "Returns the user using the Graph API"
19       if not self.accessToken():
20           return None
21       if not self.graph:
22           self.graph = GraphAPI((self.accessToken()))
23       try:
24           user = self.graph.get_object("me")
25           return dict(first_name = user['first_name'],
26                       last_name = user['last_name'],
27                       username = user['id'])
28       except GraphAPIError:
29           self.session.token = None
30           self.graph = None
31           return None
32   ## use the above class to build a new login form
33   auth.settings.login_form=FaceBookAccount()
```

LinkedIn

We have previously discussed integration with Janrain (which has LinkedIn support) and that is the easiest way to use OAuth. Yet sometime you do not want to rely on a third party service or you may want to access LinkedIn directly to get more information than Janrain provides.

Here is an example:

```
1  from gluon.contrib.login_methods.linkedin_account import LinkedInAccount
2  auth.settings.login_form=LinkedInAccount(request,KEY,SECRET,RETURN_URL)
```

LinkedInAccount requires the "python-linkedin" module installed separately.

X509

You can also login by passing to the page an x509 certificate and your credential will be extracted from the certificate. This requires M2Crypto installed from

```
1  http://chandlerproject.org/bin/view/Projects/MeTooCrypto
```

Once you have M2Cryption installed you can do:

```
1  from gluon.contrib.login_methods.x509_auth import X509Account
2  auth.settings.actions_disabled=['register','change_password','
       request_reset_password']
3  auth.settings.login_form = X509Account()
```

You can now authenticate into web2py passing your x509 certificate. How to do this is browser-dependent, but probably you are more likely to use certificates for web services. In this case you can use for example cURL to try out your authentication:

```
1  curl -d "firstName=John&lastName=Smith" -G -v --key private.key \
2      --cert  server.crt https://example/app/default/user/profile
```

This works out of the box with Rocket (the web2py built-in web server) but you may need some extra configuration work on the web server side if you are using a different web server. In particular you need to tell your web server where the certificates are located on local host and that it needs to verify certificates coming from the clients. How to do it is web server dependent and therefore omitted here.

Multiple login forms

Some login methods modify the login_form, some do not. When they do that, they may not be able to coexist. Yet some coexist by providing multiple login forms in the same page. web2py provides a way to do it. Here is an example mixing normal login (auth) and RPX login (janrain.com):

```
1  from gluon.contrib.login_methods.extended_login_form import ExtendedLoginForm
2  other_form = RPXAccount(request, api_key='...', domain='...', url='...')
3  auth.settings.login_form = ExtendedLoginForm(auth, other_form, signals=['token'])
```

If signals are set and a parameter in request matches any signals, it will return the call of other_form.login_form instead. other_form can handle some particular situations, for example, multiple steps of OpenID login inside other_form.login_form.

Otherwise it will render the normal login form together with the other_form.

9.1.7   Record versioning

You can use Auth to enable full record versioning:

```
db.enable_record_versioning(db,
    archive_db=None,
    archive_names='%(tablename)s_archive',
    current_record='current_record'):
```

This tells web2py to create an archive table for each of the tables in db and store a copy of each record when modified. The old copy is stored. The new copy is not.

The last three parameters are optional:

- archive_db allows to specify another database where the archive tables are to be stored. Setting it to None is the same as setting it to db.

- archive_names provides a pattern for naming each archive table.

- current_record specified the name of the reference field to be used in the archive table to refer to the original, unmodified, record. Notice that archive_db!=db then the reference field is just an integer field since cross database references are not possible.

Only tables with modified_by and modified_on fields (as created for example by auth.signature) will be archived.

When you enable_record_versioning, if records have an is_active field (also created by auth.signature), records will never be deleted but they will be marked with is_active=False. In fact, enable_record_versioning adds a common_filter to every versioned table that filters out records with is_active=False so they essentially become invisible.

If you enable_record_versioning, you should not use auth.archive or crud.archive else you will end up with duplicate records. Those functions do explicitly what enable_record_versioning does automatically and they will be deprecated.

9.1.8 Mail **and** Auth

One can define a mailer with

```
1 from gluon.tools import Mail
2 mail = Mail()
3 mail.settings.server = 'smtp.example.com:25'
4 mail.settings.sender = 'you@example.com'
5 mail.settings.login = 'username:password'
```

or simply use the mailer provided by auth:

```
1 mail = auth.settings.mailer
2 mail.settings.server = 'smtp.example.com:25'
3 mail.settings.sender = 'you@example.com'
4 mail.settings.login = 'username:password'
```

You need to replace the mail.settings with the proper parameters for your SMTP server. Set mail.settings.login = None if the SMTP server does not require authentication. If you don't want to use TLS, set mail.settings.tls = False

You can read more about web2py API for emails and email configuration in Chapter 8. Here we limit the discussion to the interaction between Mail and Auth.

In Auth, by default, email verification is disabled. To enable email, append the following lines in the model where auth is defined:

```
1  auth.settings.registration_requires_verification = True
2  auth.settings.registration_requires_approval = False
3  auth.settings.reset_password_requires_verification = True
4  auth.messages.verify_email = 'Click on the link http://' + \
5      request.env.http_host + \
6      URL(r=request,c='default',f='user',args=['verify_email']) + \
7      '/%(key)s to verify your email'
8  auth.messages.reset_password = 'Click on the link http://' + \
9      request.env.http_host + \
10     URL(r=request,c='default',f='user',args=['reset_password']) + \
11     '/%(key)s to reset your password'
```

In the two auth.messages above, you may need to replace the URL portion of the string with the proper complete URL of the action. This is necessary because web2py may be installed behind a proxy, and it cannot determine its own public URLs with absolute certainty. The above examples (which are the default values) should, however, work in most cases.

9.2 Authorization

Once a new user is registered, a new group is created to contain the user. The role of the new user is conventionally "user_[id]" where [id] is the id of the newly created user. The creation of the group can be disabled with

```
auth.settings.create_user_groups = None
```

although we do not suggest doing so. Notice that `create_user_groups` is not a boolean (although it can be `False`) but it defaults to:

```
auth.settings.create_user_groups="user_%(id)s"
```

It store a template for the name of the group created for user `id`.

Users have membership in groups. Each group is identified by a name/role. Groups have permissions. Users have permissions because of the groups they belong to. By default each user is made member of their own group.

You can also do

```
auth.settings.everybody_group_id = 5
```

to make any new user automatically member of group number 5. Here 5 is used as an example and we assume the group was created already.

You can create groups, give membership and permissions via **appadmin** or programmatically using the following methods:

```
auth.add_group('role', 'description')
```

returns the id of the newly created group.

```
auth.del_group(group_id)
```

deletes the group with `group_id`.

```
auth.del_group(auth.id_group('user_7'))
```

deletes the group with role "user_7", i.e., the group uniquely associated to user number 7.

```
auth.user_group(user_id)
```

returns the id of the group uniquely associated to the user identified by `user_id`.

```
auth.add_membership(group_id, user_id)
```

gives `user_id` membership of the group `group_id`. If the `user_id` is not specified, then web2py assumes the current logged-in user.

```
auth.del_membership(group_id, user_id)
```

revokes `user_id` membership of the group `group_id`. If the `user_id` is not specified, then web2py assumes the current logged-in user.

```
auth.has_membership(group_id, user_id, role)
```

checks whether `user_id` has membership of the group `group_id` or the group with the specified role. Only `group_id` or `role` should be passed to the function, not both. If the `user_id` is not specified, then web2py assumes the current logged-in user.

```
auth.add_permission(group_id, 'name', 'object', record_id)
```

gives permission "name" (user defined) on the object "object" (also user defined) to members of the group `group_id`. If "object" is a tablename then the permission can refer to the entire table by setting `record_id` to a value of zero, or the permission can refer to a specific record by specifying a `record_id` value greater than zero. When giving permissions on tables, it is common to use a permission name in the set ('create', 'read', 'update', 'delete', 'select') since these permissions are understood and can be enforced by the CRUD APIs.

If `group_id` is zero, web2py uses the group uniquely associated to the current logged-in user.

You can also use `auth.id_group(role="...")` to get the id of a group given its name.

```
auth.del_permission(group_id, 'name', 'object', record_id)
```

revokes the permission.

```
auth.has_permission('name', 'object', record_id, user_id)
```

checks whether the user identified by `user_id` has membership in a group with the requested permission.

```
rows = db(auth.accessible_query('read', db.mytable, user_id))\
    .select(db.mytable.ALL)
```

returns all rows of table "mytable" that user `user_id` has "read" permission on. If the `user_id` is not specified, then web2py assumes the current logged-in user. The `accessible_query(...)` can be combined with other queries to make more complex ones. `accessible_query(...)` is the only **Auth** method to require a JOIN, so it does not work on the Google App Engine.

Assuming the following definitions:

```
>>> from gluon.tools import Auth
>>> auth = Auth(db)
>>> auth.define_tables()
>>> secrets = db.define_table('document', Field('body'))
>>> james_bond = db.auth_user.insert(first_name='James',
                                      last_name='Bond')
```

Here is an example:

```
>>> doc_id = db.document.insert(body = 'top secret')
>>> agents = auth.add_group(role = 'Secret Agent')
>>> auth.add_membership(agents, james_bond)
>>> auth.add_permission(agents, 'read', secrets)
>>> print auth.has_permission('read', secrets, doc_id, james_bond)
True
>>> print auth.has_permission('update', secrets, doc_id, james_bond)
False
```

9.2.1 Decorators

The most common way to check permission is not by explicit calls to the above methods, but by decorating functions so that permissions are checked relative to the logged-in visitor. Here are some examples:

```
def function_one():
    return 'this is a public function'

@auth.requires_login()
def function_two():
    return 'this requires login'

@auth.requires_membership('agents')
def function_three():
    return 'you are a secret agent'

@auth.requires_permission('read', secrets)
def function_four():
    return 'you can read secret documents'

@auth.requires_permission('delete', 'any file')
def function_five():
    import os
    for file in os.listdir('./'):
        os.unlink(file)
    return 'all files deleted'
```

```
23 @auth.requires(auth.user_id==1 or request.client=='127.0.0.1', requires_login=True)
24 def function_six():
25     return 'you can read secret documents'
26
27 @auth.requires_permission('add', 'number')
28 def add(a, b):
29     return a + b
30
31 def function_seven():
32     return add(3, 4)
```

The condition argument of @auth.requires(condition) can be a callable and unless the condition is simple, it better to pass a callable than a condition since this will be faster, as the condition will only be evaluated if needed. For example

```
1 @auth.requires(lambda: check_condition())
2 def action():
3     ....
```

@auth.requires also takes an optional argument requires_login which defaults to True. If set to False, it does not require login before evaluating the condition as true/false. The condition can be a boolean value or a function evaluating to boolean.

Note that access to all functions apart from the first one is restricted based on permissions that the visitor may or may not have.

If the visitor is not logged in, then the permission cannot be checked; the visitor is redirected to the login page and then back to the page that requires permissions.

9.2.2   Combining requirements

Occasionally, it is necessary to combine requirements. This can be done via a generic requires decorator which takes a single argument, a true or false condition. For example, to give access to agents, but only on Tuesday:

```
1 @auth.requires(auth.has_membership(group_id='agents' \
2              and request.now.weekday()==1)
3 def function_seven():
4     return 'Hello agent, it must be Tuesday!'
```

or equivalently:

```
1  @auth.requires(auth.has_membership(role='Secret Agent') \
2                 and request.now.weekday()==1)
3  def function_seven():
4      return 'Hello agent, it must be Tuesday!'
```

9.2.3 Authorization and CRUD

Using decorators and/or explicit checks provides one way to implement access control.

Another way to implement access control is to always use CRUD (as opposed to SQLFORM) to access the database and to ask CRUD to enforce access control on database tables and records. This is done by linking Auth and CRUD with the following statement:

```
1  crud.settings.auth = auth
```

This will prevent the visitor from accessing any of the CRUD functions unless the visitor is logged in and has explicit access. For example, to allow a visitor to post comments, but only update their own comments (assuming crud, auth and db.comment are defined):

```
1  def give_create_permission(form):
2      group_id = auth.id_group('user_%s' % auth.user.id)
3      auth.add_permission(group_id, 'read', db.comment)
4      auth.add_permission(group_id, 'create', db.comment)
5      auth.add_permission(group_id, 'select', db.comment)
6
7  def give_update_permission(form):
8      comment_id = form.vars.id
9      group_id = auth.id_group('user_%s' % auth.user.id)
10     auth.add_permission(group_id, 'update', db.comment, comment_id)
11     auth.add_permission(group_id, 'delete', db.comment, comment_id)
12
13 auth.settings.register_onaccept = give_create_permission
14 crud.settings.auth = auth
15
16 def post_comment():
17     form = crud.create(db.comment, onaccept=give_update_permission)
18     comments = db(db.comment).select()
19     return dict(form=form, comments=comments)
20
21 def update_comment():
22     form = crud.update(db.comment, request.args(0))
23     return dict(form=form)
```

You can also select specific records (those you have 'read' access to):

```
1 def post_comment():
2     form = crud.create(db.comment, onaccept=give_update_permission)
3     query = auth.accessible_query('read', db.comment, auth.user.id)
4     comments = db(query).select(db.comment.ALL)
5     return dict(form=form, comments=comments)
```

The permissions names enforced by :

```
1 crud.settings.auth = auth
```

are "read", "create", "update", "delete", "select", "impersonate".

9.2.4 Authorization and downloads

The use of decorators and the use of `crud.settings.auth` do not enforce authorization on files downloaded by the usual download function

```
1 def download(): return response.download(request, db)
```

If one wishes to do so, one must declare explicitly which "upload" fields contain files that need access control upon download. For example:

```
1 db.define_table('dog',
2     Field('small_image', 'upload'),
3     Field('large_image', 'upload'))
4
5 db.dog.large_image.authorization = lambda record: \
6     auth.is_logged_in() and \
7     auth.has_permission('read', db.dog, record.id, auth.user.id)
```

The attribute `authorization` of upload field can be None (the default) or a function that decides whether the user is logged in and has permission to 'read' the current record. In this example, there is no restriction on downloading images linked by the "small_image" field, but we require access control on images linked by the "large_image" field.

9.2.5 Access Control and Basic Authentication

Occasionally, it may be necessary to expose actions that have decorators that require access control as services; i.e., to call them from a program or script and still be able to use authentication to check for authorization.

Auth enables login via basic authentication:

```
1   auth.settings.allow_basic_login = True
```

With this set, an action like

```
1   @auth.requires_login()
2   def give_me_time():
3       import time
4       return time.ctime()
```

can be called, for example, from a shell command:

```
1   wget --user=[username] --password=[password]
2       http://.../[app]/[controller]/give_me_time
```

It is also possible to log in by calling `auth.basic()` rather than using an `@auth` decorator:

```
1   def give_me_time():
2       import time
3       auth.basic()
4       if auth.user:
5           return time.ctime()
6       else:
7           return 'Not authorized'
```

Basic login is often the only option for services (described in the next chapter), but it is disabled by default.

9.2.6   Manual Authentication

Some times you want to implement your own logic and do "manual" user login. This can also be done by calling the function:

```
1   user = auth.login_bare(username,password)
```

`login_bare` returns user if the user exists and the password is valid, else it returns False. `username` is the email if the "auth_user" table does not have a "username" field.

9.2.7   Settings and messages

Here is a list of all parameters that can be customized for **Auth**

The following must point to a `gluon.tools.Mail` object to allow `auth` to send emails:

```
auth.settings.mailer = None
```

The following must be the name of the controller that defined the user action:

```
auth.settings.controller = 'default'
```

The following is a very important setting:

```
auth.settings.hmac_key = None
```

It must be set to something like "sha512:a-pass-phrase" and it will be passed to the CRYPT validator for the "password" field of the auth_user table. It will be the algorithm and a-pass-phrase used to hash the passwords.

By default, auth also requires a minimum password length of 4. This can be changed:

```
auth.settings.password_min_length = 4
```

To disabled an action append its name to this list:

```
auth.settings.actions_disabled = []
```

For example:

```
auth.settings.actions_disabled.append('register')
```

will disable registration.

If you want to receive an email to verify registration set this to True:

```
auth.settings.registration_requires_verification = False
```

To automatically login people after registration, even if they have not completed the email verification process, set the following to True:

```
auth.settings.login_after_registration = False
```

If new registrants must wait for approval before being able to login set this to True:

```
auth.settings.registration_requires_approval = False
```

Approval consists of setting registration_key==" via appadmin or programmatically.

If you do not want a new group for each new user set the following to False:

```
auth.settings.create_user_groups = True
```

The following settings determine alternative login methods and login forms, as discussed previously:

```
1  auth.settings.login_methods = [auth]
2  auth.settings.login_form = auth
```

Do you want to allow basic login?

```
1  auth.settings.allows_basic_login = False
```

The following is the URL of the login action:

```
1  auth.settings.login_url = URL('user', args='login')
```

If the user tried to access the register page but is already logged in, he will be redirected to this URL:

```
1  auth.settings.logged_url = URL('user', args='profile')
```

This must point to the URL of the download action, in case the profile contains images:

```
1  auth.settings.download_url = URL('download')
```

These must point to the URL you want to redirect your users to after the various possible auth actions (in case there is no referrer):

```
1   auth.settings.login_next = URL('index')
2   auth.settings.logout_next = URL('index')
3   auth.settings.profile_next = URL('index')
4   auth.settings.register_next = URL('user', args='login')
5   auth.settings.retrieve_username_next = URL('index')
6   auth.settings.retrieve_password_next = URL('index')
7   auth.settings.change_password_next = URL('index')
8   auth.settings.request_reset_password_next = URL('user', args='login')
9   auth.settings.reset_password_next = URL('user', args='login')
10  auth.settings.verify_email_next = URL('user', args='login')
```

If the visitor is not logger in, and calls a function that requires authentication, the user is redirected to auth.settings.login_url which defaults to URL('default','user/login'). One can replace this behavior by redefining:

```
1  auth.settings.on_failed_authentication = lambda url: redirect(url)
```

This is the function called for the redirection. The argument url' passed to this function is the url for the login page.

If the visitor does not have permission to access a given function, the visitor is redirect to the URL defined by

```
1  auth.settings.on_failed_authorization = \
2      URL('user',args='on_failed_authorization')
```

You can change this variable and redirect the user elsewhere.

Often on_failed_authorization is a URL but it can be a function that returns the URL and it will be called on failed authorization.

These are lists of callbacks that should be executed after form validation for each of the corresponding action before any database IO:

```
1  auth.settings.login_onvalidation = []
2  auth.settings.register_onvalidation = []
3  auth.settings.profile_onvalidation = []
4  auth.settings.retrieve_password_onvalidation = []
5  auth.settings.reset_password_onvalidation = []
```

Each callback must be a function that takes the form object and it can modify the attributes of the form object before database IO is performed.

These are lists of callbacks that should be executed after the database IO is performed and before redirection:

```
1  auth.settings.login_onaccept = []
2  auth.settings.register_onaccept = []
3  auth.settings.profile_onaccept = []
4  auth.settings.verify_email_onaccept = []
```

Here is an example:

```
1  auth.settings.register_onaccept.append(lambda form:\
2      mail.send(to='you@example.com',subject='new user',
3              message='new user email is %s'%form.vars.email))
```

You can enable captcha for any of the auth actions:

```
1  auth.settings.captcha = None
2  auth.settings.login_captcha = None
3  auth.settings.register_captcha = None
4  auth.settings.retrieve_username_captcha = None
5  auth.settings.retrieve_password_captcha = None
```

If the .captcha settings points to a gluon.tools.Recaptcha, all forms for which the corresponding option (like .login_captcha) is set to None will have a captcha, while those for which the corresponding option is set to False will not. If, instead, .captcha is set to None, only those form who have a corresponding option set to a gluon.tools.Recaptcha object will have captcha and the others will not.

This is the login session expiration time:

```
1  auth.settings.expiration = 3600  # seconds
```

You can change the name of the password field (in Firebird for example "password" is a keyword and cannot be used to name a field):

```
1  auth.settings.password_field = 'password'
```

Normally the login form tries to validate an email. This can be disabled by changing this setting:

```
1  auth.settings.login_email_validate = True
```

Do you want to show the record id in the edit profile page?

```
1  auth.settings.showid = False
```

For custom forms you may want to disable automatic error notification in forms:

```
1  auth.settings.hideerror = False
```

Also for custom forms you can change the style:

```
1  auth.settings.formstyle = 'table3cols'
```

(it can be "table2cols", "divs" and "ul")

And you can set the separator for auth-generated forms:

```
1  auth.settings.label_separator =          ':'
```

By default the login form gives the option to extend the login via "remember me" option. The expiration time can be changed or the option disabled via these settings:

```
1  auth.settings.long_expiration = 3600*24*30 # one month
2  auth.settings.remember_me_form = True
```

You can also customize the following messages whose use and context should be obvious:

```
 1  auth.messages.submit_button = 'Submit'
 2  auth.messages.verify_password = 'Verify Password'
 3  auth.messages.delete_label = 'Check to delete:'
 4  auth.messages.function_disabled = 'Function disabled'
 5  auth.messages.access_denied = 'Insufficient privileges'
 6  auth.messages.registration_verifying = 'Registration needs verification'
 7  auth.messages.registration_pending = 'Registration is pending approval'
 8  auth.messages.login_disabled = 'Login disabled by administrator'
 9  auth.messages.logged_in = 'Logged in'
10  auth.messages.email_sent = 'Email sent'
11  auth.messages.unable_to_send_email = 'Unable to send email'
12  auth.messages.email_verified = 'Email verified'
13  auth.messages.logged_out = 'Logged out'
```

```
14 auth.messages.registration_successful = 'Registration successful'
15 auth.messages.invalid_email = 'Invalid email'
16 auth.messages.unable_send_email = 'Unable to send email'
17 auth.messages.invalid_login = 'Invalid login'
18 auth.messages.invalid_user = 'Invalid user'
19 auth.messages.is_empty = "Cannot be empty"
20 auth.messages.mismatched_password = "Password fields don't match"
21 auth.messages.verify_email = ...
22 auth.messages.verify_email_subject = 'Password verify'
23 auth.messages.username_sent = 'Your username was emailed to you'
24 auth.messages.new_password_sent = 'A new password was emailed to you'
25 auth.messages.password_changed = 'Password changed'
26 auth.messages.retrieve_username = 'Your username is: %(username)s'
27 auth.messages.retrieve_username_subject = 'Username retrieve'
28 auth.messages.retrieve_password = 'Your password is: %(password)s'
29 auth.messages.retrieve_password_subject = 'Password retrieve'
30 auth.messages.reset_password = ...
31 auth.messages.reset_password_subject = 'Password reset'
32 auth.messages.invalid_reset_password = 'Invalid reset password'
33 auth.messages.profile_updated = 'Profile updated'
34 auth.messages.new_password = 'New password'
35 auth.messages.old_password = 'Old password'
36 auth.messages.group_description = \
37     'Group uniquely assigned to user %(id)s'
38 auth.messages.register_log = 'User %(id)s Registered'
39 auth.messages.login_log = 'User %(id)s Logged-in'
40 auth.messages.logout_log = 'User %(id)s Logged-out'
41 auth.messages.profile_log = 'User %(id)s Profile updated'
42 auth.messages.verify_email_log = 'User %(id)s Verification email sent'
43 auth.messages.retrieve_username_log = 'User %(id)s Username retrieved'
44 auth.messages.retrieve_password_log = 'User %(id)s Password retrieved'
45 auth.messages.reset_password_log = 'User %(id)s Password reset'
46 auth.messages.change_password_log = 'User %(id)s Password changed'
47 auth.messages.add_group_log = 'Group %(group_id)s created'
48 auth.messages.del_group_log = 'Group %(group_id)s deleted'
49 auth.messages.add_membership_log = None
50 auth.messages.del_membership_log = None
51 auth.messages.has_membership_log = None
52 auth.messages.add_permission_log = None
53 auth.messages.del_permission_log = None
54 auth.messages.has_permission_log = None
55 auth.messages.label_first_name = 'First name'
56 auth.messages.label_last_name = 'Last name'
57 auth.messages.label_username = 'Username'
58 auth.messages.label_email = 'E-mail'
59 auth.messages.label_password = 'Password'
60 auth.messages.label_registration_key = 'Registration key'
61 auth.messages.label_reset_password_key = 'Reset Password key'
62 auth.messages.label_registration_id = 'Registration identifier'
```

```
63 auth.messages.label_role = 'Role'
64 auth.messages.label_description = 'Description'
65 auth.messages.label_user_id = 'User ID'
66 auth.messages.label_group_id = 'Group ID'
67 auth.messages.label_name = 'Name'
68 auth.messages.label_table_name = 'Table name'
69 auth.messages.label_record_id = 'Record ID'
70 auth.messages.label_time_stamp = 'Timestamp'
71 auth.messages.label_client_ip = 'Client IP'
72 auth.messages.label_origin = 'Origin'
73 auth.messages.label_remember_me = "Remember me (for 30 days)"
```

add|del|has membership logs allow the use of "%(user_id)s" and "%(group_id)s". add|del|has permission logs allow the use of "%(user_id)s", "%(name)s", "%(table_name)s", and "%(record_id)s".

9.3   Central Authentication Service

web2py provides support for third party authentication and single sign on. Here we discuss the Central Authentication Service (CAS) which is an industry standard and both client and server are built-into web2py.

CAS is an open protocol for distributed authentication and it works in the following way: When a visitor arrives at our web site, our application check in the session if the user is already authenticated (for example via a session.token object). If the user is not authenticated, the controller redirects the visitor from the CAS appliance, where the user can log in, register, and manage his credentials (name, email and password). If the user registers, he receives an email, and registration is not complete until he responds to the email. Once the user has successfully registered and logged in, the CAS appliance redirects the user to our application together with a key. Our application uses the key to get the credentials of the user via an HTTP request in the background to the CAS server.

Using this mechanism, multiple applications can use a single sign-on via a single CAS server. The server providing authentication is called a service provider. Applications seeking to authenticate visitors are called service consumers.

CAS is similar to OpenID, with one main difference. In the case of OpenID, the visitor chooses the service provider. In the case of CAS, our application makes this choice, making CAS more secure.

Running a web2py CAS provider is as easy as copying the scaffolding app. In fact any web2py app that exposes the action

```
## in provider app
def user(): return dict(form=auth())
```

is a CAS 2.0 provider and its services can be accessed at the URL

```
http://.../provider/default/user/cas/login
http://.../provider/default/user/cas/validate
http://.../provider/default/user/cas/logout
```

(we assume the app to be called "provider").

You can access this service from any other web application (the consumer) by simply delegating authentication to the provider:

```
## in consumer app
auth = Auth(db,cas_provider = 'http://127.0.0.1:8000/provider/default/user/cas')
```

When you visit the login url the consumer app, it will redirect you to the provider app which will perform authentication and will redirect back to the consumer. All processes of registration, logout, change password, retrieve password, have to be completed on the provider app. An entry about the logged-in user will be created on the consumer side so that you add extra fields and have a local profile. Thanks to CAS 2.0 all fields that are readable on the provider and have a corresponding field in the auth_user table of the consumer will be copied automatically.

Auth(...,cas_provider='...') works with third party providers and supports CAS 1.0 and 2.0. The version is detected automatically. By default it builds the URLs of the provider from a base (the cas_provider url above) by appending

```
/login
/validate
/logout
```

These can be changed in consumer and in provider

```
## in consumer or provider app (must match)
auth.settings.cas_actions['login']='login'
auth.settings.cas_actions['validate']='validate'
```

```
4  auth.settings.cas_actions['logout']='logout'
```

If you want to connect to a web2py CAS provider from a different domain, you must enable them by attending to the list of allowed domain:

```
1  ## in provider app
2  auth.settings.cas_domains.append('example.com')
```

9.3.1   Using web2py to authorize non-web2py apps

This is possible but dependent on the web server. here we assume two applications running under the same web server: Apache with mod_wsgi. One of the applications is web2py with an app proving access control via Auth. The other can be a CGI script, a PHP program or anything else. We want to instruct the web server to ask permission to the former application when a client requests access to the latter.

First of all we need to modify the web2py application and add the following controller:

```
1  def check_access():
2      return 'true' if auth.is_logged_in() else 'false'
```

which returns true if the user is logged in and false otherwise. Now run a web2py process in background:

```
1  nohup python web2py.py -a '' -p 8002
```

Port 8002 is a must and there is no need to enable admin so no admin password.

Then we need to edit the Apache config file (for example "/etc/apache2/sites-available/default") and instruct apache so that when the non-web2py program is called, it should call the above check action instead and only if it returns true it should proceed and respond to the request, else if should deny access.

Because web2py and the non-web2py application run under the same domain, if the user is logged into the web2py app, the web2py session cookie will be passed to Apache even when the other app is requested and will allow credential verification.

In order to achieve this we need a script, "web2py/scripts/access.wsgi" that can play this trick. The script ships with web2py. All we need to do it tell apache to call this script, the URL of the application needing access control, and the location of the script:

```
1  <VirtualHost *:80>
2    WSGIDaemonProcess web2py user=www-data group=www-data
3    WSGIProcessGroup web2py
4    WSGIScriptAlias / /home/www-data/web2py/wsgihandler.py
5
6    AliasMatch ^myapp/path/needing/authentication/myfile /path/to/myfile
7    <Directory /path/to/>
8      WSGIAccessScript /path/to/web2py/scripts/access.wsgi
9    </Directory>
10 </VirtualHost>
```

Here "myapp/path/needing/authentication/myfile" is the regular expression that should match the incoming request and "/path/to/" is the absolute location of the web2py folder.

The "access.wsgi" script contains the following line:

```
1  URL_CHECK_ACCESS = 'http://127.0.0.1:8002/%(app)s/default/check_access'
```

which points to the web2py application we have requested but you can edit it to point to a specific application, running on a port other than 8002.

You can also change the check_access() action and make its logic more complex. This action can retrieve the URL that was originally requested using the environment variable

```
1  request.env.request_uri
```

and you can implement more complex rules:

```
1  def check_access():
2      if not auth.is_logged_in():
3          return 'false'
4      elif not user_has_access(request.env.request_uri):
5          return 'false'
6      else:
7          return 'true'
```

10

Services

The W3C defines a web service as "a software system designed to support interoperable machine-to-machine interaction over a network". This is a broad definition, and it encompasses a large number of protocols designed not for machine-to-human communication, but for machine-to-machine communication such as XML, JSON, RSS, etc.

In this chapter we discuss how to expose web services using web2py. If you are interested in examples of consuming third party services (Twitter, Dropbox, etc.) you should look into Chapter 9 and Chapter 14. web2py provides, out of the box, support for many protocols, including XML, JSON, RSS, CSV, XMLRPC, JSONRPC, AMFRPC, and SOAP. web2py can also be extended to support additional protocols.

Each of those protocols are supported in multiple ways, and we make a distinction between:

- Rendering the output of a function in a given format (for example XML, JSON, RSS, CSV)

- Remote Procedure Calls (for example XMLRPC, JSONRPC, AMFRPC)

10.1 Rendering a dictionary

10.1.1   HTML, XML, and JSON

Consider the following action:

```
1 def count():
2     session.counter = (session.counter or 0) + 1
3     return dict(counter=session.counter, now=request.now)
```

This action returns a counter that is increased by one when a visitor reloads the page, and the timestamp of the current page request.

Normally this page would be requested via:

```
1 http://127.0.0.1:8000/app/default/count
```

and rendered in HTML. Without writing one line of code, we can ask web2py to render this page using different protocols by adding an extension to the URL:

```
1 http://127.0.0.1:8000/app/default/count.html
2 http://127.0.0.1:8000/app/default/count.xml
3 http://127.0.0.1:8000/app/default/count.json
```

The dictionary returned by the action will be rendered in HTML, XML and JSON, respectively.

Here is the XML output:

```
1 <document>
2     <counter>3</counter>
3     <now>2009-08-01 13:00:00</now>
4 </document>
```

Here is the JSON output:

```
1 { 'counter':3, 'now':'2009-08-01 13:00:00' }
```

Notice that date, time and datetime objects are rendered as strings in ISO format. This is not part of the JSON standard, but rather a web2py convention.

10.1.2   Generic views

When, for example, the ".xml" extension is called, web2py looks for a template file called "default/count.xml", and if it does not find it, looks for a template called "generic.xml". The files "generic.html", "generic.xml", "generic.json" are provided with the current scaffolding application. Other extensions can be easily defined by the user.

> For security reasons the generic views are only allowed to be accessed on localhost. In order to enable the access from remote clients you may need to set the response.generic_patterns.

Assuming you are using a copy of scaffold app, edit the following line in models/db.py

- restrict access only to localhost

```
response.generic_patterns = ['*'] if request.is_local else []
```

- to allow all generic views

```
response.generic_patterns = ['*']
```

- to allow only.json

```
response.generic_patterns = ['*.json']
```

The generic_patterns is a glob pattern, it means you can use any patterns that matches with your app actions or pass a list of patterns.

```
response.generic_patterns = ['*.json','*.xml']
```

To use it in an older web2py app, you may need to copy the "generic.*" files from a later scaffolding app (after version 1.60).

Here is the code for "generic.html"

```
{{extend 'layout.html'}}

{{=BEAUTIFY(response._vars)}}

<button onclick="document.location='{{=URL("admin","default","design",
args=request.application)}}'">admin</button>
<button onclick="jQuery('#request').slideToggle()">request</button>
<div class="hidden" id="request"><h2>request</h2>{{=BEAUTIFY(request)}}</div>
<button onclick="jQuery('#session').slideToggle()">session</button>
<div class="hidden" id="session"><h2>session</h2>{{=BEAUTIFY(session)}}</div>
<button onclick="jQuery('#response').slideToggle()">response</button>
<div class="hidden" id="response"><h2>response</h2>{{=BEAUTIFY(response)}}</div>
<script>jQuery('.hidden').hide();</script>
```

Here is the code for "generic.xml"

```
{{
try:
    from gluon.serializers import xml
```

```
4    response.write(xml(response._vars),escape=False)
5    response.headers['Content-Type']='text/xml'
6  except:
7    raise HTTP(405,'no xml')
8  }}
```

And here is the code for "generic.json"

```
1  {{
2  try:
3    from gluon.serializers import json
4    response.write(json(response._vars),escape=False)
5    response.headers['Content-Type']='text/json'
6  except:
7    raise HTTP(405,'no json')
8  }}
```

Any dictionary can be rendered in HTML, XML and JSON as long as it only contains python primitive types (int, float, string, list, tuple, dictionary). response._vars contains the dictionary returned by the action.

If the dictionary contains other user-defined or web2py-specific objects, they must be rendered by a custom view.

10.1.3 Rendering Rows

If you need to render a set of Rows as returned by a select in XML or JSON or another format, first transform the Rows object into a list of dictionaries using the as_list() method.

Consider for example the following mode:

```
1  db.define_table('person', Field('name'))
```

The following action can be rendered in HTML, but not in XML or JSON:

```
1  def everybody():
2      people = db().select(db.person.ALL)
3      return dict(people=people)
```

while the following action can rendered in XML and JSON:

```
1  def everybody():
2      people = db().select(db.person.ALL).as_list()
3      return dict(people=people)
```

10.1.4   Custom formats

If, for example, you want to render an action as a Python pickle:

```
1  http://127.0.0.1:8000/app/default/count.pickle
```

you just need to create a new view file "default/count.pickle" that contains:

```
1  {{
2  import cPickle
3  response.headers['Content-Type'] = 'application/python.pickle'
4  response.write(cPickle.dumps(response._vars),escape=False)
5  }}
```

If you want to be able to render any action as a pickled file, you need only to save the above file with the name "generic.pickle".

Not all objects are pickleable, and not all pickled objects can be un-pickled. It is safe to stick to primitive Python objects and combinations of them. Objects that do not contain references to file streams or database connections are usually pickleable, but they can only be un-pickled in an environment where the classes of all pickled objects are already defined.

10.1.5   RSS

web2py includes a "generic.rss" view that can render the dictionary returned by the action as an RSS feed.

Because the RSS feeds have a fixed structure (title, link, description, items, etc.) then for this to work, the dictionary returned by the action must have the proper structure:

```
1  {'title'      : '',
2   'link'       : '',
3   'description': '',
4   'created_on' : '',
5   'entries'    : []}
```

and each entry in entries must have the same similar structure:

```
1  {'title'      : '',
2   'link'       : '',
3   'description': '',
4   'created_on' : ''}
```

For example the following action can be rendered as an RSS feed:

```
 1  def feed():
 2      return dict(title="my feed",
 3                  link="http://feed.example.com",
 4                  description="my first feed",
 5                  entries=[
 6                     dict(title="my feed",
 7                     link="http://feed.example.com",
 8                     description="my first feed")
 9                     ])
```

by simply visiting the URL:

```
 1  http://127.0.0.1:8000/app/default/feed.rss
```

Alternatively, assuming the following model:

```
 1  db.define_table('rss_entry',
 2      Field('title'),
 3      Field('link'),
 4      Field('created_on','datetime'),
 5      Field('description'))
```

the following action can also be rendered as an RSS feed:

```
 1  def feed():
 2      return dict(title="my feed",
 3                  link="http://feed.example.com",
 4                  description="my first feed",
 5                  entries=db().select(db.rss_entry.ALL).as_list())
```

The as_list() method of a Rows object converts the rows into a list of dictionaries.

If additional dictionary items are found with key names not explicitly listed here, they are ignored.

Here is the "generic.rss" view provided by web2py:

```
 1  {{
 2  try:
 3      from gluon.serializers import rss
 4      response.write(rss(response._vars),escape=False)
 5      response.headers['Content-Type']='application/rss+xml'
 6  except:
 7      raise HTTP(405,'no rss')
 8  }}
```

As one more example of an RSS application, we consider an RSS aggregator that collects data from the "slashdot" feed and returns a new web2py rss feed.

```
 1  def aggregator():
 2      import gluon.contrib.feedparser as feedparser
```

```
3    d = feedparser.parse(
4        "http://rss.slashdot.org/Slashdot/slashdot/to")
5    return dict(title=d.channel.title,
6                link = d.channel.link,
7                description = d.channel.description,
8                created_on = request.now,
9                entries = [
10                   dict(title = entry.title,
11                   link = entry.link,
12                   description = entry.description,
13                   created_on = request.now) for entry in d.entries])
```

It can be accessed at:

```
1  http://127.0.0.1:8000/app/default/aggregator.rss
```

10.1.6   CSV

The Comma Separated Values (CSV) format is a protocol to represent tabular data.

Consider the following model:

```
1  db.define_table('animal',
2      Field('species'),
3      Field('genus'),
4      Field('family'))
```

and the following action:

```
1  def animals():
2      animals = db().select(db.animal.ALL)
3      return dict(animals=animals)
```

web2py does not provide a "generic.csv"; you must define a custom view "default/animals.csv" that serializes the animals into CSV. Here is a possible implementation:

```
1  {{
2  import cStringIO
3  stream=cStringIO.StringIO()
4  animals.export_to_csv_file(stream)
5  response.headers['Content-Type']='application/vnd.ms-excel'
6  response.write(stream.getvalue(), escape=False)
7  }}
```

Notice that one could also define a "generic.csv" file, but one would have to specify the name of the object to be serialized ("animals" in the example).

This is why we do not provide a "generic.csv" file.

10.2   Remote procedure calls

web2py provides a mechanism to turn any function into a web service. The mechanism described here differs from the mechanism described before because:

- The function may take arguments

- The function may be defined in a model or a module instead of controller

- You may want to specify in detail which RPC method should be supported

- It enforces a more strict URL naming convention

- It is smarter than the previous methods because it works for a fixed set of protocols. For the same reason it is not as easily extensible.

To use this feature:

First, you must import and initiate a service object.

```
1 from gluon.tools import Service
2 service = Service()
```

> This is already done in the "db.py" model file in the scaffolding application.

Second, you must expose the service handler in the controller:

```
1 def call():
2     session.forget()
3     return service()
```

> This is already done in the "default.py" controller of the scaffolding application. Remove session.forget() if you plan to use session cookies with the services.

Third, you must decorate those functions you want to expose as a service. Here is a list of currently supported decorators:

```
1 @service.run
2 @service.xml
3 @service.json
4 @service.rss
```

```
5  @service.csv
6  @service.xmlrpc
7  @service.jsonrpc
8  @service.jsonrpc2
9  @service.amfrpc3('domain')
10 @service.soap('FunctionName',returns={'result':type},args={'param1':type,})
```

As an example, consider the following decorated function:

```
1  @service.run
2  def concat(a,b):
3      return a+b
```

This function can be defined in a model or in the controller where the call action is defined. This function can now be called remotely in two ways:

```
1  http://127.0.0.1:8000/app/default/call/run/concat?a=hello&b=world
2  http://127.0.0.1:8000/app/default/call/run/concat/hello/world
```

In both cases the http request returns:

```
1  helloworld
```

If the @service.xml decorator is used, the function can be called via:

```
1  http://127.0.0.1:8000/app/default/call/xml/concat?a=hello&b=world
2  http://127.0.0.1:8000/app/default/call/xml/concat/hello/world
```

and the output is returned as XML:

```
1  <document>
2      <result>helloworld</result>
3  </document>
```

It can serialize the output of the function even if this is a DAL Rows object. In this case, in fact, it will call as_list() automatically.

If the @service.json decorator is used, the function can be called via:

```
1  http://127.0.0.1:8000/app/default/call/json/concat?a=hello&b=world
2  http://127.0.0.1:8000/app/default/call/json/concat/hello/world
```

and the output returned as JSON.

If the @service.csv decorator is used, the service handler requires, as the return value, an iterable object of iterable objects, such as a list of lists. Here is an example:

```
1  @service.csv
2  def table1(a,b):
3      return [[a,b],[1,2]]
```

This service can be called by visiting one of the following URLs:

```
1  http://127.0.0.1:8000/app/default/call/csv/table1?a=hello&b=world
2  http://127.0.0.1:8000/app/default/call/csv/table1/hello/world
```

and it returns:

```
1  hello,world
2  1,2
```

The @service.rss decorator expects a return value in the same format as the "generic.rss" view discussed in the previous section.

Multiple decorators are allowed for each function.

So far, everything discussed in this section is simply an alternative to the method described in the previous section. The real power of the service object comes with XMLRPC, JSONRPC and AMFRPC, as discussed below.

10.2.1 XMLRPC

Consider the following code, for example, in the "default.py" controller:

```
1  @service.xmlrpc
2  def add(a,b):
3      return a+b
4
5  @service.xmlrpc
6  def div(a,b):
7      return a/b
```

Now in a python shell you can do

```
1  >>> from xmlrpclib import ServerProxy
2  >>> server = ServerProxy(
3         'http://127.0.0.1:8000/app/default/call/xmlrpc')
4  >>> print server.add(3,4)
5  7
6  >>> print server.add('hello','world')
7  'helloworld'
8  >>> print server.div(12,4)
9  3
10 >>> print server.div(1,0)
11 ZeroDivisionError: integer division or modulo by zero
```

The Python xmlrpclib module provides a client for the XMLRPC protocol. web2py acts as the server.

The client connects to the server via ServerProxy and can remotely call decorated functions in the server. The data (a,b) is passed to the function(s), not via GET/POST variables, but properly encoded in the request body using the XMLPRC protocol, and thus it carries with itself type information (int or string or other). The same is true for the return value(s). Moreover, any exception raised on the server propagates back to the client.

There are XMLRPC libraries for many programming languages (including C, C++, Java, C#, Ruby, and Perl), and they can interoperate with each other. This is one the best methods to create applications that talk to each other independent of the programming language.

The XMLRPC client can also be implemented inside a web2py action, so that one action can talk to another web2py application (even within the same installation) using XMLRPC. Beware of session deadlocks in this case. If an action calls via XMLRPC a function in the same app, the caller must release the session lock before the call:

```
1  session.forget(response)
```

10.2.2   JSONRPC

In this section we are going to use the same code example as for XMLRPC but we will expose the service using JSONRPC instead:

```
1  @service.jsonrpc
2  @service.jsonrpc2
3  def add(a,b):
4      return a+b
5
6  def call():
7      return service()
```

JSONRPC is very similar to XMLRPC but uses JSON instead of XML as data serialization protocol.

Of course we can call the service from any program in any language but here we will do it in Python.   web2py ships with a module "gluon/contrib/simplejsonrpc.py" created by Mariano Reingart. Here is an example of how to use to call the above service:

```
1  >>> from gluon.contrib.simplejsonrpc import ServerProxy
2  >>> URL = "http://127.0.0.1:8000/app/default/call/jsonrpc"
3  >>> service = ServerProxy(URL, verbose=True)
4  >>> print service.add(1, 2)
```

Use "http://127.0.0.1:8000/app/default/call/jsonrpc2" for jsonrpc2.

10.2.3 JSONRPC and Pyjamas

JSONRPC is very similar to XMLRPC, but uses the JSON-based protocol instead of XML to encode the data. As an example of application here, we discuss its usage with Pyjamas. Pyjamas is a Python port of the Google Web Toolkit (originally written in Java). Pyjamas allows writing a client application in Python. Pyjamas translates this code into JavaScript. web2py serves the JavaScript and communicates with it via AJAX requests originating from the client and triggered by user actions.

Here we describe how to make Pyjamas work with web2py. It does not require any additional libraries other than web2py and Pyjamas.

We are going to build a simple "todo" application with a Pyjamas client (all JavaScript) that talks to the server exclusively via JSONRPC.

First, create a new application called "todo".

Second, in "models/db.py", enter the following code:

```
1  db=DAL('sqlite://storage.sqlite')
2  db.define_table('todo', Field('task'))
3  service = Service()
```

(Note: Service class is from gluon.tools).

Third, in "controllers/default.py", enter the following code:

```
1   def index():
2     redirect(URL('todoApp'))
3
4     @service.jsonrpc
5     def getTasks():
6         todos = db(db.todo).select()
7         return [(todo.task,todo.id) for todo in todos]
8
9     @service.jsonrpc
10    def addTask(taskFromJson):
11        db.todo.insert(task= taskFromJson)
12        return getTasks()
13
14    @service.jsonrpc
15    def deleteTask (idFromJson):
```

```
16        del db.todo[idFromJson]
17        return getTasks()
18
19    def call():
20        session.forget()
21        return service()
22
23    def todoApp():
24        return dict()
```

The purpose of each function should be obvious.

Fourth, in "views/default/todoApp.html", enter the following code:

```
1  <html>
2    <head>
3      <meta name="pygwt:module"
4        content="{{=URL('static','output/TodoApp')}}" />
5      <title>
6        simple todo application
7      </title>
8    </head>
9    <body bgcolor="white">
10      <h1>
11        simple todo application
12      </h1>
13      <i>
14        type a new task to insert in db,
15        click on existing task to delete it
16      </i>
17      <script language="javascript"
18        src="{{=URL('static','output/pygwt.js')}}">
19      </script>
20    </body>
21  </html>
```

This view just executes the Pyjamas code in "static/output/todoapp" - code that we have not yet created.

Fifth, in "static/TodoApp.py" (notice it is TodoApp, not todoApp!), enter the following client code:

```
1  from pyjamas.ui.RootPanel import RootPanel
2  from pyjamas.ui.Label import Label
3  from pyjamas.ui.VerticalPanel import VerticalPanel
4  from pyjamas.ui.TextBox import TextBox
5  import pyjamas.ui.KeyboardListener
6  from pyjamas.ui.ListBox import ListBox
7  from pyjamas.ui.HTML import HTML
8  from pyjamas.JSONService import JSONProxy
```

```
 9
10  class TodoApp:
11      def onModuleLoad(self):
12          self.remote = DataService()
13          panel = VerticalPanel()
14
15          self.todoTextBox = TextBox()
16          self.todoTextBox.addKeyboardListener(self)
17
18          self.todoList = ListBox()
19          self.todoList.setVisibleItemCount(7)
20          self.todoList.setWidth("200px")
21          self.todoList.addClickListener(self)
22          self.Status = Label("")
23
24          panel.add(Label("Add New Todo:"))
25          panel.add(self.todoTextBox)
26          panel.add(Label("Click to Remove:"))
27          panel.add(self.todoList)
28          panel.add(self.Status)
29          self.remote.getTasks(self)
30
31          RootPanel().add(panel)
32
33      def onKeyUp(self, sender, keyCode, modifiers):
34          pass
35
36      def onKeyDown(self, sender, keyCode, modifiers):
37          pass
38
39      def onKeyPress(self, sender, keyCode, modifiers):
40          """
41          This function handles the onKeyPress event, and will add the
42          item in the text box to the list when the user presses the
43          enter key. In the future, this method will also handle the
44          auto complete feature.
45          """
46          if keyCode == KeyboardListener.KEY_ENTER and \
47              sender == self.todoTextBox:
48              id = self.remote.addTask(sender.getText(),self)
49              sender.setText("")
50              if id<0:
51                  RootPanel().add(HTML("Server Error or Invalid Response"))
52
53      def onClick(self, sender):
54          id = self.remote.deleteTask(
55                  sender.getValue(sender.getSelectedIndex()),self)
56          if id<0:
57              RootPanel().add(
```

```
58        HTML("Server Error or Invalid Response"))
59
60    def onRemoteResponse(self, response, request_info):
61        self.todoList.clear()
62        for task in response:
63            self.todoList.addItem(task[0])
64            self.todoList.setValue(self.todoList.getItemCount()-1,
65                                   task[1])
66
67    def onRemoteError(self, code, message, request_info):
68        self.Status.setText("Server Error or Invalid Response: " \
69                            + "ERROR " + code + " - " + message)
70
71 class DataService(JSONProxy):
72    def __init__(self):
73        JSONProxy.__init__(self, "../../default/call/jsonrpc",
74                           ["getTasks", "addTask","deleteTask"])
75
76 if __name__ == '__main__':
77    app = TodoApp()
78    app.onModuleLoad()
```

Sixth, run Pyjamas before serving the application:

```
1 cd /path/to/todo/static/
2 python /python/pyjamas-0.5p1/bin/pyjsbuild TodoApp.py
```

This will translate the Python code into JavaScript so that it can be executed in the browser.

To access this application, visit the URL:

```
1 http://127.0.0.1:8000/todo/default/todoApp
```

This subsection was created by Chris Prinos with help from Luke Kenneth Casson Leighton (creators of Pyjamas), updated by Alexei Vinidiktov. It has been tested with Pyjamas 0.5p1. The example was inspired by this Django page in ref. [91].

10.2.4   AMFRPC

AMFRPC is the Remote Procedure Call protocol used by Flash clients to communicate with a server. web2py supports AMFRPC, but it requires that you run web2py from source and that you preinstall the PyAMF library. This can be installed from the Linux or Windows shell by typing:

```
easy_install pyamf
```

(please consult the PyAMF documentation for more details).

In this subsection we assume that you are already familiar with ActionScript programming.

We will create a simple service that takes two numerical values, adds them together, and returns the sum. We will call our web2py application "pyamf_test", and we will call the service addNumbers.

First, using Adobe Flash (any version starting from MX 2004), create the Flash client application by starting with a new Flash FLA file. In the first frame of the file, add these lines:

```
import mx.remoting.Service;
import mx.rpc.RelayResponder;
import mx.rpc.FaultEvent;
import mx.rpc.ResultEvent;
import mx.remoting.PendingCall;

var val1 = 23;
var val2 = 86;

service = new Service(
    "http://127.0.0.1:8000/pyamf_test/default/call/amfrpc3",
    null, "mydomain", null, null);

var pc:PendingCall = service.addNumbers(val1, val2);
pc.responder = new RelayResponder(this, "onResult", "onFault");

function onResult(re:ResultEvent):Void {
    trace("Result : " + re.result);
    txt_result.text = re.result;
}

function onFault(fault:FaultEvent):Void {
    trace("Fault: " + fault.fault.faultstring);
}

stop();
```

This code allows the Flash client to connect to a service that corresponds to a function called "addNumbers" in the file "/pyamf_test/default/gateway". You must also import ActionScript version 2 MX remoting classes to enable Remoting in Flash. Add the path to these classes to the classpath settings in the Adobe Flash IDE, or just place the "mx" folder next to the newly created file.

Notice the arguments of the Service constructor. The first argument is the URL corresponding to the service that we want will create. The third argument is the domain of the service. We choose to call this domain "mydomain".

Second, create a dynamic text field called "txt_result" and place it on the stage.

Third, you need to set up a web2py gateway that can communicate with the Flash client defined above.

Proceed by creating a new web2py app called `pyamf_test` that will host the new service and the AMF gateway for the flash client. Edit the "default.py" controller and make sure it contains

```
1 @service.amfrpc3('mydomain')
2 def addNumbers(val1, val2):
3     return val1 + val2
4
5 def call(): return service()
```

Fourth, compile and export/publish the SWF flash client as `pyamf_test.swf`, place the "pyamf_test.amf", "pyamf_test.html", "AC_RunActiveContent.js", and "crossdomain.xml" files in the "static" folder of the newly created appliance that is hosting the gateway, "pyamf_test".

You can now test the client by visiting:

```
1 http://127.0.0.1:8000/pyamf_test/static/pyamf_test.html
```

The gateway is called in the background when the client connects to addNumbers.

If you are using AMF0 instead of AMF3 you can also use the decorator:

```
1 @service.amfrpc
```

instead of:

```
1 @service.amfrpc3('mydomain')
```

In this case you also need to change the service URL to:

```
1 http://127.0.0.1:8000/pyamf_test/default/call/amfrpc
```

10.2.5   SOAP

web2py includes a SOAP client and server created by Mariano Reingart. It can be used very much like XML-RPC:

Consider the following code, for example, in the "default.py" controller:

```
@service.soap('MyAdd',returns={'result':int},args={'a':int,'b':int,})
def add(a,b):
    return a+b
```

Now in a python shell you can do:

```
>>> from gluon.contrib.pysimplesoap.client import SoapClient
>>> client = SoapClient(wsdl="http://localhost:8000/app/default/call/soap?WSDL")
>>> print client.MyAdd(a=1,b=2)
{'result': 3}
```

To get proper encoding when returning a text values, specify string as u'proper utf8 text'.

You can obtain the WSDL for the service at

```
http://127.0.0.1:8000/app/default/call/soap?WSDL
```

And you can obtain documentation for any of the exposed methods:

```
http://127.0.0.1:8000/app/default/call/soap
```

10.3   Low level API and other recipes

10.3.1   simplejson

web2py includes gluon.contrib.simplejson, developed by Bob Ippolito. This module provides the most standard Python-JSON encoder-decoder.

SimpleJSON consists of two functions:

- gluon.contrib.simplesjson.dumps(a) encodes a Python object a into JSON.

- gluon.contrib.simplejson.loads(b) decodes a JavaScript object b into a Python object.

Object types that can be serialized include primitive types, lists, and dictionaries. Compound objects can be serialized with the exception of user defined classes.

Here is a sample action (for example in controller "default.py") that serializes the Python list containing weekdays using this low level API:

```
def weekdays():
    names=['Sunday','Monday','Tuesday','Wednesday',
           'Thursday','Friday','Saturday']
    import gluon.contrib.simplejson
    return gluon.contrib.simplejson.dumps(names)
```

Below is a sample HTML page that sends an Ajax request to the above action, receives the JSON message and stores the list in a corresponding JavaScript variable:

```
{{extend 'layout.html'}}
<script>
$.getJSON('/application/default/weekdays',
          function(data){ alert(data); });
</script>
```

The code uses the jQuery function $.getJSON, which performs the Ajax call and, on response, stores the weekdays names in a local JavaScript variable data and passes the variable to the callback function. In the example the callback function simply alerts the visitor that the data has been received.

10.3.2 PyRTF

Another common need of web sites is that of generating Word-readable text documents. The simplest way to do so is using the Rich Text Format (RTF) document format. This format was invented by Microsoft and it has since become a standard. web2py includes gluon.contrib.pyrtf, developed by Simon Cusack and revised by Grant Edwards. This module allows you to generate RTF documents programmatically, including colored formatted text and pictures.

In the following example we initiate two basic RTF classes, Document and Section, append the latter to the former and insert some dummy text in the latter:

```
def makertf():
    import gluon.contrib.pyrtf as q
    doc=q.Document()
    section=q.Section()
    doc.Sections.append(section)
```

```
 6    section.append('Section Title')
 7    section.append('web2py is great. '*100)
 8    response.headers['Content-Type']='text/rtf'
 9    return q.dumps(doc)
```

In the end the Document is serialized by `q.dumps(doc)`. Notice that before returning an RTF document it is necessary to specify the content-type in the header else the browser does not know how to handle the file.

Depending on the configuration, the browser may ask you whether to save this file or open it using a text editor.

10.3.3   ReportLab and PDF

web2py can also generate PDF documents, with an additional library called "ReportLab" [92].

If you are running web2py from source, it is sufficient to have ReportLab installed. If you are running the Windows binary distribution, you need to unzip ReportLab in the "web2py/" folder. If you are running the Mac binary distribution, you need to unzip ReportLab in the folder:

```
 1   web2py.app/Contents/Resources/
```

From now on we assume ReportLab is installed and that web2py can find it. We will create a simple action called "get_me_a_pdf" that generates a PDF document.

```
 1   from reportlab.platypus import *
 2   from reportlab.lib.styles import getSampleStyleSheet
 3   from reportlab.rl_config import defaultPageSize
 4   from reportlab.lib.units import inch, mm
 5   from reportlab.lib.enums import TA_LEFT, TA_RIGHT, TA_CENTER, TA_JUSTIFY
 6   from reportlab.lib import colors
 7   from uuid import uuid4
 8   from cgi import escape
 9   import os
10
11   def get_me_a_pdf():
12       title = "This The Doc Title"
13       heading = "First Paragraph"
14       text = 'bla ' * 10000
15
16       styles = getSampleStyleSheet()
```

```
17  tmpfilename=os.path.join(request.folder,'private',str(uuid4()))
18  doc = SimpleDocTemplate(tmpfilename)
19  story = []
20  story.append(Paragraph(escape(title),styles["Title"]))
21  story.append(Paragraph(escape(heading),styles["Heading2"]))
22  story.append(Paragraph(escape(text),styles["Normal"]))
23  story.append(Spacer(1,2*inch))
24  doc.build(story)
25  data = open(tmpfilename,"rb").read()
26  os.unlink(tmpfilename)
27  response.headers['Content-Type']='application/pdf'
28  return data
```

Notice how we generate the PDF into a unique temporary file, tmpfilename, we read the generated PDF from the file, then we deleted the file.

For more information about the ReportLab API, refer to the ReportLab documentation. We strongly recommend using the Platypus API of ReportLab, such as Paragraph, Spacer, etc.

10.4 Restful Web Services

REST stands for "REpresentational State Transfer" and it is a type of web service architecture and not, like SOAP, a protocol. In fact there is no standard for REST.

Loosely speaking REST says that a service can be thought of as a collection of resources. Each resource should be identified by a URL. There are four methods actions on a resource and they are POST (create), GET (read), PUT (update) and DELETE, from which the acronym CRUD (create-read-update-delete) stands for. A client communicates with the resource by making an HTTP request to the URL that identifies the resource and using the HTTP method POST/PUT/GET/DELETE to pass instructions to the resource. The URL may have an extension, for example json that specify how the protocol for encoding the data.

So for example a POST request to

```
1  http://127.0.0.1/myapp/default/api/person
```

means that you want to create a new person. In this case a person may correspond to a record in table `person` but may also be some other type of resource (for example a file).

Similarly a GET request to

```
http://127.0.0.1/myapp/default/api/persons.json
```

indicates a request for a list of persons (records from the data `person`) in json format.

A GET request to

```
http://127.0.0.1/myapp/default/api/person/1.json
```

indicates a request for the information associated to `person/1` (the record with `id==1`) and in json format.

In the case of web2py each request can be split into three parts:

- A first part that identify the location of the service, i.e. the action that exposes the service:

```
http://127.0.0.1/myapp/default/api/
```

- The name of the resource (`person`, `persons`, `person/1`, etc.)

- The communication protocol specified y the extension.

Notice that we can always use the router to eliminate any unwanted prefix in the URL and for example simplify this:

```
http://127.0.0.1/myapp/default/api/person/1.json
```

into this:

```
http://127.0.0.1/api/person/1.json
```

yet this is a matter of test and we have already discussed it at length in chapter 4.

In our example we used an action called `api` but this is not a requirement. We can in fact name the action that exposes the RESTful service any way we like and we can in fact even create more than one. For the sake of argument we will continue to assume that our RESTful action is called `api`.

We will also assume we have defined the following two tables:

```
1  db.define_table('person',Field('name'),Field('info'))
2  db.define_table('pet',Field('owner',db.person),Field('name'),Field('info'))
```

and they are the resources we want to expose.

The first thing we do is create the RESTful action:

```
1  def api():
2      return locals()
```

Now we modify it so that the extension is filtered out of the request args (so that request.args can be used to identify the resource) and so that it can handle the different methods separately:

```
1   @request.restful()
2   def api():
3       def GET(*args,**vars):
4           return dict()
5       def POST(*args,**vars):
6           return dict()
7       def PUT(*args,**vars):
8           return dict()
9       def DELETE(*args,**vars):
10          return dict()
11      return locals()
```

Now when we make a GET http request to

```
1  http://127.0.0.1:8000/myapp/default/api/person/1.json
```

it calls and returns GET('person','1') where GET is the function defined inside the action. Notice that:

- we do not need to define all four methods, only those that we wish to expose.

- the method function can take named arguments

- the extension is stored in request.extension and the content type is set automatically.

> The @request.restful() decorator makes sure that the extension in the path info is stored into request.extension, maps the request method into the corresponding function within the action (POST, GET, PUT, DELETE), and passes request.args and request.vars to the selected function.

Now we build a service to POST and GET individual records:

```
1  @request.restful()
2  def api():
3      response.view = 'generic.json'
```

```
 4    def GET(tablename,id):
 5        if not tablename=='person': raise HTTP(400)
 6        return dict(person = db.person(id))
 7    def POST(tablename,**fields):
 8        if not tablename=='person': raise HTTP(400)
 9        return db.person.validate_and_insert(**fields)
10    return locals()
```

Notice that:

- the GET and POST are dealt with by different functions

- the function expect the correct arguments (un-named arguments parsed by `request.args` and named arguments are from `request.vars`)

- they check the input is correct and eventually raise an exception

- GET perform a select and returns the record, `db.person(id)`. The output is automatically converted to JSON because the generic view is called.

- POST performs a `validate_and_insert(..)` and returns the `id` of the new record or, alternatively, validation errors. The POST variables, `**fields`, are the post variables.

10.4.1 `parse_as_rest` (experimental)

The logic explained so far is sufficient to create any type of RESTful web service yet web2py helps us even more.

In fact, web2py provides a syntax to describe which database tables we want to expose and how to map resource into URLs and vice versa.

This is done using URL patterns. A pattern is a string that maps the request args from a URL into a database query. There 4 types of atomic patterns:

- String constants for example "friend"

- String constant corresponding to a table. For example "friend[person]" will match "friends" in the URL to the "person" table.

- Variables to be used to filter. For example "{person.id}" will apply a `db.person.name=={person.id}` filter.

- Names of fields, represented by ":field"

Atomic patters can be combined into complex URL patters using "/" such as in

```
"/friend[person]/{person.id}/:field"
```

which gives a url of the form

```
http://..../friend/1/name
```

Into a query for a person.id that returns the name of the person. Here "friend[person]" matches "friend" and filters the table "person". "{person.id}" matches "1" and filters "person.id==1". ":field" matches "name" and returns:

```
db(db.person.id==1).select().first().name
```

Multiple URL patters can be combined into a list so that one single RESTful action can serve different types of requests.

The DAL has a method parse_as_rest(pattern,args,vars) that given a list of patterns, the request.args and the request.vars matches the pattern and returns a response (GET only).

So here is a more complex example:

```
@request.restful()
def api():
    response.view = 'generic.'+request.extension
    def GET(*args,**vars):
        patterns = [
            "/friends[person]",
            "/friend/{person.name.startswith}",
            "/friend/{person.name}/:field",
            "/friend/{person.name}/pets[pet.owner]",
            "/friend/{person.name}/pet[pet.owner]/{pet.name}",
            "/friend/{person.name}/pet[pet.owner]/{pet.name}/:field"
            ]
        parser = db.parse_as_rest(patterns,args,vars)
        if parser.status == 200:
            return dict(content=parser.response)
        else:
            raise HTTP(parser.status,parser.error)
    def POST(table_name,**vars):
        if table_name == 'person':
            return db.person.validate_and_insert(**vars)
        elif table_name == 'pet':
            return db.pet.validate_and_insert(**vars)
```

```
24        else:
25            raise HTTP(400)
26    return locals()
```

Which understands the following URLs that correspond to the listed patters:

• GET all persons

```
1 http://.../api/friends
```

• GET one person with name starting with "t"

```
1 http://.../api/friend/t
```

• GET the "info" field value of the first person with name equal to "Tim"

```
1 http://.../api/friend/Tim/info
```

• GET a list of pets of the person (friend) above

```
1 http://.../api/friend/Tim/pets
```

• GET the pet with name "Snoopy of person with name "Tim"

```
1 http://.../api/friend/Tim/pet/Snoopy
```

• GET the "info" field value for the pet

```
1 http://.../api/friend/Tim/pet/Snoopy/info
```

The action also exposes two POST urls:

• POST a new friend

• POST a new pet

If you have the "curl" utility installed you can try:

```
1 $ curl -d "name=Tim" http://127.0.0.1:8000/myapp/default/api/friend.json
2 {"errors": {}, "id": 1}
3 $ curl http://127.0.0.1:8000/myapp/default/api/friends.json
4 {"content": [{"info": null, "name": "Tim", "id": 1}]}
5 $ curl -d "name=Snoopy&owner=1" http://127.0.0.1:8000/myapp/default/api/pet.json
6 {"errors": {}, "id": 1}
7 $ curl http://127.0.0.1:8000/myapp/default/api/friend/Tim/pet/Snoopy.json
8 {"content": [{"info": null, "owner": 1, "name": "Snoopy", "id": 1}]}
```

It is possible to declare more complex queries such where a value in the URL is used to build a query not involving equality. For example

```
patterns = ['friends/{person.name.contains}'] maps
```

```
1 http://..../friends/i
```

into

```
1 db.person.name.contains('i')
```

And similarly:

```
patterns = ['friends/{person.name.ge}/{person.name.gt.not}'
```
maps

```
1 http://..../friends/aa/uu
```

into

```
1 (db.person.name>='aa')&(~(db.person.name>'uu'))
```

valid attributes for a field in a pattern are: contains, startswith, le, ge, lt, gt, eq (equal, default), ne (not equal). Other attributes specifically for date and datetime fields are day, month, year, hour, minute, second.

Notice that this pattern syntax is not designed to be general. Not every possible query can be described via a pattern but a lot of them are. The syntax may be extended in the future.

Often you want to expose some RESTful URLs but you want to restrict the possible queries. This can be done by passing an extra argument queries to the parse_as_rest method. queries is a dictionary of (tablename,query) where query is a DAL query to restrict access to table tablename.

We can also order results using the order GET variables

```
1 http://..../api/friends?order=name|~info
```

which order alphabetically (name) and then by reversed info order.

We can also limit the number of records by specifying a limit and offset GET variables

```
1 http://..../api/friends?offset=10&limit=1000
```

which will return up to 1000 friends (persons) and skip the first 10. limit defaults to 1000 and offset default to 0.

Let's now consider an extreme case. We want to build all possible patterns for all tables (except auth_ tables). We want to be able to search by any text field, any integer field, any double field (by range) and any date (also by range). We also want to be able to POST into any table:

In the general case this requires a lot of patterns. Web2py makes it simple:

```
1 @request.restful()
2 def api():
```

```
3    response.view = 'generic.'+request.extension
4    def GET(*args,**vars):
5        patterns = 'auto'
6        parser = db.parse_as_rest(patterns,args,vars)
7        if parser.status == 200:
8            return dict(content=parser.response)
9        else:
10           raise HTTP(parser.status,parser.error)
11   def POST(table_name,**vars):
12       return db[table_name].validate_and_insert(**vars)
13   return locals()
```

Settings `patterns='auto'` results in web2py generating all possible patterns for all non-auth tables. There is even a pattern for querying about patterns:

```
1  http://..../api/patterns.json
```

which for out `person` and `pet` tables results in:

```
1  {"content": [
2    "/person[person]",
3    "/person/id/{person.id}",
4    "/person/id/{person.id}/:field",
5    "/person/id/{person.id}/pet[pet.owner]",
6    "/person/id/{person.id}/pet[pet.owner]/id/{pet.id}",
7    "/person/id/{person.id}/pet[pet.owner]/id/{pet.id}/:field",
8    "/person/id/{person.id}/pet[pet.owner]/owner/{pet.owner}",
9    "/person/id/{person.id}/pet[pet.owner]/owner/{pet.owner}/:field",
10   "/person/name/pet[pet.owner]",
11   "/person/name/pet[pet.owner]/id/{pet.id}",
12   "/person/name/pet[pet.owner]/id/{pet.id}/:field",
13   "/person/name/pet[pet.owner]/owner/{pet.owner}",
14   "/person/name/pet[pet.owner]/owner/{pet.owner}/:field",
15   "/person/info/pet[pet.owner]",
16   "/person/info/pet[pet.owner]/id/{pet.id}",
17   "/person/info/pet[pet.owner]/id/{pet.id}/:field",
18   "/person/info/pet[pet.owner]/owner/{pet.owner}",
19   "/person/info/pet[pet.owner]/owner/{pet.owner}/:field",
20   "/pet[pet]",
21   "/pet/id/{pet.id}",
22   "/pet/id/{pet.id}/:field",
23   "/pet/owner/{pet.owner}",
24   "/pet/owner/{pet.owner}/:field"
25  ]}
```

You can specify auto patterns for some tables only:

```
1  patterns = [':auto[person]',':auto[pet]']
```

10.4.2 `smart_query` (experimental)

There are times when you need more flexibility and you want to be able to pass to a RESTful service an arbitrary query like

```
1  http://.../api.json?search=person.name starts with 'T' and person.name contains 'm'
```

You can do this using

```
1  @request.restful()
2  def api():
3      response.view = 'generic.'+request.extension
4      def GET(search):
5          try:
6              rows = db.smart_query([db.person,db.pet],search).select()
7              return dict(result=rows)
8          except RuntimeError:
9              raise HTTP(400,"Invalid search string")
10     def POST(table_name,**vars):
11         return db[table_name].validate_and_insert(**vars)
12     return locals()
```

The method `db.smart_query` takes two arguments:

- a list of field or table that should be allowed in the query
- a string containing the query expressed in natural language

and it returns a `db.set` object with the records that have been found.

Notice that the search string is parsed, not evaluated or executed and therefore it provides no security risk.

10.4.3 Access Control

Access to the API can be restricted as usual by using decorators. So, for example

```
1  auth.settings.allow_basic_login = True
2
3  @auth.requires_login()
4  @request.restful()
5  def api():
6      def GET(s):
7          return 'access granted, you said %s' % s
8      return locals()
```

can now be accessed with

```
$ curl --user name:password http://127.0.0.1:8000/myapp/default/api/hello
access granted, you said hello
```

10.5   Services and Authentication

In the previous chapter we have discussed the use of the following decorators:

```
@auth.requires_login()
@auth.requires_membership(...)
@auth.requires_permission(...)
```

For normal actions (not decorated as services), these decorators can be used even if the output is rendered in a format other than HTML.

For functions defined as services and decorated using the @service... decorators, the @auth... decorators should not be used. The two types of decorators cannot be mixed. If authentication is to be performed, it is the call actions that needs to be decorated:

```
@auth.requires_login()
def call(): return service()
```

Notice that it also possible to instantiate multiple service objects, register the same different functions with them, and expose some of them with authentication and some not:

```
public_services=Service()
private_services=Service()

@public_service.jsonrpc
@private_service.jsonrpc
def f(): return 'public'

@private_service.jsonrpc
def g(): return 'private'


def public_call(): return public_service()

@auth.requires_login()
def private_call(): return private_service()
```

This assumes that the caller is passing credentials in the HTTP header (a valid session cookie or using basic authentication, as discussed in the previous section). The client must support it; not all clients do.

11

jQuery and Ajax

While web2py is mainly for server-side development, the **welcome** scaffolding app comes with the base jQuery library [36], jQuery calendars (date picker, datetime picker and clock), the "superfish.js" menu, and some additional JavaScript functions based on jQuery.

Nothing in web2py prevents you from using other Ajax libraries such as Prototype, ExtJS, or YUI, but we decided to package jQuery because we find it to be easier to use and more powerful than other equivalent libraries. We also find that it captures the web2py spirit of being functional and concise.

11.1 web2py_ajax.html

The scaffolding web2py application "welcome" includes a file called

```
1 views/web2py_ajax.html
```

which looks like this:

```
1 {{
2 response.files.insert(0,URL('static','js/jquery.js'))
3 response.files.insert(1,URL('static','css/calenadar.css'))
4 response.files.insert(2,URL('static','js/calendar.js'))
5 response.include_meta()
6 response.include_files()
7 }}
8 <script type="text/javascript"><!--
```

```
 9   // These variables are used by the web2py_ajax_init
10       // function in web2py.js (which is loaded below).
11   var w2p_ajax_confirm_message =
12       "{{=T('Are you sure you want to delete this object?')}}";
13   var w2p_ajax_date_format = "{{=T('%Y-%m-%d')}}";
14   var w2p_ajax_datetime_format = "{{=T('%Y-%m-%d %H:%M:%S')}}";
15 //--></script>
16 <script src="{{=URL('static','js/web2py.js')}}"
17       type="text/javascript"></script>
```

This file is included in the HEAD of the default "layout.html" and it provides the following services:

- Includes "static/jquery.js".

- Includes "static/calendar.js" and "static/calendar.css", which are used for the popup calendar.

- Includes all response.meta headers

- Includes all response.files (requires CSS and JS, as declared in the code)

- Sets form variables and includes "static/js/web2py.js"

"web2py.js" does the following:

- Defines an ajax function (based on jQuery $.ajax).

- Makes any DIV of class "error" or any tag object of class "flash" slide down.

- Prevents typing invalid integers in INPUT fields of class "integer".

- Prevents typing invalid floats in INPUT fields of class "double".

- Connects INPUT fields of type "date" with a popup date picker.

- Connects INPUT fields of type "datetime" with a popup datetime picker.

- Connects INPUT fields of type "time" with a popup time picker.

- Defines web2py_ajax_component, a very important tool that will be described in Chapter 12.

- Defines web2py_websocket, a function that can be used for HTML5 websockets (not described in this book but read the examples in the source of "gluon/contrib/websocket_messaging.py").

- Defines functions to the entropy calculation and input validation of the password field.

It also includes `popup`, `collapse`, and `fade` functions for backward compatibility.

Here is an an example of how the other effects play well together.

Consider a **test** app with the following model:

```
1  db = DAL("sqlite://db.db")
2  db.define_table('child',
3      Field('name'),
4      Field('weight', 'double'),
5      Field('birth_date', 'date'),
6      Field('time_of_birth', 'time'))
7
8  db.child.name.requires=IS_NOT_EMPTY()
9  db.child.weight.requires=IS_FLOAT_IN_RANGE(0,100)
10 db.child.birth_date.requires=IS_DATE()
11 db.child.time_of_birth.requires=IS_TIME()
```

with this "default.py" controller:

```
1  def index():
2      form = SQLFORM(db.child)
3      if form.process().accepted:
4          response.flash = 'record inserted'
5      return dict(form=form)
```

and the following "default/index.html" view:

```
1  {{extend 'layout.html'}}
2  {{=form}}
```

The "index" action generates the following form:

If an invalid form is submitted, the server returns the page with a modified form containing error messages. The error messages are DIVs of class "error", and because of the above web2py.js code, the errors appears with a slide-down effect:

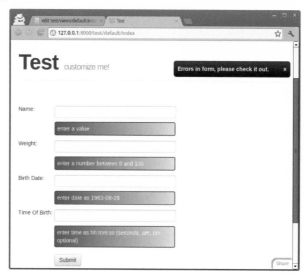

The color of the errors is given in the CSS code in "layout.html".

The web2py.js code prevents you from typing an invalid value in the input field. This is done before and in addition to, not as a substitute for, the server-side validation.

The web2py.js code displays a date picker when you enter an INPUT field of class "date", and it displays a datetime picker when you enter an INPUT field of class "datetime". Here is an example:

The web2py.js code also displays the following time picker when you try to edit an INPUT field of class "time":

Upon submission, the controller action sets the response flash to the message "record inserted". The default layout renders this message in a DIV with id="flash". The web2py.js code is responsible for making this DIV appear and making it disappear when you click on it:

These and other effects are accessible programmatically in the views and via helpers in controllers.

11.2   jQuery effects

The basic effects described here do not require any additional files; everything you need is already included in web2py_ajax.html.

HTML/XHTML objects can be identified by their type (for example a DIV), their classes, or their id. For example:

```
<div class="one" id="a">Hello</div>
```

```
2  <div class="two" id="b">World</div>
```

They belong to class "one" and "two" respectively. They have ids equal to "a" and "b" respectively.

In jQuery you can refer to the former with the following a CSS-like equivalent notations

```
1  jQuery('.one')     // address object by class "one"
2  jQuery('#a')       // address object by id "a"
3  jQuery('DIV.one')  // address by object of type "DIV" with class "one"
4  jQuery('DIV #a')   // address by object of type "DIV" with id "a"
```

and to the latter with

```
1  jQuery('.two')
2  jQuery('#b')
3  jQuery('DIV.two')
4  jQuery('DIV #b')
```

or you can refer to both with

```
1  jQuery('DIV')
```

Tag objects are associated to events, such as "onclick". jQuery allows linking these events to effects, for example "slideToggle":

```
1  <div class="one" id="a" onclick="jQuery('.two').slideToggle()">Hello</div>
2  <div class="two" id="b">World</div>
```

Now if you click on "Hello", "World" disappears. If you click again, "World" reappears. You can make a tag hidden by default by giving it a hidden class:

```
1  <div class="one" id="a" onclick="jQuery('.two').slideToggle()">Hello</div>
2  <div class="two hidden" id="b">World</div>
```

You can also link actions to events outside the tag itself. The previous code can be rewritten as follows:

```
1  <div class="one" id="a">Hello</div>
2  <div class="two" id="b">World</div>
3  <script>
4  jQuery('.one').click(function(){jQuery('.two').slideToggle()});
5  </script>
```

Effects return the calling object, so they can be chained.

When the click sets the callback function to be called on click. Similarly for change, keyup, keydown, mouseover, etc.

A common situation is the need to execute some JavaScript code only after the entire document has been loaded. This is usually done by the onload attribute of BODY but jQuery provides an alternative way that does not require editing the layout:

```
1  <div class="one" id="a">Hello</div>
2  <div class="two" id="b">World</div>
3  <script>
4  jQuery(document).ready(function(){
5    jQuery('.one').click(function(){jQuery('.two').slideToggle()});
6  });
7  </script>
```

The body of the unnamed function is executed only when the document is ready, after it has been fully loaded.

Here is a list of useful event names:

Form events

- onchange: Script to be run when the element changes

- onsubmit: Script to be run when the form is submitted

- onreset: Script to be run when the form is reset

- onselect: Script to be run when the element is selected

- onblur: Script to be run when the element loses focus

- onfocus: Script to be run when the element gets focus

Keyboard events

- onkeydown: Script to be run when key is pressed

- onkeypress: Script to be run when key is pressed and released

- onkeyup: Script to be run when key is released

Mouse events

- onclick: Script to be run on a mouse click

- ondblclick: Script to be run on a mouse double-click

- onmousedown: Script to be run when mouse button is pressed

- onmousemove: Script to be run when mouse pointer moves

- onmouseout: Script to be run when mouse pointer moves out of an element

- onmouseover: Script to be run when mouse pointer moves over an element

- onmouseup: Script to be run when mouse button is released

Here is a list of useful effects defined by jQuery:

Effects

- jQuery(...).attr(name): Returns the name of the attribute value

- jQuery(...).attr(name, value): Sets the attribute name to value

- jQuery(...).show(): Makes the object visible

- jQuery(...).hide(): Makes the object hidden

- jQuery(...).slideToggle(speed, callback): Makes the object slide up or down

- jQuery(...).slideUp(speed, callback): Makes the object slide up

- jQuery(...).slideDown(speed, callback): Makes the object slide down

- jQuery(...).fadeIn(speed, callback): Makes the object fade in

- jQuery(...).fadeOut(speed, callback): Makes the object fade out

The speed argument is usually "slow", "fast" or omitted (the default). The callback is an optional function that is called when the effect is completed. jQuery effects can also easily be embedded in helpers, for example, in a view:

```
{{=DIV('click me!', _onclick="jQuery(this).fadeOut()")}}
```

jQuery is a very compact and concise Ajax library; therefore web2py does not need an additional abstraction layer on top of jQuery (except for the ajax function discussed below). The jQuery APIs are accessible and readily available in their native form when needed.

Consult the documentation for more information about these effects and other jQuery APIs.

The jQuery library can also be extended using plugins and User Interface Widgets. This topic is not covered here; see ref. [93] for details.

11.2.1   Conditional fields in forms

A typical application of jQuery effects is a form that changes its appearance based on the value of its fields.

This is easy in web2py because the SQLFORM helper generates forms that are "CSS friendly". The form contains a table with rows. Each row contains a label, an input field, and an optional third column. The items have ids derived strictly from the name of the table and names of the fields.

The convention is that every INPUT field has an id `tablename_fieldname` and is contained in a row with id `tablename_fieldname__row`.

As an example, create an input form that asks for a taxpayer's name and for the name of the taxpayer's spouse, but only if he/she is married.

Create a test application with the following model:

```
db = DAL('sqlite://db.db')
db.define_table('taxpayer',
    Field('name'),
    Field('married', 'boolean'),
    Field('spouse_name'))
```

the following "default.py" controller:

```
def index():
    form = SQLFORM(db.taxpayer)
    if form.process().accepted:
        response.flash = 'record inserted'
    return dict(form=form)
```

and the following "default/index.html" view:

```
{{extend 'layout.html'}}
{{=form}}
<script>
jQuery(document).ready(function(){
  jQuery('#taxpayer_spouse_name__row').hide();
  jQuery('#taxpayer_married').change(function(){
      if(jQuery('#taxpayer_married').attr('checked'))
          jQuery('#taxpayer_spouse_name__row').show();
      else jQuery('#taxpayer_spouse_name__row').hide();});
});
</script>
```

The script in the view has the effect of hiding the row containing the spouse's name:

When the taxpayer checks the "married" checkbox, the spouse's name field reappears:

Here "taxpayer_married" is the checkbox associated to the "boolean" field "married" of table "taxpayer".   "taxpayer_spouse_name__row" is the row containing the input field for "spouse_name" of table "taxpayer".

11.2.2   Confirmation on delete

Another useful application is requiring confirmation when checking a "delete" checkbox such as the delete checkbox that appears in edit forms.

Consider the above example and add the following controller action:

```
def edit():
    row = db.taxpayer[request.args(0)]
    form = SQLFORM(db.taxpayer, row, deletable=True)
    if form.process().accepted:
        response.flash = 'record updated'
    return dict(form=form)
```

and the corresponding view "default/edit.html"

```
{{extend 'layout.html'}}
{{=form}}
```

The deletable=True argument in the SQLFORM constructor instructs web2py to display a "delete" checkbox in the edit form. It is False by default. web2py's "web2py.js" includes the following code:

```
jQuery(document).ready(function(){
    jQuery('input.delete').attr('onclick',
      'if(this.checked) if(!confirm(
        "{{=T('Sure you want to delete this object?')}}"))
      this.checked=false;');
});
```

By convention this checkbox has a class equal to "delete". The jQuery code above connects the onclick event of this checkbox with a confirmation dialog (standard in JavaScript) and unchecks the checkbox if the taxpayer does not confirm:

11.3 The ajax **function**

In web2py.js, web2py defines a function called ajax which is based on, but should not be confused with, the jQuery function $.ajax. The latter is much more powerful than the former, and for its usage, we refer you to ref. [36] and ref. [94]. However, the former function is sufficient for many complex tasks, and is easier to use.

The ajax function is a JavaScript function that has the following syntax:

```
ajax(url, [name1, name2, ...], target)
```

It asynchronously calls the url (first argument), passes the values of the field inputs with the name equal to one of the names in the list (second argument), then stores the response in the innerHTML of the tag with the id equal to target (the third argument).

Here is an example of a default controller:

```
def one():
    return dict()

def echo():
    return request.vars.name
```

and the associated "default/one.html" view:

```
1 {{extend 'layout.html'}}
2 <form>
3     <input name="name" onkeyup="ajax('echo', ['name'], 'target')" />
4 </form>
5 <div id="target"></div>
```

When you type something in the INPUT field, as soon as you release a key (onkeyup), the ajax function is called, and the value of the name="name" field is passed to the action "echo", which sends the text back to the view. The ajax function receives the response and displays the echo response in the "target" DIV.

11.3.1 Eval target

The third argument of the ajax function can be the string ":eval". This means that the string returned by server will not be embedded in the document but it will be evaluated instead.

Here is an example of a default controller:

```
1 def one():
2     return dict()
3
4 def echo():
5     return "jQuery('#target').html(%s);" % repr(request.vars.name)
```

and the associated "default/one.html" view:

```
1 {{extend 'layout.html'}}
2 <form>
3     <input name="name" onkeyup="ajax('echo', ['name'], ':eval')" />
4 </form>
5 <div id="target"></div>
```

This allows for more complex responses that can update multiple targets.

11.3.2 Auto-completion

Web2py contains a built-in autocomplete widget, described in the Forms chapter. Here we will build a simpler one from scratch.

Another application of the above `ajax` function is auto-completion. Here we wish to create an input field that expects a month name and, when the visitor types an incomplete name, performs auto-completion via an Ajax request. In response, an auto-completion drop-box appears below the input field.

This can be achieved via the following `default` controller:

```
def month_input():
    return dict()

def month_selector():
    if not request.vars.month: return ''
    months = ['January', 'February', 'March', 'April', 'May',
              'June', 'July', 'August', 'September' ,'October',
              'November', 'December']
    month_start = request.vars.month.capitalize()
    selected = [m for m in months if m.startswith(month_start)]
    return DIV(*[DIV(k,
                     _onclick="jQuery('#month').val('%s')" % k,
                     _onmouseover="this.style.backgroundColor='yellow'",
                     _onmouseout="this.style.backgroundColor='white'"
                     ) for k in selected])
```

and the corresponding "default/month_input.html" view:

```
{{extend 'layout.html'}}
<style>
#suggestions { position: relative; }
.suggestions { background: white; border: solid 1px #55A6C8; }
.suggestions DIV { padding: 2px 4px 2px 4px; }
</style>

<form>
 <input type="text" id="month" name="month" style="width: 250px" /><br />
 <div style="position: absolute;" id="suggestions"
      class="suggestions"></div>
</form>
<script>
jQuery("#month").keyup(function(){
     ajax('month_selector', ['month'], 'suggestions')});
</script>
```

The jQuery script in the view triggers the Ajax request each time the visitor types something in the "month" input field. The value of the input field is submitted with the Ajax request to the "month_selector" action. This action finds a list of month names that start with the submitted text (selected), builds a list of DIVs (each one containing a suggested month name), and returns a string with the serialized DIVs. The view displays the response HTML in the "suggestions" DIV. The "month_selector" action generates both the suggestions and the JavaScript code embedded in the DIVs that must be executed when the visitor clicks on each suggestion. For example when the visitor types "M" the callback action returns:

```
<div>
    <div onclick="jQuery('#month').val('March')"
         onmouseout="this.style.backgroundColor='white'"
         onmouseover="this.style.backgroundColor='yellow'">March</div>
    <div onclick="jQuery('#month').val('May')"
         onmouseout="this.style.backgroundColor='white'"
         onmouseover="this.style.backgroundColor='yellow'">May</div>
</div>
```

Here is the final effect:

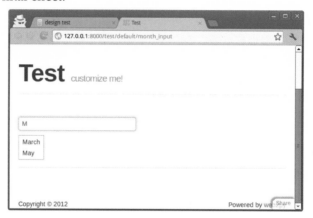

If the months are stored in a database table such as:

```
db.define_table('month', Field('name'))
```

then simply replace the month_selector action with:

```
def month_input():
    return dict()

def month_selector():
    if not request.vars.month:
        return ''
    pattern = request.vars.month.capitalize() + '%'
    selected = [row.name for row in db(db.month.name.like(pattern)).select()]
    return ''.join([DIV(k,
                _onclick="jQuery('#month').val('%s')" % k,
```

```
11        _onmouseover="this.style.backgroundColor='yellow'",
12        _onmouseout="this.style.backgroundColor='white'"
13        ).xml() for k in selected])
```

jQuery provides an optional Auto-complete Plugin with additional functionalities, but that is not discussed here.

11.3.3 Ajax form submission

Here we consider a page that allows the visitor to submit messages using Ajax without reloading the entire page. Using the LOAD helper, web2py provides a better mechanism for doing it than described here, which will be described in Chapter 12. Here we want to show you how to do it simply using jQuery.

It contains a form "myform" and a "target" DIV. When the form is submitted, the server may accept it (and perform a database insert) or reject it (because it did not pass validation). The corresponding notification is returned with the Ajax response and displayed in the "target" DIV.

Build a test application with the following model:

```
1  db = DAL('sqlite://db.db')
2  db.define_table('post', Field('your_message', 'text'))
3  db.post.your_message.requires = IS_NOT_EMPTY()
```

Notice that each post has a single field "your_message" that is required to be not-empty.

Edit the default.py controller and write two actions:

```
1  def index():
2      return dict()
3
4  def new_post():
5      form = SQLFORM(db.post)
6      if form.accepts(request, formname=None):
7          return DIV("Message posted")
8      elif form.errors:
9          return TABLE(*[TR(k, v) for k, v in form.errors.items()])
```

The first action does nothing other than return a view.

The second action is the Ajax callback. It expects the form variables in request.vars, processes them and returns DIV("Message posted") upon success or a TABLE of error messages upon failure.

Now edit the "default/index.html" view:

```
1  {{extend 'layout.html'}}
2
3  <div id="target"></div>
4
5  <form id="myform">
6    <input name="your_message" id="your_message" />
7    <input type="submit" />
8  </form>
9
10 <script>
11 jQuery('#myform').submit(function() {
12   ajax('{{=URL('new_post')}}',
13        ['your_message'], 'target');
14   return false;
15 });
16 </script>
```

Notice how in this example the form is created manually using HTML, but it is processed by the SQLFORM in a different action than the one that displays the form. The SQLFORM object is never serialized in HTML. SQLFORM.accepts in this case does not take a session and sets formname=None, because we chose not to set the form name and a form key in the manual HTML form.

The script at the bottom of the view connects the "myform" submit button to an inline function which submits the INPUT with id="your_message" using the web2py ajax function, and displays the answer inside the DIV with id="target".

11.3.4 Voting and rating

Another Ajax application is voting or rating items in a page. Here we consider an application that allows visitors to vote on posted images. The application consists of a single page that displays the images sorted according to their vote. We will allow visitors to vote multiple times, although it is easy to change this behavior if visitors are authenticated, by keeping track of the individual votes in the database and associating them with the request.env.remote_addr of the voter.

Here is a sample model:

```
1  db = DAL('sqlite://images.db')
2  db.define_table('item',
3      Field('image', 'upload'),
4      Field('votes', 'integer', default=0))
```

Here is the default controller:

```
1  def list_items():
2      items = db().select(db.item.ALL, orderby=db.item.votes)
3      return dict(items=items)
4
5  def download():
6      return response.download(request, db)
7
8  def vote():
9      item = db.item[request.vars.id]
10     new_votes = item.votes + 1
11     item.update_record(votes=new_votes)
12     return str(new_votes)
```

The download action is necessary to allow the list_items view to download images stored in the "uploads" folder. The votes action is used for the Ajax callback.

Here is the "default/list_items.html" view:

```
1  {{extend 'layout.html'}}
2
3  <form><input type="hidden" id="id" name="id" value="" /></form>
4  {{for item in items:}}
5  <p>
6  <img src="{{=URL('download', args=item.image)}}"
7      width="200px" />
8  <br />
9  Votes=<span id="item{{=item.id}}">{{=item.votes}}</span>
10 [<span onclick="jQuery('#id').val('{{=item.id}}');
11     ajax('vote', ['id'], 'item{{=item.id}}');">vote up</span>]
12 </p>
13 {{pass}}
```

When the visitor clicks on "[vote up]" the JavaScript code stores the item.id in the hidden "id" INPUT field and submits this value to the server via an Ajax request. The server increases the votes counter for the corresponding record and returns the new vote count as a string. This value is then inserted in the target item{{=item.id}} SPAN.

Ajax callbacks can be used to perform computations in the background, but we recommend using **cron** or a background process instead (discussed in chapter 4), since the web server enforces a timeout on threads. If the computation takes too long, the web server kills it. Refer to your web server parameters to set the timeout value.

12

Components and plugins

Components and plugins are relatively new features of web2py, and there is some disagreement between developers about what they are and what they should be. Most of the confusion stems from the different uses of these terms in other software projects and from the fact that developers are still working to finalize the specifications.

However, plugin support is an important feature and we need to provide some definitions. These definitions are not meant to be final, just consistent with the programming patterns we want to discuss in this chapter.

We will try to address two issues here:

- How can we build modular applications that minimize server load and maximize code reuse?

- How can we distribute pieces of code in a more or less plugin-and-play fashion?

Components address the first issue; *plugins* address the second.

12.1 Components

| A **component** is a functionally autonomous part of a web page.

A component may be composed of modules, controllers and views, but there is no strict requirement other than, when embedded in a web page, it must be localized within an html tag (for example a DIV, a SPAN, or an IFRAME) and it must perform its task independently of the rest of the page. We are specifically interested in components that are loaded in the page and communicate with the component controller function via Ajax.

An example of a component is a "comments component" that is contained into a DIV and shows users' comments and a post-new-comment form. When the form is submitted, it is sent to the server via Ajax, the list is updated, and the comment is stored server-side in the database. The DIV content is refreshed without reloading the rest of the page.

The web2py LOAD function makes this easy to do without explicit JavaScript/Ajax knowledge or programming.

Our goal is to be able to develop web applications by assembling components into page layouts.

Consider a simple web2py app "test" that extends the default scaffolding app with a custom model in file "models/db_comments.py":

```
1  db.define_table('comment_post',
2     Field('body','text',label='Your comment'),
3     auth.signature)
```

one action in "controllers/comments.py"

```
1  @auth.requires_login()
2  def post():
3      return dict(form=SQLFORM(db.comment_post).process(),
4                  comments=db(db.comment_post).select())
```

and the corresponding "views/comments/post.html"

```
1  {{extend 'layout.html'}}
2  {{for post in comments:}}
3  <div class="post">
4    On {{=post.created_on}} {{=post.created_by.first_name}}
5    says <span class="post_body">{{=post.body}}</span>
6  </div>
7  {{pass}}
8  {{=form}}
```

You can access it as usual at:

```
1  http://127.0.0.1:8000/test/comments/post
```

So far there is nothing special in this action, but we can turn it into a component by defining a new view with extension ".load" that does not extend the layout.

Hence we create a "views/comments/post.load":

```
1  {{for post in comments:}}
2  <div class="post">
3    On {{=post.created_on}} {{=post.created_by.first_name}}
4    says <blockquote class="post_body">{{=post.body}}</blockquote>
5  </div>
6  {{pass}}
7  {{=form}}
```

We can access it at the URL

```
1  http://127.0.0.1:8000/test/comments/post.load
```

This is a component that we can embed into any other page by simply doing

```
1  {{=LOAD('comments','post.load',ajax=True)}}
```

For example in "controllers/default.py" we can edit

```
1  def index():
2      return dict()
```

and in the corresponding view add the component:

```
1  {{extend 'layout.html'}}
2  {{=LOAD('comments','post.load',ajax=True)}}
```

Visiting the page

```
1  http://127.0.0.1:8000/test/default/index
```

will show the normal content and the comments component:

The {{=LOAD(...)}} component is rendered as follows:

```
1  <script type="text/javascript"><!--
2  web2py_component("/test/comment/post.load","c282718984176")
3  //--></script><div id="c282718984176">loading...</div>
```

(the actual generated code depends on the options passed to the LOAD function).

The web2py_component(url,id) function is defined in "web2py_ajax.html" and it performs all the magic: it calls the url via Ajax and embeds the response into the DIV with corresponding id; it traps every form submission into the DIV and submits those forms via Ajax. The Ajax target is always the DIV itself.

The full signature of the LOAD helper is the following:

```
1  LOAD(c=None, f='index', args=[], vars={},
2      extension=None, target=None,
3      ajax=False, ajax_trap=False,
4      url=None,user_signature=False,
5      timeout=None, times=1,
6      content='loading...',**attr):
```

Here:

- the first two arguments c and f are the controller and the function that we want to call respectively.

- args and vars are the arguments and variables that we want to pass to the function. The former is a list, the latter is a dictionary.

- extension is an optional extension. Notice that the extension can also be passed as part of the function as in f='index.load'.

- target is the id of the target DIV. If it is not specified a random target id is generated.

- ajax should be set to True if the DIV has to be filled via Ajax and to False if the DIV has to be filled before the current page is returned (thus avoiding the Ajax call).

- ajax_trap=True means that any form submission in the DIV must be captured and submitted via Ajax, and the response must be rendered inside the DIV. ajax_trap=False indicates that forms must be submitted normally, thus reloading the entire page. ajax_trap is ignored and assumed to be True if ajax=True.

- url, if specified, overrides the values of c, f, args, vars, and extension and loads the component at the url. It is used to load as components pages served by other applications (which my or may not be created with web2py).

- user_signature defaults to False but, if you are logged in, it should be set to True. This will make sure the ajax callback is digitally signed. This is documented in chapter 4.

- times specifies how many times the component is to be requested. Use "infinity" to keep loading the component continuously. This option is useful for triggering regular routines for a given document request.

- timeout sets the time to wait in milliseconds before starting the request or the frequency if times is greater than 1.

- content is the content to be displayed while performing the ajax call. It can be a helper as in content=IMG(..).

- optional **attr (attributes) can be passed to the contained DIV.

If no .load view is specified, there is a generic.load that renders the dictionary returned by the action without layout. It works best if the dictionary contains a single item.

If you LOAD a component having the .load extension and the corresponding controller function redirects to another action (for example a login form), the .load extension propagates and the new url (the one to redirect too) is also loaded with a .load extension.

If you call an action via Ajax and you want the action to force a redirect of the parent page you can do it with

```
redirect(url,type='auto')
```

Because Ajax post does not support multipart forms, i.e. file uploads, upload fields will not work with the LOAD component. You could be fooled into thinking it would work because upload fields will function normally if POST is done from the individual component's.load view. Instead, uploads are done with ajax-compatible 3rd-party widgets and web2py manual upload store commands.

12.1.1   Client-Server component communications

When the action of a component is called via Ajax, web2py passes two HTTP headers with the request:

```
1  web2py-component-location
2  web2py-component-element
```

which can be accessed by the action via the variables:

```
1  request.env.http_web2py_component_location
2  request.env.http_web2py_component_element
```

The latter is also accessible via:

```
1  request.cid
```

The former contains the URL of the page that called the component action. The latter contains the id of the DIV that will contain the response.

The component action can also store data in two special HTTP response headers that will be interpreted by the full page upon response. They are:

```
1  web2py-component-flash
2  web2py-component-command
```

and they can be set via:

```
1  response.headers['web2py-component-flash']='....'
2  response.headers['web2py-component-command']='...'
```

or (if the action is called by a component) automatically via:

```
1  response.flash='...'
2  response.js='...'
```

The former contains text that you want to be flashed upon response. The latter contains JavaScript code that you want to be executed upon response. It cannot contain newlines.

As an example, let's define a contact form component in "controllers/contact/ask.py" that allows the user to ask a question. The component will email the question to the system administrator, flash a "thank you" message, and remove the component from the page:

```
1  def ask():
```

```
 2  form=SQLFORM.factory(
 3      Field('your_email',requires=IS_EMAIL()),
 4      Field('question',requires=IS_NOT_EMPTY()))
 5  if form.process().accepted:
 6      if mail.send(to='admin@example.com',
 7                   subject='from %s' % form.vars.your_email,
 8                   message = form.vars.question):
 9          response.flash = 'Thank you'
10          response.js = "jQuery('#%s').hide()" % request.cid
11      else:
12          form.errors.your_email = "Unable to send the email"
13  return dict(form=form)
```

The first four lines define the form and accept it. The mail object used for sending is defined in the default scaffolding application. The last four lines implement all the component-specific logic by getting data from the HTTP request headers and setting the HTTP response headers.

Now you can embed this contact form in any page via

```
 1  {{=LOAD('contact','ask.load',ajax=True)}}
```

Notice that we did not define a .load view for our ask component. We do not have to because it returns a single object (form) and therefore the "generic.load" will do just fine. Remember that generic views are a development tool. In production you should copy "views/generic.load" into "views/contact/ask.load".

We can block access to a function called via Ajax by digitally signing the URL using the user_signature argument:

```
 1  {{=LOAD('contact','ask.load',ajax=True,user_signature=True)}}
```

which add a digital signature to the URL. The digital signature must then be validated using a decorator in the callback function:

```
 1  @auth.requires_signature()
 2  def ask(): ...
```

12.1.2   Trapped Ajax links

Normally a link is not trapped, and by clicking in a link inside a component, the entire linked page is loaded. Sometimes you want the linked page to be loaded inside the component. This can be achieved using the A helper:

```
{{=A('linked page',_href='http://example.com',cid=request.cid)}}
```

If cid is specified, the linked page is loaded via Ajax. The cid is the id of the html element where to place the loaded page content. In this case we set it to request.cid, i.e. the id of the component that generates the link. The linked page can be and usually is an internal URL generated using the URL command.

12.2 Plugins

A **plugin** is any subset of the files of an application.

and we really mean *any*:

- A plugin is not a module, is not a model, it is not a controller, is not a view, yet it may contain modules, models, controllers and/or views.

- A plugin does not need to be functionally autonomous and it may depend on other plugins or specific user code.

- A *plugin* is not a *plugins system* and therefore has no concept of registration nor isolation, although we will give rules to try to achieve some isolation.

- We are talking about a plugin for your app, not a plugin for web2py.

So why is it called a *plugin*? Because it provides a mechanism for packing a subset of an app and unpacking it over another app (i.e. *plug-in*). Under this definition, any file in your app can be treated as a plugin.

When the app is distributed, its plugins are packed and distributed with it.

In practice, the **admin** provides an interface for packing and unpacking plugins separately from your app. Files and folder of your application that have names with the prefix plugin_*name* can be packed together into a file called:

web2py.plugin.*name*.w2p and distributed together.

The files that compose a plugin are not treated by web2py any differently than other files except that **admin** understands from their names that they are meant to be distributed together, and it displays them in a separate page:

Yet as a matter of fact, by the definition above, these plugins are more general than those recognized as such by **admin**.

In practice we will only be concerned with two types of plugins:

- *Component Plugins.* These are plugins that contain components as defined in the previous section. A component plugin can contain one or more components. We can think for example of a `plugin_comments` that contains the *comments* component proposed above. Another example could be `plugin_tagging` that contains a *tagging* component and a *tag-cloud* component that share some database tables also defined by the plugin.

- *Layout Plugins.* These are plugins that contain a layout view and the static files required by such layout. When the plugin is applied it gives the app a new look and feel.

By the above definitions, the components created in the previous section, for example "controllers/contact.py", are already plugins. We can move them from one app to another and use the components they define. Yet they are not recognized as such by **admin** because there is nothing that labels them as plugins. So there are two problems we need to solve:

- Name the plugin files using a convention, so that **admin** can recognize them as belonging to the same plugin

- If the plugin has model files, establish a convention so that the objects it defines do not pollute the namespace and do not conflict with each other.

Let's assume a plugin is called *name*. Here are the rules that should be followed:

Rule 1: Plugin models and controllers should be called, respectively

- `models/plugin_name.py`

- `controllers/plugin_name.py`

and plugin views, modules, static, and private files should be in folders called, respectively:

- `views/plugin_name/`

- `modules/plugin_name/`

- `static/plugin_name/`

- `private/plugin_name/`

Rule 2: Plugin models can only define objects with names that start with

- `plugin_`*name*
- `Plugin`*Name*
- `_`

Rule 3: Plugin models can only define session variables with names that start with

- `session.plugin_`*name*
- `session.Plugin`*Name*

Rule 4: Plugins should include license and documentation. These should be placed in:

- `static/plugin_`*name*`/license.html`
- `static/plugin_`*name*`/about.html`

Rule 5: The plugin can only rely on the existence of the global objects defined in scaffolding "db.py", i.e.

- a database connection called `db`
- an `Auth` instance called `auth`
- a `Crud` instance called `crud`
- a `Service` instance called `service`

Some plugins may be more sophisticated and have a configuration parameter in case more than one db instance exists.

Rule 6: If a plugin needs configuration parameters, these should be set via a PluginManager as described below.

By following the above rules we can make sure that:

- **admin** recognizes all the `plugin_`*name* files and folder as part of a single entity.
- plugins do not interfere with each other.

The rules above do not solve the problem of plugin versions and dependencies. That is beyond our scope.

12.2.1   Component plugins

Component plugins are plugins that define components. Components usually access the database and define with their own models.

Here we turn the previous comments component into a comments_plugin by using the same code we wrote before, but following all of the previous rules.

First, we create a model called "models/plugin_comments.py":

```
db.define_table('plugin_comments_comment',
    Field('body','text', label='Your comment'),
    auth.signature)

def plugin_comments():
    return LOAD('plugin_comments','post',ajax=True)
```

(notice the last two lines define a function that will simplify the embedding of the plugin)

Second, we define a "controllers/plugin_comments.py"

```
def post():
    if not auth.user:
        return A('login to comment',_href=URL('default','user/login'))
    comment = db.plugin_comments_comment
    return dict(form=SQLFORM(comment).process(),
                comments=db(comment).select())
```

Third, we create a view called "views/plugin_comments/post.load":

```
{{for comment in comments:}}
<div class="comment">
  on {{=comment.created_on}} {{=comment.created_by.first_name}}
  says <span class="comment_body">{{=comment.body}}</span>
</div>
{{pass}}
{{=form}}
```

Now we can use **admin** to pack the plugin for distribution. Admin will save this plugin as:

```
web2py.plugin.comments.w2p
```

We can use the plugin in any view by simply installing the plugin via the **edit** page in **admin** and adding this to our own views

```
{{=plugin_comments()}}
```

Of course we can make the plugin more sophisticated by having components that take parameters and configuration options. The more complex the components, the more difficult it becomes to avoid name collisions. The Plugin Manager described below is designed to avoid this problem.

12.2.2 Plugin manager

The PluginManager is a class defined in gluon.tools. Before we explain how it works inside, we will explain how to use it.

Here we consider the previous comments_plugin and we make it better. We want to be able to customize:

```
db.plugin_comments_comment.body.label
```

without having to edit the plugin code itself.

Here is how we can do it:

First, rewrite the plugin "models/plugin_comments.py" in this way:

```
def _():
    from gluon.tools import PluginManager
    plugins = PluginManager('comments', body_label='Your comment')

    db.define_table('plugin_comments_comment',
        Field('body','text',label=plugins.comments.body_label),
        auth.signature)
    return lambda: LOAD('plugin_comments','post.load',ajax=True)
plugin_comments = _()
```

Notice how all the code except the table definition is encapsulated in a single function called _ so that it does not pollute the global namespace. Also notice how the function creates an instance of a PluginManager.

Now in any other model in your app, for example in "models/db.py", you can configure this plugin as follows:

```
from gluon.tools import PluginManager
plugins = PluginManager()
plugins.comments.body_label = T('Post a comment')
```

The plugins object is already instantiated in the default scaffolding app in "models/db.py"

The PluginManager object is a thread-level singleton Storage object of Storage objects. That means you can instantiate as many as you like within the same application but (whether they have the same name or not) they act as if there were a single PluginManager instance.

In particular each plugin file can make its own PluginManager object and register itself and its default parameters with it:

```
plugins = PluginManager('name', param1='value', param2='value')
```

You can override these parameters elsewhere (for example in "models/db.py") with the code:

```
plugins = PluginManager()
plugins.name.param1 = 'other value'
```

You can configure multiple plugins in one place.

```
plugins = PluginManager()
plugins.name.param1 = '...'
plugins.name.param2 = '...'
plugins.name1.param3 = '...'
plugins.name2.param4 = '...'
plugins.name3.param5 = '...'
```

When the plugin is defined, the PluginManager must take arguments: the plugin name and optional named arguments which are default parameters. However, when the plugins are configured, the PluginManager constructor must take no arguments. The configuration must precede the definition of the plugin (i.e. it must be in a model file that comes first alphabetically).

12.2.3 Layout plugins

Layout plugins are simpler than component plugins because usually they do not contain code, but only views and static files. Yet you should still follow good practice:

First, create a folder called "static/plugin_layout_*name*/" (where name is the name of your layout) and place all your static files there.

Second, create a layout file called "views/plugin_layout_*name*/layout.html" that contains your layout and links the images, CSS and JavaScript files in "static/plugin_layout_*name*/"

Third, modify the "views/layout.html" so that it simply reads:

```
1 {{extend 'plugin_layout_name/layout.html'}}
2 {{include}}
```

The benefit of this design is that users of this plugin can install multiple layouts and choose which one to apply simply by editing "views/layout.html". Moreover, "views/layout.html" will not be packed by **admin** together with the plugin, so there is no risk that the plugin will override the user's code in the previously installed layout.

12.2.4 Plugins repositories

While there is no single repository of web2py plugins you can find many of them at one of the following to URLs:

```
1 http://dev.s-cubism.com/web2py_plugins
2 http://web2py.com/plugins
3 http://web2py.com/layouts
```

Here is a screenshot from the s-cubism repository:

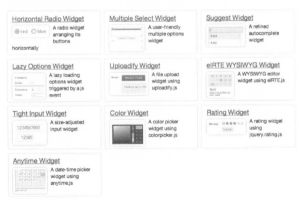

13

Deployment recipes

There are multiple ways to deploy web2py in a production environment. The details depend on the configuration and the services provided by the host.

In this chapter we consider the following issues:

- Production deployment (Apache, Nginx, Lighttpd, Cherokee)

- Security

- Scalability using Redis and a load balancer.

- Deployment on PythonAnywhere, Heroku, Amazon EC2, and on the Google App Engine platform(GAE [14])

web2py comes with an SSL [22] enabled web server, the Rocket wsgiserver [19]. While this is a fast web server, it has limited configuration capabilities. For this reason it is best to deploy web2py behind Apache [95], [96] Lighttpd [97] or Cherokee [98]. These are free and open-source web servers that are customizable and have been proven to be reliable in high traffic production environments. They can be configured to serve static files directly, deal with HTTPS, and pass control to web2py for dynamic content.

Until a few years ago, the standard interface for communication between web servers and web applications was the Common Gateway Interface (CGI) [99]. The main problem with CGI is that it creates a new process for each HTTP request. If the web application is written in an interpreted language, each HTTP request served by the CGI scripts starts a new instance of the interpreter. This is slow, and it should be avoided in a production environment. Moreover, CGI can only handle simple responses. It cannot handle, for example, file streaming. web2py provides a file `cgihandler.py` to interface to CGI.

One solution to this problem is to use the mod_python module for Apache. We discuss it here because its use is still very common, though the mod_python project has officially been abandoned by the Apache Software Foundation. mod_python starts one instance of the Python interpreter when Apache starts, and serves each HTTP request in its own thread without having to restart Python each time. This is a better solution than CGI, but it is not an optimal solution, since mod_python uses its own interface for communication between the web server and the web application. In mod_python, all hosted applications run under the same user-id/group-id, which presents security issues. web2py provides a file `modpythonhandler.py` to interface to mod_python.

In the last few years, the Python community has come together behind a new standard interface for communication between web servers and web applications written in Python. It is called Web Server Gateway Interface (WSGI) [20] [21]. web2py was built on WSGI, and it provides handlers for using other interfaces when WSGI is not available.

Apache supports WSGI via the module mod_wsgi [100] developed by Graham Dumpleton. web2py provides a file `wsgihandler.py` to interface to WSGI.

Some web hosting services do not support mod_wsgi. In this case, we must use Apache as a proxy and forward all incoming requests to the web2py built-in web server (running for example on localhost:8000).

In both cases, with mod_wsgi and/or mod_proxy, Apache can be configured to serve static files and deal with SSL encryption directly, taking the burden off web2py.

Nginx uses uWSGI instead of WSGI, a similar but different protocol which requires its own python adapter.

The Lighttpd web server does not currently support the WSGI interface, but it does support the FastCGI [101] interface, which is an improvement over CGI. FastCGI's main aim is to reduce the overhead associated with interfacing the web server and CGI programs, allowing a server to handle more HTTP requests at once.

According to the Lighttpd web site, "Lighttpd powers several popular Web 2.0 sites such as YouTube and Wikipedia. Its high speed IO-infrastructure allows them to scale several times better with the same hardware than with alternative web-servers". Lighttpd with FastCGI is, in fact, faster than Apache with mod_wsgi. web2py provides a file fcgihandler.py to interface to FastCGI. web2py also includes a gaehandler.py to interface with the Google App Engine (GAE). On GAE, web applications run "in the cloud". This means that the framework completely abstracts any hardware details. The web application is automatically replicated as many times as necessary to serve all concurrent requests. Replication in this case means more than multiple threads on a single server; it also means multiple processes on different servers. GAE achieves this level of scalability by blocking write access to the file system, and all persistent information must be stored in the Google BigTable datastore or in memcache.

On non-GAE platforms, scalability is an issue that needs to be addressed, and it may require some tweaks in the web2py applications. The most common way to achieve scalability is by using multiple web servers behind a load-balancer (a simple round robin, or something more sophisticated, receiving heartbeat feedback from the servers).

Even if there are multiple web servers, there must be one, and only one, database server. By default, web2py uses the file system for storing sessions, error tickets, uploaded files, and the cache. This means that in the default configuration, the corresponding folders have to be shared folders.

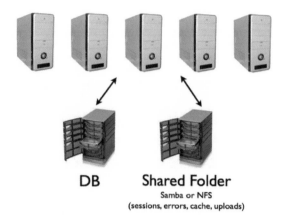

DB   **Shared Folder**
Samba or NFS
(sessions, errors, cache, uploads)

In the rest of the chapter, we consider various recipes that may provide an improvement over this naive approach, including:

- Store sessions in the database, in cache or do not store sessions at all.

- Store tickets on local filesystem and move them into the database in batches.

- Use memcache instead of cache.ram and cache.disk.

- Store uploaded files in the database instead of the shared filesystem.

While we recommend following the first three recipes, the fourth recipe may provide an advantage mainly in the case of small files, but may be counterproductive for large files.

13.1 anyserver.py

Web2py comes with a file called anyserver.py that implements WSGI interfaces to the following popular servers: bjoern, cgi, cherrypy, diesel, eventlet, fapws, flup, gevent, gnuicorn, mongrel2, paste, rocket, tornado, twisted, wsgiref

You can use any of these servers, for example Tornado, simply by doing:

```
python anyserver.py -s tornado -i 127.0.0.1 -p 8000 -l -P
```

Here -l is for logging and -P is for the profiler. For information on all the command line options use "-h":

```
1 python anyserver.py -h
```

13.2   Linux and Unix

13.2.1   One step production deployment

Here are some steps to install apache+python+mod_wsgi+web2py+postgresql from scratch.

On Ubuntu:

```
1 wget http://web2py.googlecode.com/hg/scripts/setup-web2py-ubuntu.sh
2 chmod +x setup-web2py-ubuntu.sh
3 sudo ./setup-web2py-ubuntu.sh
```

On Fedora:

```
1 wget http://web2py.googlecode.com/hg/scripts/setup-web2py-fedora.sh
2 chmod +x setup-web2py-fedora.sh
3 sudo ./setup-web2py-fedora.sh
```

Both of these scripts should run out of the box, but every Linux installation is a bit different, so make sure you check the source code of these scripts before you run them. In the case of Ubuntu, most of what they do is explained below. They do not implement the scalability optimizations discussed below.

13.2.2   Apache setup

In this section, we use Ubuntu 8.04 Server Edition as the reference platform. The configuration commands are very similar on other Debian-based Linux distribution, but they may differ for Fedora-based systems (which uses yum instead of apt-get).

First, make sure all the necessary Python and Apache packages are installed by typing the following shell commands:

```
1 sudo apt-get update
2 sudo apt-get -y upgrade
3 sudo apt-get -y install openssh-server
```

```
4  sudo apt-get -y install python
5  sudo apt-get -y install python-dev
6  sudo apt-get -y install apache2
7  sudo apt-get -y install libapache2-mod-wsgi
8  sudo apt-get -y install libapache2-mod-proxy-html
```

Then, enable the SSL module, the proxy module, and the WSGI module in Apache:

```
1  sudo ln -s /etc/apache2/mods-available/proxy_http.load \
2              /etc/apache2/mods-enabled/proxy_http.load
3  sudo a2enmod ssl
4  sudo a2enmod proxy
5  sudo a2enmod proxy_http
6  sudo a2enmod wsgi
```

Create the SSL folder, and put the SSL certificates inside it:

```
1  sudo mkdir /etc/apache2/ssl
```

You should obtain your SSL certificates from a trusted Certificate Authority such as verisign.com, but, for testing purposes, you can generate your own self-signed certificates following the instructions in ref. [102]

Then restart the web server:

```
1  sudo /etc/init.d/apache2 restart
```

The Apache configuration file is:

```
1  /etc/apache2/sites-available/default
```

The Apache logs are in:

```
1  /var/log/apache2/
```

13.2.3   mod_wsgi

Download and unzip web2py source on the machine where you installed the web server above.

Install web2py under /home/www-data/, for example, and give ownership to user www-data and group www-data. These steps can be performed with the following shell commands:

```
1  cd /home/www-data/
2  sudo wget http://web2py.com/examples/static/web2py_src.zip
3  sudo unzip web2py_src.zip
4  sudo chown -R www-data:www-data /home/www-data/web2py
```

To set up web2py with mod_wsgi, create a new Apache configuration file:

```
/etc/apache2/sites-available/web2py
```

and include the following code:

```
<VirtualHost *:80>
  ServerName web2py.example.com
  WSGIDaemonProcess web2py user=www-data group=www-data display-name=%{GROUP}
  WSGIProcessGroup web2py
  WSGIScriptAlias / /home/www-data/web2py/wsgihandler.py

  <Directory /home/www-data/web2py>
    AllowOverride None
    Order Allow,Deny
    Deny from all
    <Files wsgihandler.py>
      Allow from all
    </Files>
  </Directory>

  AliasMatch ^/([^/]+)/static/(.*) \
          /users/www-data/web2py/applications/$1/static/$2
  <Directory /users/www-data/web2py/applications/*/static/>
    Order Allow,Deny
    Allow from all
  </Directory>

  <Location /admin>
  Deny from all
  </Location>

  <LocationMatch ^/([^/]+)/appadmin>
  Deny from all
  </LocationMatch>

  CustomLog /private/var/log/apache2/access.log common
  ErrorLog /private/var/log/apache2/error.log
</VirtualHost>
```

When you restart Apache, it should pass all the requests to web2py without going through the Rocket wsgiserver.

Here are some explanations:

```
WSGIDaemonProcess web2py user=www-data group=www-data display-name=%{GROUP}
```

defines a daemon process group in context of "web2py.example.com". By defining this inside of the virtual host, only this virtual host can access this using WSGIProcessGroup, including any virtual host with the same server name but on a different port. The "user" and "group" options should be set to the user who has write access to the directory where web2py was setup. You do not need to set "user" and "group" if you made the web2py installation directory writable by the default user that Apache runs as. The "display-name" option makes the process name appears in ps output as "(wsgi-web2py)" instead of as name of Apache web server executable. As no "processes" or "threads" options are specified, the daemon process group will have a single process with 15 threads running within that process. This is usually more than adequate for most sites and should be left as is. If overriding it, do not use "processes=1" as doing so will disable any in-browser WSGI debugging tools that check the "wsgi.multiprocess" flag. This is because any use of the "processes" option will cause that flag to be set to true, even a single process, and such tools expect that it be set to false. Note: if your application code or third party extension module is not thread safe, use options "processes=5 threads=1" instead. This will create five processes in the daemon process group where each process is single threaded. You might consider using "maximum-requests=1000" if your application leaks Python objects because it is unable to garbage collect properly.

```
1  WSGIProcessGroup web2py
```

delegates running of all WSGI applications to the daemon process group that was configured using the WSGIDaemonProcess directive.

```
1  WSGIScriptAlias / /users/www-data/web2py/wsgihandler.py
```

mounts the web2py application. In this case it is mounted at the root of the web site.

```
1  <Directory /users/www-data/web2py>
2    ...
3  </Directory>
```

gives Apache permission to access the WSGI script file.

```
1  <Directory /users/www-data/web2py/applications/*/static/>
2    Order Allow,Deny
3    Allow from all
4  </Directory>
```

Instructs Apache to bypass web2py when searching static files.

```
1  <Location /admin>
2    Deny from all
3  </Location>
```

and

```
1  <LocationMatch ^/([^/]+)/appadmin>
2    Deny from all
3  </LocationMatch>
```

blocks public access to **admin** and **appadmin**

Normally we would just allow permission to the whole directory where the WSGI script file is located, but web2py places the WSGI script file in a directory which contains other source code, including the admin interface password. Opening up the whole directory would cause security issues, because technically Apache would be given permission to serve all the files up to any user who traversed to that directory via a mapped URL. To avoid security problems, explicitly deny access to the contents of the directory, except for the WSGI script file, and prohibit a user from doing any overrides from a.htaccess file to be extra safe.

You can find a completed, commented, Apache wsgi configuration file in:

```
1  scripts/web2py-wsgi.conf
```

This section was created with help from Graham Dumpleton, developer of mod_wsgi.

13.2.4   Setting password

In production it may be necessary to set the admin password programmatically. This can be done from the Bash shell with

```
1  sudo -u www-data python -c "from gluon.main import save_password; save_password(
      raw_input('admin password: '),443)"
```

13.2.5   mod_wsgi and SSL

To force some applications (for example **admin** and **appadmin**) to go over HTTPS, store the SSL certificate and key files:

```
1  /etc/apache2/ssl/server.crt
2  /etc/apache2/ssl/server.key
```

and edit the Apache configuration file web2py.conf and append:

```
1  <VirtualHost *:443>
2    ServerName web2py.example.com
3    SSLEngine on
4    SSLCertificateFile /etc/apache2/ssl/server.crt
5    SSLCertificateKeyFile /etc/apache2/ssl/server.key
6
7    WSGIProcessGroup web2py
8
9    WSGIScriptAlias / /users/www-data/web2py/wsgihandler.py
10
11   <Directory /users/www-data/web2py>
12     AllowOverride None
13     Order Allow,Deny
14     Deny from all
15     <Files wsgihandler.py>
16       Allow from all
17     </Files>
18   </Directory>
19
20   AliasMatch ^/([^/]+)/static/(.*) \
21           /users/www-data/web2py/applications/$1/static/$2
22
23   <Directory /users/www-data/web2py/applications/*/static/>
24     Order Allow,Deny
25     Allow from all
26   </Directory>
27
28   CustomLog /private/var/log/apache2/access.log common
29   ErrorLog /private/var/log/apache2/error.log
30
31 </VirtualHost>
```

Restart Apache and you should be able to access:

```
1  https://www.example.com/admin
2  https://www.example.com/examples/appadmin
3  http://www.example.com/examples
```

but not:

```
1  http://www.example.com/admin
2  http://www.example.com/examples/appadmin
```

13.2.6   mod_proxy

Some Unix/Linux distributions can run Apache, but do not support mod_wsgi. In this case, the simplest solution is to run Apache as a proxy and have Apache deal with static files only.

Here is a minimalist Apache configuration:

```
1  NameVirtualHost *:80
2  #### deal with requests on port 80
3  <VirtualHost *:80>
4    Alias / /users/www-data/web2py/applications
5    ### serve static files directly
6    <LocationMatch "^/welcome/static/.*">
7    Order Allow, Deny
8    Allow from all
9    </LocationMatch>
10   ### proxy all the other requests
11   <Location "/welcome">
12     Order deny,allow
13     Allow from all
14     ProxyRequests off
15     ProxyPass http://localhost:8000/welcome
16     ProxyPassReverse http://localhost:8000/
17     ProxyHTMLURLMap http://127.0.0.1:8000/welcome/ /welcome
18   </Location>
19   LogFormat "%h %l %u %t "%r" %>s %b" common
20   CustomLog /var/log/apache2/access.log common
21 </VirtualHost>
```

The above script exposes only the "welcome" application. To expose other applications, you need to add the corresponding <Location>...</Location> with the same syntax as done for the "welcome" app.

The script assumes there is a web2py server running on port 8000. Before restarting Apache, make sure this is the case:

```
1  nohup python web2py.py -a '<recycle>' -i 127.0.0.1 -p 8000 &
```

You can specify a password with the -a option or use the "<recycle>" parameter instead of a password. In the latter case, the previously stored password is reused and the password is not stored in the shell history.

You can also use the parameter "<ask>", to be prompted for a password.

The nohup commands makes sure the server does not die when you close the shell. nohup logs all output into nohup.out.

To force admin and appadmin over HTTPS use the following Apache configuration file instead:

```
1  NameVirtualHost *:80
2  NameVirtualHost *:443
3  #### deal with requests on port 80
```

```
 4  <VirtualHost *:80>
 5    Alias / /users/www-data/web2py/applications
 6    ### admin requires SSL
 7    <LocationMatch "^/admin">
 8      SSLRequireSSL
 9    </LocationMatch>
10    ### appadmin requires SSL
11    <LocationMatch "^/welcome/appadmin/.*">
12      SSLRequireSSL
13    </LocationMatch>
14    ### serve static files directly
15    <LocationMatch "^/welcome/static/.*">
16      Order Allow,Deny
17      Allow from all
18    </LocationMatch>
19    ### proxy all the other requests
20    <Location "/welcome">
21      Order deny,allow
22      Allow from all
23      ProxyPass http://localhost:8000/welcome
24      ProxyPassReverse http://localhost:8000/
25    </Location>
26    LogFormat "%h %l %u %t "%r" %>s %b" common
27    CustomLog /var/log/apache2/access.log common
28  </VirtualHost>
29  <VirtualHost *:443>
30    SSLEngine On
31    SSLCertificateFile /etc/apache2/ssl/server.crt
32    SSLCertificateKeyFile /etc/apache2/ssl/server.key
33    <Location "/">
34      Order deny,allow
35      Allow from all
36      ProxyPass http://localhost:8000/
37      ProxyPassReverse http://localhost:8000/
38    </Location>
39    LogFormat "%h %l %u %t "%r" %>s %b" common
40    CustomLog /var/log/apache2/access.log common
41  </VirtualHost>
```

The administrative interface must be disabled when web2py runs on a shared host with mod_proxy, or it will be exposed to other users.

13.2.7   Start as Linux daemon

Unless you are using mod_wsgi, you should setup the web2py server so that it can be started/stopped/restarted as any other Linux daemon, and so it can start automatically at the computer boot stage.

The process to set this up is specific to various Linux/Unix distributions.

In the web2py folder, there are two scripts which can be used for this purpose:

```
1  scripts/web2py.ubuntu.sh
2  scripts/web2py.fedora.sh
```

On Ubuntu, or other Debian-based Linux distribution, edit "web2py.ubuntu.sh" and replace the "/usr/lib/web2py" path with the path of your web2py installation, then type the following shell commands to move the file into the proper folder, register it as a startup service, and start it:

```
1  sudo cp scripts/web2py.ubuntu.sh /etc/init.d/web2py
2  sudo update-rc.d web2py defaults
3  sudo /etc/init.d/web2py start
```

On Fedora, or any other distributions based on Fedora, edit "web2py.fedora.sh" and replace the "/usr/lib/web2py" path with the path of your web2py installation, then type the following shell commands to move the file into the proper folder, register it as a startup service and start it:

```
1  sudo cp scripts/web2py.fedora.sh /etc/rc.d/init.d/web2pyd
2  sudo chkconfig --add web2pyd
3  sudo service web2py start
```

13.2.8 Nginx

Nginx is a free, open-source, that has rapidly been gaining popularity for its amazing perfomance.

Unlike traditional servers, Nginx does not use threads. Instead it uses an ansynchronous/event-driven architecture to handle concurrency. This architecture results in a small and predictable memory usage, even under heavy load.

Nginx is more than an HTTP server and reverse proxy, it is also an IMAP/POP3 proxy server.

Nginx is easy to configure and its configuration files and simpler and more compact than the corresponding Apache ones.

Nginx does not support WSGI but provides native support for the uWSGI [103] protocol.

On Ubuntu you can install Nginx with:

```
apt-get -y install nginx-full
```

Then you will need to create a configuration file such as the following:

```
# file /etc/nginx/sites-available/web2py
server {
        listen          80;
        server_name     $hostname;
        #to enable correct use of response.static_version
        #location ~* /(\w+)/static(?:/_[\d]+\.[\d]+\.[\d]+)?/(.*)$ {
        #     alias /home/www-data/web2py/applications/$1/static/$2;
        #     expires max;
        #}
        location ~* /(\w+)/static/ {
            root /home/www-data/web2py/applications/;
            #remove next comment on production
            #expires max;
        }
        location / {
            #uwsgi_pass       127.0.0.1:9001;
            uwsgi_pass       unix:///tmp/web2py.socket;
            include          uwsgi_params;
            uwsgi_param      UWSGI_SCHEME $scheme;
            uwsgi_param      SERVER_SOFTWARE     nginx/$nginx_version;
        }
}
server {
        listen 443 default_server ssl;
        server_name     $hostname;
        ssl_certificate          /etc/nginx/ssl/web2py.crt;
        ssl_certificate_key      /etc/nginx/ssl/web2py.key;
        ssl_prefer_server_ciphers on;
        ssl_session_cache shared:SSL:10m;
        ssl_session_timeout 10m;
        ssl_ciphers ECDHE-RSA-AES256-SHA:DHE-RSA-AES256-SHA:DHE-DSS-AES256-SHA:DHE-
            RSA-AES128-SHA:DHE-DSS-AES128-SHA;
        ssl_protocols SSLv3 TLSv1;
        keepalive_timeout   70;
        location / {
            #uwsgi_pass       127.0.0.1:9001;
            uwsgi_pass       unix:///tmp/web2py.socket;
```

```
37          include         uwsgi_params;
38          uwsgi_param     UWSGI_SCHEME $scheme;
39          uwsgi_param     SERVER_SOFTWARE    nginx/$nginx_version;
40      }
41
42  }
```

You will need to symlink the file and remove the default

```
1  ln -s /etc/nginx/sites-available/web2py /etc/nginx/sites-enabled/web2py
2  rm /etc/nginx/sites-enabled/default
```

You may also need to create the ssl folder for certificates and put certificates in there:

```
1  mkdir /etc/nginx/ssl
2  cp web2py.key /etc/nginx/ssl
3  cp web2py.crt /etc/nginx/ssl
```

You then need to install and setup uWSGI

```
1  sudo mkdir /etc/uwsgi
2  sudo mkdir /var/log/uwsgi
```

And create a configuration file "/etc/uwsgi/web2py.xml":

```
1  <uwsgi>
2      <socket>/tmp/web2py.socket</socket>
3      <pythonpath>/home/www-data/web2py/</pythonpath>
4      <mount>/=wsgihandler:application</mount>
5      <master/>
6      <processes>4</processes>
7      <harakiri>60</harakiri>
8      <reload-mercy>8</reload-mercy>
9      <cpu-affinity>1</cpu-affinity>
10     <stats>/tmp/stats.socket</stats>
11     <max-requests>2000</max-requests>
12     <limit-as>512</limit-as>
13     <reload-on-as>256</reload-on-as>
14     <reload-on-rss>192</reload-on-rss>
15     <uid>www-data</uid>
16     <gid>www-data</gid>
17     <no-orphans/>
18 </uwsgi>
```

This file assumes web2py is installed under "/home/www-data/web2py", as in the Aapache case.

You also need to edit a second configuration file "/etc/init/uwsgi-emperor.conf":

```
1 # Emperor uWSGI script
2 description "uWSGI Emperor"
3 start on runlevel [2345]
4 stop on runlevel [06]
5 respawn
6 exec uwsgi --master --die-on-term --emperor /etc/uwsgi --logto /var/log/uwsgi/uwsgi
     .log
```

Finally restart everything:

```
1 start uwsgi-emperor
2 /etc/init.d/nginx restart
```

You can reload uwsgi with

```
1 restart uwsgi-emperor
```

You can stop it with

```
1 stop uwsgi-emperor
```

You can reload web2py only (without restarting uwsgi) with

```
1 touch /etc/uwsgi/web2py.xml
```

All these steps are performed automatically by the provided scripts:

```
1 scripts/setup-web2py-nginx-uwsgi-on-centos.sh
2 scripts/setup-web2py-nginx-uwsgi-ubuntu.sh
```

13.2.9   Lighttpd

You can install Lighttpd on a Ubuntu or other Debian-based Linux distribution with the following shell command:

```
1 apt-get -y install lighttpd
```

Once installed, edit /etc/rc.local and create a fcgi web2py background process

```
1 cd /var/www/web2py && sudo -u www-data nohup python fcgihandler.py &
```

Then, you need to edit the Lighttpd configuration file

```
1 /etc/lighttpd/lighttpd.conf
```

so that it can find the socket created by the above process. In the config file, write something like:

```
1 server.modules          = (
2      "mod_access",
3      "mod_alias",
```

```
 4          "mod_compress",
 5          "mod_rewrite",
 6          "mod_fastcgi",
 7          "mod_redirect",
 8          "mod_accesslog",
 9          "mod_status",
10   )
11
12   server.port = 80
13   server.bind = "0.0.0.0"
14   server.event-handler = "freebsd-kqueue"
15   server.error-handler-404 = "/test.fcgi"
16   server.document-root = "/users/www-data/web2py/"
17   server.errorlog       = "/tmp/error.log"
18
19   fastcgi.server = (
20     "/handler_web2py.fcgi" => (
21         "handler_web2py" => ( #name for logs
22             "check-local" => "disable",
23             "socket" => "/tmp/fcgi.sock"
24         )
25     ),
26   )
27
28   $HTTP["host"] = "(^|\.)example\.com$" {
29     server.document-root="/var/www/web2py"
30        url.rewrite-once = (
31          "^(/.+?/static/.+)$" => "/applications$1",
32          "(^|/.*)$" => "/handler_web2py.fcgi$1",
33        )
34   }
```

Now check for syntax errors:

```
1 lighttpd -t -f /etc/lighttpd/lighttpd.conf
```

and (re)start the web server with:

```
1 /etc/init.d/lighttpd restart
```

Notice that FastCGI binds the web2py server to a Unix socket, not to an IP socket:

```
1 /tmp/fcgi.sock
```

This is where Lighttpd forwards the HTTP requests to and receives responses from. Unix sockets are lighter than Internet sockets, and this is one of the reasons Lighttpd+FastCGI+web2py is fast. As in the case of Apache, it is possible to setup Lighttpd to deal with static files directly, and to force some applications over HTTPS. Refer to the Lighttpd documentation for details.

Examples in this section were taken from John Heenan's post in web2pyslices.

The administrative interface must be disabled when web2py runs on a shared host with FastCGI, or it will be exposed to the other users.

13.2.10 Shared hosting with mod_python

There are times, specifically on shared hosts, when one does not have the permission to configure the Apache config files directly. At the time of writing most of these hosts still run mod_python even if it is not maintained any more in favor of mod_wsgi.

You can still run web2py. Here we show an example of how to set it up.

Place contents of web2py into the "htdocs" folder.

In the web2py folder, create a file "web2py_modpython.py" file with the following contents:

```
from mod_python import apache
import modpythonhandler

def handler(req):
    req.subprocess_env['PATH_INFO'] = req.subprocess_env['SCRIPT_URL']
    return modpythonhandler.handler(req)
```

Create/update the file ".htaccess" with the following contents:

```
SetHandler python-program
PythonHandler web2py_modpython
#PythonDebug On
```

This example was provided by Niktar.

13.2.11 Cherokee with FastCGI

Cherokee is a very fast web server and, like web2py, it provides an AJAX-enabled web-based interface for its configuration. Its web interface is written in Python. In addition, there is no restart required for most of the changes.

Here are the steps required to setup web2py with Cherokee:

Download Cherokee [98]

Untar, build, and install:

```
1  tar -xzf cherokee-0.9.4.tar.gz
2  cd cherokee-0.9.4
3  ./configure --enable-fcgi && make
4  make install
```

Start web2py normally at least once to make sure it creates the "applications" folder.

Write a shell script named "startweb2py.sh" with the following code:

```
1  #!/bin/bash
2  cd /var/web2py
3  python /var/web2py/fcgihandler.py &
```

and give the script execute privileges and run it. This will start web2py under FastCGI handler.

Start Cherokee and cherokee-admin:

```
1  sudo nohup cherokee &
2  sudo nohup cherokee-admin &
```

By default, cherokee-admin only listens at local interface on port 9090. This is not a problem if you have full, physical access on that machine. If this is not the case, you can force it to bind to an IP address and port by using the following options:

```
1  -b,  --bind[=IP]
2  -p,  --port=NUM
```

or do an SSH port-forward (more secure, recommended):

```
1  ssh -L 9090:localhost:9090 remotehost
```

Open "http://localhost:9090" in your browser. If everything is ok, you will get cherokee-admin.

In cherokee-admin web interface, click "info sources". Choose "Local Interpreter". Write in the following code, then click "Add New".

```
1  Nick: web2py
2  Connection: /tmp/fcgi.sock
3  Interpreter: /var/web2py/startweb2py.sh
```

Finally, perform the following remaining steps:

- Click "Virtual Servers", then click "Default".

- Click "Behavior", then, under that, click "default".

- Choose "FastCGI" instead of "List and Send" from the list box.

- At the bottom, select "web2py" as "Application Server"

- Put a check in all the checkboxes (you can leave Allow-x-sendfile). If there is a warning displayed, disable and enable one of the checkboxes. (It will automatically re-submit the application server parameter. Sometimes it doesn't, which is a bug).

- Point your browser to "http://yoursite", and "Welcome to web2py" will appear.

13.2.12 Postgresql

PostgreSQL is a free and open source database which is used in demanding production environments, for example, to store the.org domain name database, and has been proven to scale well into hundreds of terabytes of data. It has very fast and solid transaction support, and provides an auto-vacuum feature that frees the administrator from most database maintenance tasks.

On an Ubuntu or other Debian-based Linux distribution, it is easy to install PostgreSQL and its Python API with:

```
sudo apt-get -y install postgresql
sudo apt-get -y install python-psycopg2
```

It is wise to run the web server(s) and the database server on different machines. In this case, the machines running the web servers should be connected with a secure internal (physical) network, or should establish SSL tunnels to securely connect with the database server.

Edit the PostgreSQL configuration file

```
sudo nano /etc/postgresql/8.4/main/postgresql.conf
```

and make sure it contains these two lines

```
...
track_counts = on
...
autovacuum = on   # Enable autovacuum subprocess?  'on'
...
```

Start the database server with:

```
sudo /etc/init.d/postgresql restart
```

When restarting the PostgreSQL server, it should notify which port it is running on. Unless you have multiple database servers, it should be 5432.

The PostgreSQL logs are in:

```
/var/log/postgresql/
```

Once the database server is up and running, create a user and a database so that web2py applications can use it:

```
sudo -u postgres createuser -PE -s myuser
postgresql> createdb -O myself -E UTF8 mydb
postgresql> echo 'The following databases have been created:'
postgresql> psql -l
postgresql> psql mydb
```

The first of the commands will grant superuser-access to the new user, called myuser. It will prompt you for a password.

Any web2py application can connect to this database with the command:

```
db = DAL("postgres://myuser:mypassword@localhost:5432/mydb")
```

where mypassword is the password you entered when prompted, and 5432 is the port where the database server is running.

Normally you use one database for each application, and multiple instances of the same application connect to the same database. It is also possible for different applications to share the same database.

For database backup details, read the PostgreSQL documentation; specifically the commands pg_dump and pg_restore.

13.2.13 Start the scheduler as a Linux service (upstart)

To install the scheduler as a permanent daemon on Linux (w/ Upstart), put the following into /etc/init/web2py-scheduler.conf, assuming your web2py instance is installed in <user>'s home directory, running as <user>, with app <myapp>, on network interface eth0.

```
description "web2py task scheduler"
start on (local-filesystems and net-device-up IFACE=eth0)
```

```
3 stop on shutdown
4 respawn limit 8 60 # Give up if restart occurs 8 times in 60 seconds.
5 exec sudo -u <user> python /home/<user>/web2py/web2py.py -K <myapp>
6 respawn
```

You can then start/stop/restart/check status of the daemon with:

```
1 sudo start web2py-scheduler
2 sudo stop web2py-scheduler
3 sudo restart web2py-scheduler
4 sudo status web2py-scheduler
```

13.3   Windows

13.3.1   Apache and mod_wsgi

Installing Apache, and mod_wsgi under Windows requires a different procedure. Here are assuming Python 2.5 is installed, you are running from source and web2py is located at c:/web2py.

First download the requires packages:

- Apache apache_2.2.11-win32-x86-openssl-0.9.8i.msi from [104]

- mod_wsgi from [105]

Second, run apache...msi and follow the wizard screens. On the server information screen

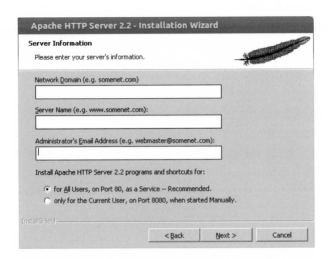

enter all requested values:

- **Network Domain**: enter the DNS domain in which your server is or will be registered in. For example, if your server's full DNS name is server.mydomain.net, you would type mydomain.net here

- **ServerName**: Your server's full DNS name. From the example above, you would type server.mydomain.net here. Enter a fully qualified domain name or IP address from the web2py install, not a shortcut, for more information see [106].

- **Administrator's Email Address**. Enter the server administrator's or webmaster's email address here. This address will be displayed along with error messages to the client by default.

Continue with a typical install to the end unless otherwise required

The wizard, by default, installed Apache in the folder:

```
C:/Program Files/Apache Software Foundation/Apache2.2/
```

From now on we refer to this folder simply as Apache2.2.

Third, copy the downloaded mod_wsgi.so to Apache2.2/modules written by Chris Travers, published by the Open Source Software Lab at Microsoft, December 2007.

Fourth, create server.crt and server.key certificates (as discussed in the previous section) and place them in the folder Apache2.2/conf. Notice the cnf file is in Apache2.2/conf/openssl.cnf.

Fifth, edit Apache2.2/conf/httpd.conf, remove the comment mark (the # character) from the line

```
LoadModule ssl_module modules/mod_ssl.so
```

add the following line after all the other LoadModule lines

```
LoadModule wsgi_module modules/mod_wsgi.so
```

look for "Listen 80" and add this line after it

```
Listen 443
```

append the following lines at the end changing drive letter, port number, ServerName according to your values

```
NameVirtualHost *:443
<VirtualHost *:443>
  DocumentRoot "C:/web2py/applications"
  ServerName server1

  <Directory "C:/web2py">
    Order allow,deny
    Deny from all
  </Directory>

  <Location "/">
    Order deny,allow
    Allow from all
  </Location>

  <LocationMatch "^(/[\w_]*/static/.*)">
    Order Allow,Deny
    Allow from all
  </LocationMatch>

  WSGIScriptAlias / "C:/web2py/wsgihandler.py"

  SSLEngine On
  SSLCertificateFile conf/server.crt
  SSLCertificateKeyFile conf/server.key

  LogFormat "%h %l %u %t "%r" %>s %b" common
  CustomLog logs/access.log common
</VirtualHost>
```

Save and check the config using: [Start > Program > Apache HTTP Server 2.2 > Configure Apache Server > Test Configuration]

If there are no problems you will see a command screen open and close. Now you can start Apache:

[Start > Program > Apache HTTP Server 2.2 > Control Apache Server > Start] or better yet start the taskbar monitor

```
[Start > Program > Apache HTTP Server 2.2 > Control Apache Server]
```

Now you can right-click on the red feather-like taskbar icon to "Open Apache Monitor" and then start, stop and restart Apache as required.

This section was created by Jonathan Lundell.

13.3.2 Start as Windows service

What Linux calls a daemon, Windows calls a service. The web2py server can easily be installed/started/stopped as a Windows service.

In order to use web2py as a Windows service, you must create a file "options.py" with startup parameters:

```
 1  import socket, os
 2  ip = socket.gethostname()
 3  port = 80
 4  password = '<recycle>'
 5  pid_filename = 'httpserver.pid'
 6  log_filename = 'httpserver.log'
 7  ssl_certificate = "
 8  ssl_private_key = "
 9  numthreads = 10
10  server_name = socket.gethostname()
11  request_queue_size = 5
12  timeout = 10
13  shutdown_timeout = 5
14  folder = os.getcwd()
```

You don't need to create "options.py" from scratch since there is already an "options_std.py" in the web2py folder that you can use as a model.

After creating "options.py" in the web2py installation folder, you can install web2py as a service with:

```
 1  python web2py.py -W install
```

optionally you can specify an options.py file:

```
1 python web2py.py -W install -L options.py
```

You can start/stop the service with:

```
1 python web2py.py -W start
2 python web2py.py -W stop
```

13.3.3   Start the scheduler as a Windows service

Running the scheduler as a Windows service makes a lot of sense. The easiest approach is to download nssm (from htp://www.nssm.cc). nssm is an open source scheduling helper. It wraps around an executable command to turn it into a service. The command to start the scheduler is *pythonw.exe -K <appname>* We use nssm to wrap around this, becoming a service. Before doing this, you need to choose a name for your service. There are strong advantages to creating a specific service for each app which needs a scheduler. Therefore, your naming convention for services may be web2py_scheduler_app1

After extracting the zip file, open a Windows command prompt in the folder containing the version for your architecture, and type

```
1 nssm install web2py_scheduler_app1
```

This shows a dialog asking you to enter Application and Options. Application is the pythonw.exe executable from your Python installation. Options is -K app1 where app1 is the name of your application.

It is possible to invoke the scheduler with multiple applications. However, in this mode, web2py detaches each application's scheduler into a subprocess. Therefore, the process started by the service will not die if one of the scheduler instances runs into problems; rather, that child process would die. We then can't take advantage of automatic restarting of services in case of failure. Using one app per service avoids this weakness.

13.4   Securing sessions and admin

It is very dangerous to publicly expose the **admin** application and the **appadmin** controllers unless they run over HTTPS. Moreover, your password and credentials should never be transmitted unencrypted. This is true for web2py and any other web application.

In your applications, if they require authentication, you should make the session cookies secure with:

```
session.secure()
```

An easy way to setup a secure production environment on a server is to first stop web2py and then remove all the parameters_*.py files from the web2py installation folder. Then start web2py without a password. This will completely disable admin and appadmin.

```
nohup python web2py --nogui -p 8001 -i 127.0.0.1 -a '' &
```

Next, start a second web2py instance accessible only from localhost:

```
nohup python web2py --nogui -p 8002 -i 127.0.0.1 -a '<ask>' &
```

and create an SSH tunnel from the local machine (the one from which you wish to access the administrative interface) to the server (the one where web2py is running, example.com), using:

```
ssh -L 8002:127.0.0.1:8002 username@example.com
```

Now you can access the administrative interface locally via the web browser at localhost:8002.

This configuration is secure because **admin** is not reachable when the tunnel is closed (the user is logged out).

> This solution is secure on shared hosts if and only if other users do not have read access to the folder that contains web2py; otherwise users may be able to steal session cookies directly from the server.

13.5   Efficiency and scalability

web2py is designed to be easy to deploy and to setup. This does not mean that it compromises on efficiency or scalability, but it means you may need to tweak it to make it scalable.

In this section we assume multiple web2py installations behind a NAT server that provides local load-balancing.

In this case, web2py works out-of-the-box if some conditions are met. In particular, all instances of each web2py application must access the same database servers and must see the same files. This latter condition can be implemented by making the following folders shared:

```
1  applications/myapp/sessions
2  applications/myapp/errors
3  applications/myapp/uploads
4  applications/myapp/cache
```

The shared folders must support file locking. Possible solutions are ZFS (ZFS was developed by Sun Microsystems and is the preferred choice.), NFS (With NFS you may need to run thenlockmgr daemon to allow file locking.), or Samba (SMB).

It is possible to share the entire web2py folder or the entire applications folder, but this is not a good idea because this would cause a needless increase of network bandwidth usage.

We believe the configuration discussed above to be very scalable because it reduces the database load by moving to the shared filesystems those resources that need to be shared but do not need transactional safety (only one client at a time is supposed to access a session file, cache always needs a global lock, uploads and errors are write once/read many files).

Ideally, both the database and the shared storage should have RAID capability. Do not make the mistake of storing the database on the same storage as the shared folders, or you will create a new bottleneck there.

On a case-by-case basis, you may need to perform additional optimizations and we will discuss them below. In particular, we will discuss how to get rid of these shared folders one-by-one, and how to store the associated data in the database instead. While this is possible, it is not necessarily a good solution. Nevertheless, there may be reasons to do so. One such reason is that sometimes we do not have the freedom to set up shared folders.

13.5.1 Efficiency tricks

web2py application code is executed on every request, so you want to minimize this amount of code. Here is what you can do:

- Run once with `migrate=True` then set all your tables to `migrate=False`.

- Bytecode compile your app using **admin**.

- Use `cache.ram` as much as you can but make sure to use a finite set of keys, or else the amount of cache used will grow arbitrarily.

- Minimize the code in models: do not define functions there, define functions in the controllers that need them or - even better - define functions in modules, import them and use those functions as needed.

- Do not put many functions in the same controller but use many controllers with few functions.

- Call `session.forget(response)` in all controllers and/or functions that do not change the session.

- Try to avoid web2py cron, and use a background process instead. web2py cron can start too many Python instances and cause excessive memory usage.

13.5.2 Sessions in database

It is possible to instruct web2py to store sessions in a database instead of in the sessions folder. This has to be done for each individual web2py application, although they may all use the same database to store sessions.

Given a database connection

```
db = DAL(...)
```

you can store the sessions in this database (db) by simply stating the following, in the same model file that establishes the connection:

```
session.connect(request, response, db)
```

If it does not exist already, web2py creates, under the hood, a table in the database called `web2py_session_appname` containing the following fields:

```
1  Field('locked', 'boolean', default=False),
2  Field('client_ip'),
3  Field('created_datetime', 'datetime', default=now),
4  Field('modified_datetime', 'datetime'),
5  Field('unique_key'),
6  Field('session_data', 'text')
```

"unique_key" is a uuid key used to identify the session in the cookie. "session_data" is the cPickled session data.

To minimize database access, you should avoid storing sessions when they are not needed with:

```
1  session.forget()
```

Sessions are automatically forgotten is unchanged.

With sessions in database, "sessions" folder does not need to be a shared folder because it will no longer be accessed.

> Notice that, if sessions are disabled, you must not pass the session to form.accepts and you cannot use session.flash nor CRUD.

13.5.3   HAProxy a high availability load balancer

If you need multiple web2py processes running on multiple machines, instead of storing sessions in the database or in cache, you have the option to use a load balancer with sticky sessions.

Pound [107] and HAProxy [108] are two HTTP load balancers and Reverse proxies that provides sticky sessions. Here we discuss the latter because it seems to be more common on commercial VPS hosting.

By sticky sessions, we mean that once a session cookie has been issued, the load balancer will always route requests from the client associated to the session, to the same server. This allows you to store the session in the local filesystem without need for a shared filesystem.

To use HAProxy:

First, install it, on out Ubuntu test machine:

```
1  sudo apt-get -y install haproxy
```

Second edit the configuration file "/etc/haproxy.cfg" to something like this:

```
1  ## this config needs haproxy-1.1.28 or haproxy-1.2.1
2
3  global
4        log 127.0.0.1    local0
5        maxconn 1024
6        daemon
7
8  defaults
9        log        global
10       mode       http
11       option  httplog
12       option  httpchk
13       option  httpclose
14       retries 3
15       option redispatch
16       contimeout      5000
17       clitimeout      50000
18       srvtimeout      50000
19
20 listen 0.0.0.0:80
21       balance url_param WEB2PYSTICKY
22       balance roundrobin
23       server  L1_1 10.211.55.1:7003  check
24       server  L1_2 10.211.55.2:7004  check
25       server  L1_3 10.211.55.3:7004  check
26       appsession WEB2PYSTICKY len 52 timeout 1h
```

The listen directive tells HAProxy, which port to wait for connection from. The server directive tells HAProxy where to find the proxied servers. The appsession directory makes a sticky session and uses the a cookie called WEB2PYSTICKY for this purpose.

Third, enable this config file and start HAProxy:

```
1  /etc/init.d/haproxy restart
```

You can find similar instructions to setup Pound at the URL

```
1  http://web2pyslices.com/main/slices/take_slice/33
```

13.5.4 Cleaning up sessions

You should be aware that on a production environment, sessions pile up fast. web2py provides a script called:

```
1  scripts/sessions2trash.py
```

that when run in the background, periodically deletes all sessions that have
not been accessed for a certain amount of time. Web2py provides a script
to cleanup these sessions (it works for both file-based sessions and database
sessions).

Here are some typical use cases:

- Delete expired sessions every 5 minutes:

```
nohup python web2py.py -S app -M -R scripts/sessions2trash.py &
```

- Delete sessions older than 60 minutes regardless of expiration, with
  verbose output, then exit:

```
python web2py.py -S app -M -R scripts/sessions2trash.py -A -o -x 3600 -f -v
```

- Delete all sessions regardless of expiry and exit:

```
python web2py.py -S app -M -R scripts/sessions2trash.py -A -o -x 0
```

Here app is the name of your application.

13.5.5 Uploading files in database

By default, all uploaded files handled by SQLFORMs are safely renamed and
stored in the filesystem under the "uploads" folder. It is possible to instruct
web2py to store uploaded files in the database instead.

Now, consider the following table:

```
db.define_table('dog',
    Field('name')
    Field('image', 'upload'))
```

where dog.image is of type upload. To make the uploaded image go in the
same record as the name of the dog, you must modify the table definition by
adding a blob field and link it to the upload field:

```
db.define_table('dog',
    Field('name')
    Field('image', 'upload', uploadfield='image_data'),
    Field('image_data', 'blob'))
```

Here "image_data" is just an arbitrary name for the new blob field.

Line 3 instructs web2py to safely rename uploaded images as usual, store
the new name in the image field, and store the data in the uploadfield called

"image_data" instead of storing the data on the filesystem. All of this is be done automatically by SQLFORMs and no other code needs to be changed.

With this tweak, the "uploads" folder is no longer needed.

On Google App Engine, files are stored by default in the database without the need to define an uploadfield, since one is created by default.

13.5.6   Collecting tickets

By default, web2py stores tickets (errors) on the local file system. It would not make sense to store tickets directly in the database, because the most common origin of error in a production environment is database failure.

Storing tickets is never a bottleneck, because this is ordinarily a rare event. Hence, in a production environment with multiple concurrent servers, it is more than adequate to store them in a shared folder. Nevertheless, since only the administrator needs to retrieve tickets, it is also OK to store tickets in a non-shared local "errors" folder and periodically collect them and/or clear them.

One possibility is to periodically move all local tickets to the database.

For this purpose, web2py provides the following script:

```
scripts/tickets2db.py
```

By default the script gets the db uri from a file saved into the private folder, **ticket_storage.txt**. This file should contain a string that is passed directly to a **DAL** instance, like:

```
mysql://username:password@localhost/test
postgres://username:password@localhost/test
...
```

This allows to leave the script as it is: if you have multiple applications, it will dynamically choose the right connection for every application. If you want to hardcode the uri in it, edit the second reference to db_string, right after the *except* line. You can run the script with the command:

```
nohup python web2py.py -S myapp -M -R scripts/tickets2db.py &
```

where myapp is the name of your application.

This script runs in the background and moves all tickets every 5 minutes to a table and removes the local tickets. You can later view the errors using the admin app, clicking on the "switch to: db" button at the top, with the same exact functionality as if they were stored on the file system.

With this tweak, the "errors" folder does not need to be a shared folder any more, since errors will be stored into the database.

13.5.7 Memcache

We have shown that web2py provides two types of cache: `cache.ram` and `cache.disk`. They both work on a distributed environment with multiple concurrent servers, but they do not work as expected. In particular, `cache.ram` will only cache at the server level; thus it becomes useless. `cache.disk` will also cache at the server level unless the "cache" folder is a shared folder that supports locking; thus, instead of speeding things up, it becomes a major bottleneck.

The solution is not to use them, but to use memcache instead. web2py comes with a memcache API.

To use memcache, create a new model file, for example `0_memcache.py`, and in this file write (or append) the following code:

```
from gluon.contrib.memcache import MemcacheClient
memcache_servers = ['127.0.0.1:11211']
cache.memcache = MemcacheClient(request, memcache_servers)
cache.ram = cache.disk = cache.memcache
```

The first line imports memcache. The second line has to be a list of memcache sockets (server:port). The third line defines `cache.memcache`. The fourth line redefines `cache.ram` and `cache.disk` in terms of memcache.

You could choose to redefine only one of them to define a totally new cache object pointing to the Memcache object.

With this tweak the "cache" folder does not need to be a shared folder any more, since it will no longer be accessed.

This code requires having memcache servers running on the local network. You should consult the memcache documentation for information on how to setup those servers.

13.5.8   Sessions in memcache

If you do need sessions and you do not want to use a load balancer with sticky sessions, you have the option to store sessions in memcache:

```
from gluon.contrib.memdb import MEMDB
session.connect(request,response,db=MEMDB(cache.memcache))
```

13.5.9   Caching with Redis

[109] An alternative to Memcache is use Redis.

Assuming we have Redis installed and running on localhost at port 6379, we can connect to it using the following code (in a model):

```
from gluon.contrib.redis_cache import RedisCache
cache.redis = RedisCache('localhost:6379',db=None, debug=True)
```

where 'localhost:6379' is the connection string and db is not a DAL object but a Redis database name.

We can now use cache.redis in place of (or along with) cache.ram and cache.disk.

We can also obtain Redis statistics by calling:

```
cache.redis.stats()
```

13.5.10   Sessions in Redis

If you have Redis in your stack, why not use it for sessions ?

```
from gluon.contrib.redis_session import RedisSession
sessiondb = RedisSession('localhost:6379',db=0, session_expiry=False)
session.connect(request, response, db = sessiondb)
```

The code has been tested with 1M sessions. As long as Redis can fit in memory, the time taken to handle 1 or 1M sessions is the same. While against file-based sessions or db-based sessions the speedup is unnoticeable for 40K sessions, over that barrier the improvement is remarkable. You'll end up with

1 key per session, plus 2 keys, one holding an integer (needed for assigning different session keys) and the other holding the set of all sessions generated (so for 1000 sessions, 1002 keys).

If session_expiry is not set, sessions will be handled as usual, you'd need to cleanup sessions as usual once a while.

However, when session_expiry is set will delete automatically sessions after n seconds (e.g. if set to 3600, session will expire exactly one hour later having been updated the last time) You should however occasionally run sessions2trash.py just to clean the key holding the set of all the sessions previously issued (for 1M sessions, cleaning up requires 3 seconds)

13.5.11   Removing applications

In a production setting, it may be better not to install the default applications: **admin**, **examples** and **welcome**. Although these applications are quite small, they are not necessary.

Removing these applications is as easy as deleting the corresponding folders under the applications folder.

13.5.12   Using replicated databases

In a high performance environment you may have a master-slave database architecture with many replicated slaves and perhaps a couple of replicated servers. The DAL can handle this situation and conditionally connect to different servers depending on the request parameters. The API to do this was described in Chapter 6. Here is an example:

```
from random import sample
db = DAL(sample(['mysql://...1','mysql://...2','mysql://...3'], 3))
```

In this case, different HTTP requests will be served by different databases at random, and each DB will be hit more or less with the same probability.

We can also implement a simple Round-Robin

```
def fail_safe_round_robin(*uris):
    i = cache.ram('round-robin', lambda: 0, None)
```

```
3    uris = uris[i:]+uris[:i] # rotate the list of uris
4    cache.ram('round-robin', lambda: (i+1)%len(uris), 0)
5    return uris
6 db = DAL(fail_safe_round_robin('mysql://...1','mysql://...2','mysql://...3'))
```

This is fail-safe in the sense that if the database server assigned to the request fails to connect, DAL will try the next one in the order.

It is also possible to connect to different databases depending on the requested action or controller. In a master-slave database configuration, some action performs only a read and some person both read/write. The former can safely connect to a slave db server, while the latter should connect to a master. So you can do:

```
1 if request.function in read_only_actions:
2     db = DAL(sample(['mysql://...1','mysql://...2','mysql://...3'], 3))
3 if request.action in read_only_actions:
4     db = DAL(shuffle(['mysql://...1','mysql://...2','mysql://...3']))
5 else:
6     db = DAL(sample(['mysql://...3','mysql://...4','mysql://...5'], 3))
```

where 1,2,3 are slaves and 3,4,5 are masters.

13.5.13 Compress static files

Browsers can decompress content on-the-fly, so compressing content for those browsers saves your bandwidth and theirs, lowering response times. Nowadays most web servers can compress your content on the fly and send it to the browsers requesting gzipped content. However, for static files, you are wasting CPU cycles to compress the same content over and over.

You can use *scripts/zip_static_files.py* to create gzipped versions of your static files and serve those without wasting CPU. Run as `python web2py.py -S myapp -R scripts/zip_static_files.py` in cron. The script takes care to create (or update) the gzipped version and saves them along with your files, appending a.gz to their name. You just need to let your webserver know when to send those files [110] [111]

13.6 Deploying on PythonAnywhere

PythonAnywhere

PythonAnywhere is the simplest way to deploy web2py applications.

PythonAnywhere is a Python development and hosting environment that displays in your web browser and runs on cloud servers. They are already set up with everything you need to run Python and they support web2py specifically. In our experience PythonAnywhere is easy to use, fast, and powerful. They also provide MySQL databases, python shells and Dropbox integration. Professional hosting is available if the free basic one is not enough for you.

In order to use PythonAnywhere you need to create an account, login, then use the provided web Dashboard to add a new Web App of type web2py.

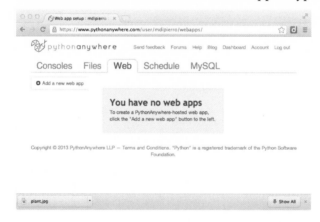

The interface also ask you for an admistrative password.

The web2py folder will be created in your user folder.

Alternatively, you can also use the web based BASH shell to install web2py as you normally do:

```
1 wget http://www.web2py.com/examples/static/web2py_src.zip
2 unzip web2py_src.zip
```

Always from the shell you should create an admin password for later use:

```
1 python -c "from gluon.main import save_password; save_password(raw_input('admin
      password: '),433)"
```

Then visit the "Web" panel using the web interface and edit the "/var/www/<username>_pythonanywhere_com_wsgi.py" file. This is the entry point for your program (in our case web2py) and, as you may guess, it is based on the WSGI protocol.

Edit the "/var/www/<username>_pythonanywhere_com_wsgi.py" file and write in it:

```
1 import sys
2 path = '/home/<username>/web2py'
3 if path not in sys.path: sys.path.append(path)
4 from wsgihandler import application # the web2py handler
```

Here "<username>" is your PythonAnywhere username.

After you've installed web2py, notice that you do not need to start or configure a web server. PythonAnywhere provides one and it is reloaded when you edit the above config file. or press the "Reload web app" button on the Dashboard. Everyone can immediately access it at the url:

```
1 http://yourusername.pythonanywhere.com/
```

They also provide a secure version of the site, and you're forced to use it for using the web2py Administrative interface at:

```
1 https://yourusername.pythonanywhere.com/admin/default/index
```

We thank the PythonAnywhere team for their help and support.

13.7 Deploying on Heroku

[112]

Heroku is a modern and agile multiplatform hosting solution. It allows to push your applications to a server cloud using Git. In order to user Heroku you must have Git installed and you must have the Heroku SDK installed. You interact heroku using the SDK locally and your commands will be pushed and executed on the server.

Applications running on Heroku cannot rely on a persistent filesystem since it is refreshed periodically. For this reason only the application code can be stored on the file system. All data must be stored in the database. Heroku relies on PostgreSQL. Yet the PostgreSQL is also configured using the Heroku SDK and the URI for the database is assigned dynamically at run-time and stored in an environment variable.

This means that web2py applications must be modified to work on Heroku in order to use the database.

Web2py provides a "heroku.py" script to help you. All you need to do is replace:

```
1 db = DAL(...)
```

in your code with:

```
1 from gluon.contrib.heroku import get_db
2 db = get_db(name=None, pool_size=10)
```

Here name is the environment variable containing the Heroku PostgreSQL URI (something like HEROKU_POSTGRESQL_RED_URL). It defaults to None and if there is only one HEROKU_POSTGRESQL_*_URL environment variable it will use that. pool_size is the usual DAL pool size.

When non-running on the Heroku platform get_db will use a development database "sqlite://heroku.test.sqlite".

In both cases sessions will be stored in database.

Web2py provides a script "scripts/setup-web2py-heroku.py" to deploy your web2py installation on heroku. It performs the following steps:

It installs virtualenv and the psycopg2 driver:

```
1 sudo pip install virtualenv
2 sudo pip install psycopg2
```

It creates and activates a virtualenv

```
1 virtualenv venv --distribute
2 source venv/bin/activate
```

Then creates a requirement file:

```
1 pip freeze > requirements.txt
```

And creates a "Procfile" which tells Heroku how to start web2py:

```
1 echo "web: python web2py.py -a 'yourpassword' -i 0.0.0.0 -p \$PORT" > Procfile
```

You can change this line to use a different server. You must edit it to select your own admin password. \$PORT is a variable which is correctly escaped since its value is set at runtime. You should also consider starting web2py with gnuicorn using anyserver.py since this is one of the recommended web servers for Python.

Finally the script creates a Git repository:

```
1 git init
2 git add .
3 git add Procfile
4 git commit -a -m "first commit"
```

pushes everything to Heroku, and starts it:

```
1 heroku create
2 git push heroku master
3 heroku addons:add heroku-postgresql:dev
4 heroku scale web=1
5 heroku open
```

heroku here is a shell command part of the Heroku SDK.

We thank Craig Krestiens from Heroku for his help with this recipe.

13.8 Deploying on EC2

Amazon Elastic Compute Cloud (Amazon EC2) is a web service that provides resizable computing capacity in the cloud. It is one of the largest and most popular clouds. Many other cloud platforms run on EC2. You can run any application on EC2 by creating and deploying a disk image. Amazon then provides API to replicate the image while sharing part of the file system.

A description of the entire process is beyond the scope of this book but, assuming you have an existing Amazon EC2 account, you can use the Turnkey Hub find and deploy a ready made web2py image:

```
https://hub.turnkeylinux.org/amazon/launch/web2py/
```

Once your image is deployed you can login into it as a normal VPS and you can manage (backup/restore/copy) it via the Amazon EC2 web interface.

13.9 Deploying on Google App Engine

It is possible to run web2py code on Google App Engine (GAE) [14], including DAL code.

GAE supports two versions of Python: 2.5 (default) and 2.7 (beta). web2y supports both but uses 2.5 by default (this may change in the future). Look into the "app.yaml" file described below for configuration details.

GAE also supports a Google SQL database (compatible with MySQL) and a Google NoSQL (referred to as "Datastore"). web2py supports both. If you wish to use Google SQL database follow the instructions on Chapter 6. This section assumes you will be using the Google Datastore.

The GAE platform provides several advantages over normal hosting solutions:

- Ease of deployment. Google completely abstracts the underlying architecture.

- Scalability. Google will replicate your app as many times as it takes to serve all concurrent requests.

- One can choose between a SQL and a NoSQL database (or both together).

But also some disadvantages:

- No read or write access to the file system.

- No HTTPS unless you use the appspot.com domain with a Google certificate.

and some Datastore specific disadvantages:

- No typical transactions.

- No complex datastore queries. In particular there are no JOIN, LIKE, and DATE/DATETIME operators.

- No multiple OR sub-queries unless they involve one and the same field.

Because of the read-only filesystem, web2py cannot store sessions, error tickets, cache files and uploaded files in the filesystem; they must be stored in the datastore and not in the filesystem.

Here we provide a quick overview of GAE and we focus on web2py specific issues, we refer you to the official GAE documentation online for details.

Attention: At the time of writing, GAE supports only Python 2.5. Any other version will cause problems. You also must run the web2py source distribution, not a binary distribution.

13.9.1   Configuration

There are three configuration files to be aware of:

```
1 web2py/app.yaml
2 web2py/queue.yaml
3 web2py/index.yaml
```

app.yaml and queue.yaml are most easily created by using the template files app.example.yaml and queue.example.yaml as starting points. index.yaml is created automatically by the Google deployment software.

app.yaml has the following structure (it has been shortened using...):

```
 1 application: web2py
 2 version: 1
 3 api_version: 1
 4 runtime: python
 5 handlers:
 6 - url: /_ah/stats.*
 7   ...
 8 - url: /(?P<a>.+?)/static/(?P<b>.+)
 9   ...
10 - url: /_ah/admin/.*
11   ...
12 - url: /_ah/queue/default
13   ...
14 - url: .*
15   ...
16 skip_files:
17   ...
```

app.example.yaml (when copied to app.yaml) is configured to deploy the web2py welcome application, but not the admin or example applications. You must replace web2py with the application id that you used when registering with Google App Engine.

url: /(.+?)/static/(.+) instructs GAE to serve your app static files directly, without calling web2py logic, for speed.

url:.* instructs web2py to use the gaehandler.py for every other request.

The skip_files: session is list of regular expressions for files that do not need to deployed on GAE. In particular the lines:

```
(applications/(admin|examples)/.*)|
((admin|examples|welcome)\.(w2p|tar))|
```

tell GAE not to deploy the default applications, except for the unpacked welcome scaffolding application. You can add more applications to be ignored here.

Except for the application id and version, you probably do not need to edit app.yaml, though you may wish to exclude the welcome application.

The file queue.yaml is used to configure GAE task queues.

The file index.yaml is automatically generated when you run your application locally using the GAE appserver (the web server that comes with the Google SDK). It contains something like this:

```
indexes:
- kind: person
  properties:
  - name: name
    direction: desc
```

In this example it tells GAE to create an index for table "person" that will be used to sort by "name" in reversed alphabetical order. You will not be able to search and sort records in your app without corresponding indexes.

It is important to always run your apps locally with the appserver and try every functionality of your app, before deployment. This will be important for testing purposes, but also to automatically generate the "index.yaml" file. Occasionally you may want to edit this file and perform cleanup, such as removing duplicate entries.

13.9.2 Running and deployment

Linux

Here we assume you have installed the GAE SDK. At the time of writing, GAE runs on Python 2.5.2. You can run your app from inside the "web2py" folder by using the appserver command:

```
python2.5 dev_appserver.py ../web2py
```

This will start the appserver and you can run your application at the URL:

```
http://127.0.0.1:8080/
```

In order to upload your app on GAE, make sure you have edited the "app.yaml" file as explained before and set the proper application id, then run:

```
python2.5 appcfg.py update ../web2py
```

Mac, Windows

On Mac and Windows, you can also use the Google App Engine Launcher. You can download the software from ref. [14].

Choose [File][Add Existing Application], set the path to the path of the top-level web2py folder, and press the [Run] button in the toolbar. After you have tested that it works locally, you can deploy it on GAE by simply clicking on the [Deploy] button on the toolbar (assuming you have an account).

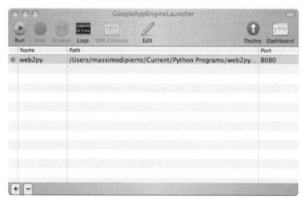

On GAE, the web2py tickets/errors are also logged into the GAE administration console where logs can be accessed and searched online.

13.9.3   Configuring the handler

The file gaehandler.py is responsible for serving files on GAE and it has a few options. Here are their default values:

```
LOG_STATS = False
APPSTATS = True
DEBUG = False
```

LOG_STATS will log the time to serve pages in the GAE logs.

APPSTATS will enable GAE appstats which provides profiling statistics. They will be made available at the URL:

```
http://localhost:8080/_ah/stats
```

DEBUG sets debug mode. It make no difference in practice unless checked explicitly in your code via gluon.settings.web2py_runtime.

13.9.4   Avoid the filesystem

On GAE you have no access to the filesystem. You cannot open any file for writing.

For this purpose, on GAE, web2py automatically stores all uploaded files in the datastore, whether or not "upload" Field(s) have a uploadfield attribute.

You also should store sessions and tickets in the database and you have to be explicit:

```
if request.env.web2py_runtime_gae
    db = DAL('gae')
    session.connect(request,response,db)
else:
    db = DAL('sqlite://storage.sqlite')
```

The above code checks whether you are running on GAE, connects to BigTable, and instructs web2py to store sessions and tickets in there. It connects to a sqlite database otherwise. This code is already in the scaffolding app in the file "db.py".

13.9.5 Memcache

If you prefer, you can store sessions in memcache:

```
from gluon.contrib.gae_memcache import MemcacheClient
from gluon.contrib.memdb import MEMDB
cache.memcache = MemcacheClient(request)
cache.ram = cache.disk = cache.memcache

db = DAL('gae')
session.connect(request,response,MEMDB(cache.memcache))
```

Notice that on GAE cache.ram and cache.disk should not be used, so we make them point to cache.memcache.

13.9.6 Datastore issues

The absence of multi-entity transactions and typical functionalities of relational databases are what sets GAE apart from other hosting environment. This is the price to pay for high scalability. GAE is an excellent platform if these limitations are tolerable; if not, then a regular hosting platform with a relational database should be considered instead.

If a web2py application does not run on GAE, it is because of one of the limitations discussed above. Most issues can be resolved by removing JOINs from web2py queries and de-normalizing the database.

Google App Engine supports some special field types, such as ListProperty and StringListProperty. You can use these types with web2py using the following old syntax:

```
from gluon.dal import gae
db.define_table('product',
    Field('name'),
    Field('tags', type=gae.StringListProperty()))
```

or the equivalent new syntax:

```
db.define_table('product',
    Field('name'),
    Field('tags', 'list:string'))
```

In both cases the "tags" field is a StringListProperty therefore its values must be lists of strings, compatibly with the GAE documentation. The second notation is to be preferred because web2py will treat the field in a smarter way in the context of forms and because it will work with relational databases too.

Similarly, web2py supports list:integer and list:reference which map into a ListProperty(int).

list types are discussed in more detail in Chapter 6.

13.9.7   GAE and https

If you application has id "myapp" your GAE domain is

```
http://myapp.appspot.com/
```

and it can also be accessed via HTTPS

```
https://myapp.appspot.com/
```

In this case it will use an "appspot.com" certificate provided by Google.

You can register a DNS entry and use any other domain name you own for your app but you will not be able to use HTTPS on it. At the time of writing, this is a GAE limitation.

14

Other recipes

14.1 Upgrading

In the "site" page of the administrative interface there is an "upgrade now"
button. In case this is not feasible or does not work (for example because of
a file locking issue), upgrading web2py manually is very easy.

┃ Simply unzip the latest version of web2py over the old installation.

This will upgrade all the libraries as well as the applications **admin**,
examples, welcome. It will also create a new empty file "NEWINSTALL".
Upon restarting, web2py will delete the empty file and package the welcome
app into "welcome.w2p" that will be used as the new scaffolding app.
web2py does not upgrade any file in other existing applications.

14.2 How to distribute your applications as binaries

It is possible to bundle your app with the web2py binary distribution and
distribute them together. The license allows this as long you make clear in
the license of your app that you are bundling with web2py and add a link to
the web2py.com.

Here we explain how to do it for Windows:

- Create your app as usual

- Using **admin**, bytecode compile your app (one click)

- Using **admin**, pack your app compiled (another click)

- Create a folder "myapp"

- Download a web2py windows binary distribution

- Unzip it in folder "myapp" and start it (two clicks)

- Upload using **admin** the previously packed and compiled app with the name "init" (one click)

- Create a file "myapp/start.bat" that contains "cd web2py; web2py.exe"

- Create a file "myapp/license" that contains a license for your app and make sure it states that it is being "distributed with an unmodified copy of web2py from web2py.com"

- Zip the myapp folder into a file "myapp.zip"

- Distribute and/or sell "myapp.zip"

When users will unzip "myapp.zip" and click "run" they will see your app instead of the "welcome" app. There is no requirement on the user side, not even Python pre-installed.

For Mac binaries the process is the same but there is no need for the "bat" file.

14.3 WingIDE, Rad2Py, and Eclipse

You can use web2py with third party IDEs with as WingIDE, Rad2Py, and Eclipse.

Here is a screenshot of using web2py with WingIDE:

The general problem with these IDEs (except Rad2Py which is designed specifically to work with web2py) is that they do not understand the context in which models and controllers are executed and therefore autocompletion does not work out of the box.

To make autocompletion work the general trick consists in editing your models and controllers and adding the following code:

```
1  if False:
2      from gluon import *
3      request = current.request
4      response = current.response
5      session = current.session
6      cache = current.cache
7      T = current.T
```

it does not change the logic as this is never executed but it forces the IDE to parse it and understand where the objects in the global namespace come from (the gluon module) thus making autocompletion work.

14.4 SQLDesigner

There is a software called SQLDesigner which allows you to build web2py models visually and then generate the corresponding code. Here is a screenshot.

The version of SQLDesigner which works with web2py can be found here:

`https://github.com/elcio/visualdal`

14.5   Publishing a folder

Consider the problem of sharing a folder (and subfolders) on the web.
web2py makes this very easy. You just need a controller like this:

```
from gluon.tools import Expose
def myfolder():
    return dict(files=Expose('/path/to/myfolder'))
```

which you can render in a view with {{=fiels}}. It will create an interface to
view the files and folders, and navigate the tree structure. Images will have
a preview.

The path prefix "/path/to/myfolder" will be hidden to the visitors. For
example a file called "/path/to/myfolder/a/b.txt" and replaced with
"base/a/b.txt".   The "base" prefix can be specified using the basename
argument of the Expose function. Using the argument extensions can specify
a list of file extensions to be listed, other files will be hidden. For example:

```
def myfolder():
    return dict(files=Expose('/path/to/myfolder',basename='.',
                    extensions=['.py', '.jpg']))
```

Files and folders that contain the word "private" in the path or have file that
start with "." or terminate in " " are always hidden.

14.6 Functional testing

web2py comes with a module `gluon.contrib.webclient` which allows functional testing of local and remote web2py applications. Actually, this module is not web2py specific and it can be used for testing and interacting programmatically with any web application, yet it is designed to understand web2py session and web2py postbacks.

Here is an example of usage. The program below creates a client, connects to the "index" action in order to establish a session, registers a new user, then logouts, and logins again using the newly created credentials:

```
from gluon.contrib.webclient import WebClient

client = WebClient('http://127.0.0.1:8000/welcome/default/',
                   postbacks=True)

client.get('index')
# register
data = dict(first_name = 'Homer',
            last_name = 'Simpson',
            email = 'homer@web2py.com',
            password = 'test',
            password_two = 'test',
            _formname = 'register')
client.post('user/register',data = data)

# logout
client.get('user/logout')

# login again
data = dict(email='homer@web2py.com',
            password='test',
            _formname = 'login')
client.post('user/login',data = data)

# check registration and login were successful
client.get('index')
assert('Welcome Homer' in client.text)
```

The WebClient constructor takes a URL prefix as argument. In the example that is "http://127.0.0.1:8000/welcome/default/". It does not perform any network IO. The `postbacks` argument defaults to `True` and tells the client how to handle web2py postbacks.

The WebClient object, client, has only two methods: get and post. The first argument is always a URL postfix. The full URL for the GET of POST request is constructed simply by concatenating the prefix and the postfix. The purpose of this is imply making the syntax less verbose for long conversations between client and server.

data is a parameter specific of POST request and contains a dictionary of the data to be posted. Web2py forms have a hidden _formname field and its value must be provided unless there is a single form in the page. Web2py forms also contain a hidden _formkey field which is designed to prevent CSRF attacked. It is handled automatically by WebClient.

Both client.get and client.post accept the following extra arguments:

- headers: a dictionary of optional HTTP headers.

- cookies: a dictionary of optional HTTP cookies.

- auth: a dictionary of parameters to be passed to urllib2.HTTPBasicAuthHandler().add_password(**auth) in order to perform basic authentication. For more information about this we refer to the Python documentation for the urllib2 module.

The client object in the example carries on a conversation with the server specified in the constructor by making GET and POST requests. It automatically handles all cookies and sends them back to maintain sessions. If it detects that a new session cookie is issued while an existing one is already present, it interprets it as a broken session and raises an exception. If the server returns an HTTP error, it raises an exception. If the server returns an HTTP error which contains a web2py ticket, it returns a RuntimeError exception containing the ticket code.

The client object maintains a log of requests in client.history and a state associated with its last successful request. The state consists of:

- client.status: the returned status code

- client.text: the content of the page

- client.headers: a dictionary of parsed headers

- `client.cookies`: a dictionary of parsed cookies

- `client.sessions`: a dictionary of web2py sessions in the form {appname: session_id}.

- `client.forms`: a dictionary of web2py forms detected in the client.text. The dictionary has the form {_formname,_formkey}.

The WebClient object does not perform any parsing of the `client.text` returned by the server but this can easily be accomplished with many third-party modules such as BeautifulSoup. For example here is an example code that finds all links in a page downloaded by the client and checks all of them:

```
from BeautifulSoup import BeautifulSoup
dom = BeautifulSoup(client.text)
for link in dom.findAll('a'):
    new_client = WebClient()
    new_client.get(a.href)
    print new_client.status
```

14.7 Building a minimalist web2py

Some times we need to deploy web2py in a server with very small memory footprint. In this case we want to strip down web2py to its bare minimum.

An easy way to do it is the following:

- On a production machine, install the full web2py from source

- From inside the main web2py folder run

```
python scripts/make_min_web2py.py /path/to/minweb2py
```

- Now copy under "/path/to/minweb2py/applications" the applications you want to deploy

- Deploy "/path/to/minweb2py" to the small footprint server

The script "make_min_web2py.py" builds a minimalist web2py distribution that does not include:

- admin

- examples

- welcome

- scripts

- rarely used contrib modules

It does include a "welcome" app consisting of a single file to allow testing deployment. Look into this script. At the top it contains a detailed list of what is included and what is ignored. You can easily modify it and tailor to your needs.

14.8   Fetching an external URL

Python includes the urllib library for fetching urls:

```
import urllib
page = urllib.urlopen('http://www.web2py.com').read()
```

This is often fine, but the urllib module does not work on the Google App Engine. Google provides a different API for downloading URLs that works on GAE only. In order to make your code portable, web2py includes a fetch function that works on GAE as well as other Python installations:

```
from gluon.tools import fetch
page = fetch('http://www.web2py.com')
```

14.9   Pretty dates

It is often useful to represent a datetime not as "2009-07-25 14:34:56" but as "one year ago". web2py provides a utility function for this:

```
import datetime
d = datetime.datetime(2009,7,25,14,34,56)
from gluon.tools import prettydate
pretty_d = prettydate(d,T)
```

The second argument (T) must be passed to allow internationalization for the output.

14.10   Geocoding

If you need to convert an address (for example: "243 S Wabash Ave, Chicago, IL, USA") into geographical coordinates (latitude and longitude), web2py provides a function to do so.

```
from gluon.tools import geocode
address = '243 S Wabash Ave, Chicago, IL, USA'
(latitude, longitude) = geocode(address)
```

The function geocode requires a network connection and it connects to the Google geocoding service for the geocoding. The function returns (0,0) in case of failure. Notice that the Google geocoding service caps the number of requests, so you should check their service agreement. The geocode function is built on top of the fetch function and thus it works on GAE.

14.11   Pagination

This recipe is a useful trick to minimize database access in case of pagination, e.g., when you need to display a list of rows from a database but you want to distribute the rows over multiple pages.

Start by creating a **primes** application that stores the first 1000 prime numbers in a database.

Here is the model db.py:

```
db = DAL('sqlite://primes.db')
db.define_table('prime',Field('value','integer'))
def isprime(p):
    for i in range(2,p):
        if p%i==0: return False
    return True
if len(db().select(db.prime.id))==0:
    p=2
    for i in range(1000):
        while not isprime(p): p+=1
        db.prime.insert(value=p)
        p+=1
```

Now create an action list_items in the "default.py" controller that reads like this:

```
1  def list_items():
2      if len(request.args): page=int(request.args[0])
3      else: page=0
4      items_per_page=20
5      limitby=(page*items_per_page,(page+1)*items_per_page+1)
6      rows=db().select(db.prime.ALL,limitby=limitby)
7      return dict(rows=rows,page=page,items_per_page=items_per_page)
```

Notice that this code selects one more item than is needed, 20+1. The extra element tells the view whether there is a next page.

Here is the "default/list_items.html" view:

```
1  {{extend 'layout.html'}}
2
3  {{for i,row in enumerate(rows):}}
4  {{if i==items_per_page: break}}
5  {{=row.value}}<br />
6  {{pass}}
7
8  {{if page:}}
9  <a href="{{=URL(args=[page-1])}}">previous</a>
10 {{pass}}
11
12 {{if len(rows)>items_per_page:}}
13 <a href="{{=URL(args=[page+1])}}">next</a>
14 {{pass}}
```

In this way we have obtained pagination with one single select per action, and that one select only selects one row more than we need.

14.12 httpserver.log and the Log File Format

The web2py web server logs all requests to a file called:

```
1  httpserver.log
```

in the root web2py directory. An alternative filename and location can be specified via web2py command-line options.

New entries are appended to the end of the file each time a request is made. Each line looks like this:

```
1  127.0.0.1, 2008-01-12 10:41:20, GET, /admin/default/site, HTTP/1.1, 200, 0.270000
```

The format is:

```
1  ip, timestamp, method, path, protocol, status, time_taken
```

Where

- ip is the IP address of the client who made the request

- timestamp is the date and time of the request in ISO 8601 format, YYYY-MM-DDT HH:MM:SS

- method is either GET or POST

- path is the path requested by the client

- protocol is the HTTP protocol used to send to the client, usually HTTP/1.1

- status is the one of the HTTP status codes [113]

- time_taken is the amount of time the server took to process the request, in seconds, not including upload/download time.

In the appliances repository [24], you will find an appliance for log analysis.

This logging is disabled by default when using mod_wsgi since it would be the same as the Apache log.

14.13 Populating database with dummy data

For testing purposes, it is convenient to be able to populate database tables with dummy data. web2py includes a Bayesian classifier already trained to generate dummy but readable text for this purpose.

Here is the simplest way to use it:

```
from gluon.contrib.populate import populate
populate(db.mytable,100)
```

It will insert 100 dummy records into db.mytable. It will try to do intelligently by generating short text for string fields, longer text for text fields, integers, doubles, dates, datetimes, times, booleans, etc. for the corresponding fields. It will try to respect requirements imposed by validators. For fields containing the word "name" it will try to generate dummy names. For reference fields it will generate valid references.

If you have two tables (A and B) where B references A, make sure to populate A first and B second.

Because population is done in a transaction, do not attempt to populate too many records at once, particularly if references are involved. Instead, populate 100 at a time, commit, loop.

```
for i in range(10):
    populate(db.mytable,100)
    db.commit()
```

You can use the Bayesian classifier to learn some text and generate dummy text that sounds similar but should not make sense:

```
from gluon.contrib.populate import Learner, IUP
ell=Learner()
ell.learn('some very long input text ...')
print ell.generate(1000,prefix=None)
```

14.14   Accepting credit card payments

There are multiple ways to accept credit card payments online. web2py provides specific APIs for some of the most popular and practical ones:

- Google Wallet [50]

- PayPal paypalcite

- Stripe.com [51]

- Authorize.net [52]

- DowCommerece [53]

The first two mechanisms above delegate the process of authenticating the payee to an external service. While this is the best solution for security (your app does not handle any credit card information at all) it makes the process cumbersome (the user must login twice; for example, once with your app, and once with Google) and does not allow your app to handle recurrent payments in an automated way.

There are times when you need more control and you want to generate yourself the entry form for the credit card info and than programmatically ask the processor to transfer money from the credit card to your account.

For this reason web2py provide integration out of the box with Stripe, Authorize.net (the module was developed by John Conde and slightly modified) and DowCommerce. Stripe is the simplest to use and also the cheapest for low volume of transactions (they charge no fix cost but charge about 3% per transaction). Authorize.net is better for high volumes (has a fixed yearly costs plus a lower cost per transaction).

Mind that in the case of Stripe and Authorize.net your program will be accepting credit cards information. You do not have to store this information and we advise you not to because of the legal requirements involved (check with Visa or MasterCard), but there are times when you may want to store the information for recurrent payments or to reproduce the Amazon one-click pay button.

14.14.1   Google Wallet

The simplest way to use Google Wallet (Level 1) consists of embedding a button on your page that, when clicked, redirects your visitor to a payment page provided by Google.

First of all you need to register a Google Merchant Account at the url:

```
https://checkout.google.com/sell
```

You will need to provide Google with your bank information. Google will assign you a merchant_id and a merchant_key (do not confuse them, keep them secret).

Then you simply need to create the following code in your view:

```
{{from gluon.contrib.google_wallet import button}}
{{=button(merchant_id="123456789012345",
        products=[dict(name="shoes",
                    quantity=1,
                    price=23.5,
                    currency='USD',
                    description="running shoes black")])}}
```

When a visitor clicks on the button, the visitor will be redirected to the Google page where he/she can pay for the items. Here products is a list of products and each product is a dictionary of parameters that you want to pass describing your items (name, quantity, price, currency, description, and other optional ones which you can find described in the Google Wallet documentation).

If you choose to use this mechanism, you may want to generate the values passed to the button programmatically based on your inventory and the visitor shopping chart.

All the tax and shipping information will be handled on the Google side. Same for accounting information. By default your application is not notified that the transaction has been completed therefore you will have to visit your Google Merchant site to see which products have been purchased and paid for, and which products you need to ship to your buyers there. Google will also send you an email with the information.

If you want a tighter integration, you have to use the Level 2 notification API. In that case you can pass more information to Google and Google will call your API to notify about purchases. This allows you to keep accounting information within your application but it requires you expose web services that can talk to Google Wallet.

This is a considerable more difficult problem but such API has already been implemented and it is available as plugin from

```
http://web2py.com/plugins/static/web2py.plugin.google_checkout.w2p
```

You can find the documentation of the plugin in the plugin itself.

14.14.2   Paypal

Paypal integration is not described here but you can find more information about it at this resource:

```
http://www.web2pyslices.com/main/slices/take_slice/9
```

14.14.3   Stripe.com

This is probably one of the easiest way and flexible ways to accept credit card payments.

You need to register with Stripe.com and that is a very easy process, in fact Stripe will assign you an API key to try even before you create any credentials.

Once you have the API key you can accept credit cards with the following code:

```
from gluon.contrib.stripe import Stripe
stripe = Stripe(api_key)
d = stripe.charge(amount=100,
                  currency='usd',
                  card_number='4242424242424242',
                  card_exp_month='5',
                  card_exp_year='2012',
                  card_cvc_check='123',
                  description='the usual black shoes')
if d.get('paid',False):
    # payment accepted
elif:
    # error is in d.get('error','unknown')
```

The response, d, is a dictionary which you can explore yourself. The card number used in the example is a sandbox and it will always succeed. Each transaction is associated to a transaction id stored in d['id'].

Stripe also allows you to verify a transaction at a later time:

```
d = Stripe(key).check(d['id'])
```

and refund a transaction:

```
r = Stripe(key).refund(d['id'])
if r.get('refunded',False):
    # refund was successful
elif:
    # error is in d.get('error','unknown')
```

Stripe makes very easy to keep the accounting within your application.

All the communications between your app and Stripe go over RESTful web services. Stripe actually exposes even more services and provides a larger set of Python API. You can read more on their web site.

14.14.4   Authorize.Net

Another simple way to accept credit cards is to use Authorize.Net. As usual you need to register and you will obtain a `login` and a transaction key (`transkey`. Once you have them it works very much like Stripe does:

```
from gluon.contrib.AuthorizeNet import process
if process(creditcard='4427802641004797',
           expiration="122012,
           total=100.0,cvv='123',tax=None,invoice=None,
           login='cnpdev4289', transkey='SR2P8g4jdEn7vFLQ',testmode=True):
    # payment was processed
else:
    # payment was rejected
```

If you have a valid Authorize.Net account you should replace the sandbox `login` and `transkey` with those of your account, set `testmode=False` to run on the real platform instead of the sandbox, and use credit card information provided by the visitor.

If `process` returns `True`, the money has been transferred from the visitor credit card account to your Authorize.Net account. `invoice` is just a string that you can set and will be store by Authorize.Net with this transaction so that you can reconcile the data with the information in your application.

Here is a more complex example of workflow where more variables are exposed:

```
from gluon.contrib.AuthorizeNet import AIM
payment = AIM(login='cnpdev4289',
              transkey='SR2P8g4jdEn7vFLQ',
              testmod=True)
payment.setTransaction(creditcard, expiration, total, cvv, tax, invoice)
payment.setParameter('x_duplicate_window', 180) # three minutes duplicate windows
payment.setParameter('x_cust_id', '1324')       # customer ID
payment.setParameter('x_first_name', 'Agent')
payment.setParameter('x_last_name', 'Smith')
payment.setParameter('x_company', 'Test Company')
payment.setParameter('x_address', '1234 Main Street')
payment.setParameter('x_city', 'Townsville')
payment.setParameter('x_state', 'NJ')
payment.setParameter('x_zip', '12345')
payment.setParameter('x_country', 'US')
payment.setParameter('x_phone', '800-555-1234')
payment.setParameter('x_description', 'Test Transaction')
payment.setParameter('x_customer_ip', socket.gethostbyname(socket.gethostname()))
```

```
19 payment.setParameter('x_email', 'you@example.com')
20 payment.setParameter('x_email_customer', False)
21
22 payment.process()
23 if payment.isApproved():
24     print 'Response Code: ', payment.response.ResponseCode
25     print 'Response Text: ', payment.response.ResponseText
26     print 'Response: ', payment.getResultResponseFull()
27     print 'Transaction ID: ', payment.response.TransactionID
28     print 'CVV Result: ', payment.response.CVVResponse
29     print 'Approval Code: ', payment.response.AuthCode
30     print 'AVS Result: ', payment.response.AVSResponse
31 elif payment.isDeclined():
32     print 'Your credit card was declined by your bank'
33 elif payment.isError():
34     print 'It did not work'
35 print 'approved',payment.isApproved()
36 print 'declined',payment.isDeclined()
37 print 'error',payment.isError()
```

Notice the code above uses a dummy test account. You need to register with Authorize.Net (it is not a free service) and provide your own login, transkey, testmode=True or False to the AIM constructor.

14.15   Dropbox API

Dropbox is a very popular storage service. It not only stores your files but it keeps the cloud storage in sync with all your machines. It allows you to create groups and give read/write permissions to the various folders to individual users or groups. It also keeps version history of all your files. It includes a folder called "Public" and each file you put in there will have its own public URL. Dropbox is a great way to collaborate.

You can access dropbox easily by registering at

```
1 https://www.dropbox.com/developers
```

you will get an APP_KEY and an APP_SECRET. Once you have them you can use Dropbox to authenticate your users.

Create a file called "yourapp/private/dropbox.key" and in it write

```
1 <APP_KEY>:<APP_SECERT>:app_folder
```

where <APP_KEY> and APP_SECRET are your key and secret.

Then in "models/db.py" do:

```
1 from gluon.contrib.login_methods.dropbox_account import use_dropbox
2 use_janrain(auth,filename='private/dropbox.key')
3 mydropbox = auth.settings.login_form
```

This will allow users to login into your app using their dropbox credentials, and your program will be able to upload files into their dropbox account:

```
1 stream = open('localfile.txt','rb')
2 mydropbox.put('destfile.txt',stream)
```

download files:

```
1 stream = mydropbox.get('destfile.txt')
2 open('localfile.txt','wb').write(read)
```

and get directory listings:

```
1 contents = mydropbox.dir(path = '/')['contents']
```

14.16 Twitter API

Here are some quick examples on how to post/get tweets. No third-party libraries are required, since Twitter uses simple RESTful APIs.

Here is an example of how to post a tweet:

```
1 def post_tweet(username,password,message):
2     import urllib, urllib2, base64
3     import gluon.contrib.simplejson as sj
4     args= urllib.urlencode([('status',message)])
5     headers={}
6     headers['Authorization'] = 'Basic '+base64.b64encode(
7         username+':'+password)
8     req = urllib2.Request(
9         'http://twitter.com/statuses/update.json',
10        args, headers)
11    return  sj.loads(urllib2.urlopen(req).read())
```

Here is an example of how to receive tweets:

```
1 def get_tweets():
2     user='web2py'
3     import urllib
4     import gluon.contrib.simplejson as sj
5     page = urllib.urlopen('http://twitter.com/%s?format=json' % user).read()
6     tweets=XML(sj.loads(page)['#timeline'])
7     return dict(tweets=tweets)
```

For more complex operations, refer to the Twitter API documentation.

14.17 Streaming virtual files

It is common for malicious attackers to scan web sites for vulnerabilities. They use security scanners like Nessus to explore the target web sites for scripts that are known to have vulnerabilities. An analysis of web server logs from a scanned machine or directly in the Nessus database reveals that most of the known vulnerabilities are in PHP scripts and ASP scripts. Since we are running web2py, we do not have those vulnerabilities, but we will still be scanned for them. This is annoying, so we like to respond to those vulnerability scans and make the attacker understand their time is being wasted.

One possibility is to redirect all requests for.php,.asp, and anything suspicious to a dummy action that will respond to the attack by keeping the attacker busy for a large amount of time. Eventually the attacker will give up and will not scan us again.

This recipe requires two parts.

A dedicated application called **jammer** with a "default.py" controller as follows:

```
class Jammer():
    def read(self,n): return 'x'*n
def jam(): return response.stream(Jammer(),40000)
```

When this action is called, it responds with an infinite data stream full of "x"-es. 40000 characters at a time.

The second ingredient is a "route.py" file that redirects any request ending in.php,.asp, etc. (both upper case and lower case) to this controller.

```
route_in=(
 ('.*\.(php|PHP|asp|ASP|jsp|JSP)','jammer/default/jam'),
)
```

The first time you are attacked you may incur a small overhead, but our experience is that the same attacker will not try twice.

Index

Bibliography

[1] http://www.web2py.com

[2] http://www.python.org

[3] http://en.wikipedia.org/wiki/SQL

[4] http://www.sqlite.org/

[5] http://www.mysql.com/

[6] http://www.postgresql.org/

[7] http://www.microsoft.com/sqlserver

[8] http://www.firebirdsql.org/

[9] http://www.oracle.com/database/index.html

[10] http://www-01.ibm.com/software/data/db2/

[11] http://www-01.ibm.com/software/data/informix/

[12] http://www.ingres.com/

[13] http://www.mongodb.org/

[14] http://code.google.com/appengine/

[15] http://en.wikipedia.org/wiki/HTML

[16] http://www.w3.org/TR/REC-html40/

[17] http://www.php.net/

[18] http://www.owasp.org

[19] https://launchpad.net/rocket

[20] http://en.wikipedia.org/wiki/Web_Server_Gateway_Interface

[21] http://www.python.org/dev/peps/pep-0333/

[22] http://en.wikipedia.org/wiki/Secure_Sockets_Layer

[23] http://www.pythonsecurity.org

[24] http://www.web2py.com/appliances

[25] http://www.web2py.com/examples/default/usergroups

[26] http://www.web2py.com/AlterEgo

[27] http://www.python.org/dev/peps/pep-0008/

[28] http://www.gnu.org/licenses/lgpl.html

[29] http://www.cdolivet.com/editarea/

[30] http://pypi.python.org/pypi/simplejson

[31] http://pyrtf.sourceforge.net/

[32] http://www.dalkescientific.com/Python/PyRSS2Gen.html

[33] http://packages.python.org/feedparser/

[34] https://github.com/trentm/python-markdown2

[35] http://www.tummy.com/Community/software/python-memcached/

[36] http://jquery.com/

[37] http://www.network-theory.co.uk/docs/pytut/

[38] http://oreilly.com/catalog/9780596158071

[39] http://www.python.org/doc/

[40] http://en.wikipedia.org/wiki/Cascading_Style_Sheets

[41] http://www.w3.org/Style/CSS/

[42] http://www.w3schools.com/css/

[43] http://en.wikipedia.org/wiki/JavaScript

[44] http://www.amazon.com/dp/0596000480

[45] http://www.xmlrpc.com/

[46] http://oembed.com/

[47] http://code.google.com/p/rad2py/wiki/
     QdbRemotePythonDebugger

[48] http://en.wikipedia.org/wiki/Hypertext_Transfer_Protocol

[49] http://www.w3.org/Protocols/rfc2616/rfc2616.html

[50] https://wallet.google.com/manage

[51] https://stripe.com/

[52] http://www.authorize.net/

[53] http://www.dowcommerce.com/

[54] http://en.wikipedia.org/wiki/Pluggable_Authentication_
     Modules

[55] http://docs.python.org/2/library/cookie.html#id2

[56] http://en.wikipedia.org/wiki/Cron#CRON_expression

[57] http://peak.telecommunity.com/DevCenter/EasyInstall

[58] http://www.pip-installer.org

[59] http://en.wikipedia.org/wiki/XML

[60] http://www.w3.org/XML/

[61] http://en.wikipedia.org/wiki/XHTML

[62] http://www.w3.org/TR/xhtml1/

[63] http://www.w3schools.com/xhtml/

[64] http://www.modernizr.com/

[65] http://twitter.github.com/bootstrap/

[66] http://sourceforge.net/projects/zxjdbc/

[67] http://pypi.python.org/pypi/psycopg2

[68] http://pybrary.net/pg8000/

[69] https://github.com/petehunt/PyMySQL

[70] http://sourceforge.net/projects/mysql-python

[71] http://python.net/crew/atuining/cx_Oracle/

[72] http://pyodbc.sourceforge.net/

[73] http://kinterbasdb.sourceforge.net/

[74] http://informixdb.sourceforge.net/

[75] http://pypi.python.org/simple/ingresdbi/

[76] http://www.cubrid.org/

[77] http://www.sybase.com/

[78] http://www.teradata.com/products-and-services/database

[79] http://www.sapdb.org/

[80] http://pypi.python.org/pypi/pymongo/

[81] http://docs.python.org/library/imaplib.html

[82] http://docs.python.org/library/csv.html#csv.QUOTE_ALL

[83] http://www.faqs.org/rfcs/rfc2616.html

[84] http://www.faqs.org/rfcs/rfc2396.html

[85] http://tools.ietf.org/html/rfc3490

[86] http://tools.ietf.org/html/rfc3492

[87] ttp://mail.python.org/pipermail/python-list/2007-June/
      617126.html

[88] ttp://mail.python.org/pipermail/python-list/2007-June/
      617126.html

[89] http://www.recaptcha.net

[90] http://www.google.com/recaptcha

[91] http://gdwarner.blogspot.com/2008/10/
brief-pyjamas-django-tutorial.html

[92] http://www.reportlab.org

[93] http://ui.jquery.com/

[94] http://www.learningjquery.com/

[95] http://www.apache.org/

[96] http://wiki.nginx.org/Main

[97] http://www.lighttpd.net/

[98] http://www.cherokee-project.com/download/

[99] http://en.wikipedia.org/wiki/Common_Gateway_Interface

[100] http://code.google.com/p/modwsgi/

[101] http://www.fastcgi.com/

[102] http://www.openssl.org/

[103] http://projects.unbit.it/uwsgi/

[104] http://httpd.apache.org/download.cgi

[105] http://adal.chiriliuc.com/mod_wsgi/revision_1018_2.3/mod_
wsgi_py25_apache22/mod_wsgi.so

[106] http://httpd.apache.org/docs/2.2/mod/core.html

[107] http://www.apsis.ch/pound/

[108] http://haproxy.1wt.eu/

[109] http://redis.io/

[110] http://httpd.apache.org/docs/2.2/content-negotiation.html

[111] http://wiki.nginx.org/HttpGzipStaticModule

[112] https://devcenter.heroku.com/articles/python

[113] http://en.wikipedia.org/wiki/List_of_HTTP_status_codes